EMPIRE OF LETTERS

Eighteenth-century English, Scottish and American letter manuals, among the most frequently reprinted books of the era, spread norms of polite conduct and communication, helping not only to connect and unify different regions of the British Atlantic world, but to foster very different local and regional cultures and values. By teaching secret writing, they also enabled transatlantic correspondents to communicate what they wanted despite interception, censorship and the practice of reading private letters in company. Eve Tavor Bannet uncovers what people knew then about letters that we have forgotten, revolutionizing our understanding of eighteenth-century letters, novels, periodicals, and other kinds of writing that used the letter form in print as well as manuscript. This lively, widely re-searched interdisciplinary study will change the ways we read and interpret eighteenth-century letters and think about the book in the Atlantic world.

EVE TAVOR BANNET is Professor of English at the University of Oklahoma. Her previous books include *The Domestic Revolution* (Baltimore, 2000) and *Structuralism and the Logic of Dissent* (London, 1989, 1991). Her work appears in journals including *Eighteenth-Century Studies*, *The Eighteenth-Century Novel*, *Huntington Library Quarterly* and *New Literary History*.

THE
Young Secretary's Guide:
OR, A
Speedy Help to Learning.

In Two Parts.

Part I. Containing the moſt curious Art of inditing familiar Letters, relating to Buſineſs in Merchandize,
Trade, Correſpondence, Familiarity, Friendſhip, and
on all Occaſions : Alſo Inſtructions for Directing, Su-
perſcribing and Subſcribing of Letters, with due Re-
ſpect to the Titles of Perſons of Quality and others.
Rules for Pointing and Capitalling in Writing, &c.
Likewiſe a ſhort *Engliſh* Dictionary, explaining hard
Words.

Part II. Containing the Nature of Writings Obligato-
ry, &c. with Examples of Bonds, Bills, Letters of
Attorney, Deeds of Sale, Deeds of Mortgage, Relea-
ſes, Acquittances, Warrants of Attorney, Deeds of
Gift, Aſſignments, Counter Security, Bills of Sale,
Letters of Licence, Apprentices Indentures, Bills of
Exchange, and all other Writings made by Scrive-
ners, &c. With a Table of Intereſt, &c. &c.

By J. Hill.

Made ſuitable to the People of New-England ; *but with
a ſmall Alteration, may ſuit all Parts of* America.

The Twenty Fourth Edition,
With large Additions.

BOSTON:
Printed and ſold by *Thomas Fleet,* at the *Heart* & *Crown*
in Cornhill. 1750.

Frontiſpiece Thomas Fleet's imprint on an American edition of John Hill's *Young
Secretary's Guide* (1750), reproduced by permission of the Beinecke Rare Book and
Manuscripts Library, Yale University.

EMPIRE OF LETTERS

Letter Manuals and Transatlantic Correspondence, 1688–1820

EVE TAVOR BANNET

CAMBRIDGE
UNIVERSITY PRESS

CAMBRIDGE UNIVERSITY PRESS
Cambridge, New York, Melbourne, Madrid, Cape Town, Singapore,
São Paulo, Delhi, Dubai, Tokyo

Cambridge University Press
The Edinburgh Building, Cambridge CB2 8RU, UK

Published in the United States of America by Cambridge University Press, New York

www.cambridge.org
Information on this title: www.cambridge.org/9780521123525

First published 2005
This digitally printed version 2009

A catalogue record for this publication is available from the British Library

ISBN 978-0-521-85618-8 Hardback
ISBN 978-0-521-12352-5 Paperback

Cambridge University Press has no responsibility for the persistence or
accuracy of URLs for external or third-party internet websites referred to in
this publication, and does not guarantee that any content on such websites is,
or will remain, accurate or appropriate.

Contents

Acknowledgments

A number of individuals and organizations have materially supported the research and writing of this book.

A fellowship at the Institute for Advanced Study in the Humanities at the University of Edinburgh during the spring of 2002 provided access to the excellent resources of the National Library of Scotland and to a variety of stimulating colleagues, both at the Institute and in the English Department of the University of Edinburgh, who taught this Londoner that the so-called "periphery" was always, in reality, another integral and passionately interesting center. I thank Susan Manning, Faith Hope, John Frow, Cairns Craig and Anthea Taylor for all that the visit became and for sharing some of Scotland with me.

A long-term NEH fellowship at the Huntington Library during the year 2003–4 gave me access to an invaluable transatlantic library, a congenial group of colleagues, and time to think, rethink, work and rework this book. I am grateful to the National Endowment for the Humanities and to the Huntington for making that year possible, and to all the people in Pasadena and San Marino who made it so pleasant and so productive. I am particularly indebted, in very different ways, to Jean Howard, Paulina Kewes, Richard Terdiman, Roy Richie, Susan Green Suzie Krasnoo and Mona Schulman.

Paul Bell and David Mair at the University of Oklahoma gave this project "legs" by arranging for additional funding and for release time, more often than not after the last minute. My students at Oklahoma got me thinking about transatlantic connections by revealing just how much of what I was presenting to them as "Eighteenth-Century British" had been passed down in their own families, often by the women, and was still familiar. The responses of colleagues at conferences to various bits of this book have been particularly helpful, as was a memorable discussion over a long weekend with Jessica Munns and Philip Woodvine. I also thank the University of Delaware Press for permission to reprint parts of my article "Epistolary Commerce in Steele's *Spectator*" from Don Newman's collection, *Emerging Discourses in the Spectator*.

This study is hugely better for the careful reading, acute questions and constructive criticism of Susan Manning, Robert Hume and Daniel Cottom, for Cambridge University Press's anonymous readers, and for Linda Bree's crash course in editorial streamlining. I have been very fortunate in their readiness to share their expertise and in their encouragement and support.

None of this would have been possible, however, without the determination, courage, devotion and extraordinary generosity of our son, Alan Bannet and my husband, Jacob, during a very difficult and challenging time. To them, with love and gratitude, I therefore dedicate this book.

Prologue

Despite renewed interest in letter-writing practices and widespread agreement that letters were central to eighteenth-century culture, the manuals which taught those practices and disseminated them down the social hierarchy have been almost entirely overlooked. Eighteenth-century British and American letter manuals taught codes, conventions and practices of letter-writing and letter-reading that have now largely been forgotten, together with the proper conduct of conversation and of familial, social, sexual, professional and commercial life. They were masterpieces of Enlightenment taxonomy that combined, in little space, examples of polite domestic, social, professional and commercial correspondence, instruction in Standard English and proper forms, and conduct book teaching in manners and morals. They often included as models the epistles of now canonical authors, several of whom also wrote manuals of their own. Self-consciously addressed to a broad and mobile public of gentlemen, merchants, tradesmen, military officers and professionals, as well as mariners, maidservants, apprentices and schoolchildren, women of all ages and provincials of all ranks, letter manuals were among the most frequently reprinted books on both sides of the Atlantic throughout the long eighteenth century. They were readily available from provincial as well as London booksellers, and in America from mid-century, could be borrowed from subscription libraries in most colonies or states. Inscriptions in surviving copies show that personal copies were treasured by successive owners, lent to friends, and handed down from generation to generation until they fell apart. The influence of letter manuals may be said to have rivaled even novels as popular as *Clarissa* or *Betsy Thoughtless* in these regards.

In this, their new populist incarnation, letter manuals began to proliferate in England and in British-America at the end of the seventeenth century, at the inception of English efforts to unite the three kingdoms and the American mainland and island colonies within a growing, and increasingly far-flung, commercial empire, when letters were the only available technology for distance communication. Extension of "the art of letter-writing" to all manner and ranks of people ensured that, in time, town and country, metropolis and English, Scottish and American provinces, would be firmly, if not always reliably, linked by a multiplicity of epistolary networks permitting trade, war, exchanges of "intelligence," and putative government control. With population moving back and forth through the three kingdoms and across the Atlantic highway, dissemination of the art of letter-writing also made it possible to maintain what contemporaries called "a good correspondency" among the many families and friends that schooling, apprenticeships, service, indentures, urbanization, emigration, trade, war, government posts and colonization, separated and dispersed. The redeployment of the letter both in its manuscript and print forms – not, as has been argued, print capitalism *per se* – made "administrative centralization" possible, "created unified fields of exchange and communication," and enabled Englishmen, Scotsmen, and British-Americans to imagine themselves as one transatlantic community.[1] To borrow Alison Gilbert Olson's suggestive title, letters made the empire work.[2]

One of the functions of letter manuals during the long eighteenth century was to unite dispersed localities by facilitating the "mutual communication" of persons with different local and regional dialects, pronunciations, mores, memories, levels of education and ranks. Manuals supplied the lacks in a gentleman's Latinate education, supplemented the limits of a petty school education in the provinces and among the lower orders, and helped produce the many "writers by trade" required by the burgeoning new bureaucracies and by Britain's commercial and military expansion into the Atlantic world. By disseminating a single standard language, method and culture of polite communication, letter manuals created common ground for the written commerce of people in different counties, kingdoms, provinces and estates in all the old senses of the word commerce – exchange, conversation, traffic, intercourse and trade. They therefore contributed to forging the nation and the first British empire as much as improved roads and transportation, the institution of the post office and of regular shipping routes, the periodical press, and national

See the Bibliography for full title and publication details.
1 Anderson, *Imagined Communities*, 42, 47; Grasso, *A Speaking Aristocracy*, 211.
2 Olson, *Making Empire Work*.

days of celebration or commemoration.[3] It should not therefore surprise us to find that their value was still appreciated in America in the 1790s, when strategic thinking was dominated by the daunting size of the country and by the goal of increasing patriotism through education, and consensus through communication.

Nevertheless, the story of letter manuals is not a depressing tale of enforced uniformity and inexorable standardization. As we will see, the migration of letter-writing models down the social hierarchy and across different regions of Britain and America was mediated by repeated translations both of individual letters and of individual manuals into different cultural registers. This happened both centrally in London and locally in the provinces, but in somewhat different ways. Writers and compilers of letter manuals for London printers and booksellers most often imitated and rewrote extant epistolary models to adapt available formulae and conventions to their changing sense of the culture, the fashion, and their target audience. Both descriptive and prescriptive, they also sought to "improve" their users by offering examples of whatever conduct and sentiments they considered proper to people of different ranks, ages and genders with different relative duties and concerns. Local Scottish and American printers, who adapted London manuals for their local markets with similar goals in mind, generally proceeded by selection and reordering rather than by rewriting, using such devices of *compilatio* and *ordinatio* as excision (or abridgement), juxtaposition, clustering, reclassification, sequencing and recontextualization to alter the ideological bent, and even the stylistic choices, of their London "copy." In these longstanding, traditional ways, they created, often under the same title, what was in many cases an entirely different text. Indeed, some manuals were altered and revised so thoroughly or so frequently from edition to edition that over time, they became quite different from themselves.

In this case, therefore, print was not a fixed and reifying technology. Letter manuals belie the modern opposition between the manuscript environment where "texts are malleable and social" and the print culture where texts are "fixed and possessively individualistic"; and they prevent centralization of printing in London from figuring without qualification as "a politically centrifugal force, designed to serve the core interests of the politically centralized nation-state."[4] Thanks to the changing

---

3 Colley, *Britons*; Clive and Bailyn, "England's Cultural Provinces"; Bailyn, *Peopling*; Pagden, *Lords of all the World*; Landsman, "Provinces and the Empire."
4 Marotti and Bristol (eds.), *Print, Manuscript and Performance*, 5, 5–6.

compilations and adaptations of regional printers, the same models of writing and conduct circulated differently in different parts of Britain and America, at once promoting mutual identification and strengthening distinct provincial identities. For regional and American printers, "anglicization" and "exceptionalism" went hand in hand.

Imitation, with which we will be repeatedly concerned, did not mean copying in the eighteenth century, though it could. Accusations of plagiarism abounded in literary circles at the end of the seventeenth century as theaters, printers and booksellers began to treat literary texts as potentially profitable literary property. Grammarians at the end of the eighteenth century complained that everyone was repeating the same epistolary forms, expressions, sentiments and models. And early nineteenth-century American writers who sought to construct a distinctly American literature treated imitations of English writings with hostility as "a servile aspect of dependency."[5] But during the long eighteenth century, imitation as such was not proscribed even by the most rabid critics of plagiarism. It continued to link Europe and the Atlantic world across difference, because everyone was still being taught to write by imitating models. Especially where letter-writing instruction was concerned, it was a commonplace that imitating examples was more efficacious than applying precepts. This did not necessarily make for sameness. As a method of teaching epistolary writing and of generating new letters, imitation was conceived and practiced as a system that only *began* with a phase of transcription and copying. Imitation was supposed to advance, with a pupil's growing proficiency, through rewording and then through the variation, correction, amplification, inversion or radical adaptation of the model or models in use, to their "improvement" and creative transformation. Familiarity with the same basic models and classes of letter meant that one of the pleasures of reading a letter, as well as an important way of interpreting meaning, involved recognition of the implicit model and of the changes that had been introduced. In these more advanced forms, moreover, imitation was an old, classical and humanist, techne that, in Derridean terms, permitted writers to re-mark their letters both inside and outside the culture, conventions and expressions inscribed in their model texts. Inasmuch as the writers and printers of letter manuals themselves used imitation to produce new letters and new compilations of letters, these too represent – and require of us – readings in terms of repetition and difference, in which new manuals are articulated on old,

---

5 Granqvist, *Imitation as Resistance*, 11; Kewes, *Authorship*; Griffin, *Faces of Anonymity*.

and letters written in the present are placed in dialogue with letters of the past.

Neither letters nor letter manuals were new in the eighteenth century. The letter or epistle was a classical genre, and the first letter manuals in English date from the Renaissance. Most early English manuals were heavily influenced by Erasmus in the sixteenth century and by Frenchman, Puget de la Serre, in the seventeenth century. Indeed, many model letters in early English manuals were more or less direct translations from classical, humanist or French sources. Until after the Restoration, letter manuals in English generally offered models geared to courtly occasions or to a classically educated readership. They treated letters as a branch of eloquence, and surrounded them with models of oral conversation, or with lists of commonplaces and discussions of rhetorical figures and tropes. Some features of these early manuals were carried over into the late seventeenth and eighteenth centuries. For instance, classical, humanist and French letters continued to figure as models in some mid-eighteenth-century manuals. Sixteenth-century manuals like William Fulwood's *Enimie of Idleness* (1568) or Angel Day's *English Secretorie* (1599) exemplified different kinds of epistolary writing by using both real and fictive models, and employed humanist methods of classification and instruction. Eighteenth-century manuals followed suit. During the Renaissance and seventeenth century, there were also one or two early exemplars of manuals designed for a non-courtly and non-learned readership, such as *The Merchant's Avizo* (1589) which contained models for all the letters a Bristol factor or apprentice might need to write his master during a short business trip to Portugal or Spain, or *The Secretaries Study Containing New Familiar Epistles Wherein Ladies, Gentlemen and all that are ambitious to write and speak elegantly, and elaborately, in a succinct and facetious strein, are furnished with fit Phrases, Emphaticall expressions, and various directions for the most polish'd and judicious way of inditing Letters, Whether Amorous, Civill, Houshold, Politick, Chiding, Excusing, Requesting, Gratulatory, Or Nuncupatory* by S. S. Gent. (1652). But even here those who are not ladies or gentlemen are merely subsumed under "all that are ambitious." The model letters within are dominated by flowery gallantries and letters of compliment after the manner of the popular seventeenth-century *Academies of Complement*, which were heavily influenced by the French. And the few household or domestic letters that are offered assume possession of a fairly comfortable country estate.

This book opens at the beginning of the long eighteenth century, when most letter manuals began to address the needs of a wider and more diverse public, to associate letter-writing with grammar and spelling as well as with rhetoric, to include business letters and legal forms, and to act as conduct books for polite domestic, social, professional and commercial manners and morals. I will place this beginning in 1687, when John Hill's trend-setting manual and transatlantic best-seller, *The Young Secretary's Guide, or A Speedy Help to Learning*, was officially licensed. I will conclude around 1820, when the last eighteenth-century models of epistolary writing began, slowly, to go out of print. I do not wish to claim that these dates represent clear-cut beginnings and endings. When we are considering manuals that made a habit of rewriting and reassembling their predecessors' letters, we inevitably enter and leave history *in medias res*. But it does appear that between these dates there was fairly widespread agreement about the format of *Secretaries* and *Letter-Writers*, whom they should address, what they should contain, and what they should do.

During the long eighteenth century, British and American letter manuals were miscellanies of fragments, which came in a variety of related forms. All centered on an anthology of heterogeneous and apparently discontinuous model letters between fictional generic characters or social types (such as landlord and tenant, merchant and apprentice, sister and brother or father and son), that were designed to teach the art of letter-writing by imitation.

Secretaries and *Complete Letter-Writers* generally bound their model letters together in a compendium with a variety of legal forms and precedents and with everything else a person might need to write a polite letter in "proper" English: a short grammar, rules for punctuation, some brief directions for letter-writing, a guide to the forms of polite address, a dictionary of hard words, a spelling dictionary for homonyms, a list of contractions, and instructions for the formatting, appearance and folding of letters. They sometimes also included formulae for cards or for petitions, and verse epistles. As we will see, all these elements of what I will call *compendia* were ideologically weighted in different ways, and the values they persistently conveyed were as important as their utilitarian functions.

Compendia were also truncated into what I will call *Letter-miscellanies*. Letter-miscellanies such as Samuel Richardson's *Letters Written to and for Particular Friends on the most Important Occasions* (1741),[6] Eliza Haywood's *Epistles for the Ladies* (1749), *The Ladies Complete Letter-Writer*

---

6 *Familiar Letters on Important Occasions* is the title Brian W. Downs gave his 1928 edition of this work.

(1763) or Vicesimus Knox's *Elegant Epistles* (1790) were simply collections of model letters without the compendium's outwork of supporting materials. Some were designed to instruct letter-writers in a more indirect and entertaining manner or for the improvement of style. Some, like *The Art of Letter-Writing* (1762) or *The Correspondent* (1790), offered critical or explanatory comments between letters and sizable introductions to letter-writing practices. Most silently reproduced the kinds of model letters that might otherwise be found in compendia. *Secretaries* and *Complete Letter-Writers* often purloined letters from *Letter-miscellanies*, as well as from each other.

Abbreviated *Secretaries* or *Letter-Writers* were also inserted into even more compendious *vade mecums*, such as William Mather's *Young Man's Companion, or Arithmetic Made Easy* (1710), George Fisher's *The Instructor, or Young Man's Best Companion* (1735) or Thomas Wise's *The Newest Young Man's Companion* (1758). These taught numeracy, bookkeeping, measuring and surveying and other practical skills as well as epistolography, and gave directions for making and preserving ink, for cutting the nibs on quill pens, and for writing secret letters.

Finally, there was an ongoing tradition of "Merriments" or witty take-offs on standard letters, that can be traced back to translations and imitations of Frenchman Nicholas Breton's *A Poste with a madde Packet of Letters* (1602). During the eighteenth century, the popularity of merriments declined in the wake of stern warnings by moralists and conduct book-writers that ridicule was more likely to offend than instruct and amuse. Because merriments like Charles Gildon's *A Postboy robb'd of his Mail* (1692, 1693) or epistolary parts of the *Spectator* (1711) often used a thin fictional thread to connect disparate letters, twentieth-century New Critics tended to read the few they admired as "literature" and to overlook their character as letter manuals as a result. Merriments performed the same functions as other letter manuals – if anything their introduction of a guide, fictional critic or group of critics to comment on the letters they presented enabled them to make their instructions more explicit than compendia could. The difference is that merriments were directed to a double audience: while giving some plain instruction to the epistographically challenged, they used satire, wit and comic distance to recycle manual materials for a more elite, learned or sophisticated readership. Compendia and letter-miscellanies often included a few sample letters of merriment.

The great achievement of the new "English school," and of the letter manuals that publicized its teachings, was to disseminate letter-writing down the social hierarchy and to make epistolary kinds, codes and conventions familiar to all manner and ranks of people. One might say that the eighteenth century naturalized the idea that anyone can (or should be able to) read and write a letter. Together with the persistence of some of the eighteenth-century letter's formal features into the present day, this long misled us into believing that we still knew all the codes, and that eighteenth-century letters could be read as straightforward historical evidence, or as giving us privileged insights into what people privately thought and truly felt. These preconceptions are being altered by a growing number of excellent, cultural and historical, studies of particular early modern or romantic epistolary practices, of surviving epistolary exchanges and collections of family letters, and of novels using epistolary form.[7] We now realize that "letters are not unmediated historical arte-facts."[8] We have become increasingly aware that there is still a great deal that we do not know about letter-writing and letter-reading. But we have not gone back to letter manuals to investigate the epistolary codes, practices, presuppositions and ideologies that were taught and assumed.

The only three sustained modern studies of either British or American letter manuals during either the seventeenth or eighteenth centuries are long New Critical and bibliographical essays which date from the 1930s and 1940s.[9] There have been some important related studies since then: Roger Chartier's ground-breaking work on seventeenth-century French letter manuals, Jonathan Goldberg's brilliant analysis of the writing of letters (in both senses) during the English Renaissance, and Ian Michael's encyclopedic investigation of the teaching of English from the sixteenth to the nineteenth centuries.[10] But the voluminous corpus of British and American letter manuals during the long eighteenth century remains as close to a completely untapped resource as it is possible to get in eight-eenth-century studies. Closer acquaintance with this material will subvert any comfortable assurance that eighteenth-century letters can be read

7 For instance, Daybell, *Early Modern Women Letter Writers*; Earle (ed.), *Epistolary Selves*; Goldgar, *Impolite Learning*; Goodman, *Republic of Letters*; Harrison, *Until Next Year*; Jagodzinski, *Privacy and Print*; Barton and Hall (eds.), *Letter-Writing*; Cook, *Epistolary Bodies*; Favret, *Romantic Correspondence*; Gilroy and Verhoeven (eds.), *Epistolary Histories*; How, *Epistolary Spaces*; Lowenthal, *Lady Mary*.
8 Earle (ed.), *Epistolary Selves*, 1.
9 Hornbeak, "Complete Letter-Writer in English, 1568–1800" (1934); Robertson, *The Art of Letter-Writing* (1943); Weiss, *American Letter-Writers, 1698–1943* (1945). There are some acute insights in Altman's "Political Ideology in the Letter Manual," and a chapter on letter manuals in Dierks, "Letter-Writing, Gender and Class in America."
10 Roger Chartier (ed.), *Correspondence*; Goldberg, *Writing Matter*; Michael, *Teaching of English*.

reliably either as "a window in the bosom" or as transparent historical documents. Manuals show that letters inhabited an extremely complex and highly developed cultural and rhetorical system which offers a very different interpretative box of tools.

The questions driving this study relate primarily to how letter manuals may be read, how they transmitted and altered discursive practices and cultural norms, and what they can tell us about Enlightenment epistolography and about how to read an eighteenth-century correspondence. I am coining the term "letteracy" to designate the collection of different skills, values, and kinds of knowledge beyond mere literacy that were involved in achieving competency in the writing, reading and interpreting of letters. Under letteracy, I include associated cultural information, such as common conceptions of letter-writing, awareness of current epistolary practices, basic knowledge about where letter-writing was taught and about how it was taught or to be learned, even how to "read" and use a letter manual. The three parts of this book approach the question of what letteracy consisted of, how it was transmitted and how it was practiced, in different but complementary ways, each of which will be introduced more fully at the beginning of each part.

Part I explores the recurrent features of *Secretaries* and *Letter-Writers* on the basis of a wide variety of *London* manuals. Chapter 1 discusses how English manuals represented their target audiences, their contexts and functions, and their relations to everyday life. It also considers the questions relating to literacy and schooling and to the uses and accessibility of the post that arise as soon as one begins to evaluate English manuals' surprisingly broad sense of their public. Chapter 2 deciphers the now unfamiliar architectonics of eighteenth-century compendia. It explains the content and significance of their various taxonomies, the organization of their letter-collections and the relations between their outwork and model letters. It also describes the epistolary conventions and practices of reading and interpretation that manuals taught, the methods they employed to teach reading and convey ideology, and different ways in which they might be used by people with different levels of education and ability. The emphasis throughout is on what these features of manuals teach us about how to write and read a letter. One of the important things to understand at the outset is that letters were not construed by eighteenth-century manuals, or indeed by writing masters, as a primarily private or closeted genre. When they spoke of reading, they meant reading aloud. The letter, which was conceived as issuing from speech and as returning to speech at the point of oral delivery, was a shape-changer. It reconfigured itself through a variety of media – manuscript, print and voice – as it traveled across space and time.

Part II examines the ways in which letter manuals themselves were changed from printing to printing and from place to place as they traveled the Atlantic to America and were redesigned by local printers for different local audiences. Along with bibles, psalters, primers and grammars, letter manuals were among the earliest types of book that were not only printed in Britain and regularly imported into the American provinces, but also reprinted and consciously "fitted" by local American printers to the values and needs of their local customers. The importation, reprinting and adaptation of British letter manuals continued well into the early Republic. It is therefore surprising that so little attention has been paid to them by early Americanists or by historians of the book in the Atlantic world.

A fairly large number of different letter manuals were produced for London booksellers between 1688 and 1820, but relatively few were steady sellers in the sense that the market for them justified more than two or three London editions and encouraged repeated reprints and adaptations in the provinces. The manuals that dominated the English, Scottish and American markets in both these ways – by dissemination from London and repeated reproduction and adaptation in the provinces – and which consequently familiarized comparatively large numbers of people with what letters ought to say and do, are those which have been selected for analysis in this part of the book, which focuses primarily on the collections of letters in each case. Chapters 3, 4 and 5 are organized by the successive London manuals which dominated the home market and gave rise to American and Scottish adaptations. Chapter 3 covers the period from 1688 to around 1740, when John Hill's and Thomas Goodman's *Secretaries* were widely reprinted, adapted and altered in America. Chapter 4 covers the second half of the eighteenth century, when Scottish versions of Crowder's and Dilworth's *Complete Letter-Writers* were preferred and used as bases for American adaptations. And Chapter 5 considers diverse uses made of Cooke's popular *Universal Letter-Writer; or Art of Correspondence* from the 1790s on. I have followed a certain number of conduct book subjects across all these manuals to facilitate comparison and highlight change. These include representations of friendship between men, professional life, trade and commerce, the household, apprenticeship and domestic service, the role of women, marriage, education, travel, absence and conversation.

Together, these chapters offer ideological and stylistic analyses of the letter-collections in the compendia that were most frequently reprinted in

Britain, and cover the surprisingly large number of American imprints that were not mere reprints. The fact that manuals were frequently altered, even by their original printers, means that each manual title represented a variable "series" of versions rather than the label for a fixed book. This has understandably led to some bibliographical confusion in the ESTC. One of the things that Chapters 3 to 5 do, in conjunction with the bibliography at the end, is establish filiations between manuals and show which were versions of which.

Having examined the architectonics and recurrent features of letter manuals, and the ways in which London manuals were transformed and translated into different cultural registers by printers in America and Scotland, this book goes on in Part III to comply with eighteenth-century injunctions that to be adequate, book learning must be complemented by an acquaintance with the world. In a segment on "The Principles of Politeness," *The New Letter-Writer, or The Art of Correspondence* (1775) insisted that "Secrecy is a characteristic of Good-Breeding." Other manuals warned their reader-writers to be wary of putting their real thoughts down on paper for more practical reasons of discretion in the face of publicity, interception and censorship. *Vade mecums* gave instruction in secret writing. Chapter 6 addresses such instructions by exploring the culture of secrecy that issued from the codes of politeness and that was reinforced both by the practice of reading letters aloud to one's "company" and by justified fears of interception and censorship. Without pretending to be exhaustive, it shows how the epistolary *Doppelganger* of simultaneously public and hidden transcripts manifested itself in various public and private forms of transatlantic communication, and explores some of the ways in which letters communicated what they could not say, and alerted their recipients to what they concealed. Chapter 7 concludes with brief analyses of three canonical literary texts – Crevecoeur's first *Letter from an American Farmer*, *The Spectator*, and Franklin's *Autobiography* – which review and illustrate the matter discussed in each part of the book. This respects and underlines the fact that the eighteenth century assumed a continuity between letters in different areas and levels of culture. Rather than aiming at closure, these texts open letter manuals onto what we have considered "good literature," by showing that they can alter the way we understand familiar texts.

Novels too presupposed the letteracy to be explored in this book, and were often preoccupied by it. At the beginning of our period, for instance, in *Love Letters between a Nobleman and his Sister* (1684–87), which was roughly contemporaneous with Hill's manual, Aphra Behn

uses a narrative frame in Part II to describe her characters' reflections and/
or conversations about the letters they read and write. The narrative
punctures that naive credulity in the immediacy and sincerity of letters
which was allowed Silvia (and the reader) in Part I, by underscoring the
difference between what characters think, desire or mean and what they
actually write. The narrative repeatedly shows that letters can be manipu-
lative and deceptive even when they are as essentially true in content,
sincere in style, and dutiful in sentiment, subscriptions and compliments,
as the following letter to Philander:

> . . .I conclude [Octavio] a Lover, tho' without Success; what Effects that may
> have upon the Heart of *Silvia*, only Time can render an Account of: And whose
> Conduct I shall the more particularly observe from a Curiosity natural to me, to
> see if it may be possible for Silvia to love again, after the adorable Philander,
> which Levity in one so perfect would cure me of the Disease of Love, while I liv'd
> amongst the fickle Sex: But since no such Thought can yet get Possession of my
> Belief, I humbly beg your Lordship will entertain no Jealousie, that may be so
> fatal to your Repose, and to that of Silvia; doubt not but my Fears proceed
> perfectly from the Zeal I have for your Lordship, for whose Honour and
> Tranquility none shall venture so far as, my Lord, your Lordship's most Humble
> and Obedient Servant, Brillard.

The narrative undercuts this letter's *prima facie* meaning by explaining
that Brillard's purpose is to "hint" at Silvia's "Levity" in such a way as to
stir his addressee's resentment without giving him any suspicion that
Brillard's own motive is anything but "Duty and Respect to Philander."
Its descriptions of Brillard's calculations prior to writing about "how to
manage [Philander] to his best Advantage" and of his critical re-reading of
his letter "to see whether he had cast it to his Purposes," remind the reader
that epistolography was an art of rhetoric, which educated men used to
persuade and move others in predetermined ways, and that women
generally lacked such classical rhetorical schooling.[11] This is also the
terminus ad quem of Silvia's education in Part II. Silvia's transformation
from the "controlled woman" of Part I into the "controlling woman who
manipulates her desirability"[12] in Part II, is mediated by a series of
realizations about the artifice of the "Rhetoric of Love" as expressed in
the language, style, tone, repetitions, flattery and conventions of love
letters. These realizations make Silvia an increasingly resisting reader,
and teach her to write letters as carefully crafted rhetorical instruments

11 Behn, *Love Letters* (London, 1708), 168, 169.
12 Todd, "Hot brute," 278.

for particular effects, rather than as "unthinking, artless Speaking" that expresses the true "Sense of her Soul."[13] Letter manuals begin from here.

Towards the end of our period, Jane Austen assumed far greater familiarity with epistolary matters and expected readers, once primed, to be able to determine the character and meaning of interpolated letters for themselves. In *Pride and Prejudice* (1813), for instance, readers are primed through a conversation in Bingley's drawing room, where Darcy is writing a letter, about how letter-writers betray not only their character, but also their attitude to friendship, through their "stile of writing." Miss Bingley reminds us that "stile" is manifest, among other things, in the letter's length, handwriting, formatting, and vocabulary; in the speed or deliberation, ease or restraint of the writing; and in epistolary representations of the degree of familiarity between the parties – all manual topics. One of the ironies of this scene is that Miss Bingley has just betrayed her own character and attitude to friendship in her letter of invitation to Jane:

My dear friend,

If you are not so compassionate as to dine today with Louise and me, we shall be in danger of hating each other for the rest of our lives, for a whole day's tête-à-tête between two women can never end without a quarrel. Come as soon as you can on the receipt of this. My brother and the gentlemen are to dine with the officers. Yours ever, Caroline Bingley.[14]

The narrator generally focalizes the meaning of letters through characters' interpretations and reactions, leaving the reader to measure the latter against her own reading of the interpolated letters. In this case, Lydia seizes on Miss Bingley's reference to officers, Mrs. Bennett laments the gentlemen's absence, and Jane turns the conversation to questions of transportation. Their reading characterizes them. Letterate readers will notice, however, that all ignore Caroline's "stile of writing." They fail to notice that the suggestion in the superscription and subscription that Caroline will consider Jane her "dear friend" for "ever" is belied in the body of the letter by her careless over-familiarity and fashionable posturing ("tête-à-tête") and by the implication in her use of the imperative ("Come. . .") that Caroline views Jane as very much her social inferior. Caroline's friendship is also belied by the disrespect and lack of consideration indicated through her omission of the proper sentiments for letters of this kind: "I hope you are not engaged"; "your company you know how we value"; "I am sure I need not tell you we shall do all we can to

13 Behn, *Love Letters*, 211.
14 Austen, *Pride and Prejudice*, 77.

render [your visit] agreeable. . ." Jane discovers only during a much later visit to London that she has been "entirely deceived in Miss Bingley's regard for me." She insists in a letter to her sister that her misplaced "confidence" in Caroline has been "natural" and that in "the same circumstances. . . I am sure I should be deceived again."[15] But letterate readers, who have understood the value of Caroline's "regard" from her first letter, will think: "You would be deceived again only if you again ignored stile of writing."

The bridge between letter manuals and novels is not necessarily to be sought in "the literary familiar letter." Like Caroline's letter of invitation or Jane's letter of news, letters in novels often belong to those apparently insignificant classes of familiar letter which were modeled in letter manuals and did the everyday business of life. Letter manuals and novels both exemplified the same complex eighteenth-century culture of letters, and can also shed light on one another in other ways. I suggest some as I go along. Readers will, I hope, make other connections of their own.

The overall structure of this book assumes as a given the position now taken by both British and American scholars of the Atlantic world, who explore the networks of politics, commerce, culture and communication that crossed national borders and national literatures, and who argue that during the long eighteenth century, America, the West Indies and Scotland were all cultural provinces of England. I am profoundly indebted to the work of Bernard Bailyn, Jack P. Green, David Shields, Richard Bushman, William Spengeman, Susan Manning, Barbara de Wolfe, David Hackett Fischer, Ian Steele, Angus Calder, Ned Landsman and others, who have opened transatlantic studies to the movement of people, ideas, books and goods in important and interesting new ways. Taking a transatlantic perspective alters what we are able to see of our own English, Scottish or American cultures, and repositions what we thought we knew.

Letter manuals were interdisciplinary compilations. I am therefore also heavily indebted to scholars in a variety of disparate literary, cultural and historical fields working on a variety of English, Scottish, French, and American materials, whose work has shown me how to approach, contextualize, or understand the history of, particular aspects of these manuals. I have drawn on modern studies of letters, politeness, censorship, rhetoric, grammar, manuscript culture, conduct books and the art of conversation, on the history of the book and the history of reading, on

15 *Ibid.*, 184.

social, economic and imperial history, the history of education and literacy, and histories of language, law, urbanization and institutions. My major debts will be evident in the bibliography and notes.

This book can only claim to make some preliminary inroads into as yet largely uncharted territory. I hope that it will draw attention to the interest and importance of eighteenth-century British and American letter manuals and to the further work they invite from a variety of scholarly perspectives.

PART I

Letter manuals and eighteenth-century letteracy

Introduction

In the introduction to his best-selling letter manual, *The Young Secretary's Guide, or Speedy Help to Learning* (1687), John Hill still thought it necessary to explain the purposes and uses of letter-writing. He stressed the importance of letters to "Empires, Kingdoms, Estates and Provinces." The art of letter-writing "immediately shewed its Serviceableness in the negotiating and managing important Affairs throughout the habitable World, especially in all civiliz'd Nations, where Traffick, Trade, or Commerce, relating to the Profit, Pleasure, or Well-being of humane Societies, take place, or where the Necessity of conversing with one another, though at the greatest Distance imaginable, is requisite and commendable." For families and friends, especially in the English or American provinces, letters were "the maintainer of Love, Amity and Correspondency" and the preserver of human societies across space and time, because they enabled those who were separated to converse in writing and "created the same Effects and right Understanding, as if the Sender or Writer were present."[1]

More remarkable than the need to explain why anyone would want to write a letter, was the function that Hill conceived for letter manuals. Hill suggested that *Secretaries* such as his could enable everyone, and especially provincials, to "save themselves the Charge, if not (as in Country Towns and Villages often happens) the tedious fruitless Search of a Secretary or Scrivener," and allow them to keep their affairs more secret.[2] In other words, Hill made the revolutionary suggestion that printed *Secretaries* could supply the place earlier occupied by human secretaries and scribes and (in the words of another manual a century later) make *Every Man his own Letter-Writer* – and every woman too.[3] Printed manuals would offer

1 John Hill, *The Young Secretary's Guide*, 7th ed. (London, 1796), 2.
2 *Ibid.* and Preface, n.p.
3 James Wallace, *Every Man his own Letter-Writer* (London, 1782).

3

the public an abacus or techne that they could use to generate new letters without any intermediary but themselves. Epistolary compendia like Hill's would meet the working needs of "Empires, Kingdoms, Estates and Provinces," and the personal, social and professional needs of those within them, by modeling "Forms and Precedents" for all the letters and legal documents that anyone might need to write, by offering instruction in grammar, spelling, and reading, and by demonstrating the proper language, codes, sentiments and forms of address to be used on different occasions to correspondents of different ranks in letters of different kinds. Printed *Secretaries* would thereby become the means of empowering people of all ages and all ranks. In conjunction with the new academies and "English" venture schools, epistolary compendia throughout the century would disseminate "the sundry measures taken in Inditing Letters" to "the Younger Sort of either Sex." But they also would also serve the needs of those "of Elder Years" who had "Business and import-ant Affairs" to transact but were not yet "fully qualified in this kind," and "prove in some kind serviceable even to the Learned" by offering them the means of epistolary, moral and stylistic "Improvement."[4]

The extension of letter-writing to all manner and ranks of people in late seventeenth- and eighteenth-century Britain and British-America by means of manuals such as Hill's coincided with the expansion of empire, and was its *sine qua non*. The first ten editions of *The Young Secretary's Guide*, which appeared between 1687 and 1699, were contemporaneous with the turn of English merchants from Europe to the Atlantic trade, with the financial revolution of the 1690s, with the Glorious Revolution and beginning of a century of almost constant foreign war, and with a huge expansion of government departments and bureaucracies.[5] They accompanied the reorganization of the Board of Trade and Plantations under the Secretaries of State which made colonization and commerce affairs of state; the institution of new academies and "English" schools, which made letter-writing in the vernacular a fundamental part of the curriculum for the first time, and the establishment of a single national and transatlantic government-run post. Indeed, John Hill, Gent, may himself have been a provincial lawyer seeking a government job in the post office at York.[6]

4 Hill, *Young Secretary's Guide*, Preface.
5 Sacks, *Widening Gate*; O'Brien, "Inseparable Connections"; Dickson, *Financial Revolution*; Brewer, *Sinews of Power*; Stone, *Imperial State*.
6 Robinson, *British Post Office*, 45.

These developments, which increased the demand for competent letter-writers in government and administration as much as in commerce and trade, preceded the Union with Scotland of 1707 and what Linda Colley has called "forging the nation" from disparate and culturally distinct counties and kingdoms.[7] Without precluding nation-building in Britain, these administrative, commercial and military developments also subsumed and enveloped it. Empire, in the sense of extension of English government and dominion, proceeded in the opposite direction from that assumed by later, ideologically charged, oppositions between nation (at the center close to home) and "empire" (distantly out there on the periphery).[8] It began in the seventeenth century with colonization and with political and military struggles for dominion far from home, and turned back in the eighteenth century, during intervals between foreign wars, to ensure that England was not vulnerable to her enemies and colonial rivals through other kingdoms in the British Isles. The Scots agreed to Union largely to gain commercial access to England's colonies, and went on to play important roles both as migrants to America and as actors in the colonial administrative and war machines. Empire, in the narrower sense of overseas dominions, was one of the interests that united the three kingdoms.[9]

The needs of this expanding mercantile empire both at home and abroad appear to have set the terms that enabled *English* manuals to conceive their functions more broadly than merely in relation to the interests of a single rising middle or "middling" trading or commercial class. As we will see, at the upper end of the social hierarchy, English manuals addressed and portrayed the epistolary needs of the lesser gentry, professionals (including military officers) and well-to-do merchants, while at the lower end they served apprentices, clerks, sailors, servants and maidservants. Unlike American adaptations we will examine in Part II, English manuals did not limit their target audiences or the letters they modeled to the needs, concerns and families of tradesmen and merchants;

---

7 Colley, *Britons: Forging the Nation 1707–1837*. England's colonization of America and the Sugar Islands began a century before Union with Scotland. The "Union of Crowns" at the accession of James VI of Scotland and James I of England did not integrate Scotland and England economically or politically. The Act of Union with Ireland only took place in 1800, almost a century after Hill. For a different view, see Armitage, *Greater Britain*.

8 "Empire, community and realm were treated, to all intents and purposes, as identical." Miller, *Defining the Common Good*, 66.

9 For changing models of empire, Pagden, *Lords of All the World*; Wilson, *Sense of the People*; Marshall, "Empire and Authority." For views from the provinces, Calder, *Revolutionary Empire*; Fry, *Scottish Empire*; Green, *Periphery and Center*.

and well before the Revolution, this "middle class" of successful tradesmen, merchants and professionals was part of America's political and
social elite.

As instruments of public instruction, letter manuals were outgrowths,
and translations into the vernacular for popular use, of a longstanding,
European-wide, pedagogical system based on the commonplace book,
and on what Mary Thomas Crane has described as "the collection and
redeployment of textual fragments."[10] Far from declining at the end of the
seventeenth century as early modernists have supposed, the humanist
method of pedagogy associated with it was, if anything, given a new lease
of life in the eighteenth century by Locke and by Rollin, who were widely
influential both in Britain and in America. Rollin's *Method of Teaching
and Studying the Belles Lettres* (1734) taught composition and writing from
pre-selected commonplace book excerpts using a method that he rightly
claimed was only "an exact account of what has for a long time been
constantly performed."[11] Printed commonplace books inspired by Locke's
directions for their use and organization were still being published and
used in England at the turn of the nineteenth century.[12]

Commonplace books were compiled by what Crane calls "gathering"
and "framing." Gathering, which was represented for centuries in the
figure of a bee collecting honey from chosen flowers, involved the selection and collection of exemplary extracts from authoritative texts.
Framing consisted of the reordering and rearrangement of those fragments under commonplace headings or *tituli* to make the extracts easier
to locate and to use. Writing in this system was a matter of reusing and
recycling the matter and style of extracts by imitating, rewording, varying,
inverting or combining them both on the level of sentiment or argument, and on the level of language and imagery. Compilation by
gathering and framing was also still viewed as a form of writing and "as
an authorial activity."[13] The writer-compilers of London's seventeenth-
and eighteenth-century letter manuals, who often signaled that they were
themselves products of this kind of learned education, composed the
"original letters" of which their manuals consisted by using these methods
of imitation, variation, inversion, and correction to produce new letters

---

10 Crane, *Framing Authority*, 6. Also Parkes, "Influence of the Concepts"; Moss, *Printed
   Commonplace Books.*
11 Rollin, *Belles Lettres*, 64, 67.
12 Beal, "Nations in Garrison."
13 Crane, *Framing Authority*, 138.

from old, to alter matter, change applications, and modernize style. They also expected their most educated readers to treat their manuals as they would the extracts in a printed commonplace book. John Hill, for instance, informed "the Learned" that they might "without any prejudice to their Knowledge and Understanding of higher Matters, gather from the sundry choice Flowers scattered in this Garden of profitable Recreation, some Honey of Improvement to add to their larger Store."[14] On the other hand, like some important London compilers at mid-century, provincial American printers worked exclusively from pre-printed materials and did not significantly alter individual letters. Instead they used traditional methods of gathering and framing to adapt manuals and to generate "new" letter manuals from old. They used selection, exclusion, rearrangement, recontextualization and other such devices to produce abridged or adapted manuals that were remarkably different in ideological content, in target audience, and sometimes even in style from the London manual or manuals from which they worked. They made compilation a convincingly "authorial activity."

Late seventeenth- and eighteenth-century letter manuals preserved other traces of their filiation to commonplace books too. All letter manuals created titles for letters, and later for the larger sections that contained them, just as commonplace books did. And from the 1750s on, when manuals had begun to construct themselves as a "copious well-stocked portable library"[15] in addition to their other functions, they frequently used abstract commonplace headings on their title-pages to advertise the range and variety of the subjects addressed by the letters they contained. Henry Hogg's *New and Complete Universal Letter-Writer, or Whole Art of Polite Correspondence* (*c.* 1790) and Hogan's Philadelphia manual, *The New Universal Letter-Writer, or Complete Art of Polite Correspondence* (1804), both listed the "important, instructive and entertaining subjects" that they "*particularly*" addressed in alphabetical order on their title-pages as: "*Advice, Affection, Affluence, Benevolence, Business, Children to Parents, Compliments, Condolence, Courtship, Diligence, Education, Fidelity, Folly, Friendship, Generosity, Happiness, Humanity, Humour, Industry, Justice, Love, Marriage, Masters to Servants, Modesty, Morality, Oeconomics, Parents to Children, Paternal Affection, Piety, Pleasure, Prodigality, Prudence, Religion, Retirement, Servants to Masters, Trade, Truth, Virtue, Wit etc. etc.*" Like conventional commonplace book categories,

---

14 "Epistle to the Reader." This epistle was later omitted.
15 Moss, *Printed Commonplace Books*, 159.

this mixed catalogue of moral virtues (benevolence, diligence, fidelity, justice, generosity, modesty, prudence, etc.), of topics (business, courtship, love, friendship, marriage, piety, religion, oeconomics, retirement, trade), and of relations (children to parents, masters to servants, servants to masters), was a way of dividing up the world that had implicit ideological content. This mixed catalogue also invited readers to study the letters within as extracts collected and rearranged in commonplace books were studied, namely both for their matter and their manner: as treasuries of information and guides to moral conduct, as well as models of style and expression and loci for arguments or proper sentiments.

Chapter 1 begins by looking at some of the obvious questions that arise as soon as one considers letter-writing and the market for epistolary manuals in these contexts: the state of literacy, education and national and imperial posts, and the relation of letter manuals to them; why printers and compilers thought there was a market for their manuals among members of certain occupations and ranks; why letter manuals used the language of the family and household as well as that of occupation and rank to represent their potential readers; and how they used the old Ciceronian definition of correspondence as "written conversation" to put letter-writing within the reach of a broad readership and to relate letter-writing to everyday conversation and social life.

The focus in Chapter 2 is on the elements of letter manuals. This chapter explores the composition and complex taxonomies common to a large variety of London manuals throughout the eighteenth century. It shows what these taught about letter-writing and social conduct, how they taught it, and the different ways in which they might be read, imitated and used by a public with different levels of education and competence.

CHAPTER I

Empire of letters

EDUCATION FOR THE POST

The post office became a single, integrated, government-run service in England only in 1685. The service was extended to the American provinces in 1693, and to post-Union Scotland in 1711.[1] The late seventeenth- and eighteenth-century postal service was still comparatively slow, seasonal, uneven, and where shipping was involved, subject to disruption by war. In the early years, posts only ran a limited number of routes: from London to the outports on the west coast of England and on to Ireland; from London to Edinburgh; and between the major towns on America's eastern seaboard. The mail generally crossed the Atlantic to Britain's American mainland and island colonies on whatever merchant ships were heading that way. Before the postal reforms in America under Benjamin Franklin during the 1750s, it could take as long for mail to travel from New York to Philadelphia as from London to New York – forty-nine days on average, *if* the winds were fair, *if* the season was right, and *if* the vessel happened to be going directly to New York. For much of the eighteenth century, therefore, "remoter areas of Scotland and Ireland were as far from London news as Barbados or Massachusetts," and news of Boston often reached Britain before it reached Philadelphia.[2] But there had never before been a postal service as comprehensive, and service was expanded and improved throughout the eighteenth century.

Despite obvious shortcomings, the post office created "a communications revolution" that was, in the words of one scholar, "as profound in

---

1 Post Office Acts, each of which have also been called the beginning of the Post, were passed by the Cromwellian Parliament in 1653 and by the Restoration Parliament in 1660; but the post office was not a direct source of government revenue and a single system under government control until the dates I indicate. The first Parliamentary Act for the whole system was Queen Anne's 1711 Post Office Act.
2 Steele, *English Atlantic*, 6. Also Robinson, *Carrying British Mail*; Pred, *Urban Growth*.

its consequences. . .as the subsequent revolutions that came to be associated with the telegraph, the telephone and the computer."[3] Historians have identified three major areas that were impacted by this communications revolution. These can also give us some notion of the scope and importance of letter-writing in the empire if we bear in mind that historians of the post tend to attribute to the institution and to its administrative and vehicular infrastructure, functions performed by the written and printed letters it carried. The first area revolutionized by the post was political and administrative. The post "enhanced England's ability to govern her colonies"; it helped to weld the kingdoms of England, Ireland and Scotland into "an artificial nation"; and it ushered in the fatal era of English administrative centralization.[4] Many of the decisions about where to run English post roads or government mail-carrying packets at sea were made for strategic, political and military reasons by a succession of governments which sought to achieve for Britain absolute dominion over the seas, primacy in commerce, and triumph over its European rivals for wealth and power in the new world. The political and strategic importance of the eighteenth-century post was also recognized by American patriots when they created their own "Constitutional Post" in 1774 as war with Britain approached, and made "the best means of establishing posts for conveying letters and intelligence through this Continent" one of the first priorities of the Continental Congress of 1775. The second area impacted by the post was commerce. Institution of an integrated, government-run postal system preceded and accompanied the great commercial and financial revolutions of the 1690s, and was instrumental in improving the pace and efficiency both of inland and of foreign trade throughout the period. The post facilitated coordination between merchants, wholesalers, manufacturers, retailers and factors in this essentially mercantile empire where new wealth on both sides of the Atlantic grew from overseas trade.[5] Indeed, some said that government supported the American colonial post (which ran at a loss for about fifty years) primarily "for the increase and preservation of trade and commerce."[6] The third area affected by the communications revolution, and the one that has been of most interest to recent scholars, has to do with the transmission of news and information. Despite time-lags, the post did

---

3 John, *Spreading the News*, vii.
4 Fuller, *American Mail*, 30; Colley, *Britons*, 56.
5 Gauci, *Politics of Trade*; Holderness, *Preindustrial England*.
6 Quoted in Konwiser, *Colonial and Revolutionary Posts*, 16.

quite efficiently distribute throughout the British Isles and the British Atlantic, heavily subsidized commercial newsletters and newspapers, as well as royal proclamations and the official government infomercial, *The London Gazette* (all of which either included letters or took epistolary form). The rise and proliferation of the newspaper and with it, of the provincial press, would have been unthinkable without this postal delivery system.[7] The post circulated and disseminated printed information, joining isolated settlements in the British Isles and American provinces into one information network with feedback loops more or less regularly for the first time. Historians have therefore emphasized the role of the post in creating an informed citizenry, in forging "bonds of union" between different regions of Britain and her empire, and in "reinforcing colonists' identity as British subjects."[8]

As a carrier of written letters, however, the post office also represented a communications revolution in a more grassroots sense. One of the most remarkable and new things about the late seventeenth- and eighteenth-century postal system was that it was open to the public at large, and more or less within most peoples' means. The postal rates set by Parliament were altered several times, but one can say that during the first half of this period, carriage of a "single" letter (a letter consisting of a single sheet) generally cost 3 pence, or in America 4 pence, for a letter traveling within sixty miles, double within a hundred-mile radius, and treble within 200 miles. Under George III, the base fee (carriage of a single within sixty miles) went up to 6 pence on both sides of the Atlantic, but was subsequently brought back down. Carriage of a letter between New York and London cost 9 pence at the end of the seventeenth century and 1 shilling in the middle of the eighteenth century. In Britain, the number of letters and packets carried by the post increased exponentially every few years from the last decade of the seventeenth century for, high as they seem, these charges made postage at least for an occasional letter affordable to an unexpectedly wide swathe of the paying population.[9]

---

7 In America, many postmasters were also printers of newspapers, even when running the post involved financial losses. For the press in the Atlantic world, see Clark, *Public Prints*; Warner, *Letters of the Republic*; Sommerville, *News Revolution in England*.
8 Kiebowicz, *News in the Mail*, 9; Fuller, *American Mail*, 29.
9 Robinson calculates on the basis of post office revenue that the numbers of letters carried rose from around 800,000 in 1697–8 to almost 100,000 four years later; and Ellis notes that revenue rose from £121,800 in 1715 to £186,500 in 1764. However, this only indicates overall trends. The accounting system was poor, and reported revenue did not include the pensions that were taken out of it or the large amounts of franked mail carried gratis. These calculations also involve

Using Peter Earle's calculation that £50 per annum constituted a reasonable competence in London prior to 1730 together with his estimate of annual incomes, these rates put letter carriage within the reach not only of gentry, merchants, wholesalers, "men of business" and professionals of all kinds, but also of small shopkeepers, artisans, and domestic servants who are not included in Earle's "middling class."[10] At mid-century, journeymen in the several trades which payed a guinea a week could also afford occasional postage. Robert Campbell's figures show that these included journeyman notaries, drapery painters, engravers, pattern drawers, statuary makers, goldsmiths, snuff-box makers, gilders, builders, coach carvers, engineers, and watchmakers.[11] Letter manuals were very affordable too. They generally cost 1 shilling in London during the late seventeenth and for most of the eighteenth century, rising to 2 shillings only in the 1790s. They were cheaper than novels, and generally printed in duodecimo to keep them widely affordable. Especially during the first half of the eighteenth century, *vade mecums* and epistolary compendia on both sides of the Atlantic often contained lists of prices for letter carriage by post, as well as information about the days on which the post left and arrived at various destinations.

The fact that the post placed letter carriage within the means of a wide swathe of the population was the aspect of this traffic that most troubled eighteenth-century governments in Britain, in Revolutionary America and in the early Republic, who had a paranoid fear of insurgencies and criminal correspondence. For it meant that news and information was being transmitted through the post by the handwritten letters of ordinary people. News and information (collectively known as "intelligence") traveled between mercantile correspondents throughout the empire, who regularly exchanged local political and economic news. Intelligence was also transmitted in the descriptive letters that travelers, settlers, soldiers and wives wrote to their friends at home. For instance, Henrietta Lipton, who was an acquaintance of Martha Washington, conveyed some of the same information about the political lay of the land in America in letters to her uncle in Scotland, as her ambassador husband was sending in reports to Secretary of State, Lord Grenville, in London. News was much in demand, and few correspondents omitted to share some with

dubious assumptions – for instance that the average letter cost 6 pence because most people were sending letters with two sheets. Robinson, *British Post Office*; Ellis, *Post Office*.

10 Earle, *Making of the English Middle Class*.

11 Campbell, *London Tradesman* (1747).

family, patrons and friends. Intelligence also obviously circulated in correspondence between government officials, between members of the opposition and their supporters, between London agents or informants and their provincial or colonial employers, and between ambassadors and their courts. Throughout the long eighteenth century, therefore, successive governments routinely treated the post office as a convenient depot of intelligence, by detaining, opening, copying and when necessary deciphering "private letters" in transit to find out what was going on in the nation, in the empire and in the world.[12]

As a result, throughout the long eighteenth century, government, agents, merchants and private correspondents sent mail by messengers, couriers, friendly captains, acquaintances and friends rather than through the post, wherever and whenever they could. Benjamin Franklin was still defending this practice before Parliament in 1774. The letter mail carried by the post was therefore only a part, and most likely quite a small part, of the whole correspondence circulating in the empire and the nation. We might therefore say that many of the achievements now attributed to the post office (or sometimes to the press), such as creating bonds of union, circulating information, unifying regions and provinces, and coordinating political, commercial and interpersonal action, can only be attributed to the post metonymically. Attributing such nation- and empire-building achievements to the post also makes it all too easy to take for granted, and therefore to overlook, the fact that as an institution, a post office assumes a fairly widespread ability to write letters – or the production of such ability where it has been lacking. As Ian Steele has pointed out, this was "a literate empire, a paper empire" which "rewarded literacy, even required it."[13]

The extent of eighteenth-century literacy is still uncertain. Modern estimates vary widely, and so do the criteria for literacy. There was clearly a significant surge in literacy between the middle of the seventeenth century and the middle of the eighteenth – David Cressy confirms that almost 70 per cent of English men and 90 per cent of English women in mid-seventeenth-century England could not sign their names, whereas a century later these figures had dropped to 40 per cent and 60 per cent.[14] However,

---

12 Ellis, *Post Office*; Fowler, *Unmailable*; John, *Spreading the News*. In the early Republic, opening letters in the post was, in principle, prohibited by law; but contemporaries testify that it went on happening.
13 Steele, *English Atlantic*, 265.
14 Cressy, "Literacy in Context," 305.

estimates such as this which are based on signatures found on surviving legal documents have been put in question by the realization that reading was taught prior to and separately from writing, and that many more people may therefore have been able to read than to write. There is also a problem with modern assessments of the distribution of literacy. Estimates on the higher end are that by mid-century 70 per cent of white men in British urban centers, and 60 per cent of white men in Puritan New England were literate, and that literacy was far greater in towns and among the trading classes than in rural areas, among the lower classes or among women. But this is hard to reconcile with the work that has been done, by scholars in a different field, on schooling and on schools. As Geoffrey Holmes has pointed out, "the more that is discovered about basic educational provision of every kind in Augustan England," the more it seems likely to bear out the truth of Francis Brokesby's words, written in 1701, "that there are few country villages where some or other do not get a livelihood by teaching school."[15] The same has frequently been said of the American provinces.[16] Besides the sheer increase in the numbers of elementary and secondary schools both in Britain and in America during this period, it is noteworthy that, on both sides of the Atlantic, parishes and local governments made it one of the conditions of indenture for the many poor or orphaned young people of both sexes that they placed in apprenticeships, that their masters ensure that they be taught to read and write. There were some free places for sons of the poor in most grammar schools, and some of the most prominent men in the eighteenth century came up that way. On both sides of the Atlantic, there was also provision of education for girls both with boys in "petty" or elementary schools and in private and boarding schools for girls. It therefore seems reasonable to assume, at the very least, that in England, "by the time of Walpole (1722–42), most tradesmen, shopkeepers and small farmers could read, and within twenty years so could about 40 per cent of all laborers and women."[17]

However, imperial problems of communication at this time went far beyond mere technical literacy. Even setting aside the different languages

---

15 Holmes, *Augustan London*, 55; Money, "Teaching in the Market Place." In 1755, Bristol had twenty schoolmaster and seventeen schoolmistresses running private schools alone. Alnwick in Northumberland was supporting fifteen private schools.

16 Cohen, *History of Colonial Education*; Cremin, *American Education*; Bailyn, *Education in the Forming of American Society*.

17 Hay and Rogers, *Eighteenth-Century English Society*, 9. Other evidence includes the institution and expansion of the provincial press. See Feather, *Provincial Book Trade*, 33.

spoken on the so-called Celtic fringe, local and regional differences in pronunciation, vocabulary, syntax, customs and forms of address were still making it difficult for people in different parts of England – let alone of Britain or the empire – to understand one another's manners and speech. At the beginning of the eighteenth century, Defoe found the Devonshire dialect incomprehensible, and grammarian Hugh Jones observed that the speech of Yorkshire and that of Somerset were unintelligible to one another. At the end of the century, James Adams (a Scot) declared that Suffolk outdid all the counties in England in "queer cant," and Noah Webster observed that "the people of distant counties in England can hardly understand one another, so various are their dialects."[18] Transcribing a transatlantic letter from one Tonal Mackepherson to his father in the Highlands in a letter he wrote to a friend in London in the 1730s, Edmund Burt illustrated the difficulty of reading letters across linguistic and cultural regions by contrasting the ease and enjoyment with which Mackepherson's letter was circulated in his native Highland speech community, with the difficulty that those outside it had in deciphering a letter written and spelled as Mackepherson would have spoken and pronounced the words:

Tear lofen kynt Fater,

Dis is te let ye ken dat I am in quid Healt, plessed be Got for dat, houpin te here de lyk frae yu as I am yer nane Sin. . .De Skep dat I kam in was a lang tym in de See cumin oure heir, but plissit pi Got for a ting wi a kepit our Heels unco weel, pat ShonieMagwillivrey da hat ay a Seir Heet.[19]

Efforts to rectify this communication problem by instituting "Standard English" and standard spelling during this period went hand in hand with efforts to disseminate standard epistolary forms and standard (often known as "polite") cultural practices.[20] This point was graphically underlined by the inclusion in late seventeenth- and eighteenth-century letter manuals of grammars, spellers, dictionaries of hard words, and directions for manners and epistolary etiquette, in place of the collections of commonplaces and rhetorical tropes that letter manuals had offered until

---

18 Quoted in Knowles, *Cultural History of the English Language*, 134; Gorlach, "Regional and Social Variation," 499.
19 *Burt's Letters*, 112.
20 "The codifiers and advocates of Standard English belonged to an educated class and cultivated a standard reflecting their own linguistic forms, communicative practices, and social privileges." Ullman, *Things*, 26. Codifiers also criticized and satirized the upper ranks for not adhering to the models of language and conduct they were promulgating.

quite late in the seventeenth century.[21] To prevent local dialects and eccentric local practices from impeding "commerce" across counties and provinces – in all the word commerce's eighteenth-century senses of exchange, intercourse, traffic, conversation and trade – standardized spelling had to replace words spelled phonetically however the writer pronounced them and standard written English had to replace the writing and printing of local dialects. The dissemination of standard epistolary forms and polite norms therefore took precedence over the elocution movement's efforts during the second half of the eighteenth century to regularize the pronunciation of spoken English. It has been argued that standardization was a function of printing, since "written forms are particularly amenable to the most effective technology of standardization, printing."[22] Printers and booksellers who traded in books certainly had an interest in establishing a form of written language that could be bought and read with ease outside their own particular localities. But it is clearly also the case that, both for a government which used printed and handwritten letters to make empire work and for a nation of shopkeepers whose commerce had begun to depend upon trafficking with correspondents elsewhere in the British Isles and across the Atlantic, standard forms of letters written in Standard English – preferably in a legible "secretary's hand" – facilitated commerce of all kinds by streamlining communication, and by making letters easier to understand and quicker to write.[23]

This period therefore witnessed a concerted program of public pedagogy, undertaken both in schools and in print, that was designed to inculcate and promote manuscript letter-writing in the vernacular among people at all ranks. As early as 1649, during the lengthy seventeenth-century debate about replacing the grammar schools' traditional Latin-based classical curriculum with a more widely practical and vernacular education, George Snell had included letter-writing under "useful knowledge" on the grounds that he who could "attain Abilitie to express neatly and cautiously all sorts of Affairs in missive Letters, is in a readie waie to

---

21 For language's impact on national unity, Noah Webster, *Dissertations on the English Language* (1789); Tennenhouse, "A Language for the Nation"; Crowley, *Language in History*. Most scholars agree that standardization was in process during the eighteenth century and achieved in the nineteenth – though "dialects" like Cockney continued well into the early twentieth century as the accompaniment of Standard English. But see Bailey, *Images of English*, and Crowley, *Standard English*.

22 Ullman, *Things*, 26.

23 Hence, during the early Republic, Noah Webster insisted that national unity and "political harmony" were "concerned in a uniformity of language," and initiated the new nation's distinct system of language by introducing new "American" standardized spellings.

be assumed to anie imploiment of the highest importance."[24] By the 1690s, in the wake of the Toleration Act and the birth of the Charity School movement, the new "English" curriculum had begun to produce what would become virtually an alternative school system on both sides of the Atlantic, composed of an array of dissenting and other academies, private and boarding schools, writing schools, mathematical schools, charity schools and evening schools, which taught letter-writing in the vernacular as "a practical skill," along with *pronunciation* or reading aloud, grammar and spelling.[25] The new "English schools" also taught geography, history, arithmetic and book-keeping, geometry and drawing (for surveying). Many added options in natural philosophy, the history of trade and commerce, ethics, government and French, which was the commercial and diplomatic *lingua franca* of Europe.[26]

In his transatlantically popular and much reprinted version of the English school curriculum, *The Preceptor* (1748), which was notably dedicated to George II and firmly oriented to empire, printer Robert Dodsley explained the value of such subjects to men in agriculture, in commerce and in the professions as well as to men with landed fortunes. He explained, for instance, that such men needed to study geography "to know the situation of nations on which their interests generally depend." They needed to study the history of trade and commerce to understand "when the Balance of Trade is on our Side, what are the Products or Manufactures of other countries, and how far one Nation may in any Specie of Traffic obtain or preserve Superiority over another." They needed to study the principles of law and government because every Englishman is "a secondary Legislator, as he gives his Consent of his Representatives, to all the Laws by which he is bound, and has a Right to Petition the great Council of the Nation, whenever he thinks they are deliberating on an Act detrimental to the Interests of the Community."[27] But having indicated the purpose of all other subjects, Dodsley began

---

24 Cited in Mitchell, *Grammar Wars*, 77.
25 Michael, *Teaching of English*, 269.
26 This curriculum is sometimes misleadingly described as "vocational," by contrast with that of Latin grammar schools. The classical curriculum of Latin grammar schools and later university merely prepared students for different vocations – the Church, the learned professions, government. All education in the eighteenth century was overwhelmingly utilitarian, both in the sense that it taught particular vocational skills, and in the sense that it was supposed to be geared to the station in life that the student was intended to occupy.
27 Letters of petition were the way to get bounties, lobby for bills or government action, or discourage government measures viewed as detrimental to the interest of one's social or economic group.

with the fundament – a long chapter on "Reading, Speaking and Writing Letters" – because, he insisted, the ability to write letters had become "equally useful to the highest and the lowest," and was now "in most Stations of Life indispensably required."[28] Once the privileged instrument of kings, courts and papal nuncios, letter-writing had become the basis of any "General Course of Education wherein the first principles of Polite Learning are laid down. . .for the Instruction of Youth."

There were affinities between the materials selected for compendia and *vade mecums* and the curricula of the new English-based and arithmetic-based education in the new "English" schools. Letter manuals have therefore sometimes, mistakenly, been conflated with school-texts.[29] *Vade mecums* like *The Instructor, or Young Man's Best Companion* (1735), which taught numeracy, book-keeping, measuring and surveying and other practical skills as well as epistolography, mirrored the principal school subjects in mercantile and dissenting academies and private "English" schools. *Secretaries* and *Letter-writers*, by contrast concentrated on the verbal parts of this instruction. These compendia often summarized or reprinted as part of their miscellany, works like Dilworth's *Speller*, Lowth's *Grammar* and Blair's *Instructions for Pronunciation*, that had begun life as school-texts. They also usually tactfully suggested on their title-pages that they were designed "for the instruction of youth," despite the fact that the preface or introduction inside marketed them to adults of all ages and ranks. Some compendia and letter-miscellanies also included letters offering general information about school subjects.

There are suggestions that letter-miscellanies or compendia may have been employed in the classroom. For instance, Henry Hogg observed in his Preface to *The New and Complete Universal Letter-Writer or Whole Art of Polite Correspondence* (1790?) that "it is presumed that it [the manual] should be universally introduced into all schools, for the purpose of making young Ladies and Gentlemen (at stated times) transcribe a letter upon whatever Subject they might think proper, and address them each to their little friends." Writing letters to one's fellow pupils or friends by imitating models one had read and transcribed was one frequently recommended way of learning to write them. Hogg was no doubt hoping to supply the place of *The Spectator* which, throughout the eighteenth century, *was* regularly used as a school-text both in Dissenting Academies

---

28 Dodsley, *Preceptor* (1754), xix, xxviii, xxix, xvi.
29 Michael, *Teaching of English*. Historians of the book also often include epistolary manuals among school-texts.

in Britain (such as Philip Doddridge's) and in the academies sprouting throughout the American provinces on the British model.[30] Over half the *Spectator* papers consisted of letters conveniently and entertainingly organized into a letter manual. Later letter manuals frequently recommended that their readers practice letter-writing by imitating and rewording the letters in *The Spectator* – as indeed, Benjamin Franklin did. *The Instructive Letter-Writer and Entertaining Companion* (1769), for instance, instructed its readers that "The Guardian and Spectators should be read often, especially the letters that are interspersed in those valuable volumes."[31]

Compendia and letter-miscellanies could be used in the classroom to teach a wide variety of subjects in addition to epistolary composition, as John Buchanan explained:

The Method I take, and I find it so far effectual to the End proposed, is, having got what I judged the best Book of Letters, I make several young Gentlemen stand up, and one of them read a Letter gracefully; after which I read it to them myself, making Observations on the Sentiment and Style, and asking their Opinions with Respect to both. And if the Letter has an Answer, I ask them before they read it, what Answer they would make to this or that Passage? If their Answer happens to tally with that of the Author, it gives them great Spirits. And on the whole, a deep and lasting Impression is made on their Memories, and their Understandings improved.[32]

Buchanan used a single book of letters with impressive economy to teach graceful elocution or delivery (reading aloud), the different styles of epistolary writing and of epistolary address, conduct book ideas and morals ("Sentiment"), and correspondence or communication skills, as well as to cultivate the memory and the understanding by means of the information they contained. It is feasible to suppose, therefore, that especially in country areas and in American provinces where books were scarce, epistolary compendia which included spellers and grammars, and *vade mecums* which offered guides to mathematics, book-keeping, and surveying, and some rudimentary history and geography as well as epistolography, may have been used for home or local schooling.[33] "Books," as Isaac Watts pointed out, "are a sort of dumb teachers."[34]

---

30 Bailyn, *Education in the Forming of American Society*.
31 [George Seymour], *The Instructive Letter-Writer*, 9. *Tatlers* are sometimes mentioned too.
32 Buchanan, *English Grammar* (1762), xxviii–xxix.
33 Gilmore, *Reading becomes a Necessity of Life*; Cremin, *American Education*; Davidson, *Reading in America*; Houston, *Scottish Literacy*.
34 In Wilson Smith (ed.), *Theories of Education*, 103.

But though epistolary compendia may have been used as a vehicle for formal schooling, they were not primarily designed either for children or for schools. They were self-help and self-improvement manuals for mature as well as young adults, which targeted a wide range of publics.

LETTER MANUALS' TARGET AUDIENCES

London manuals did not only profile their target audiences explicitly on title-pages, in prefaces and in introductions. Because users were expected to imitate the example of characters like themselves, manuals also indicated their target audiences by their choices of fictional generic letter-writing characters in the collections of model letters they contained. These generic characters or social types were so many representatives within the text of the reader-writers manuals were targeting outside it. Together with such information as we have about who actually owned letter manuals, sketchy as it admittedly still is, understanding manuals' identifications of their potential audiences is a useful first step towards puncturing dismissive modern assumptions that *London* manuals were designed exclusively for the "partly literate"[35] or for the trading middle class. At the same time, manuals' identifications of their potential users must be treated with some caution: they indicate where printers or compilers considered letter-writing an important, and perhaps relatively new, requirement and where they hoped to find potential buyers; but we cannot assume that all the audiences manuals identified actually bought or used them in writing letters, or if they did, that they did so in any number. Moreover, as we will see in Part II, American and Scottish adaptations of London manuals frequently had different target audiences than the *London* manuals I will be considering here, many of which were imported into the American provinces.

Typical entries in letter-collections looked like this:

A Letter of Excuse for Silence, and Assurance twas not out of Disrespect

There are Times, Madam, in which it is failing in Care, not to write to one's Friends; there are others in which it is Prudence. Methinks it better becomes an unhappy Man to be silent than to speak; for he tires if he speaks of his Misery, or he is ridiculous if he attempts to be diverting. I have not done myself the Honour of writing to you since my Departure, to avoid one or other of these Inconveniences. I have too much Respect for you, Madam, to importune you with my Griefs; and I am not Fool enough to have a Mind to laugh. I know very

---

35 Robertson, *Art of Letter-Writing*, 66.

well that there may be a Mean between these two Extremes; but after all, the Correspondence of the unhappy are seldom pleasing to those who are in Prosperity. And yet, Madam, there are Duties with which one ought not to dispense; and it is to acquit myself of them, that I now assure you that no one can be with more Esteem and Respect than I am,

Your faithful and affectionate Servant,

I. B.

A Letter from a Servant in London, to his Master in the Country

Sir,

    As I find you are detained longer in the Country than you expected, I thought it my Duty to acquaint you that we are all well at Home; and to assure you that your Business shall be carried on with the same Care and Fidelity as if you were personally present. We all wish for your Return as soon as your Affairs will permit; and it is with Pleasure that I take this Opportunity of subscribing myself,

Sir,

Your most obedient, and faithful Servant,

Sam. Trusty.[36]

    The titles given to letters by compilers usually indicated the occasion for the letter, the kind of letter that followed, and which generic characters were corresponding. I have transcribed two letters which directly followed one another in Crowder's *Complete Letter-Writer* (1755) to offer a sense of what these collections looked like. It was fairly characteristic for them to juxtapose heterogeneous letters written in different styles and designed for reader-writers of different ranks – as here *The Complete Letter-Writer* juxtaposed a gentleman's complemental letter of excuse to a lady with a clerk or servant's courteous but more matter-of-fact letter of advice to his master. Generic characters were broadly identified by occupation or rank, or by family relationships.

    In their prefaces and introductions, London manuals sought to cast their net as widely as possible. Hill's allusion to the needs of those who lived in the country and in country towns where secretaries and scriveners were scarce, marketed his printed *Secretary* to the more than 70 per cent of

---

36 Crowder's *Complete Letter-Writer or Polite English Secretary* (London, 1768), 80–1. This was anonymous, but repeatedly reprinted for Stanley Crowder in London, from the time he set up in business on London Bridge in 1755 until his death in 1798. Since several different manual series call themselves *Complete Letter-Writers*, I call this one Crowder's to avoid confusion. Also, "many booksellers acted as editors or compilers of extracted or commissioned material." Raven, *Judging New Wealth*, 64.

the population both in the British Isles and in the American colonies who still lived in rural and small provincial urban settings.[37] Subsequent London manuals sought to make their manuals "equally useful to the highest and the lowest." Crowder's *Complete Letter-Writer, or Polite English Secretary* (1755) explained that it was describing itself as "complete" not only to indicate the range of subjects and occasions for letter-writing for which it offered models, but also to show that it was designed to "answer the Purpose almost of every Individual, from the Boy at School to the Secretary of State." This included "many Epistles of the lower Class" because these "could not be omitted without deviating from the grand Point of View, namely General Utility."[38] Charles Johnson likewise advertised his *Compleat Introduction to the Art of Writing Letters* (1758) as "universally adapted to all Classes and Conditions of Life." Even at the end of the century, Henry Hogg observed in his Preface to *The New Universal Letter-Writer Or, Complete Art of Polite Correspondence* (c. 1790), that there were still "many grown up persons of all occupations, professions and degrees, who need in a great measure the assistance of [a] Letter-Writer."

The number of editions and reprints of the most popular manuals in London alone confirm that a very large number of people were buying letter manuals throughout the long eighteenth century. Even the least regarded manuals generally managed three or four London editions. The most popular London compendia and *vade mecums* were reprinted upwards of twenty or thirty times. They were both exported to America and adapted by local printers there, and usually went through several editions in American adaptations as well. From the 1760s on, some popular London manuals were also reprinted multiple times in Scotland. The fact that manuals were "steady sellers"[39] on both sides of the Atlantic and that people were buying letter manuals in London and all over the provinces in quantity cannot be doubted. But we must look to the generic characters in the letter collections to see how printers and compilers broke these broad audiences down, and try to understand why they elected to offer epistolary models for the specific social groups they chose.

---

37 Corfield, *Impact of English Towns*, Ellis, *Georgian Town*, and Kussmaul, *Rural Economy*.
38 Crowder's *Compleat Letter-Writer*, Preface. In later editions, *Compleat* became *Complete*.
39 Steady sellers are "books that went through five or more editions in New England in a period of at least 50 years"; and "printers in New England relied on steady sellers for their business." Hall, "Uses of Literacy," 29, 31.

Virtually all compendia that claimed to be "for the instruction of youth" on their title-pages included dutiful letters from schoolboys and schoolgirls to their parents, as well as apprentice letters and maidservant letters. Schoolboy letters were a nod at schools, where masters required their students to write a letter home once a week both to practice letter-writing and to demonstrate to fee-paying parents that their offspring were making improvements in handwriting and letteracy. They also made a more polemical point when they had schoolboys describe their progress in the Latin curriculum. Why, after all, would printers and compilers think they had a market for letter-writing models and English grammars and spellers among children (or indeed gentlemen) who had the benefit of a classical education? The answer of advocates of "English schools" and English masters throughout the seventeenth and eighteenth centuries was that the classical education offered by Latin schools did not adequately teach their pupils to write letters in the vernacular. Robert Campbell summed up commonly repeated sentiments when he observed in 1747 that graduates of public schools and Latin grammar schools "can render, it is true, their Words into English [i.e. translate from Latin into English], but they can speak their noble Sentiments in no Language; and whatever Progress they have made in Greek and Latin, it is certain they often know no more of their Mother Tongue (except the mere Sound) than if they had been born in Japan, or on the Cape of Good Hope."[40] By including grammar schoolboy letters, letter manuals presented themselves as poten-tial supplements to a Latin education, while implicitly promoting the virtues of the English school.

Campbell added that those employed to teach in public schools and in Latin grammar schools "are mere Pedants. . .without any knowledge of useful Literature, and profoundly ignorant of Men and Things." Famil-iarizing their readers with contemporary "Men and Things" was another of the educational functions assumed by manuals and letter-miscellanies. As John Buchanan put it in 1762, books of model letters taught "the Rules of private and public Conduct" as well as "the Snares and Temptations of the World," and served to "introduce [their users] to the knowledge of Mankind, and prepare them for appearing on the Stage of public Life with Honour and Advantage."[41] Teaching "politeness" and "civility" was an important part of this preparation. Letter manuals thus contributed to

---

40 Campbell, *London Tradesman*, 85.
41 *The British Grammar*, xxvi–xxvii.

the construction of Britons as what Paul Langford has described as "a polite and commercial people," as well as to what Americanists have called the "anglicization" of America.[42]

Collections of letters in compendia also invariably included apprentice letters, for apprentices represented a very compendious category of potential readers. Apprenticeship for young men, which began between the ages of fourteen and seventeen, was the principal means of training for the civil service and for most of the professions, as well as for the different forms of trade, artisanal manufacture, retailing and commerce. Commerce, the "new professions" (such as the army, navy, surveying and estate management), and the middle and lower strata of two of the learned professions (solicitors and scriveners in law, surgeons and apothecaries in medicine) were all rapidly expanding their ranks during this period. The new civil service, with its multiplying government departments and commissions, clerks, secretaries, customs officers, excise officers, Exchequer officials, postal officials, colonial administrators and more, was likewise growing apace, and requiring "an unprecedented expansion in the number of transcribers, copyists and record keepers."[43] Letter manuals at mid-century recommended the security and gentility of such employments over artisan manufacture and trade.

Young women were apprenticed too: to artisans like milliners, glovers and mantua makers; to manufacturers in the textile industry; to tradesmen like vintners, victuallers, "upholders," pawnbrokers and innkeepers; and to professional teachers.[44] Adult women worked in a variety of trades. But their wages were small – earnings of 8 shillings a week were exceptional for a woman in manufacture or trade at a time when the common wage for men was 12 to 15 shillings a week. Letter manuals therefore ignored female apprentices and women who worked in trade, and focused on maidservants instead. The wages for maidservants were considered "high" even during the 1770s when trade and commerce declined; and the fact that they received bed and board meant that they had money to spare for frills and furbelows, or other purchases – much to the annoyance of male moralists who castigated them for extravagance and for dressing

---

42 Langford, *A Polite and Commercial People.* For "anglicization," see Bushman, *Refinement of America*; Wood, *Radicalism of the American Revolution*; Green, *Imperatives, Behaviors, and Identities* and *The Intellectual Construction of America*; Shields, *Civil Tongues*; Landsman, *From Colonials to Provincials.*
43 Brewer, *Sinews of Power*, xvi.
44 Simonton, "Apprenticeship."

above their station.[45] A maidservant who began work at the age of fourteen or fifteen and saved her earnings over a number of years had a dowry which could enable her to marry a tradesman; or she could marry a footman who had saved his earnings too and set up with him in "a substantial business." Thomas Mortimer, who used this phrase, reported in 1772 that "a list was lately put into my hands of upwards of one thousand ale-house keepers, green-grocers, chandlers, oil shops, and other retail trades in London, and the villages adjacent, all of whom were originally footmen and servant maids."[46] London manuals therefore almost invariably included standard maidservant letters about marrying tradesmen – the letter a maidservant might write to inform her parents in the country of a proposal of marriage from a young tradesman, and another to let them know that such a marriage had occurred.

Compendia not unexpectedly included numerous model letters to and from fictional clerks, country chapmen, shopkeepers, tradesmen, merchants, town landlords and urban tenants, who represented commerce and trade. The letter collections in compendia and *vade mecums* invariably included "letters of business," though the emphasis placed on commercial issues varied considerably from manual to manual. That manuals, schoolmasters and writers on commerce and trade stressed the importance of letter-writing to merchants and tradesmen will come as no surprise: we now take it for granted that merchants and tradesmen were the first group in society outside the Court and the Church to need letters and to know how to write them. Merchants had, after all, been using writing for commercial purposes since the Phoenicians. But matters may not have been so clear cut. Campbell indicates that in the middle of the eighteenth century, tradesmen and shop-keepers in profitable businesses such as linen-drapery were hiring clerks, at wages far higher even than those of their highly skilled foreman or "finisher," to write their letters and keep their books for them, because they were not capable of doing so themselves. He also attempted to persuade such people to change their ways by urging that "the Art of writing a Letter genteely, is a necessary and ornamental Qualification to a Tradesman, as much as to any man else: Nay it is more useful than to many Gentlemen, because their Correspondence is larger, and their Ignorance more exposed. I often wonder to see a Man who can write his Name to a note of ten thousands pounds, yet cannot dictate a common Letter of Business with any kind of Propriety of

45 Defoe, *Law of Subordination.*
46 Mortimer, *Elements of Commerce, Politics and Finances* (1772), 93.

Language, or write one Line free of false Grammar or bad Spelling."[47] Perhaps eighteenth-century schoolmasters and writers on commerce and trade who touted letter-writing were not preaching to the choir. And perhaps a man who could read, but not write much beyond his name, could at least learn from letter manuals how to "dictate a common Letter of Business" which expressed what he wanted to say in the proper way.

Equally interesting are the terms in which the importance of letter-writing was urged on men in commerce and trade. In the 1720s, for instance, Thomas Watts, master of an English school on Abchurch Lane in London which prepared students for trade, commerce, public offices, clerkships and stewardships, insisted that "whoever would be a *Man of Business* must be a *Man of Correspondence*" because "to speak and write with *Propriety* and *Elegance* has too great an *Influence* on *business* to be neglected." William Webster, a noted writing-master and accountant who kept a boarding school in London, likewise insisted that the man of business needed "above all, a good *narrative Style* or a facility to express himself handsomely by Letter." Like Campbell, these schoolmasters emphasized the importance of expressing oneself handsomely or genteelly in a letter. William Milns, an Oxford graduate and migrating London schoolmaster who opened a private academy in New York in the 1790s, offers a partial explanation: "There is nothing perhaps upon which the character of the merchant so much depends as on the language of his Letters; he is known to many of his correspondents by no other means." The anonymous author of *The Accomplish'd Merchant* was even more explicit: "For as Trade can only be carry'd on by an Intercourse of Letters between the *Merchants* of one Country with those of another, their Letters will ever be the *Touchstone* of their Ability, discover who have heads well turn'd for Business, are actuated by rational Views and Motives, and take wise Measures to support and extend their Credit."[48] When trade and commerce were conducted *in absentia*, at a distance, and on credit rather than in cash, and a man's financial credit depended on others' belief in his ability, integrity and adherence to mercantile custom, a man's credit in both senses depended on the way he presented himself in his correspondence.

47 *London Tradesman*, 195.

48 Sheldahl, *Education for the Mercantile Counting House*. Watts, *Method for forming a Man of Business*, 19, 25; Webster, *Education of Youth*, 87; Milns, *Plan of Instruction for Private Classes*, 5; *Accomplish'd Merchant*, 16.

But why was it necessary – at a time when people were told to write letters as they would speak – to write elegantly and genteelly to make the proper impression on one's fellow tradesmen, merchants, factors and commercial correspondents? Why was it not sufficient just to express oneself in a matter-of-fact, clear and concise manner – to display, in other words, what everyone agreed were the fundamental virtues of a commercial letter? The most salient answer appears to be that merchants and tradesmen were competing with gentry within their own ranks. Increasing numbers of gentry were apprenticing their sons in commerce and trade: by the 1720s, parents had to pay several hundred pounds to apprentice their sons to the most reputable masters in the more desirable trades or in the most profitable mercantile houses, effectively pricing out the poor and middling sorts; and by the middle of the century, these men who had been bred in the upper ranks were active in the City. It was therefore not merely, as we have generally argued, that wealthy merchants sought to acquire the language and manners of their betters for them-selves, or failing that for their sons, in order to be able to "pass" amongst the gentry once they had retired from the city and bought a country estate. The sons of the gentry were speaking their genteel English, dis-playing their genteel manners, and writing letters that reflected these, within the City itself. They were competing amongst merchants and tradesmen from more modest backgrounds, and thus to some extent setting the standard of language and conduct in commerce and trade. This may be why Malachy Postlewayt, who has been described as a "fountain of mid-century British political commonplaces,"[49] backed up his injunction to merchants to learn to write letters by stressing the importance of successful competition in letter-writing: "We have heard a worthy and ingenious merchant declare, That his being able to corres-pond in a manner something superior to the generality was the means of getting him a very good estate, from very small beginnings; this talent having brought him a very large commission business. . ."[50] Writing masters therefore advertised their difference from the "mere pedants" in Latin grammar schools by promising to remove the impediments of those

---

49 Miller, *Defining the Common Good*, 163.
50 Postlethwayt, *Universal Dictionary of Trade and Commerce* (1755), II: 221. Secondarily, there were trades which were thought to require genteel speech and manners not because they were populated by the sons of gentlemen, but because they depended almost entirely on ladies for their business. Campbell said tradesmen such as mercers, who sold silks, velvets and brocades to ladies must be "very polite and skilled in all the Punctilios of City Good-Breeding," "affect a Court air," and "have much of the Frenchman in their manners."

whose regional, provincial, or class culture prevented them from "corresponding in a manner something superior to the generality."

Finally, London compendia included among their model correspondents generic characters who represented the professions and the gentry. British manuals invariably included one or two soldiers and sailors – not surprisingly since Britain spent two-thirds of the long eighteenth century at war. These are generally shown writing letters home to their wives or sweethearts, and receiving letters in return. Manuals also included estate stewards, who often had to correspond with absentee landlords as well as with tenants and others on matters related to the estate.[51] These were generally shown in manuals demanding rent from tenant farmers who were unable to pay on time. Particularly prominent in manuals at the end of the eighteenth century, though present here and there throughout, was the clergy – always useful for letters of advice or consolation and uplifting religious thoughts.

Professionals in the civil service, doctors and lawyers were represented by the generic character "gentleman"– as indeed was the landed gentry. In some respects, the letters each might need to write overlapped. From this point of view, it is significant that contemporaries throughout the eighteenth century echoed Guy Miege's observation that a gentleman was either such by birth or anyone "with a liberal or genteel education that looks gentleman-like (whether he be so or not) and has the wherewithal to live freely," and that professionals were invariably granted the status of gentlemen whatever their class of origin.[52] In professions like government or the civil service where preferment depended on patronage and cliency, and in professions like the law or medicine where success depended on a good social network as well as on patronage, the ambitious had to be able to write appropriate letters to their patrons and "friends" in the word's eighteenth-century sense which "spanned kinship ties, sentimental ties, economic ties, occupational connections, intellectual and spiritual attachments, sociable networks and political alliances."[53] London manuals specialized in modeling the sort of letters that such people needed to write to remind their "friends" of their existence when there were benefits to be conferred, to congratulate a patron or friend on a promotion or recovery from sickness, to accompany a small gift, to ask for help, to thank a friend for benefits received, and otherwise to ingratiate themselves and keep

51 Beckett, "Estate Management."
52 Borsay, "English Urban Renaissance," 176.
53 Tadmor, *Family and Friends*, 167.

useful connections alive. We often mistake such letters for letters of friendship in the modern sense; but as Gordon Wood has put it, in the eighteenth century, "friendships were euphemisms for all kinds of dependencies."[54] The ability to write apparently "social" letters to one's "friends" was a professional skill, which mimed and adapted the social conventions and letter-writing practices of the court.

The civil service, the professions, commerce, the armed services, apprenticeship and domestic service were all channels for both social and geographical mobility.[55] Apprenticeships were frequently taken up a long way from home, and young men and women came in large numbers from the English, Scottish and Irish provinces to work as servants in London. Members of the army and navy, merchant and marine, were obviously much traveled. And alongside migrants to the new world and the English on the Grand Tour, there were already career structures in place in administration, government, commerce and trade for competent letter-writers, many of which might involve a tour of duty in the colonies. A man who began as a "Writer" or lowly clerk in commerce could rise to "Correspondent" or factor abroad, and eventually to partner. There were hierarchies of clerks in each government office leading to a permanent secretaryship at the top and hierarchies of colonial administrators and customs officers who were sent out from London.[56] Even "professional qualifications increasingly constituted a passport to travel – not just in Britain but throughout its expanding empire."[57] As Vicesimus Knox observed in 1783, in a manual designed for the "Improvement of Epistolary Style," for the many seeking to make or mend their fortunes overseas, letteracy was the passport to success:

Many natives of this country spend their youth in foreign climes. How greatly does it contribute to raise their characters at home, when they are able to write judicious letters to their relations, their friends, their patrons, their employers? A clear, a discreet, an elegant letter, establishes their character in their native country, while perhaps their persons are at a distance of the antipodes, raises esteem among all who read it, and often lays a foundation for future eminence. It goes before them like a pioneer, smoothes the road and levels the hill that leads up to honour and fortune.[58]

---

54 Wood, *Radicalism of the American Revolution*, 58.
55 Corfield, *Power and the Professions*; Holmes, *Augustan England*; Haber, *Quest for Authority*.
56 Brewer, *Sinews of Power*, xvi. Also Steele, *English Atlantic*, and Hancock, *Citizen of the World*. For a different view, see Brooks, "Apprenticeship."
57 Corfield, *Power and the Professions*, 219.
58 Knox, *Elegant Epistles*, vi.

Irishman Richard Steele had argued over sixty years before that the "new men" of the eighteenth century – the rising men of sense and ability from outside the upper ranks and often from outside London too, who were used, promoted and integrated by the elite because they brought needed skills – would be competent writers of letters, uniquely or in addition to whatever else they did.[59] And indeed, many important figures of the Scottish Enlightenment began their careers as secretaries. As Franklin pointed out, manuscript or print letteracy in government service was an alternative path to a knighthood, to the House of Commons, to the Cabinet, to high colonial Office, to the Bench and to advancement in the Church at a time when individuals were rising from the lower and mechanick ranks well as from middle and mercantile classes.[60]

Letter manuals answered Jon Klancher's interesting question about "how an individual reader became aware of belonging to a greater social audience" by juxtaposing images in the text of reader-writers in diverse ranks and occupations in a manner reminiscent of the Prologue to *The Canterbury Tales.*[61] No one who even leafed through one of these collections of letters could doubt that he or she belonged to a larger society, or fail to perceive where they fit into it. For instance, the servant-reader and the master-reader of the *Letter from a Servant in London to his Master in the Country* in *The Complete Letter-Writer, or Polite English Secretary* (above, pp. 20–21) could each see their proper relative positions in that letter, and how they were placed in society relative to the gentleman addressing his excuses to a lady in the letter just above. By the same token, while recognizing their relative positions in the gentleman's merely polite deference to the lady, lady and gentleman readers of the latter's letter of excuse would be forcibly reminded by the letter immediately below of the presence in society of the tradesmen, merchants and servants who supplied Britain's material needs. The gap between social reality and the harmonious vision in this paper society, of everyone juxtaposed performing the proper relative duties of their place and rank in the language and style considered proper to them, was the space of prescription, instruction and ideological work.

---

59 Siskin, *Power of Writing*; Griffin, *Literary Patronage*; Solomon, *Rise of Robert Dodsley*; Bauman, *Legislators and Interpreters.*
60 Franklin, "English School," note. Both in Britain and in America, letteracy permitted men who began life as apprentices to glue- or stocking-makers, footmen, poor scholars or lowly "mechanicks" – like Addison and Steele, or printers Robert Dodsley, William Strahan and Benjamin Franklin – to rise in the world to become MPs or members of provincial assemblies.
61 Klancher, *English Reading Audiences*, 6.

The cross-section of society represented by the parade of letter-writing *dramatis personae* in London manuals was broader than even the compendious class that has been called "the middling sort," which has proved almost impossible to define.[62] A more practical way of characterizing the social representation in London letter manuals may be to identify the top and the bottom, and leave the middle to take care of itself. Here the discovery of several recent historians that in eighteenth-century Britain, urban merchants, professionals and the urban gentry associated with one another socially and frequently intermarried is particularly useful, as is the fact that this group often constituted the elite in English and Scottish, as well as American, provincial towns.[63] Amanda Vickery has found the same pattern of social interaction and intermarriage among the rural commercial elite, rural professionals and the lesser landed gentry. This group has variously been called the "pseudo-gentry" and "the genteel."[64] Contemporaries certainly saw merchants, professionals and gentlemen as a group related by a common interest in trade and commerce. Richard Rolt, for instance, designed his *New Dictionary of Trade and Commerce* "for the use of the Merchants and Tradesmen of Great Britain, as well as of Private Gentlemen"; Roger North's *The Gentleman Accountant* argued that book-keeping was "as profitable to a Man of an Estate as to one of a gainful Profession, the one getting, the other Preserving an Estate"; and Thomas Mortimer addressed his treatise on the elements of commerce to gentlemen, to prevent recurrence of the "imbecility of entire administrations when departments in charge of commercial affairs have been filled with gentlemen without any mercantile knowledge."[65] I think we can say that this related group of wealthy merchants, professionals and lesser gentry marks the top of the social hierarchy in most London compendia and letter-miscellanies, and that a substantial number of model letters are geared to them.[66]

---

62 Compare the different definitions in Hunt, *The Middling Sort*; Earle, *Making of the English Middle Class*; Corfield, *Impact of English Towns*; Holderness, *Preindustrial England*; Barry and Brooks, *The Middling Sort of People*. Blackstone identified forty different finely graded ranks in Britain. Efforts to reduce them to a nineteenth-century tripartite structure may not be productive. See Wahrman, *Imagining the Middle Class*; Corfield, "Class by Name and Number"; Wrightson, "Class."

63 Phillipson, "Culture and Society in the Eighteenth-Century Province."

64 Vickery, *Gentleman's Daughter*, 1; Holderness, *Preindustrial England*.

65 Rolt, *New Dictionary of Trade and Commerce*, title-page; Mortimer, *Elements of Commerce*, vi.

66 Peers occasionally appeared in mid-century London manuals but, with few exceptions, as authors of real letters in sections designed for the Improvement of Epistolary style.

At the bottom, London manuals addressed a group that can broadly be defined as servants, if we bear in mind that during the eighteenth century "servant" was a term that covered people of very various social status. Along with domestics like housekeepers, companions, tutors, governesses, footmen, coachmen, gardeners, cooks, dancing masters and maidservants, the category of "servant" included apprentices, clerks, journeymen, estate agents and some agricultural workers. It essentially meant any employee, but the laboring poor. Jonathan Clark has therefore gone so far as to argue that, in Britain, more than 50 per cent of the British population was in service of one kind or another.[67] Nor were servants confined to a few gentry or aristocratic households. Attorneys, doctors, clergy, tradesmen, shopkeepers, artisans, farmers and even cottagers employed some servants too.

This representation of society in London manuals would be recognizable, even appealing, to buyers in the American provinces, since generally in these letter manuals, as in America, "the entire top of the European status order was missing," and "gentlemen were broadly defined as great merchants and planters, the clergy, the professionals, [and] officers of the courts and government."[68] Commerce and trade were key elements in the growth of port towns, and the vast majority of British migrants during the eighteenth century came to America as indentured servants, so these dimension of London manuals would be eminently recognizable too. As we will see in Part II, American adaptations changed the *dramatis personae* of London manuals to accord with the different social "markings" and uses of politeness in New England, Philadelphia and New York. But the particular, not to say peculiar, representation of society in London manuals may explain why imported letter manuals also worked perfectly well for Americans throughout the eighteenth century.

We cannot, at present, be sure whether all the publics that epistolary compendia targeted actually bought or used them. Unfortunately, little research has yet been done either in the history of the book or in the history of reading which makes more than passing reference to letter manuals. But we do have some pointers.

Our best evidence to date relates to servants. Frances Austin's and Jan Fergus's separate case studies of the letter-writing and book-buying habits of specific groups of provincial servants in England show that servants both bought such manuals and used them when they wrote letters.

67　Clark, *English Society*, 83; Hecht, *Domestic Servant Class*; Hill, *Servants*.
68　Green, *Intellectual Construction of America*, 107; Bushman, *Refinement of America*, xiii.

Fergus, who subsumes manuals like Crowder's *Complete Letter-Writer* under conduct books and self-improvement literature, found that "servants who were prepared to buy print shared a higher proportion of interest in conduct books than did other provincial customers," either because they were hoping to move up in the world or, more interestingly, because their employers expected them to know how to behave.[69] Surviving letters also show that by the late eighteenth century, classical rhetorical epistolary conventions of salutation and signature, address and self-representation, narration and response, had ceased to be the privileged possession of the elite, of male secretaries and of men of letters. Some or all of these conventions recur in the surviving letters of provincial servants, laborers and gardeners, as well as in the epistles of women, soldiers, sailors, shopkeepers, merchants, factors and clerks. Thanks to the recovery work of Douglas Hay, Frances Austin and Barbara De Wolfe among others, it has become clear that among non-elite and non-middle class groups, a letter was not the exceptional phenomenon we once thought it, and that by the end of the century "ordinary working people . . . took the writing of letters as a matter of course."[70] This language may be a little hyperbolic. But spelling, punctuation and grammar apart, surviving letters from "ordinary working people" do show them observing many or all of the principal formal epistolary conventions. Here, for example, is a letter written in England in 1779 by a British-African servant to Mr. Lincoln, a West African musician of African descent:

To Mr. L[incoln]

May 4, 1779

My dear child,

I am truly sorry to address this letter to you at this season in the English channel – the time considered that you have left us, you ought in all good reason to have been a seasoned Creole of St. Kitt's – but we must have patience – what cannot be cured – must be endured. – I dare believe you bear the cruel delay with resignation – and make the best and truest use of your time by steady reflection and writing. – I. would wish you to notedown the occurrences of every day – to which add your own observation of men and things – the more you habituate yourself to minute investigation, the stronger you will make your mind. . . Dear boy, 'tis my love preaches; N— begged me to write a line for him, as he said you wanted news. – I have none but what you know as well as myself – such as the regard and best wishes of Mrs. Sancho – the girls and myself – such as wishing a

69 Fergus, "Provincial Servants' Reading," 216.
70 Austin, "Letter Writing in a Cornish Community," 44; Hay, *Albion's Fatal Tree*, Appendix III.

happy end to your long-protracted voyage. . .and in order to leave room for friend N—, I here assure you I am your affectionate friend, I. Sancho.[71]

And here is part of a letter written in South Carolina by a sixteen-year-old Scottish indentured servant in 1775:

Dear Godfather,

I am very sorry that I did not take your Advise and stay at home with you as I have found to my sad Experience that I ought not to hav slightig your Advise Mr Gordon was vere good to me but Mr Brown us'd me vere ill and I Runaway from them & wint to the Armey that was marching up to the Back parts of South Carolina against a sett of people they call Torrys in this Country and when I came back I went to One Mr LeRoy Hammond a Merchant in So. Carolina & he Bought my time which I am vere glad of for he & his Lady uses me vere will & gives me Cloaths & I Ride with my Master & Loves them Both You'l Please send me all the Money you can Colect that is my Due by the first safe oppertunity that I may be enabled to Buy my time & Put myself to some Tradesman to Learn his calling for a Tradsman has good Wages in this Country I beg that none of my Relation may come to this Country Except they are able to pay their passage thir Selves. . .Pray Remember me to my Dear freind Mr James Riddoh Mrs Gordon Madam Allin Madam Young My Uncle & Aunt & all their Femily & in perticular Mr John Gordon – I am Dear Godfather Your Most Obident and Huml Godson, Baikia Harvey.[72]

These letters do more than reproduce clichéd expressions and epistolary formulae. They take standard forms modeled in letter manuals: Sancho's epistle is a version of the much reprinted "Letter to a friend who has embarked, but is detained by contrary winds" which goes back at least to *The Postboy robb'd of his Mail*, while Baikia Harvey has adopted the form of *The Complete Letter-Writer*'s "Apprentice's how I go on" letter. Both writers also display the sentiments proper to the forms they have chosen. Such familiarity with epistolary forms and conventions among non-elite groups with little formal education is noteworthy, to say the least. It was an effect of the widespread identification of letters with ordinary speech; of the universal practice of hearing personal letters, periodical letters, fictional letters and public addresses read aloud;[73] and

---

71 *Letters of the Late Ignatius Sancho*, 158–9. Compositors and printers often "corrected" spelling and punctuation even for now canonical authors; since Sancho's letters were printed at the end of his life to raise money for his subsistence, their correctness in these respects may well be due to some now forgotten eighteenth-century compositor.

72 De Wolfe, *Discoveries of America*, 211–12.

73 David Hall and Rhys Isaac have shown how hearing material read aloud led to reading. Hall, "Uses of Literacy" and Isaac, "Books and the Social Authority of Learning," in Joyce *et al.* (eds.), *Printing and Society*.

above all, of a vigorous, century-long campaign of public education in epistolary forms, styles and conventions carried on in print.

Our best source of information about the market for *London* letter manuals above the servant ranks comes from Americanists. However, here the information is still largely anecdotal. Richard Beale Davis found that in colonial America, "small collections generally included a layman's legal manual such as *The Complete Lawyer* or *The Complete Attorney* or *The Young Secretary's Guide*" – the latter being John Hill's letter manual with its legal forms at the end. Edwin Wolf mentions that a copy of *Familiar Letters of Love, Gallantry and Several Occasions* was owned by one Henry Clarke, a mariner, in 1726, and that a copy of the 1717 edition of *A New Academy of Compliments* was found in the library of Frances Daniel Pastorius, who founded Germantown in 1683 and was unquestionably a learned man (a student of Paracelsus and mystical tracts).[74] Richard Bushman records that in 1751–4, the Ridgeley letters show a father in Dover, Delaware, sending his son a copy of *The Young Man's Companion*, and his son writing his father a letter that sounds as if it came straight out of it. Though bearing on an American adaptation, it is suggestive too that William Hunter, printer and bookseller in provincial Williamsburg, took forty-five copies of a *vade mecum*, George Fisher's *American Instructor or Young Man's Best Companion*, from Franklin and Hall in 1751, at a time when "even sales of popular school books rarely exceeded a dozen copies a year."[75]

Surviving American catalogues offer interesting information of a different kind. They tell us that American subscription libraries, whose membership generally consisted of tradesmen, local gentlemen and professionals like doctors and lawyers, contained copies of *English* letter manuals and *vade mecums*.[76] In 1741, for instance, the Library Company of Philadelphia owned *Letters of Wit, Politics and Morality, Love, Friendship and Gallantry, Ancient and Modern* (London, 1701). By 1757, it had acquired *Polite Epistolary Correspondence* (London, 1751) and *Voiture's Works, containing Letters and Characters of the most Eminent Persons* (London, 1736). In 1770, it also had Richardson's *Letters written to and for Particular Friends on the most Important Occasions*, Howell's *Familiar*

---

74 Davis, *Colonial Southern Bookshelf*, 24; Wolf, *Book Culture*, 24, 26.

75 Bushman, *Refinement of America*, 10; Stiverson and Stiverson, "The Colonial Retail Book Trade," in *Printing and Society*, 156. Letter manuals are included among chapbooks in Neuberg, "Chapbooks," in Davidson (ed.), *Reading in America*.

76 Franklin's *Autobiography*; Raven, *London Booksellers and American Customers*.

Letters, A Collection of Original Letters written by the most Eminent Persons on various entertaining Subjects and *Letters on the most common as well as important occasions of Life by writers of the most Merit.* American bookseller catalogues show that English manuals like Hill's *Young Secretary's Guide* and Crowder's *Complete Letter-Writer* were frequently imported and sold in Philadelphia and New York to 1771, and that the same American printers whose printing shops had designed or reprinted American adaptations of English manuals also imported and sold the original English versions. For instance, William Bradford's catalogue of imported books for 1760 included *The Young Secretary's Guide, The Academy of Compliments,* an unspecified *Familiar Letter-Writer* and *The Young Man's Companion;* and in 1761, Hugh Gaine in New York imported Johnson's *Introduction to the Art of Letter-Writing* (whose author he mistook for Dictionary Johnson) and Haywood's *Epistles to the Ladies.*[77]

This information is sketchy and bears on the provinces. But it does appear to confirm that letter manuals did have a market, at least in the provinces, among people of different ranks with different social and occupational needs. It suggests that London printers and compilers may have been fairly realistic in their assessment of their target audiences and in their arguments for the practical utility of printed *Secretaries, Letter-Writers* and *Letter-Miscellanies* to schoolboys, servants, tradesmen and merchants, professionals and gentlemen.

Late seventeenth- and eighteenth-century letter manuals were small books. Once they had included grammars, spellers and the rest of their outwork, compendia only had space for a limited number of letters. Hill's *Secretary* contained 120 letters, Crowder's *Complete Letter-Writer* at mid-century was positively huge at 145. But most compendia and *Letter-Miscellanies* contained far fewer letters than this. *Vade mecums'* collections of epistolary models were positively sparse, twenty or twenty-five being a handsome complement; and many American adaptations of London manuals managed to do the necessary quite brilliantly with between thirty-five and sixty letters in the early years. The question is how compilers succeeded in supplying the needs of so many diverse publics for models of letters that could be written on "all the most common occasions of life" in minimal space. This is the question to which we now turn.

---

77 Winans observes that catalogues are scarce before the 1750s; the vast majority thereafter were published in Pennsylvania. *Descriptive Catalogue*, xvii.

REPRESENTING THE HOUSEHOLD-FAMILY

Though some letter manuals identified and represented narrower target audiences such as ladies or clerks, most compendia and many letter-miscellanies condensed and focused the range and variety of ranks and occupations in their target audiences into manageable proportions by foregrounding family relationships and offering letters that answered the question: "What kinds of letters might all the members of a family, in all their diverse relations to others inside and outside the family, have occasion to write?" In the middle of the seventeenth century, Thomas Blount's *Academie of Eloquence* had included among the tropes and commonplaces of its "Compleat English Rhetoric," a collection of model epistles abounding in ceremonial letters of compliment, thanks and excuse, that were suited to "the *mode*" and to the "Emergent Occasions" of an aristocratic court.[78] But by the beginning of the eighteenth century, most compendia were adapted to the needs of a family, understood in its broad eighteenth-century sense to include servants, apprentices and kin, and designed to supply models of *familiar* letters, understood in the word's now obsolete sense of "pertaining to the family." Naomi Tadmor has dubbed the family conceived as "a household including its diverse dependents, such as servants, apprentices and co-resident relatives," the "household-family." Unlike the modern nuclear family or the eighteenth-century lineage family, the household-family included people who were not related by kinship and who might not remain in that "family" or household for more than a year or two, as well as uncles, aunts or other relatives.[79]

Generic letter-writing characters drawn from family relationships, as father, son, daughter, mother, brother, sister, uncle or aunt, could also be merchant, schoolgirl, tenant, landlord, maidservant, apprentice, gentleman, lady or sailor. And it was possible to bring the two taxonomies together in model correspondences, for instance, by offering model letters from an uncle who was a tradesman to his nephew apprenticed to a tradesman in town, from a mother to a school-child, or from a maidservant in town to her parents in the country, that simultaneously discussed apprenticeships, work or schooling, and exemplified ideal family relationships.

---

78 See extended title.
79 Tadmor, *Family and Friends*, 19. Also, O'Day, *Family and Family Relationships*, esp. Chapter 4. Apprentices were live-in members of someone's household-family until very late in the century.

Both in Britain and in the American provinces, household-families (not individuals) were considered the fundamental building-blocks of society.[80] They performed roles later taken over by separate state agencies. Household-families were urban and rural society's most basic economic and administrative unit: under the jurisdiction of its master, the household-family was supposed to feed, employ, sustain, socialize, discipline and govern all its members. The household-family was society's major employer, and the source of all formal and informal education: it taught children their letters or arranged for them to be taught; it determined whether children were to be sent to school or to apprenticeships; decided on the careers and marriages of offspring or at least approved them; took in apprentices to train and socialize; and integrated servants and journeymen as members of its own "little society."[81] The family also often functioned as a bank and insurance company for its members. The household-family's failings were therefore of major concern to moralists, ministers and conduct book writers throughout the eighteenth century. Using the household-family as one of their several organizing principles meant that letter manuals also unobtrusively performed important, ideological, social and political functions by providing examples of, and laying down rules for, the improvement of the household-family's conduct and interactions. More aggressively from mid-century on, manuals also focused on the control of young women in courtships, on the disposal of daughters in marriage, and on the proper marital choices for men at different ranks. One might note that domestic and courtship novels occupied the same ground.[82]

Despite differences in the proportional space given to different common everyday occasions for letter-writing in different collections of letters, compendia and many letter-miscellanies generally treated the same basic aspects of everyday life. They usually began with letters between parents or kin and children who were away at school, visiting friends, working as apprentices or servants in town or otherwise embarking on adult life. They included model letters of courtship and marriage, and letters of friendship and advice between "friends." They also included

80 For the family's centrality as a unit of social and economic organization in rural and urban England and in America, see Clark, *English Society*; Amussen, *An Ordered Society*; Wilson, *Gentlemen Merchants*; Norton, *Liberty's Daughters*; Burchell, "The Role of the Upper Class."

81 For the family's central role in education in Britain and America, see Bailyn, *Education*; Cremin, *American Education*; O'Day, *Professions*.

82 See, for instance, Armstrong, *Desire and Domestic Fiction*; Bannet, *Domestic Revolution*; Langland, *Nobody's Angels*; Sobba Green, *The Courtship Novel*; Yeazell, *Fictions of Modesty*.

model letters of business, both such as might be written between "friends," among the gentry and in the professions and such as commercial correspondents might write. Sometimes the latter would grow out of the apprentice letters between kin and children, giving examples of the commercial letters an apprentice would be required to write before moving on to letters useful to beginners in business, factors, tradesmen, estate agents, merchants, wholesale dealers, and landlords; sometimes business letters would include or overlap with letters of friendship in the modern sense (for instance, letters asking for or offering a loan to a friend or acquaintance); and in compendia, business letters for all possible occasions were capped by the forms for a variety of bills, bonds, letters of attorney, indentures, deeds of sale, and other legal documents in the compendium's second part.

Even after they began to divide up letter collections into "subjects" such as duty, amusement, friendship, courtship and marriage at mid-century, letter manuals tended to jumble business letters of both types together with family correspondence. In her study of eighteenth-century Colchester, Shani D'Cruze found that "the business household where the divide between working and domestic arrangements was minimal and the labor of all household persons contributed to both the economic and domestic tasks" was a distinctive feature of the town gentry, merchants, traders, superior artisans, clergy and other professionals she studied.[83] "Lack of divide between working and domestic arrangements" also accurately describes the presentation of family and business letters in most eighteenth-century compendia, letter-miscellanies and *vade mecums*. But it would be a mistake to assume that this sort of "business household" was as restricted socially as the parameters of D'Cruze's research imply.

Both in Britain and in British-America, as other scholars have shown, household-families lived in villages *and* in towns; on plantations, on country estates, and on yeoman farms; above or behind the commercial "house," the shop or the artisanal workshop; and in the establishments of provincial lawyers, doctors and clerical men. Even quite lowly families, such as small artisans, kept a servant and constituted a modest household-family. Worth noting, too, is the fact that wittingly or unwittingly, modern archivists have found that the surviving papers of the great eighteenth-century landlords conveniently fall into domains that broadly

---

83 D'Cruze, "The Middling Sort in Eighteenth-Century Colchester," 181. Also Davidoff and Hall, *Family Fortunes*, who argue that the work place was not fully separated from the home until well into the nineteenth century.

correspond to those found in eighteenth-century epistolary compendia. The Fletcher of Saltoun Papers and the Maxwell of Monreith Papers in the National Library of Scotland, for instance, are catalogued under "family correspondence," "letters to friends," "letters on estate business," "letters to and from lawyers and accountants," and "legal papers." Letters of courtship and marriage are generally put in among the family correspondence. Many family collections also contain commercial letters of business, about mills or factories owned and run by the great landowner in question, and trading correspondence with agents and factors at home or abroad about the purchase of raw materials or the sale of produce. Besides reminding us that on both sides of the Atlantic, "farmers" could also be, and often were, manufacturers, traders and transatlantic merchants too, modern archivists' organization of surviving letters from the great eighteenth-century landlords suggests that the domains addressed in letter manuals, and the occasions for letter-writing that they modeled, were not limited to urban spaces or to any single propertied class.

Using the household-family as a principle of architectonic economy permitted compendia, letter-miscellanies and *vade mecums* to simultaneously address the epistolary needs of households at different ranks, and of the people of different ranks who composed them. It enabled manuals to be serviceable to what Vicesimus Knox called "sometime letter-writers" as well as to be responsive (albeit to different degrees) to the specific needs of the prolifically epistolary, clerking-factoring-and-trading fraternity, and of the gentleman with estate or other private business to transact. It meant both that an entire family could use them, and that a lone man or woman at whatever rank could find in them models for letters suited to "all the relative situations" of his or her life.

Modern accounts of the household-family tend to envision it permanently under one roof, even if the particular individuals composing it came and went. Letter manuals, however, necessarily foregrounded the geographical mobility of its members – the occasions when those serving as apprentices, maidservants, schoolchildren, siblings or factors, soldiers, sailors or government officers were far from home, and when husbands and wives, parents and children, were apart. Absence had, of course, always been fundamental to the concept of letters. In 1599, in a manual that was heavily indebted to Erasmus's *De Epistolis Scribendis*, Angel Day defined an epistle as "the familiar and mutuall talke of one absent friende to another."[84] In his *Principles of Letter-Writing*, Justus Lipsius

84 Day, *English Secretary*, 8.

likewise defined a letter as "a message of the mind to someone who is absent or regarded as absent," citing as his authority Cicero's observation that letter-writing "was devised so that we might inform those who are absent of anything that they should know." In his influential courtesy book a century later, Courtin was still defining correspondence as "the discourse of the absent."[85] By the eighteenth century, absence was a familiar, albeit still productive topos, for letters and letter-writers to use and imaginatively elaborate in their letters.

Another, more remarkable, facet of letters as the discourse of the absent was Turpilius's maxim that letters are "the one thing which makes the absent present."[86] It was in Turpilius's oscillating, and merely virtual, epistolary space between absence and presence, that letter manuals inscribed their household-families. Paradoxically, perhaps, letter manuals made present the composition and structure of the household-family by collecting together all the letters that every possible member of a household-family might write to absent fathers, mothers, uncles, aunts, sisters, brothers and friends who were also shopkeepers, traders, merchants, professionals, gentlemen, or their wives, daughters and servants. In the process, they also portrayed each household-family as being linked in innumerable social and mercantile ways, by innumerable cords of concern and affection, to other household-families both in the larger society and "beyond the sea."

Even the earliest Renaissance and seventeenth-century British letter manuals that were written in the vernacular, and designed to bring the older Latin epistolary formularies and *ars dictaminis* out of schools and colleges, included at least one model letter to or from a correspondent "beyond the Sea." Seventeenth-century manuals offered models for describing sea voyages plagued by dreadful storms or for writing to a friend who had embarked but whose ship was detained by contrary winds, a letter "from a Commander in War to his Mistress" or a letter "to a Lady residing in a Town that had lately been besieged." One early manual, *The Merchant's Avizo* (1607), offered commercial correspondents "a briefe forme of all such letters as you shall need to write during your whole voyage," including forms for "a letter to be written to your Master, if your Ship be forced by weather into any place, before you come to your Port of

---

85 Courtin, *Rules*, 170.
86 Lipsius, *Principles*, 9. For absence made present in Erasmus, see Jardine, "Reading and the Technology of Textual Effect," in Raven *et al.* (eds.), *Practice and Representation of Reading*, and Goldberg, *Writing Matter*.

discharge" and for "a letter to be written to a friend, giving him thanks for some pleasure he had done for you and requesting againe some farther good turne of him."[87]

During the early and mid-seventeenth century, "beyond the Sea" letters often bore reference to countries in Europe – *The Merchant's Avizo*, for instance, speaks of Portugal and Spain. References to specific places abroad were frequently eliminated once Britain's sights expanded to the New World, as if to open manuals to infinite new conquests and to correspondence with as yet unthought of places on the globe. The number of "beyond the Sea" letters in each manual also grew to include other stock letters: a letter from a wife to her soldier or sailor-husband abroad, with his reply; a letter from a young woman to her betrothed overseas asking to be released from their engagement, with his reply; letters "to a Friend beyond the Sea" to "inquire after his Health and Welfare" or to reproach him or her for not writing, together with letters of excuse for failing to write; letters of news or intelligence, describing places and events for the information or edification of persons elsewhere. For the rest, "beyond the Sea letters" could, and in peoples' actual historical practice did, adopt the forms that were situated in manuals as letters from someone in town to someone in the country (or vice versa). The town-and-country construct was applicable both to rural areas in relation to the nearest provincial town, and to the provinces near and far which figured as "the country" in relation to London. The importation and reprinting of British letter manuals in colonial America during the eighteenth century indicates that letter formulae such as these were viewed as being broadly applicable to epistolary exchanges within provincial America, as well as within Britain and across the seas.

FAMILIAR LETTERS AND EVERYDAY CONVERSATION

Sixteenth- and seventeenth-century elites, who kept human secretaries to compose and copy their correspondence, deployed a semiology of the letter borrowed from the ancient Romans which made the act of writing a letter in one's own hand a mark of special favor.[88] But eighteenth-century teachers and writers, who sought to extend the art of letter-writing to "all at least above the lowest rank," developed a semiology of style and correctness that made the ability to write one's own letters with propriety,

---

87 Marchant, *Merchant's Avizo*, 8; Blount, *Academie of Eloquence*; Gildon, *Postboy*, II.
88 Daybell, *Early Modern Women* Writers, esp. introduction and essays by Daybell and Truelove.

elegance and ease a mark of personal distinction. To make this point, manuals from the middle of the eighteenth century regularly cited or paraphrased a philosopher who was himself a secretary and thoroughly implicated in empire, both as a member of the Board of Trade and Plantations, and via his employer who owned land in the Carolinas. *The Accomplished Letter-Writer or Universal Correspondent* (1779) went so far as to make Locke's observations on letter-writing in *Thoughts on Education* the epigraph on its title-page:

The Writing of Letters has so much to do in all the Occurrences of Humane Life, that no Gentleman can avoid shewing himself in this Kind of Writing. Occasions daily force him to make use of his Pen. . .[for the well or ill-managing] of all his Affairs. . .[A man's letters] lay him open to severer Examination of his Breeding, Sense and Abilities than Oral discourse, whose transient Faults, dying for the most part with the Sound that gives them Life, and so not subject to strict Review, more easily escape Observation and Censure.[89]

Such identifications of epistolography with gentility, together with the derision to which demotic letters were sometimes subjected in *merriments* and canonical novels, led many twentieth-century scholars of eighteenth-century letters to produce in their own work an artificial and unhistorical segregation of "polite" letters from the whole range of familiar letters, and to underwrite this segregation in aesthetic or literary terms.[90] But derision of demotic letters can also be read as an index of the very novelty of finding that one's "inferiors" were suddenly writing letters, while assertions about the gentility of letter-writing can be seen as a way of motivating people to acquire the proper skills. A "familiar letter" was not exclusively an intimate letter between well-bred friends or lovers, and all familiar letters were supposed to be polite.

The term "familiar letters" encompassed letters of business and letters of news, as well as letters of friendship, family, amusement and courtship. Angel Day observed that "familiar epistles" were named familiar "for the ordinary causes and matters of handling in themselves contained."[91] Eighteenth-century letter manuals echoed this on their title-pages (when they were not actually entitled *Familiar Letters*) by claiming that they contained letters for "all the most common occasions of life." William Fulwood defined familiar letters as "domesticall or household letters"

---

89 Locke, *Thoughts*, 243 (no. 189).
90 For instance, Stewart, "Towards Defining an Aesthetic"; Anderson *et al.*, *Familiar Letter*; Irving, *Providence of Wit*.
91 Day, *The English Secretary*, II: 58.

which "let our friends understand our estate and our businesse, be it health, prosperity, sickness, adversitie or any other domesticall and familiar things."[92] Eighteenth-century writers likewise described a familiar letter as "a letter which touches our affairs, or the affairs of those around us" and the means "by which a great Part of the Commerce of human Life is carried on." As Dr. Johnson pointed out, it could therefore be "written on all subjects, in all states of mind" on any "present occasion."[93] Cicero's dictum *Ad Familiares* that letters were "written conversation" served as the foundation of eighteenth-century epistolary theory, and was everywhere repeated. As William Walsh put it in 1692, "the style of letters ought to be as near approaching familiar conversation as possible."[94] Letter manuals likewise insisted: "That is a true familiar letter which expresseth our Meaning the same as if we were discoursing with the Party to whom we write in succinct and easy Terms."[95] Familiar letters supplied the place of speech or conversation in all the everyday personal, domestic, social, professional and commercial intercourse of life.

As manuals indicated in their laconic directions for letter-writing, however, there was a contradiction in characterizing letters as "written conversation" and as a graphical representation of "natural" everyday speech, while self-consciously teaching epistolography as an "art" with rules and conventions. This could, of course, be papered over by falling back on the old chestnut that letter-writing was the "Art of all others, [that] requires the greatest Art to conceal it" and by demanding that the rigidly conventional forms of letters be written in an "easy" and "natural" manner that turned them into a sort of second nature. But letter manuals generally dealt with this contradiction – as we will see in the next chapter they also dealt with other conflicting imperatives – by incorporating both terms of the opposition. One of several paradoxes that letter manuals re-presented and held in balance was that between assuring their readers that: "when you sit down to write a Letter, remember that this sort of Writing should be like Conversation. . .and you will be no more at Loss to write than you will be to speak"[96] – and assuring them that manuals were the means of "instructing" and "improving" their users in "the art of letter-writing."

---

92 *Enimie of Idleness*, 69.
93 Lipsius, *Principles*, 21; Johnson, *Rambler*, no. 152.
94 Preface to *Letters and Poems*.
95 *The Complete Letter-Writer* (London, 1778), 32.
96 *Ibid.*, 31.

Some manuals drew attention to the contradiction to heighten the value of what they offered. The "General Directions for Writing Letters," reprinted in several manuals, reiterated that "the surest rule for writing well is to write as we speak, deliberately, without art, and without affectation." But it also warned that "to succeed in this kind of composition, is far more difficult than is generally imagined, as experience daily affords convincing proofs. Out of an hundred good speakers scarce ten will be found who write in the same degree of perfection, though it should seem nothing more was wanting to commit our thoughts to paper. Far greater exactness is required for writing than speaking."[97] Some manuals showed more discomfort. Another frequently reprinted preface, which I am taking here from *The Accomplished Letter-Writer or Universal Correspondent* (1779), cited and paraphrased without attribution Johnson's essay on letters in *Rambler* 152: "That Letters should be written in strict conformity to Nature is true. . .But it is Natural to depart from Familiarity of Language upon Occasions not familiar." Moreover, "wherever we are studious to please, we are afraid of trusting our first Thoughts, and endeavour to recommend our Opinions by studied Ornaments, Accuracy of Method, and Elegance of Style."[98] This last point was particularly telling, since the first rule of politeness was to please. Some manuals simply skirted the difficulty. Dilworth's Preface to his *Complete Letter-Writer, or Young Secretary's Instructor* (Glasgow, 1783) observed in successive sentences, without a blink, that you must "write letters on all occasions with elegance and propriety" and that "when you write to a friend, your letter should be a picture of your heart."

In defense of these compilers, it must be said that their ambivalence embodied the best academic thinking of the time. Hugh Blair's *Lectures on Rhetoric and Belles Lettres*, for instance, suddenly develop the same quirk when he turns to "Epistolary Writing." On the one hand, Blair observes that the "first and fundamental requisite" of letter-writing "is to be natural and simple," and that "a stiff and laboured manner is as bad in a Letter as it is in Conversation." But on the other hand, he insists that "the first requisite, both in conversation and correspondence, is to attend to all the proper decorums which our own character, and that of others demand" and that even "in writing to the most intimate friend, a certain degree of attention, both to the subject and the style is becoming." Blair argues that in letters, "we expect. . . to discover somewhat of [the writer's]

---

97 *The Court Letter-Writer*, 43, 42.
98 *The Accomplished Letter-Writer*, iii.

real character. . .[and] please ourselves with beholding the writer in a situation which allows him to be at his ease, and to give vent occasionally to the overflowings of his heart." But he also points out that "it is childish indeed to expect that in Letters we are to find the whole heart of the Author unveiled. Concealment and disguise take place, more or less, in all human intercourse." Blair states that the best letters are those "written with most facility" which "flow readily" from the mind, heart or imagination; but he also warns that "the liberty of writing letters with too careless a hand, is apt to betray persons into imprudence in what they write."[99] Thus, conversation and correspondence were supposed both to reveal and to mask: they were to seem "natural and simple," even sincere, in order to more successfully guard their secrets. Letters must show ease and not be "too highly polished," but they must pay careful attention to those conventions bearing on subject, style, self-representation and decorum, which constituted worldly polish.

Perhaps the best way of understanding such ambivalences is to ask why teachers, academics and manual compilers could afford to abandon neither term of these oppositions between speech and writing, nature and art, sincerity and decorum.

The link between epistolary writing and ordinary speech, and between correspondence and everyday conversation, could not be abandoned because in practice, *pace* Derrida, letters were a site where speech and writing were constantly rotating into each other's places. At the point of generation and conception, letter-writers were advised to imagine that they were speaking to their correspondents as they wrote, to write as they would speak, and to listen to the sound of their words and sentences as they put them down on the page: "In the Placing of Words we must consult the Ear and judge whether its Satisfaction be complete. . .".[100] The completed letter would thus become in every possible sense "silent speech." Again, at the point of reception, the "silent speech" of the letter reverted to audible speech. "The discourse of the absent" was "made present" through the voice of a person reading the letter aloud. Reading a letter aloud in company acted as a vocalization of the absent writer's speech act within the conversation that it stimulated among the company who heard it. This completed the circle by making the letter a form of silent speech that both issued from conversation and returned to it. Letters participated in ritual and collective aspects of social life that

99 Blair, *Rhetoric and Belles Lettres*, II: 62–4.
100 [Anon.], *The New Art of Letter-Writing* (London, 1762), 8.

made correspondence a performative event. In company, to borrow a term from painting, a letter often served as a 'conversation piece,' and the ability to read a letter aloud competently was an important and ingratiating social skill.

Guglielmo Cavello and Roger Chartier have pointed out that "orality. . . varies according to whether it reflects simply spoken discourse or is a vocalized version of writing, oralized by the reader."[101] This bears on all forms of discourse in the seventeenth and eighteenth centuries, when visual signs on the page increasingly supplied the place of the envisioned mnemonic signs that rhetoricians had traditionally taught orators to engrave in their memories, as the preserver of silent speech awaiting vocalization by the speaker.[102] Substitution of writing for memory meant that traditional orations such as speeches, sermons, addresses, declarations and petitions, that had once been produced from memory as "spoken discourses," came increasingly to be read aloud from a handwritten or printed text; they became a "vocalized version of writing." Writing thus became a script. The need to produce vocalized versions of writing was responsible for a new emphasis in rhetoric during the second half of the eighteenth century on *pronunciatio* or delivery – on teaching potential parliamentary speakers, clergymen and gentlemen to *speak* and *perform* written texts. It also gave rise to a corresponding interest in the convergence between reading and acting, which overlaid and fed out of a prior concern with performance in conversation. What has been forgotten – both by historians of rhetoric and by literary critics who followed a limited reading of Richardson in identifying letters with the solitude of the closet and the secret converse of the heart[103] – is that vocalized reading practices extended to the reading of letters. Letters too were a script.[104] The expectation in the eighteenth century was still that letters would be read aloud to family, friends and acquaintance, and/or shown around, to give everyone something to talk about.

101 Cavello and Chartier, *History of Reading*, 6.
102 Enders, "Rhetoric of Memory."
103 For the limits of this view, Gillis, *Paradox of Privacy*. We might also remember that the justification for letter-writing with which the novel opens is that of enabling Clarissa's friends, and the public at large, to know what is transpiring in the Harlowe household.
104 For reading practices in which the oral and written converged, Tadmor, "In the even my wife read to me"; Coleman, *Public Reading*; St. George, "Massacred Language"; Gustafson, *Eloquence is Power*; Fliegelman, *Declaring Independence*; Hall, "Readers and Writers in New England"; and Hugh Amory, "The New England Book Trade 1713–1790," both in Amory and Hall (eds.), *The Colonial Book*.

As a genre, the eighteenth-century letter was therefore a shape changer, not very different in this regard from the drama which alternated between written, oral and printed forms. During its trajectory from one corres-pondent to another, the letter successively occupied each place on a continuum that ran from oral speech to the silent speech of manuscript (and thence potentially to print), from the silent speech of writing to vocalized writing or scripted speech – and back the same way when the speech or conversation that a letter stimulated in its reader or among the company at its point of reception produced a new letter. No distinction appears to have been made between reading aloud from a printed or a handwritten letter, and the same people who read handwritten letters aloud to their family and friends also read aloud novels, pamphlets and periodicals which frequently took epistolary form.[105] The expectation that letters would be read aloud whether they took written or printed form, made the press a preserver and disseminator of the voice and the voice an agent of the press – like writing.[106] This is what John Markland was suggesting in *Typographia*, when he praised those "Who first contriv'd the *wondrous Frame* / That to *dead Types* supply'd a *Tongue*, / And Speech to *lifeless Characters* could give."[107] This is also how Franklin seemed to be conceiving the matter when he insisted on the importance of teaching pupils in his English school to read aloud effectively: "For Want of Good Reading, Pieces published with a View to influence the Minds of Men for their own or the public Benefit, lose half their Force. Were there one good Reader in a Neighbourhood, a public Orator might be heard throughout a Nation with the same Advantages, and have the same effect on his Audience, as if they stood within the Reach of his Voice."[108]

Speech, manuscript and print were still what D. F. McKenzie called "complementary modes."[109] Letters constructed a spectacular world where what was given to the ear was made available to the eye, and where the hand transmitted what the eye had perceived and the voice would render with a vivid and visible, but also dangerous and promiscuous durability. Eighteenth-century letters inhabited an episteme of re-presentation and surrogation where presence was married to absence, where the hand, the

---

105 Studies stressing the primacy either of the voice or the press in early America include Warner, *Letters of the Republic*; Fliegelman, *Declaring Independence*; Looby, *Voicing America*; Williams, *Significance of the Printed Word*; Grasso, *Speaking Aristocracy*.
106 Peters, *Theatre of the Book*.
107 Quoted in Crain, "Print and Everyday Life," 53.
108 In Smith, *Theories of Education*, 179.
109 McKenzie, "Speech–Manuscript–Print," 88.

eye, the ear and the voice rotated into one another's places, and where speech, manuscript and print were inexorably linked.

Compilers of printed manuals could not abandon the connections between speech and writing, and between correspondence and conversation, therefore, because these informed every stage of the letter's trajectory, embraced familiar social practices and entered into the very imaginary of epistolary form.

Manual printers and compilers could not give up on treating letter-writing as an art either, or desist from inculcating learned decorums and worldly polish. As late as 1807, *The Monthly Review* described the problem thus: "At Paris and at Court, talking well was become a habit, and it was commonly observed that we ought to write a letter as we speak; the meaning of which expression [the Editor] takes to be that the style of letters should resemble that of the conversation of well-bred persons; that it should be equally remote from the manner of provincial wits, the stiffness of the inferior literati and the awkwardness of the ill-educated."[110] Once one broadened the social base of letter-writers, and made it a skill requisite for different ranks, one could no longer rely on people being able to "talk well" or on their being "well-bred" as a basis for letter-writing. It was useless and implicitly contradictory to repeat Cicero's doctrine that letters were "written conversation" by telling people to write letters as they would talk, without addressing the issue of how they talked, what they said, and how they conducted themselves in the process. Seductive as the identification of politeness with the refined and courtly upper class has proved to be, therefore, here again the dissemination of politeness to wider and wider sectors of the population through schooling, letter manuals and conduct books during this period, has to be understood as a way of standardizing conduct, and of creating a common culture, within which communication, mutual comprehension and harmonious "correspondence" across regions and across ranks in the nation and in the empire could more easily occur. As Lawrence Klein has pointed out, "conversation was the paradigmatic arena of politeness," because politeness was "a set of discursive norms for the operation of discourse," and "an art or techne governing the 'how' of social relations."[111]

Capitalizing on the factitious, acquired, rule-bound and decorous character of epistolary writing to promote and market manuals, compendia

---

110 Quoted in Irving, *Providence of Wit*, 88.
111 Klein, *Shaftesbury and the Culture of Politeness*, 4, 10; Klein, "Gender," 108.

printers and compilers acted as impresarios for a whole range of sophisticated, old and newer, language arts. Prescriptive as much as descriptive,
letter manuals reproduced the work of the learned in their grammars,
guides to punctuation, rhetorical teachings, and instructions about secret
writing. They used "writers by trade or profession" as "experts" on letters,
much they used grammarians as experts on grammar, and rhetoricians as
experts on rhetoric.

Budgell's point in *The Spectator* that getting a first-class classical education did not make a man capable of writing a good English letter was
relevant here too: "many Learned Persons, who, while they are admiring
the Styles of Demosthenes or Cicero, want Phrases to express themselves
on the most common Occasions," and "writing but rarely and with some
Reluctance, most People are embarrassed when obliged to take up the
pen."[112] Writers by trade or profession were those who did not want
phrases to express themselves, and who could provide phrases and model
letters for others to borrow. Especially after mid-century, therefore,
epistolary compendia often marketed themselves by pointing out on their
title-pages, that many of the model letters in their compilations were
taken from the major, all but canonical, epistolary writers. The list of
authors on the title-page of John Tavernier's *Newest and Most Complete
Polite Familiar Letter-Writer* (4th ed.; 1768) reads: "Pliny, Cicero, Voiture,
Locke, Balzac, Addison, Steele, Pope, Gay, Swift, Voltaire, Rochester,
Temple, the King of Prussia and Queen Anne." George Seymour's
Instructive Letter-Writer and Entertaining Companion (1769) extended this
list to include Plutarch, Sir Walter Raleigh, The Duke and Dutchess of
Marlbro' [*sic*], Tillotson, Atterbury, Molyneux, Dr. Blackwell, Richardson,
Mr. and Mrs. Rowe and several more kings and queens. Men and women
of letters (in the literal sense) were brandished as the primary sources or
designers of epistolary models for less able writers; and in letter manuals
from mid-century, the fictive letters of professional writers often appeared
cheek by jowl with real letters that writers had once sent.

Entire letter manuals were also produced by some of "the best modern
authors" themselves. Long before Samuel Richardson's *Letters Written to
and for Particular Friends on the most Important Occasions* (1741), Voiture
(a leading and fashionable French writer of epistolographical models) was
virtually drowned out in Tom Browne's English translations both of his
Familiar Letters and of his *Works*, by the preponderance in the same

---

112 *The New Art of Letter-Writing* (London, 1762), 231, 2.

volumes of model letters by Dryden, Dennis, Wycherley, Congreve and others. Eliza Haywood's *Epistles for the Ladies*, Richard Steele's *Spectator Letters*, and David Fordyce's *New and Complete British Letter-Writer*[113] are other cases in point. These texts were also frequently rifled by compendia, usually without attribution. Both Haywood's *Epistles*, which was a bestseller on both sides of the Atlantic, and Richardson's *Letters*, which was not, were widely reprinted, adapted or rewritten in other manuals. Crowder's *Complete Letter-Writer or Polite English Secretary* (London, 1755) and Dilworth's *Complete Letter-Writer or Young Secretary's Instructor* (Glasgow, 1783), for instance, used or adapted several of Richardson's *Letters* without attribution. Crowder's *Complete Letter-Writer* also included five of Haywood's *Epistles* verbatim, without attribution and with changes in the names of their fictional writers and addressees which further disguised their provenance. Letters from Crowder's *Complete Letter-Writer* together with a large number of letters from Haywood's *Epistles* also formed the bulk of *The Ladies Complete Letter-Writer* (1763) and of Lady Dorothea du Bois' *The Ladies' Polite Secretary, or New Female Letter-Writer* (1771). *The Correspondent* borrowed heavily from Chesterfield and Steele. Richardson himself had borrowed letters and occasions for letter-writing from earlier manuals, such as G. F.'s *Secretary's Guide* (1734). And so it went. Professional and canonical writers were harnessed or harnessed themselves to the task of national and imperial epistolographical composition and improvement.

At the same time, the classical idea of correspondence as "written conversation" was adapted to an Enlightenment ideology particularly conducive to empire. As Robert Dodsley observed, echoing Locke and his followers, "Society subsists among Men by a mutuall Communication of their Thoughts to each other. Words, Looks, Gesture and the Different Tones of Voice are the Means of Communication."[114] Conversation, defined as the mutual communication of men's thoughts to each other by words, looks, gesture and tones of voice, re-marked the Lockean doctrine that the mere existence of language proved that God and nature had designed man for society, and that man was not made to exist alone. Conversations – and correspondences as their written re-presentation – were quintessentially the language of man as a social being who was dependent on others for all his needs and wants. Conversational exchange

113 For Fordyce, see Bannet, "Empire and Occasional Conformity."
114 Dodsley, *Preceptor*, 9.

among men served at once as figure and instrument for the "mutual dependence" and "mutual good offices" that political thinkers described as the "cement" of society, and that economists represented as the foundation of commercial exchange. Indeed, this figure came to be imbedded in the language: in the eighteenth century, conversation meant "commerce, sociability, having dealings with others, intercourse, intimacy"; in one of its eighteenth-century senses, "commerce" meant "to have intercourse or converse, to hold communication with"; and correspondence meant "answering each other with fitness or mutual adaptation, congruity, harmony."

Once societies depended on written as well as on oral communication among men for their existence, the dictum that letters were "written conversation" and the doctrine that "Society subsists among Men by mutuall Communication of their Thoughts" conveniently extended these Enlightenment ideas about society to societies large and small, domestic and political, when their members were not physically present to one another. Letters were the means by which Society could subsist *in absentia* and be maintained among people separated by geographical distance. Letters, as Turpilius said, made the absent present, or as Lord Kames put it, through letters, "ideal presence supplies the place of real presence, and in idea we perceive people acting and suffering precisely as in an original survey."[115] While inhabiting a system of communication which turned on mutual adaptation and address, the idea that handwritten letter exchanges were "written conversations" that enabled Society to subsist among men without their physical presence, made it possible for written correspondences to construct imaginary publics and "imaginary societies" with real-world effects. Indeed, by encouraging reader-writers to "imagine" that their correspondents were present before them as they wrote, manuals encouraged them to create, "in idea" and *in absentia* – by the power of words to summon up images before the mind – imaginary transatlantic families, imaginary circles of friends, imaginary guardianships or courtships, imaginary trading firms and – transatlantic correspondence by transatlantic correspondence – an imaginary transatlantic nation joined by "the same language, the same culture, and the same religion." By offering real and fictional exchanges of letters cheek by jowl, letter manuals signaled and naturalized the collusion of the imaginary with the real that was inseparable from written

115 Kames, *Elements*, 70.

conversation and epistolary commerce, whether in manuscript or in print. Letter-writing had political, social, domestic, cultural and economic consequences, *because* it had fictional force even in its most "real" or utilitarian manifestations.

Speech and writing, nature and art, imagination and reality, simplicity and sociality, were intertwined in the letter-form. Letter manuals therefore held on to their paradox: people should write letters as they would naturally speak, and learn from manuals how to write letters and how to speak.

CHAPTER 2

Manual architectonics

Eighteenth-century letter manuals were vocal about their usefulness, silent about how a reader-writer was supposed to use them. They thought it necessary to expound upon the importance of letter-writing to people of all ranks, as we saw; but assumed a public that was capable, without instruction, of reading "a book the Object of which is to teach by Specimens," and of learning to write from scattered heterogeneous fragments.[1] We have the opposite problem. The fragmentary and miscellaneous composition of many early books, together with issues related to what Robert Hume has called "collective authorship," constitute primary interpretative difficulties for anyone working in areas such as this today.[2] Better attuned to the continuities of narrative and of expository prose, we are having to relearn how to read medieval and early modern anthologies, miscellanies, and commonplace books.

Epistolary compendia and letter collections "worked" by superimposing multiple taxonomies on fragments of diverse kinds and by incorporating a variety of binary oppositions. This created a grid, simple in appearance but complex in design, that could be traversed in different ways for different purposes, and translated quite variously by reader-writers with different levels of education and skill. Modeling letters between fictionally generic characters in specific circumstances, as all the manuals did, provided them with a convenient shorthand for inscribing these taxonomies and for exemplifying opposite aspects of the letter form. As we will see below, many of the taxonomies exemplified in model letters were also signaled and supported by the more expository outwork that *Compendia* bound up with them: grammars, spellers, directions for punctuation, directions for addressing people at various ranks, directions for folding letters and more. Understanding these recurrent taxonomies

---

1 *Correspondent*, iv.   2 Hume, "Editing a Nebulous Author," 249.

and their import is the first step both in learning to "read" an eighteenth-century letter manual, and in discovering what manuals have to tell us about the conventions of reading and writing in eighteenth-century correspondences. Among other things, they tell us a great deal about how to read style and tone, how to gauge the relative ranks of writer and recipient/s, and how to dig for commonplaces.

LETTER CLASSES

Perhaps the most fundamental taxonomy in eighteenth-century letter manuals was increasingly obscured as the century wore on, and is easiest to miss today. Eighteenth-century manuals used a classification of letters by function that had been adapted from early seventeenth-century French epistolographers, rather than from English humanist epistolographers, who classified letters according to the different kinds of classical oration. Classifications of letters were highly visible in Renaissance letter manuals, and some seventeenth-century handbooks still organized their entire collections by grouping letters together under kind or class.[3] But only rare manuals during the long eighteenth century organized their letters this way, and only four manuals still openly invoked letter classes to explain the "Endes and Designs" of each. They are the London version of Hill's *Young Secretary's Guide; or Speedy Help to Learning* (1687); Thomas Goodman's *The Experienc'd Secretary* (1699); *The New Art of Letter-Writing* (1762), which was dedicated to the "Noblemen and Gentlemen educated at Marybone School"; and *The Correspondent* (1796), which sought to rival Vicesimus Knox's popular *Elegant Epistles* (1791) by offering the explanations and critical commentaries that his volume lacked. Conveniently distributed throughout the period, these more expository manuals show remarkable unanimity despite the more than a century that separates the first from the last.

The recognized classes of familiar letter made a formidable list. They included: letters of business; letters of advice; letters of praise or commendation; letters of recommendation; letters of remonstrance; letters of exhortation; letters of entreaty, request or petition; letters of

---

3 Stylistically, letters were grave, learned or jocular; functionally, they were "exhortatorie, accusatorie, commendatorie, excusatorie, congratulatorie, resonsorie, consolatorie, jocatorie, nunciatore, criminatorie, lamentatorie, mandatorie, dehortatorie, objurgatorie, petitorie, comminatorie, expostulatorie, ematorie, conciliatorie, laudatorie, or intercessorie." See Lipsius, *Principles*; Day, *English Secretary.*

counsel; letters of complaint; letters of reproof; letters of excuse; letters of thanks; letters of invitation; letters of congratulation; letters of consolation, comfort or condolence; letters of visit; letters of compliment; letters proffering assistance; letters of merriment or raillery; and letters mixing two or more of the above. All eighteenth-century manuals gave examples of letters belonging to each of the different classes; but manuals after Hill – including otherwise faithful American reprints of Hill – generally omitted the expository chapter and retained only the practice of indicating the letter's class in the titles they affixed to their model letters. Titles such as "from a Brother at Home, to his Sister abroad on a Visit, complaining of her not writing," "from a Daughter to her Mother, by way of Excuse for having neglected to write to her," or "a Letter from a Nephew to an Uncle, who wrote him a Letter of Rebuke," which I have taken from Crowder's *Complete Letter-Writer or Polite English Secretary* (1755), indicate, for instance, that the first is a letter of complaint, and the other two, letters of excuse.

Letter classes were fundamental to eighteenth-century letter-writing because the function of each class of letter determined its matter and proper subjects, the commonplaces it was supposed to express, and the kinds of occasion to which it applied. One general rule for letter-writing was "to say what the Occasion dictates."[4] Specimen letters in manuals were therefore written or selected with a view to demonstrating the subjects and sentiments proper to each class of letter, and letter-writers were expected to repeat what the class of letter they were writing required them to say – preferably in their own words. What was thought to distinguish one letter from another within any particular class was not what it said, but how far the writer had managed to "follow Horace's advice to express common Things and Subjects as if they are not,'" and thus to "make what we say our own, and heighten it with the Graces of Novelty, though a Thousand others have said it before."[5] A frequently repeated phrase was that "A fine letter does not consist in saying fine things, but expressing ordinary ones in an uncommon manner."[6] The Art of Letter-Writing was therefore the art of saying "What oft was thought, but ne'er so well expressed." A good letter disguised its repetition of the commonplaces that writing a familiar letter dictated, or it reinscribed them by denying that the writer needed, wished or was going to use them

---

4 *Correspondent*, iv.   5 *New Art of Letter-Writing*, 8.
6 This appears for instance in Robert Dodsley's *Preceptor*, and in *The Instructive Letter-Writer and Entertaining Companion*, 3rd ed. (London, 1769), 11.

again. A good familiar letter can make its readers forget for the duration of a reading that they have heard the same sentiments and ideas before, and overlook the insistence of the class of letter to which it belongs, rather than read it in the proper way with a view to enjoying the new twists that they have been given. A good familiar letter was what we would call a "literary familiar letter," insofar as we expect the "literary" to involve defamiliarization.

Eighteenth-century letter classes are not as obvious as they may initially seem. In some cases, they contained types of letter that we do not now think of together. We should take note of two in particular. Letters of Advice, Hill explains, are "such as are sent to Friends or Correspondents to give them notice of their own Affairs, and the Affairs of others, wherein they are concerned, or of which we think they are desirous to be informed." But they are also "those of an Indulgent parent to his Children, as to the good Government of their Lives and well Managing of their Affairs, etc.," *and* such as are "much used amongst Merchants, to give their Factors, or Correspondents in other Countries an Account of the Prices of Goods, Customs, and Exchanges that thereby they may regulate their Affairs accordingly" (4–5). The common element was clearly that all these letters provided their correspondents with necessary information or intelligence; but only in Hill's second sense do letters of advice contain what we would call advice today. Letters of advice in Hill's first sense are what the eighteenth century also (increasingly) called letters of intelligence or letters of news. They were the most frequent, and among the most prized, of eighteenth-century letters, in part because nation and empire ran on intelligence, and in part because "a new subject is of infinite use in the country," as one of Elizabeth Griffith's characters pointed out.[7] Letters of news or intelligence required skills of description and narration that grew out of traditional divisions both of the oration and of the letter, but they began to be modeled explicitly only in mid-eighteenth-century manuals. The word advice continued to be used in Hill's third sense for merchants' letters covering the subjects he describes throughout the eighteenth century.

Letters of Business likewise constituted a far more compendious category than we might assume today. Hill described letters of business both as "Trustees of all the Trading Part of Mankind and the silent Messengers of their Affairs" *and* as no less "useful in matters of State, as

7 Griffith, *Delicate Distress*, 165.

having reference to War and Peace, With many other Things of high concern and Moment" (4). Business letters dealt with court, political, administrative or government business, as well as with commercial affairs. *The New Art of Letter-Writing* pointed out that since business letters were "those that treat of important matters," they could include letters of advice, counsel, remonstrance, command, request, recommendation, offering assistance, complaint, reproach and excuse. This extended business to cover the sort of household-family business and business between friends or acquaintance that figured prominently in this and other letter manuals, for instance in the form of letters requesting a loan from acquaintance or kin, letters offering financial assistance to a nephew or fellow trader, letters reproaching a son, brother or nephew for irresponsible conduct at work, letters of excuse from an apprentice to his master and even letters of visit, compliment or friendship of certain kinds.

Another reason that letter classes can be less obvious than they may seem is that without knowing what had to be said in each class of letter, and how, convention can easily be mistaken for sincerity, or repetition for originality. Letters of condolence, which have been used by more than one historian as evidence of the religious sentiments of whole communities, and letters of visit or friendship, which have been prized by literary critics, illustrate some of the limits on free self-expression as well as the unreliability of tone as a touchstone of sincerity.

The function of letters of consolation or condolence was to offer comfort in the event of any calamity, from banishment or loss of estate to sickness or death. In the event of death, the reader-writer was supposed to begin by saying "that we cannot but *participate* with our *Friend* therein by condoling his *Misfortune*, and as we shared in his Joy, so we can do no less in his Sorrow."[8] He was to continue thus:

We may say that we are under the deepest Concern for his Affliction; and taking so great a part as we do therein. . .we do not design to advise him not to mourn and afflict himself. . .But that he should moderate his Grief, and shew some Fortitude by supporting courageously what he cannot correct, and making, as it is said, a Virtue of Necessity. . .That the time now is to show the Advantages he has reaped, perhaps from the Study of Philosophy or Christian Resignation; and that it is not reasonable for Nature to change her Course, and exempt him from the Laws all the World is subject to; and that he should submit without murmuring to the will of God.[9]

---

8 *Young Secretary's Guide*, 10.   9 *New Art of Letter-Writing*, 32.

The New Art of Letter-Writing stressed that "Sentiments of Piety are properly inserted into Letters of Consolation" and that "it is chiefly in Letters of Consolation that we are allowed to use moral Sayings and Maxims or Sentiments of Piety."[10] Unless all religious elements have been excluded in favor of positively atheistic maxims, therefore, the presence of moral maxims, of Christian consolation and of quotations from the Scriptures in contemporary letters of condolence should tell us more about the education and politeness of the writer than about the piety and religious convictions of anyone involved. The religious and philosophical note was dictated – as was the tone of sincerity. In a letter of this kind, the reader-writer was instructed, "the Heart must appear touched," and consequently, choice must be made of "tender and natural Expressions" rather than of witty or studied ones.[11] Even some of the letter's insincerities were dictated from mid-century on. Earlier manuals often included a jocular letter of consolation to someone who had more reason to rejoice than to grieve at the death of a parent or spouse. But from mid-century these disappeared from letter manuals, and writers were advised that "we are not allowed to adapt our discourse openly to the secret Sentiments of the Heart; Decency forbids it."[12] If the reader-writer believed that his or her addressee was not really grieving, he or she was merely to moderate the expressions of religious consolation. The difference between this letter of condolence and the one addressing real grief was thus a subtle matter of degree rather than of sentiment or style. For the people directly involved, this subtle difference might signal the unsaid, but it can be difficult for a third party to be sure which kind of letter they are reading. And, of course, a clergyman on his high horse, a pompous or tactless writer, or one who was not in the know, might earnestly or ponderously press on with the whole array of conventional consolatory arguments regardless of the merely performative character of the mourner's sorrow.[13]

Letters of Visit, which were often anthologized in manuals after mid-century in sections called "Letters of Friendship," have consistently

10 *Ibid.*, 46, 48.
11 This does not mean that no one ever wrote a sincere letter of condolence; only that it was proper to sound sincere even if one was not.
12 *New Art of Letter-Writing*, 48.
13 Another standard format for letters of condolence included encomiums to the departed, but these were more dependent on the rhetorical places and less easy to generalize in models, and therefore appear less frequently in manuals.

been read by twentieth-century critics as genuine literary testimonies to homosocial friendships. However, they too had their fixed topoi. These stemmed from the conviction that to be far from sight was to be far from mind; and from the fear, in this face-to-face and highly personalized patronage society, that being far from mind meant being forgotten when benefits or sinecures were being handed out. As *The Correspondent* stressed: "The only Means of keeping alive the Warmth of Friendship in Absence is by an epistolary Correspondence; that neglected, no warmth of Esteem is able to resist the unvarying effects of time, which by the Introduction of new Connections, new Scenes of Pleasure, and new Circumstances of Embarrassment, must necessarily supersede an Interest which the holder is too indolent or too busy to claim."[14] This sense of the practical importance of keeping in touch with one's "friends" became as pervasive among traders, country gentry and transatlantic families, as among the literati or members of the government or court. Writing letters when one was far away was essential in order to keep the memory of oneself before one's "friends" – both in the larger eighteenth-century sense of kin, patrons, colleagues and potential business partners or helpers, and in the more restricted sense of erstwhile intimates or companions – as well as in order to find out what was going on in one's absence. The topoi in such letters therefore turned on issues of remembering and forgetting, often as demonstrated by whether or not letters had been written or answered. They also often turned on the traditional complemental or philosophical topoi of "friendship," "love" and service between men. The writer of a letter of visit or friendship had to reassure his absent correspondent that their erstwhile affection remained unaffected by absence, time or distance; that the writer fully understood the importance and pleasures of friendship or continued to appreciate and value the high merit of his correspondent; and above all, that he remained willing to "serve" him if necessary. However eloquently they might be written and however philosophical they might wax about the charms of friendship, such letters had a fundamentally politique, conventional and phatic function. Among sophisticated epistolary writers and readers, the sincerity of such letters was therefore always in question. This is evident, for example, in the convention of denying the conventionality of such civilities, as in the following model letter:

14 *Correspondent*, 222

Sir,

    If our mutual Friendship had no other Way of being maintained but by Letters, I should be constantly employed in writing them, to give you fresh Assurances of its Stability; but, well knowing that it is kept up of itself, and by the solid Ground-work it is built upon, I despise all the Artifices of Civility and Compliment. By the slender Acquaintance you have with your own Merit and my Humour, you may know, without being a Prophet, how much I esteem you; and, as Science has Truth for its Object, you may have all the Reason in the World to believe, that I am truly and sincerely, etc.[15]

    Phrases, such as "I despise all the Artifices of Civility and Compliment," "I am a sworn Enemy of Civilities and Courtesies, in Regard to Persons, whom I honour to the Degree I do you," or "[believe] that I am, without Compliment, Sir, Your most humble Servant," were attempts to reinscribe the presumption of sincerity on which the function of such letters depended.[16] But skepticism and suspicion were the proper reactions for reader-receivers of such letters, as we will see in the section on "responsive reading" below and again in Chapter 3. To express sincerity less equivocally, "Romantic subjectivity" had ultimately to cut through the proprieties, and seek devices (like the broken sentence) to profile its difference against the norms.

    Finally, some letter classes employed now unfamiliar codes. For instance:

Letters of *Recommendation*, or Letters *Recommendatory*, are those that one Friend sends to another, to prefer any Person or Business; and therein he insinuates the Honesty, or Ability of the Person, and the Employments he is capable of undertaking, and the Reason why he recommends him, acknowledging what is done to the Party as done to himself. (5)

    As this paragraph mentions in passing, letters of recommendation as a class included letters recommending one policy or piece of business over another (which also made it a particular form of letter of counsel or advice), as well as letters recommending persons for employment. The now unfamiliar code is indicated in the last phrase. Stating that the job or preferment given to the party recommended would be viewed as a favor to the person writing the letter, signaled that the recommendation was seriously meant. Without it, there would be a suspicion that the letter had been written under duress or as an unavoidable *politesse*, and that the addressee could safely give the job or preferment to someone else. Inclusion of this phrase made the letter of recommendation a form of patronage, rather than just a testimonial.

---

15 *New Art of Letter-Writing*, 158.   16 *Ibid.*, 155.

Similar codes occur in letters of request or petition and in letters of thanks. It was essential to conclude a letter of request or a letter of thanks with "a promise of due Acknowledgment of the Favour." The writer had to demonstrate his recognition that granting the favor or request put him under an obligation to perform some service in return. This was also implicit in the letter of recommendation's acknowledgment that the writer would view what was done for the person he was recommending as a favor to himself. As Enlightenment philosophers and political economists liked to say, society was sustained by an "exchange of mutual good Offices." You scratch my back, I'll scratch yours. Substitution by an assurance that remembrance of the favor granted would be expunged only by death, or by an assurance that God would be sure to remember and reward the kindness given, signaled the writer's conviction that his misfortunes or his inferior position in society relative to his correspondent were such that he was not, might not again be, or would never be, in a position to return the favor.

Both *The New Art of Letter-Writing* and *The Correspondent* pointed out that "in the intercourse of life, necessity compels almost every individual, at some period, to apply for the advice, friendly interference or pecuniary assistance of another." A letter of request, solicitation, or entreaty was a basic, bread-and-butter letter. Letters of petition, which were often included in a special section at the end of manuals from mid-century, eventually became more specifically letters of application for jobs, government relief, or institutional or individual charity. *The Correspondent* insisted that it was better to make all such requests, entreaties and applications by letter than in person. For the writer, a letter "spares the pain and confusion attendant on verbal requests," and for his correspondent, "it affords time and deliberation and permits him to arrange matters so as to facilitate compliance or soften refusal."[17] Manuals usually offered specimens both of letters complying with requests and of letters refusing them. The former were considered particularly elegant and politique when they expressed their compliance "with so much delicacy and force, as to render the most valuable gifts, and advantageous occasions, more valuable and agreeable," thus in such a way as to increase the obligation while pretending to minimize it. The art of the latter lay in refusing without offending.[18]

17 *Correspondent*, 308.   18 *Ibid.*, 309.

Letters of thanks were also coded in the sense that they had to be nicely proportioned to the magnitude of the gift or favor received and to the extent of the obligation. In the case of smaller favors or gifts, they were supposed to convey both gratitude and pleasure, by describing the many uses or beauties of the gift or how a letter (often referred to in correspondences as "your favor") had been read and appreciated. In the case of larger favors, like the procurement of a post or a living, "all the graces of eloquence" were to be brought into play and the extent of the obligation had to be stressed. A letter of thanks could easily offend if one did not get the magnitude of the gift or favor and the extent of the obligation incurred quite right. *The New Art of Letter-Writing* therefore recommended that "Whatever may be the Quality of the Benefit or Benefactor, it is necessary we should seem sensible of it, and withal *exaggerate* its Circumstances, making appear the Utility or Honour that has accrued to us from it, and protesting in concluding our Letter, that we shall preserve it for perpetual Remembrance."[19] Here again, of course, exaggeration notwithstanding, one was supposed to choose expressions that would sound sincere.

The fact that there were so many classes of letters with different prescribed subjects, sentiments and styles meant that letters could not "altogether be reduced to one common or constant Standard."[20] The associated imperative, which was to treat the letter as an address and to "regulate yourself by a due Attention to the Station in Life of those you address and your own," diversified the standard even further, as we will see in the next section.[21]

THE PARADOX OF POLITENESS

Manuals identified, and in some sense created, the particular occasions for letter-writing they also modeled by seeking opportunities in the everyday for writing all the traditional kinds or classes of letter. Besides the class of letter, the titles given to letters indicated the occasion for which a particular class of letter had been adapted, and indeed, the sort of everyday occasion on which a particular class of letter might be used. As we saw in the previous chapter, they also gave expression to each manual's taxonomy of characters and social roles. London compendia used these

---

19 *New Art of Letter-Writing*, 66.
20 *Young Secretary's Guide*, Chapter II. Johnson makes the same point in *Rambler*, 152.
21 *Correspondent*, 9.

taxonomies to inscribe and reinforce what I am going to a call a paradox of politeness: on the one hand, the popularization of polite letteracy and the democratic extension of polite manners to everyone above the laboring poor, and on the other hand, insistence on observance of the customary, deferential, non-egalitarian forms.[22]

Situating generic kinds of letters between fictionally generic characters or social types in specific circumstances enabled manuals to demonstrate that kinds or classes of letter ignored distinctions of rank and gender, and crossed any line we might wish to draw between the public and the private, or the family and the workplace. Manuals situated letters of complaint and letters of excuse, for instance, between a parent and child, a brother and sister, or an uncle and nephew, between friends, tradesmen, masters and servants, landlords and tenants, between men and women during courtship, and between husband and wife after marriage. Similarly, they showed that there could be occasion for letters of entreaty (requesting a favor) and letters of thanks (for a favor rendered) between tradesmen, between commercial correspondents, between gentlemen, across ranks, and in all the more social and domestic situations of life (such as a lady inviting a friend to stay at her house in the country, or a son at school asking his father for dancing lessons). The fact that manuals also intermixed generic names indicating ranks, such as "gentlewoman" or "young lady," with names representing familial relations, such as mother or daughter, also indicated the applicability of most letter classes across ranks. Letter manuals thus demonstrated that classes of letters were both hugely adaptable and remarkably democratic. By situating classes of model letters at all ranks, and in all the diverse circumstances of public, commercial and domestic life, compilers quietly reinforced and illustrated their prefatory marketing message: that "the art of letter-writing" was "equally useful to the highest and the lowest," "to the younger Sort of either Sex," "to those of Elder years," to "every Age, Sex and Profession," and indeed to "all, at least above the lowest rank," since "the daily intercourse of common life cannot be duly preserved without this mode of communication."[23]

But if classes of letters were presented as equally suited to the everyday intercourse of all ranks, styles and forms of address were not. Situating letters between social types in fictional circumstances also enabled manuals to model the different language, sentiments and expressions

---

22 In the eighteenth century, "democratic" was a synonym for "leveling" or egalitarian.
23 Dodsley, *Preceptor*, x, xvi; *Young Secretary's Guide*, 2; Knox, *Elegant Epistles*, v.

requisite for different addressees in societies that remained profoundly hierarchical, both in the public and domestic spheres. Manuals, both in Britain and in America even after Independence, repeatedly warned letter-writers that "regard must always be shewn to time, place and person," and that "we must endeavour to suit our expressions to the nature of the subject, and the rank of our correspondent, being careful not to seem haughty when addressing our superiors, nor demean ourselves when writing to an inferior, and hold an equal rank with equals."[24] Manuals therefore presented different versions of the same kind of letter as it should be written to persons of different ranks and degrees of familiarity.

Demonstrating how the quality, rank and character of the addressee determined the language, style and sentiments of the letter one wrote, and modeling the customary "*Distances, Familiarities, Condescensions or Humiliations* according as the Letters refer to *Superiors, Equals or Inferiors*,"[25] reinforced the message conveyed in compendia by the "Instructions for Outside and Inside Superscriptions and Subscriptions of Letters." These listed the formal terms of address to be used for people at different ranks from the king down, and the order of precedence among ranks as well. Superscriptions (My Lord, Sir, Dear Sir) and subscriptions (your humble servant, your most humble and obedient servant, your brother) indicated the hierarchical relationship and the degree of familiarity in which correspondents thought they stood relative to each other (or in which they were pretending to stand, in order to please, flatter or persuade their addressee). Subscriptions, in particular, were "no other than the Compliments of Writers, to which their Names are affixed, yet ought to express some measure of the *Quality* of the person, by owning Superiority in him to whom the Letter is Directed, or a Power and Authority in Him who Writes it, over Him to whom it is Written; and on the other Hand, *Friendship, Equality or Familiarity*."[26] In other words, superscriptions and subscriptions registered hierarchies and acknowledged relations of power. They can constitute the key to the interpretation of an eighteenth-century letter, and substantially change its *prima facie* reading.

One piece of etiquette that manuals taught in this regard was that the hierarchically superior correspondent always named the relationship in which he or she stood to the addressee in the superscription, while the hierarchically inferior correspondent named it only in the subscription.

---

24 Knox, *Elegant Epistles*, vi; "General Directions" from *The Court Letter-Writer*, 43.
25 *Young Secretary's Guide*, 2.   26 *Ibid.*, 81.

For instance, an older brother began his letter "Dear Brother," while his younger brother ended his letter "I am . . . your loving Brother, James"; a father might begin "Son," but his son would begin "Sir" or "Honoured Sir." Another piece of etiquette distinguished among ranks in the very formulae for subscriptions, for instance by using "Your Servant" to an inferior; "Your humble and affectionate Servant," or "Your friend and humble Servant" to an equal; and "Your most humble and obedient Servant" or "Your most obliged and humble Servant" to a Superior. In subscriptions to the great and to persons of quality, one added My Lord, My Lady, Your Lordship, Your Ladyship, Sir, Madam or Miss in a separate line before "Your most humble and obedient Servant." Although there were fixed forms such as these, in practice subscriptions also lent themselves to considerable creative variation, in part because run-on subscriptions – subscriptions growing out of the letter's last sentence – were fashionable throughout the period, and in part because the adjectives chosen to precede the word "servant" or the named relationship (brother, daughter) could be varied at will.

It should be noted that American manuals after Independence eventually replaced English "Instructions for the Inside and Outside Superscriptions and Subscriptions of Letters" with an equally hierarchical list of American dignitaries from the President down, tabulated with the proper terms of respect with which each should be addressed. During the last decades of the eighteenth century, manuals on both sides of the Atlantic also began to use "Dear" as a superscription far more frequently, and to a far wider variety of addressees, than before.

Compendia for most of the century also included among their "Instructions for Inside and Outside Superscriptions and Subscriptions of Letters," cognate rules for the material culture and appearance of the letter:

Letters should be wrote on *quarto* fine post paper, whether gilt or plain is a matter of no consequence, when addressed to a superior; if to an equal or inferior, the writer may use what sort or size he pleases: but be careful never to seal your letter with a wafer, except to the latter. When you write to a superior, let your letter be as short as the subject or occasion will permit, especially when a favour is requested; and be extremely careful never to abbreviate any of your words, as *I've* for *I have*, *can't* for *cannot* etc. Such abbreviations are both disrespectful and too familiar.[27]

27 *Court Letter-Writer*, 45. *The Complete Letter-Writer* and *Young Secretary's Guide* say the same less concisely.

It was possible to write a familiar letter too familiarly, even to inferiors. Postscripts too were discouraged in letters to superiors and equals, as less respectful and less affectionate than including the "compliments" (regards to Lady M– or Aunt Dottie) and "services" expressed in them in the body of the letter, because postscripts suggested that the person/s mentioned had earlier been forgotten.

There was also a semiotics of blank spaces. Correspondents were told to represent graphically the social distance in which they stood relative to their correspondents at the beginning the letter by the amount of space they left on the page between the superscription and body of the text, and again at the end, by the distance they left on the page between the text of the letter and the subscription of their own name. Mindful of the frequent interceptions of letters during this period, some manuals warned that signing one's name "at a considerable distance below the conclusion of the letter" and "leaving a large vacant space over the names, though customary, is much better avoided, because it is putting it in the power of anyone who has your letter, to write what he pleases over your name, and to make you, in all appearance, sign a writing you would by no means have set your hand to."[28] On the left-hand side of the page, a one-inch margin represented the minimum benchmark of respect. In practice, letters to or among the great might leave a two- or three-inch margin, while those writing to intimates or family members might eliminate the margin altogether to save space, or "cross" their letters – write the letter, then turn the page to its side and write at a right angle across the lines they had written before. Just looking at a letter that one held in one's hands and noting the quality of paper, the length of the text, the presence or absence of abbreviations, the quantity or absence of blank spaces, and the formatting of the manuscript page, could signal all one needed to know *a priori* about the rank and importance of its addressee and the education or "good-breeding" of its writer, as well as about the relative power and degree of familiarity subsisting between them.

The date, which it was proper to write either above or below the body of the letter, could also offer indications of the relationship between correspondents, since reader-writers were generally advised that politeness, affection and respect dictated a speedy response, and that they could use delay in responding to signify displeasure, indifference or contempt. This convention certainly underlay some of the anxiety expressed in

---

28 *Ibid.*, 51. *The Complete Letter-Writer* made the same point.

letters of visit or friendship about a friend's failure to write or to answer letters with any dispatch.

What we call the address, and the eighteenth century called the letter's direction, was coded too. It was not just that letters to superiors were supposed to be enclosed in a "cover," where other letters could be folded and sealed so that one small blank piece of a page was left to serve as the space for the direction. Letter-writers also needed tact to decide what to put in the direction. Manuals advised that when directing a letter to a person who was eminent, important or well known, whether as a merchant or as a gentleman, it was considered impolite to specify his or her location too closely, for this suggested that the person was too obscure to be easily found. This obviously presented a problem if one's correspondent was in reality comparatively obscure, especially if they lived in a city, for though it might be more flattering, or more polite, to direct the letter as if one's addressee were well known, one incurred the risk of the letter going astray.

Suiting a letter to the station of one's addressee relative to oneself also impacted the body of the epistolary text. Letters from an inferior to a superior were supposed to express themselves in a more elevated style, and in a manner that was deferential without appearing obsequious or servile, and flattering without appearing fulsome or insincere. Praise, which formed a significant part of letters of friendship too, was always tricky in this regard. In letters of advice, letters of counsel, letters recommending a particular course of action, and letters of remonstrance, complaint or reproach, relative station determined whether or not it was permissible to express one's sentiments directly. A person with authority over his addressee, such as father writing to his son, a master to his servant, a mother to her daughter, or a minister of state to his minion, could be as direct as they liked when offering advice or remonstrance. For the same reason, letters of Command could only be written by a superior to an inferior. But among equals, and especially among friends or familiars, reader-writers were told to convey their advice or reproaches more indirectly, by resorting to wit or teasing, or by making moral or philosophical observations about the virtues or vices of people in general, in the hope that their correspondent would recognize that these were meant for himself. Narrative was also highly recommended as a way of conveying meaning without giving offense and without creating jealousy or resentment in one's interlocutors or correspondents, because everyone assumed they could tell a good story too and because narratives remained suitably indirect. In letters of accusation, the reader-writer was advised to use indirection of a more traditionally rhetorical sort: "Those who undertake to accuse one of a considerable Fault, often begin their Letters with the good Qualities of the Person they intend to blame. This artifice makes them appear sincere, whereas, if they were thought prejudiced by Aversion, they would not persuade so easily."[29] Here again, the appearance of sincerity is an effect of the writing rather than of the heart.

Letters of news, compliment, friendship and such, the function of which was to please, were supposed to reflect the interests, humor, age, sex and character of their addressees, rather than those of the writer. A man's interests might lie in the sciences, but it was improper to write to a woman about them. A person might be a great wit, but it was improper (and unsafe) to write a witty or jocular letter to a person without wit or humor. One did not write to an honest man as to a cunning one, or to a coquette as to a lady of sense and virtue. The content and style of a letter might therefore tell a third party as much or more about its addressee, than about its writer.

PROPER SENTIMENTS AND PROPER CONDUCT

On the level of the individual letter, there were several ways in which manuals taught proper conduct. One way was to use exemplifications of proper conduct to fill out the commonplaces for particular classes of letter and to transmit both together, as in the following two examples:

From a young Apprentice to his Father, to let him know how he likes his Place, and goes on

Honoured Sir,

I know it will be a great Satisfaction to you, and my dear Mother, to hear that I go on very happy in my Business; and my Master, seeing my Diligence, puts me forward, and encourages me in such a Manner, that I have great Delight in it; and hope I shall answer in Time your good Wishes and Expectations, and the Indulgence which you have always shewn me. There is such good Order in the Family, as well on my Mistress's Part as my Master's, that every Servant, as well as I, knows his Duty, and does it with Pleasure. So much Evenness, Sedateness, and Regularity, is observed in all they enjoin or expect, that it is impossible but it should be so. My Master is an honest, worthy Man; every Body speaks well of him. My Mistress is a chearful sweet-tempered Woman, and rather heals Breaches than widens them. And the Children, after such Examples, behave to us all like one's own Brothers and Sisters. Who can but love such a Family? I wish,

29 *New Art of Letter-Writing*, 68.

when it shall please God to put me in such a Station, that I may carry myself just as my Master does; and if I should ever marry, have just such a Wife as my Mistress: And then, by God's Blessing, I shall be as happy as they are, and as you, Sir, and my dear Mother have always been. If any Thing can make me happier than I am, or continue to me my present Felicity, it will be the Continuance of yours, and my good Mother's Prayers, for,

Honoured Sir,

Your very dutiful Son.

This letter of news or "advice" in Hill's first sense derived from Richardson's *Letters Written to and for Particular Friends* (1741) and was reprinted again and again in multiple manuals throughout the eighteenth century; I have taken it here from Charles Johnson's *The Complete Art of Writing Letters, adapted to All Classes and Conditions of Life* (London, 1779).[30] This model letter fulfils the function of letters of this class, which is for writers to give their "Friends or Correspondents Notice of their own Affairs, and the Affairs of others wherein they are concerned, or which we think they are desirous to be informed" by modeling all three. The topos of giving his parents notice of "the affairs of others wherein he is concerned" is filled out by the young apprentice's highly idealistic portrayal of the well-ordered family in which he finds himself, where everyone knows their proper place and performs their relative duties each to each in the prescribed ways. This ideal family embodies the injunctions of conduct books from Fleetwood's *Relative Duties of Parents and Children, Husbands and Wives, Masters and Servants* to Gisbourne's *Inquiry into the Duties of the Female Sex*. Lest anyone miss the point, the young man observes that his master and mistress's children dutifully model themselves upon their parents' example, and that he hopes to do the same when he has a household-family of his own. This ideal family is normalized by the indication that the young man's parents run their household-family in the same way and by the young man's use, in the style and mode of address of this letter, of the expressions of duty and deferential forms considered proper for sons writing to their fathers. These include the respectful acknowledgment of the hierarchical distance between father and son signaled by the "honoured Sir" in superscription and subscription and the naming of their relationship only in the subscription; the expressions of obedience and of duty, and

---

30 Pp. 33–4.

the expression of gratitude for "the Indulgence you have always shewn me" – which is by way of being a set phrase for dutiful letters to parents. While demonstrating the proper epistolary forms for letters between sons and fathers, the young man's use of them implicitly confirms both that his parents have a well-ordered family in which children know their proper place, and that he is also likely to be conducting himself properly in the family in which he has been placed; they are therefore also performatives of character.

The conduct book elements of this letter are directed as much at any masters and mistresses who may be using the manual as at apprentices or servants more generally. Complaints about the carelessness and laziness of apprentices and about the impudence and dishonesty of servants were rampant throughout the eighteenth century, which may account for the popularity of this letter among compilers of manuals. Like Defoe, who described at length the "Degeneracy of *English* Servants" through lack of proper subordination to their masters, this letter suggests that "the Want of Family Government is the Ruin of Servants" and that the remedy lies in masters' and mistresses' "Reformation of Family Discipline."[31] To masters and mistresses, the message of this letter is that if they were to conduct themselves as the master and mistress do in this letter, their example would be followed by everyone in their household-family, and children, apprentices and servants would all be as dutiful, diligent and happy as they would be themselves.

From a country Chapman to the Person he deals with in London

Sir,

   Though I have not lately had any Occasion for Goods, yet thinking it necessary to keep up your former Correspondence, I have given you the Trouble of a few Lines, desiring to hear from you how Trade moves at London; and what the Price is now of those Commodities in which you know I principally deal: And to prevent your too much trouble, I should be glad if you would send me down a very useful Paper, which I remember I have seen in *London*, containing the Price current of all Goods and Merchandizes; and I will gladly satisfy you for it; and esteem it a kindness to,

Sir,

Your Friend and Chapman,
JW

---

31 Defoe, *Law of Subordination*, 293, 299.

While demonstrating the sorts of things to write in a tradesman's "letter of visit," this model letter provides instruction about proper trading practices. It tells provincial retailers to keep up their contacts with London even when these are not immediately needed and to make sure they are informed about the London prices for goods. Printed lists of London prices were a relatively new phenomenon at the beginning of the eighteenth century. They saved London wholesalers or their clerks from laboriously having to write out lists of prices for each of their correspondents as part of their letters of advice, as they had been wont to do. However, provincial correspondents were still obliged to write out local prices for their London correspondents by hand during the first half of the eighteenth century, and the writer of this model letter is assuming that a country chapman (or shopkeeper) might not be aware of the existence of printed price lists for London goods, or realize that this service now cost money and that he should offer to pay for it.

Another way in which manuals conveyed conduct book teachings on the level of the individual letter was by means of letters of advice. Many conduct books throughout the century took the form of letters of advice from a father to a son or daughter, or from a mother to her child, and letters such as these were easily integrated into letter manuals. The following is an example of a letter that does double duty: it fulfilled its function as a letter of advice from "an indulgent Parent to his Children, as to the good Government of their Lives and well managing of their Affairs," by instructing his son on how to well manage his conversation:

A Father to his Son, on Conversation

Dear Charles,
    Though Good-humour, Sense and Discretion seldom fail to make a Man agreeable; it may be no ill Policy sometimes to prepare yourself in a particular Manner for Conversation, by looking a little farther than your Neighbours, into whatever is become a reigning Subject. If our Armies are besieging a Place of Importance abroad, or our House of Commons debating a Bill of Consequence at home, you can hardly fail of being heard with Pleasure, if you have nicely informed yourself of the Strength, Situation and History of the first, or of the Reasons for and against the latter. It will have the very same Effect, if, when any single Person begins to make a Noise in the World, you can learn some of the smallest Accidents in his Life or Conversation, which, though they are too fine for the Observation of the Vulgar, give more Satisfaction to Men of Sense, (as they are the best Opening to a real Character) than the Recital of his most glaring Actions. I know but one ill Consequence to be feared from this Method, namely, that coming full charged into Company, you should resolve to unload, whether an handsome Opportunity offers or not.

Though the asking of Questions may plead for itself the specious Name of Modesty, and a desire for Information; it affords little Pleasure to the rest of the Company, who are not troubled with the same Doubts; besides which, he who asks a Question would do well to consider, that he lies wholly at the Mercy of another, before he receives an Answer. Nothing is more silly, than the Pleasures some People take in what they call *speaking their Minds*. A Man of this Make will say a rude Thing for the mere Pleasure of saying it; when an opposite Behaviour, full as innocent, might have preferred his Friend or made his Fortune.

It is not impossible for a Man to form to himself as exquisite a Pleasure in complying with the Humour and Sentiments of others, as of bringing others over to his own: since it is the certain Sign of a superior Genius, that can take and become whatever Dress he pleases.

I shall only add, that besides what I have here said, there is something that never can be learnt but in the Company of the Polite. The Virtues of Men are catching as well as their Vices, and our own Observations, added to these will soon discover what it is that commands attention in one Man, and makes you tired and displeased with the Discourse of another. I remain yours etc.[32]

The same preparation that qualified a man for conversation, qualified him to write good letters of news or intelligence, and made him a desirable companion and correspondent: collecting information or news about public affairs or public men that was currently of interest to others, and discovering something about them that most people did not know but would wish to know, to tell them about. Horace Walpole made a career of this sort of letter. This letter of advice stresses, however, that news and information were polite subjects, opinions were not. For politeness prescribed that a man make himself agreeable, that he seek to please others rather than himself, and that he avoid giving offense. A man made himself agreeable by good humor, by discretion, and by agreeing with the humor and opinions of others. To make himself agreeable, a man had to be able "to take and become whatever Dress he pleases." This made friends and brought him preferment; speaking his mind did not. A polite letter, like a polite conversation, was less informative than it seemed and any opinions or prejudices it contained might, once again, reflect those of its addressee more than of its author.

A third way in which manuals conveyed conduct book teaching on the level of the individual letter was by means of each letter's characterization of one or more social or generic type. The three letters above describe and/or silently present the traits of the "good apprentice," "the good tradesman" and "the gentleman," as well as those of the "good master

---

32 C. Johnson, *Art of Writing Letters*, 32–3.

and mistress" and "the good son." Repeated characterization of the same social or generic types in different letters throughout each collection, and identification of their traits both by affirmation as above and by negatives – for instance in letters of reproach to a bad apprentice or failed trades-man – provided at once a more rounded characterization of each social type for the imitation of the manual's readers, and a more insistent conduct book lesson. Repeated characterization of particular social or generic types was also one way in which the heterogeneous and discon-tinuous letters in each collection were linked.

THE LETTER AS COMPOSITION AND AS CONVERSATION

In letter manuals, the binary opposition between the democracy of kinds of letters and the hierarchy of styles of address, was overlaid by another between the letter as conversation and the letter as rhetorical composition or text.

Imitation of epistolary models in books designed to teach by specimens focused attention on model letters as text, and taught by repetition what Lipsius characterized as the "conventionally fixed," as opposed to the "variable," aspects of the letter form.[33] The fixed elements of a letter were not restricted to the formulae for superscriptions and subscriptions, or indeed to the subjects and sentiments prescribed by the different classes of letter. What Crevecoeur's farmer, James, called "the difficulty" of letter-writing, namely "how to collect, digest and arrange what I know," had long since been addressed in the rhetorical tradition by adapting the "parts" of a classical oration (*exordium, narratio, divisio, confirmatio, refutatio, peroratio*) to the composition and structuring of letters.[34] Though adjusted to classical and eighteenth-century character-izations of the familiar letter as a comparatively informal, conversational genre, the letter had a proper rhetorical form; and there were correct, rhetorically informed, ways of writing opening and closing paragraphs, and of ordering the matter between:

The *exordium* or introduction should be employed, not indeed with the formality of rhetoric, but with the ease of natural politeness and benevolence, in conciliating esteem, favour and attention; the proposition or narrative, in stating business with clearness and precision; the conclusion in confirming what has

---

33 Lipsius, *Principles*, 11ff.
34 Kennedy, *Classical Rhetoric*; Howell, *Eighteenth-Century British Logic and Rhetoric*.

been premised, in making apologies, extenuating offence, and in cordial expressions of respect and affection.[35]

The "Letter from the young Apprentice to his Father, to let him know how he likes his Place, and goes on" (above, p. 69) models these three parts of the letter. The young man's *exordium*, which ends with "the Indulgence which you have always shewn me," is designed to capture the favor, esteem and benevolence of his parents. The narrative, which begins "There is such good Order in the Family," clearly communicates the business of the letter, which is to convey news about his affairs and inform his parents of how he goes on. The conclusion, which begins "I shall be as happy as they are, and as you, Sir, and my dear Mother have always been," offers the necessary cordial expressions of respect and affection.

Like *exordium*, "proposition" and "narrative" were terms taken from classical rhetoric. Mainwaring defined the narration as "expound[ing] that which is or is not transacted" in such a way as to make it "evident" by making it "appear," and the proposition as a statement of the argument or case.[36] The anonymous author of *The New Art of Letter-Writing* is even more insistent on the structural similarities between letters and classical orations:

We have first Recourse to Civilities, whether we are obliged to thank the person we write to or to excuse ourselves; or that we have some favour to ask, or some Affair to recommend to him. These first Civilities may be deemed what is called the Exordium in a Harangue: They serve to insinuate us into his Mind, and dispose him to receive favorably what we have to say to him. When we enter upon our matter, we make appear to him, according to the Difference of Subjects, either the Justice of our Pretensions or the Share we take in whatever affects him. . .It will be easy to comprehend that the Exposition of the Subject serves as a Narration, and that the Reasons for justifying our Request, hold the place of a Proof or Confirmation. If we conclude by Protestations of a perfect Submission, or eternal Gratitude, it is in order to touch the Heart, and to persuade. Such is the intent of the Peroration of a Discourse, wherein the most vehement Figures are used for gaining a powerful Ascendent over the Minds of the Auditory. Now though this Order may be observed, yet it will be better to disregard than to endeavour to make it appear. Nothing must shew Restraint or Affectation in a Letter; every particular in it ought to breathe the Liberty that reigns in common Conversation.[37]

---

35 Knox, *Elegant Epistles*, vii.   36 Mainwaring, *Institutes*, 38.
37 *New Art of Letter-Writing*, 10–11.

Clearly, this was an area that lent itself to different levels of proficiency. "Elegant letters" by "the best authors" which we class as literary and which were designed in manuals for the improvement of style, often demonstrated more advanced techniques for ordering, transposing, combining, eliding and disguising the letter's rhetorical "parts" in such a way as to give it that appearance of ease, naturalness and "Liberty" which were so highly valued. Advanced techniques could also be modeled more modestly. In "A Father to his Son, on Conversation" (above, pp. 72–3), for instance, the father disposes of the Exordium, which is designed to induce his son to receive what he has to say favorably, by rapidly indicating in the first half of the first sentence the practical utility to his son of the advice which follows. He continues with a series of four propositions about conversation, developing which conveys the "Share [he] takes" in "whatever affects" his son. And though he seems to conclude without properly concluding, the conclusion's function of persuading his son of the justice of his propositions and of gaining an ascendancy over his mind is implicitly performed in the last paragraph by his recommendation that his son observe the conversational practices of the polite, since this will confirm the truth and value to his son of what he has advised.

The perceived difference between oratory and epistolography lay not in structure, but in style or "dress." A letter was "simple" and "natural" in comparison to stylistic features more proper to oratory. A letter that was written "simply" and "naturally" contained no figures, no fables, no proverbs, no sententiae, no digressions, no affectations of eloquence, no parentheses, no tautologies, no expletives. It was clear, conversational and to the point. It was "so constructed as to give [the reader] no difficulty in the perusal, in searching for obscure and ambiguous meanings, reconciling paradoxical assertions or developing concealed metaphors." It demonstrated "a facility of diction which prevents doubt and gratifies curiosity in the very moment of exciting it." And this, of course, was "not to be done by carelessness or inattention, but by the use of a style in the highest degree finished."[38] Writers were advised to revise their letters, and to practice letter-writing as much as they could. However spontaneous or casual it might be made to seem, therefore, there was nothing casual or spontaneous about a good letter. It was only that in a

38 *Correspondent*, 15–16.

letter, like the effort that had gone into it, the "Art ought to be absolutely concealed."[39]

What was viewed as simple and conversational in prose style changed over time. The conversational note, both in the form of implied apostrophe or direct address to the recipient in the body of the letter and in the form of references to preceding and possible succeeding letters or conversations, was generally retained; but everyone was conscious that there were fashions in epistolary style as in dress. London compilers marketed their manuals by promising that their letters modeled the most modern, current or fashionable style of epistolary writing and by casting aspersions on the style of manuals previous to themselves. As we will see in Part II, differences over style among manuals, which involved American adapters as well as London writer-compilers, were about ways of constructing national identities as well as of projecting or identifying character and rank. Style was used to differentiate French from English letters which imitated and corrected them. Especially during the first half of the eighteenth century, style was also one of the features differentiating London, Boston or Philadelphia manuals from each other. There was a long battle, which played out differently in English and American manuals, about how far French or Frenchified compliments were proper to the style and content of letters. By the turn of the nineteenth century, compliments had by common agreement been relegated to cards at the back of the manual. But the fact that multiple styles, old and new, were circulating simultaneously both in Britain and in America for most of the century, with different ideological connotations in different places, should be factored into the reading of letters.

Throughout the century, manuals likewise insisted that letters also differed from orations by their length. They recommended brevity in epistolary writing as an expression of politeness and respect, especially in letters to persons of superior rank. In manuals, commercial letters, which called virtually every correspondent Sir and treated everyone with equal respect in this regard, always remained fairly short. But for other classes of letter, how long "brevity" was, varied considerably, and in general, brief letters got longer as the century progressed. Among real correspondents, commercial letters were often mixed in with letters of news or friendship, which lengthened them to the limits of the available sheet.[40]

---

39 *Ibid.*, 5.   40 For Philadelphia merchants, see Ditz, "Formative Ventures."

The interest of earlier twentieth-century critics in letters as esthetically pleasing texts led many to read them as if "in the letter there is no interlocutor."[41] The fact that contemporaries insisted that it was "the *propria communia dicere*, the art of giving grace and elegance to familiar occurrences that constitutes the merit of this kind of writing" certainly produced plenty of "literary" features to admire in the language and style of eighteenth-century letters.[42] But reading them merely as texts ignored that the interlocutor was everywhere inscribed in the text, as well as the eighteenth century's constant identification of correspondence and conversation. Modeling letters between characters in specific situations was, in addition to its other functions, a way for letter manuals to foreground the dialogical character of correspondence conceived as "written conversation."

Letter manuals had modeled "Answers" to letters since the Renaissance, and did so increasingly as the eighteenth century progressed. The "Instructions for writing Letters" that were reprinted in several manuals informed reader-writers that "in answering letters, no particular, especially in letters of business, should be disregarded. Begin with the first, and proceed regularly till you have gone thro' the whole."[43] A well-written answer "mirrored" the letter to which it was responding, by reproducing the substance of each point that had been made in it, but without using the same words. This rule made it possible to read one side of a correspondence and get a fairly good idea of what had been said in the letter or letters one had not seen. This made it possible to read a single letter aloud to one's "company," as was the practice, without having to go into long, boring explanations about what had transpired in the preceding letter or letters, for it made each letter at once dialogical or responsive, and relatively self-contained. By the same token, vague or implied mirroring was one way of limiting comprehension of parts of a letter one did not want widely understood. These rules for answers were exploited by some epistolary novelists who made them governing devices of their fictions by offering their readers only one side of a correspondence – Mary Collyer's *Felicia to Charlotte* and Henry MacKenzie's *Julia de Roubigne* being notable cases in point.

The conversational character of letters as embodied in fictional answers and in model correspondences was supported by emphasis on the

---

41 Saintsbury, *Letter Book*, 3.
42 *Instructive Letter-Writer and Entertaining Companion* 3rd ed. (London, 1769), 8.
43 *Ibid.*, 10.

conversational nature of language in the grammars that compendia included alongside their model letters. Dilworth and Lowth's grammars were those most frequently reprinted or summarized in compendia; both were also widely reprinted on both sides of the Atlantic as free-standing texts. Harvard and Yale used Lowth's *Grammar* from the early 1770s to the mid-nineteenth century; and Lowth's and Dilworth's influence were further spread in America by Lindley Murray, who defined grammar as they did, and cited both of the passages below.[44] Dilworth and Lowth taught grammar as "the art of speaking and writing the English language with propriety" – once again equating speech and writing – and they represented language as a system that derived from and opened onto conversation: "How many persons belong to a pronoun noun?" asked Thomas Dilworth:

There are *three persons* in both numbers [singular and plural]: the first, [I] who is always he that speaketh; the second [thou/you], who is always the person or thing spoken to; and the third who is always the person or thing spoken of.[45]

And here is Lowth's explanation for the lack of gender distinctions in first- and second-person pronouns:

The person speaking and spoken to being at the same time the subjects of discourse, are supposed to be present; from which, and other circumstances, their sex is commonly known, and need not be marked by a distinction of gender: but the third person or thing spoken of, being absent, and in many respects unknown, it is necessary that it should be marked by a distinction of gender. . . accordingly the pronoun singular of the third person hath three genders: he, she, it.[46]

Neither Dilworth nor Lowth can describe pronouns without reference to a dynamic conversational situation in which an I is addressing a You about a he, she or it. The assumption was that "language is always 'addressed' to someone else, even if that someone is not immediately present" and that, whether oral or written, "all utterances can be seen as replies to other utterances."[47]

While linking grammar, conversation and correspondence and displaying the everyday origins of each, letter manuals showed how one class of letter could be used to answer another. They demonstrated, for instance,

---

44 Murray, *English Grammar*, 30.
45 Dilworth, *New Guide*, 101. First published in London and Ireland in 1740, and reprinted both by Franklin and Bradford, this had forty American editions between 1747 and 1840.
46 Lowth, *English Grammar*, 21.   47 Leith and Myerson, *Power of Address*, xii.

that letters of thanks were the proper response to letters of congratulation, or letters of excuse to letters of complaint or reproach, by modeling answers that took these forms. But more interestingly, they also coupled answers with letters to teach readers how to read below the commonplace surfaces of letters.

RESPONSIVE READING

"S. Johnson" demonstrated particular artistry in teaching purchasers of his manual to become better readers by using answers to make them look back at letters and read them again with more insight; so I am going to take my two examples of this method of manual instruction from his *Compleat Introduction to the Art of Writing Letters* (1758). Though he included some of the usual apprentice and tradesman letters, more than half of Johnson's compilation consisted of "real" letters between eminent people, largely I think in his case because he was angling several sections of his manual towards men in administration and government. The fact that the following were "real" letters also implicitly warned such men about how treacherous letters could be in government circles.

The first example begins with a letter of thanks from "Queen Anne to the Duke of Marlborough after the Victory of Oudenarde":

I want Words to express the Joy I have that you are well after your glorious Success, for which, next to Almighty God, my thanks are due to you: And indeed I can never say enough for all the great and faithful Services you have ever done me. But be so Just as to believe I am as truly Sensible of them as a grateful Heart can be, and shall be ready to show it upon all occasions. I hope you cannot doubt of my Esteem and Friendship for you, nor think, because I differ with you in some Things, it is for want of either. No; I do assure you, if you were here, I am sure you would not think me so much in the Wrong in some things, as I fear you do now. I am afraid my Letter should come too late to London, and therefore dare say no more, but I pray God Almighty to continue his Protection over you, and send you safe home again; and be assured I shall ever be sincerely, etc.[48]

This seems a particularly gracious letter of thanks. It conforms to the rules for such letters by finding several synonymous ways of expressing the magnitude of the Queen's gratitude for Marlborough's services, and her willingness to make a due return by conferring favors upon him. While she never allows him to forget that this is a letter from a superior to her servant, the Queen introduces a personal note by mentioning her joy that

---

48 Johnson, *Art of Writing Letters*, 45.

he survived the battle, her prayers that he will return home safely, and her desire to ensure that her letter reaches him in a timely manner. She also uses a conversational style that increases the familiarity ("No, I do assure you. . ." "Be so Just as to believe. . ."), and indicates that this letter is part of an ongoing relationship by referring back to a previous occasion on which they had disagreed and forward to their next meeting. The Queen's letter is followed in Johnson's manual by the following answer:

Duke of Marlborough to Queen Anne

Madam,

By what I hear from London, I find your Majesty is pleased to think, that when I have reflected, I may be of Opinion, that you are in the Right of giving Mr. Hill the Earl of Essex's Regiment. I beg your Majesty will be so just to me, as not to think I can be so unreasonable as to be mortified to the Degree that I am, if it proceed only from this one Thing; for I shall always be ready and glad to do every Thing that is agreeable to you, after I have represented what may be a Prejudice to your Service. But this is only one of a great many mortifications that I have met with. And as I may not have many Opportunities of Writing to you, let me beg of your Majesty to reflect what your own People and the rest of the World must think, who have been Witnesses of the Love, Zeal and Duty with which I have served you, when they shall see, that after all I have done, it has not been able to protect me against the Malice of a Bed-Chamber Woman. Your Majesty will allow me on this Occasion to remind you of what I Writ to you the last Campaign, of the certain Knowledge I had of Mrs. Masham's having assured Mr. Harley, that I should receive such constant Mortifications as should make it impossible for me to continue in your Service. God Almighty and the whole World are my witnesses, with what Care and Pains, I have served you more than twenty Years; and I was resolved, if possible, to have struggled with Difficulties to the End of this War. But the many Instances I have had of your Majesty's great change to me, has so broke my spirits, that I must beg, as the greatest and last Favour, that you will approve of my retiring, so that I may employ the little Time I have to Live, in making my just Acknowledgments to God, for the Protection he has been pleased to give me: and your Majesty may be assured that my Zeal for you and my Country is so great that in my Retirement I shall daily Pray for your Prosperity, and that those who shall serve you as faithfully as I have done, may never feel the hard Return that I have met with.[49]

One does not expect the Queen's letter to be followed by a letter of resignation. The fact that it is, indicates that what Marlborough has read and taken seriously in the Queen's letter is only what is *not* commonplace for letters of thanks, namely, the phrase about their difference and the

---

49 *Ibid.*, 46.

indication that she has not changed her mind. Foregrounding these brief comments in reading the letter belies the Queen's assurance that she has a grateful heart and is "ready to show it on all occasions." It profiles such sentiments as an empty and merely conventional form of words, just as giving a regiment to Mr. Hill (who was Mrs. Masham's brother) without consulting the victorious commander-in-chief of the army and against his objections, belies the appreciation the Queen claims to have for "all his great and faithful services." The Queen has swathed her demonstration of just how little influence Marlborough now has with her in polite phrases, in the expected personal letter of thanks for a major victory against the French. Marlborough's response is unintelligible without going back to read the Queen's letter in this way. Going back to reread the Queen's letter to discover what prompted such an extreme reaction on Marlborough's part and to perceive how he read it, offers a reading lesson about the need to pay attention to what is commonly and uncommonly said in classes of letters, and about how much can be conveyed in the briefest, dullest and most conventional epistolary forms. So much for manner. The matter is something else again.

For though this exchange of letters has historical truth, it does not have historical accuracy. The letters selected by Johnson identify what historians still agree was the real moment of Marlborough's fall (the argument about the appointment of Colonel Hill). They demonstrate the reasons for his fall: the replacement of the Duchess of Marlborough by Mrs. Masham as the Queen's bedchamber favorite, the role of Harley in Masham's influence over the Queen, the Marlboroughs' vain protests about Masham, the Queen's wish to get the upper hand over Marlborough who had dominated her from her youth, and her willingness to set aside Marlborough's great services for England, past and future, to go her own way (which, in the event, meant making peace with France). But this letter of Marlborough's was not, in actual historical fact, an answer to that letter of the Queen's. Marlborough reported to his wife that after Oudenarde, the Queen had not "shown some concern for my being safe" as she normally did.[50] The victory at Oudenarde took place in November of 1708, the fuss over Hill in January of 1710, and Marlborough and the Queen exchanged several letters in between. Marlborough did not leave office after the fuss – indeed he got his way over Hill; and in December 1711, when he did leave office, the Queen dismissed him.

50 Churchill, Vol. VI: 177.

This exchange of letters between the Queen and Marlborough was the statement of the compiler acting as an author. In Victor Kaufman's terms, it was the compiler "perform[ing] an act of interception and ventriloquism."[51] Johnson "gathered" or culled these two letters from their original historical and textual contexts, and "framed" or recontextualized them by adding the reference to Oudenarde in the title he gave the Queen's letter; by putting the two letters together in his manual as if one were answering the other; and by giving them an entirely new thematic context through the letters he chose to precede and succeed them. These include Ann Boleyn's letter to Henry VIII from the Tower just prior to her execution; a letter from Charles I to the Earl of Strafford expressing his gratitude for Strafford's services and promising to keep him safe, followed by the Earl of Strafford's letter to his son from the Tower immediately before his execution; a brief letter from Charles II to his brother James, Duke of York, sending him into exile in France; and a letter from Pope to Dr. Atterbury upon his banishment. The common element and unstated theme of all these letters is clearly the insecurity even of the highest offices and greatest men, the ingratitude of English monarchs to those closest to them as well as to those who have rendered them the greatest services, and the folly of believing otherwise. These are also points forcibly made by the exchange Johnson has constructed between the Queen and Marlborough when read in this context. The context Johnson gave them in his compilation thus highlighted and reinforced a particular reading and a particular lesson.

My second example of Johnson's mastery in using answers to teach readers to look below the surface of letters is part of this same thematic series. It begins with two letters, one from Pope and one from Bolingbroke, to Dean Swift, now banished in Ireland.

Mr. Pope to Swift

Aug. 1723

I find a Rebuke in a late Letter of yours that both stings and pleases me extremely. Your saying that I ought to have writ a Postscript to my Friend Gay's, makes me not content to write less than a whole Letter; and your seeming to take his kindly, gives me Hopes you will look upon this as a sincere Effect of Friendship. Indeed, as I cannot but own the Laziness with which you tar me, and with which I may equally charge you, for both of us have had a Surfeit of Writing; so I really thought you would know yourself to be so certainly intitled

---

51 Kaufmann, *Post Scripts*, 128.

to my Friendship, that it was a Possession you could not imagine stood in Need of any farther Deeds or Writings to assure you of it. Whatever you seem to think of your withdrawn and separate State, at this Distance, and in this Absence *Dean Swift* lives still in *England*, in every Place and Company where he would chuse to live, and I find him in all the Conversations I keep, and in all the Hearts in which I desire any Share.

We have never met these many Years without Mention of you. Besides my old Acquaintance, I have found that all my Friends of a later Date are such as were yours before: Lord *Oxford*, Lord *Harcourt*, and Lord *Harley*, may look upon me as one intailed upon them by you: Lord *Bolingbroke* is now returned (as I hope) to take Me with all his other Hereditary Rights; and indeed, he seems grown so much a Philosopher, as to set his Heart upon some of them as little, as upon the Poet you gave him. It is sure an ill Fate, that all those I most loved, and with whom I have most lived, must be banished: After both of you left *England*, my constant Host was the Bishop of *Rochester*. This is a Nation that is cursedly afraid of being overrun with too much Politeness, and cannot regain one great Genius, but at the Expense of another. I tremble for my Lord *Peterborough* (whom I now lodge with) he has too much Wit, as well as Courage, to make a solid General; and if he escapes being banished by others, I fear he will banish himself. This leads me to give you some Account of my Life and Conversation, which has been infinitely more various and dissipated, than when you knew me and cared for me; and among all Sexes, Parties and Professions. A Glut of Study and Retirement in the first Part of my Life, cast me into this; and this, I begin to think, will throw me again into Study and Retirement.

The Civilities I have met with from opposite Setts of People, have hindred me from being violent or sour to any Party; but at the same Time the Observations and Experiences I cannot have but collected, have made me less fond of, and less surprized at any: I am therefore the more afflicted, and the more angry, at the Violences and Hardships I see practised by either. The merry Vein you knew me in, is sunk into a Turn of Reflection that has made the World pretty indifferent to me; and yet I have acquired a Quietness of Mind which by Fits improves into a certain Degree of Chearfulness, enough to make me just so good-humoured as to wish that World well. My Friendships are increased by new ones, yet no Part of the Warmth I felt for the old is diminished. Aversions I have none but to Knaves (for Fools I have learned to bear with) and such I cannot be commonly civil to; for I think those Men are next to Knaves who converse with them. The greatest Man in Power of this Sort shall hardly make me bow to him, unless I had a personal Obligation, and that I will take Care not to have. The top Pleasure of my Life is one I learned from you, both how to retain and how to use the Freedom of Friendship with Men much my Superiors. To have pleased great men, according to *Horace*, is a Praise; but not to have flattered them, and yet not to have displeased them, is a greater. I have carefully avoided all Intercourse with Poets and Scribblers, unless where, by great Chance, I have found a modest one. By these Means I have had no Quarrels with any personally; none have been Enemies, but who were also Strangers to me; and as there is no great Need of an

Eclaircissement with such, whatever they writ or said I never retaliated; not only never seeming to know, but often really never knowing any Thing of the Matter. There are very few Things that give me the Anxiety of a Wish; the strongest I have would be to pass my Days with you, and a few such as you. But fate has dispersed them all about the World; and I find to wit as vain, as to wish to see the Millennium and the Kingdom of the Just upon Earth.

If I have sinned in my long Silence, consider there is one to whom you yourself have been as great a Sinner. As soon as you see his Hand, you will learn to do me Justice, and feel in your Heart how long a Man may be silent to those he truly loves and respects.[52]

This letter of friendship, which is also a letter of consolation, runs through the required commonplaces in elegantly uncommon ways. Hence (paradoxically) its value as an example. The necessary affirmation that the friendship endures despite distance and silence is covered in the first and last paragraphs by a joking reversal of Swift's reproach for not writing, and by Pope's expression of surprise that he needed "farther Deeds or Writings" to assure him that he was "so certainly intitled to my Friendship." The assurance that Swift has not been forgotten is flatteringly conveyed through the image of Swift's still living in England in the conversations and hearts of everyone that Pope encounters. The topos about the charms and importance of friendship is expressed by Pope's insistence that his strongest wish "would be to pass my Days with you, and a few such as you." And consolation for Swift's banishment to Ireland is offered both in the form of commonplace reflections about the wise man's indifference to the world and refusal to flatter the great, and by showing Swift that he is not alone in having been banished, indeed that banishment might be viewed as a distinction. Compiler Johnson followed Pope's letter by another from Bolingbroke, which restated the same topoi, and which I will not transcribe here because it is equally long. The main difference between the two letters is that Bolingbroke claims that his indifference to the world and value for true friendship have caused him to voluntarily choose "Retirement from the World." This leads him into many of the usual commonplaces about contentment in retirement and country pleasures: "The hoarse Voice of Party was never heard in this quiet Place; Gazettes and Pamphlets are banished from it . . Perfect Tranquility is the general Tenour of my Life. . ."[53] Here is Swift's response to both letters.

---

52 S. Johnson, *Art of Letter-Writing*, 60–2.   53 *Ibid.*, 63, 64.

Dr. Swift to Mr. Pope

Dublin, Sept. 1723

Returning from a Summer Expedition of four Months on Account of my Health, I found a Letter from you, with an Appendix longer than yours from Lord *Bolingbroke.* I believe there is not a more miserable Malady than an Unwillingness to write Letters to our best Friends, and a Man might be Philosopher enough in finding out Reasons for it; one Thing is clear, that it shews a mighty Difference betwixt Friendship and Love, for a Lover (as I have heard) is always scribbling to his Mistress. If I could permit myself to believe what your Civility makes you say, that I am still remembered by my Friends in *England,* I am in the Right to keep myself here – *Non sum qualis eram.* I left you in a period of Life, when one Year does more Execution than three at yours, to which, if you add the Dulness of the Air, and of the People, it will make a terrible Sum. I have no very strong Faith in you Pretenders to Retirement; you are not of an Age for it, nor have gone through either good or bad Fortune enough to go into a Corner, and form Conclusions *de contemptu mundi et fuga faeculi,* unless a Poet grows weary of too much Applause, as Ministers do of too much Weight of Business.

Your Happiness is greater than your Merit, in chusing your Favourites so indifferently among either Party; this you owe partly to your Education, and partly to your Genius, employing you in an Art in which Faction has nothing to do, for, I suppose, *Virgil* and *Horace* are equally read by Whigs and Tories. You have no more to do with the Constitution of Church and State, than a Christian in *Constantinople*; and you are so much the wiser and happier, because both Parties will approve your Poetry, as long as you are known to be of neither.

Your Notions of Friendship are new to me: I believe every man is born with his *quantum,* and he cannot give to one without robbing another. I very well know to whom I would give the first Places in my Friendship, but they are not in the Way. I am condemned to another Scene, and therefore I distribute it in Pennyworths to those about me, and who displease me least: and should do the same to my Fellow-Prisoners, if I were condemned to Jail. I can likewise tolerate Knaves much better than Fools, because their Knavery does me no Hurt in the Commerce I have with them, which however I own is more dangerous, though not so troublesome, as that of Fools. I have often endeavoured to establish a Friendship among all Men of Genius, and would fain have done it: they are seldom above three or four Contemporaries, and if they could be united, would drive the World before them. I think it was so among the Poets in the Time of Augustus; but Envy and Party, and Pride, have hindered it among us. I do not include the Subalterns, of which you are seldom without a large Tribe. . .

I would describe to you my Way of living, if any Method could be called so in this Country. I choose my Companions among those of least Consequence, and most Compliance: I read the most trifling Books I can find, and whenever I write, it is upon the most trifling Subjects: But riding, walking and sleeping, take up eighteen of the twenty-four Hours. I procrastinate more than I did twenty

Years ago, and have several Things to finish, which I put off to twenty Years hence; *Haec est vita Solutorum, etc.* I send you the Compliments of a Friend of yours, who hath passed four Months this Summer with two grave Acquaintance at his Country-house, without ever once going to *Dublin*, which is but Eight Miles distant; yet when he returns to *London*, I will engage you shall find him as deep in the Court of Requests, the Park, the Opera's and the Coffee House, as any Man there. I am now with him for a few Days.

You must remember me with great Affection to Dr. *Arbuthnot*, Mr. *Congreve*, and *Gay*. . . .

Swift had not failed to notice that, though they included every *other* commonplace required by the epistolary genres they had chosen and raided their commonplace books for appropriate reflections about friend-ship and retirement, neither Pope nor Bolingbroke mentioned their willingness to serve him. That is certainly part of what set him off. By writing one answer to both letters, and calling one an appendix to the other, Swift indicated that he read them as rewritings of each other. By going on not only to mirror the letters he was answering, but also to puncture each topos in turn, he indicated that he also read their letters as tissues of empty commonplaces: "If I could permit myself to believe what your Civility makes you say, that I am still remembered by my Friends in *England*, I am in the Right to keep myself here"; "Your notions of Friendship are new to me. . . " Swift attacks the topoi of remembering and forgetting and the topoi of friendship to suggest that if his friends (i.e. immediate correspondents and those London lords or patrons) had genuine notions of friendship or genuine love for him, they would show it in deeds as well as in words, and he would not now still be banished in Ireland. Swift also punctures Pope's and Bolingbroke's claim that they positively prefer the pleasures of retirement to which Swift had been condemned: "I have no very strong Faith in you Pretend-ers to Retirement. . . "[54] He points out that their concept of the pleasures of retirement with companions of their choice has no bearing on his banishment to the barren company of Irish country hicks, and suggests that their ideas resemble those of the friend, who brought some acquain-tances of his down to his country house for a few months and saw no need to stir from it, because he knew he would soon be back in London. So far Swift's reading of Pope's and Bolingbroke's letters only repeats the lesson of Marlborough's letter, which is to look below the gracious,

54 *Ibid.*, 60–7.

charming or cleverly phrased surfaces of letters to read them in terms of what is commonly said in the class of letters to which they belong, as well as in terms of what they have omitted from or added to the expected forms.

But Swift's repeated indications of the inapplicability of what Pope and Bolingbroke have written to his situation in Ireland ("employing you in Art in which Faction has nothing to do," "I am condemned to another Scene," "I would describe to you my Way of living") also contains a far more damning reproach: that his correspondents have ignored the first rule of polite epistolography, which is to write a letter agreeable to the humor, interests and concerns of the person to whom one is writing. Rereading Pope's letter from the point of view of someone in Swift's situation as he describes it, one can see that Pope has written like a fool (as indeed Swift points out). Pope's letter does not contain even one iota of news or information about what is going on in town, about their common friends, or even about some new book that people are talking about in London, to relieve Swift's dull round of riding, walking and sleeping. Instead, Pope has allowed himself to get so carried away by pride and by his own fine restatements of commonplace sentiments that he has failed to ask himself what pleasure or entertainment Swift could possibly get from hearing at length about the favor Pope was enjoying from Lord Oxford, Lord Harcourt and everyone else in London, or what possible satisfaction it could give Swift to be told of Pope's success in avoiding the pitfalls of party into which Swift had fallen. Instead of writing an agreeable, Pope has written an insulting letter. Swift's letter is indisputably "rude" in that it uncompromisingly speaks his mind; but both in its rudeness and in addressing each of Pope's commonplaces in turn, it also "mirrors" the letter it is answering.

By culling them from their contexts and juxtaposing them without comment (thus also without the preconceptions about Pope's or Swift's characters or careers which accompany modern critical readings of their letters), Johnson turned Swift's answer into an object lesson about the importance of thinking carefully about the applicability of commonplaces when writing letters, and about the various ways in which one can be rude. He also teaches that one is unwise to trust one's reading of a letter unless one has seen, and factored in, its correspondent's answer. One might add that using answers to make readers look back at the letter that is being answered, and reread it differently, is an under-analyzed technique of the epistolary novel. Richardson draws attention to the technique in *Clarissa*, by having Anna Howe respond to two or three of Clarissa's apparently descriptive letters of news with the charge that they show her to be secretly in love with Lovelace. That does not mean that this is the only place where it applies.

THE LETTER AS WRITING AND VOCALIZED SPEECH

In letter manuals, binary oppositions between the democracy of letter classes and the hierarchy of styles of address, and between letters as compositions and letters as conversation, were overlaid by that between speech and writing. This too is a modernist binary. In the eighteenth century, as we saw in Chapter 1, the expectation was that both written and printed letters would be read aloud either to a "public" or "in company" to family, friends, neighbors and acquaintances, and that they would thus be returned to the speech from which they had issued.

Schools and letter manuals both emphasized the reading of letters, and when they used the term "reading," they generally meant reading aloud. *The Preceptor*, for instance, explained that reading aloud in "the familiar style" meant that "he that reads is only to talk with a Paper in his Hand, and to indulge himself in all the lighter Liberties of Voice, as when he reads the common Articles of a Newspaper, or a cursory Letter of Intelligence or Business," and printed letters on which students could practice reading in this way.[55] The "new eloquence" which taught people to reproduce in reading the tones and cadences of ordinary speech, and condemned the older and more "artificial" manner of declamatory speaking and reading, played right into the letter-writer's hands. Thomas Sheridan describes the nature of the shift:

The true source of the bad manner of reading and speaking in public that so far generally prevails [is that] we are taught to read in a different way, in different tones and cadences from those we use in speaking; and this artificial manner, is used instead of the natural one, in all recitals and repetitions at school, as well as in reading.[56]

Whether conceived as "the discourse of the absent" or as "written conversation," the familiar letter was an obvious form of writing to pronounce with the tones and cadences that people used in everyday speech. Reading a letter aloud in the familiar style lent body and what

---

55 *Preceptor*, pp. xvi–xvii.
56 Sheridan, *Lectures on Elocution*, 4. Also Potkay, *Fate of Eloquence*; Fliegelman, *Declaring Independence*.

Thomas Sheridan and John Rice both called a "living voice" to the "silent speech" of the letter by reenacting the various rhythms, pauses, emphases, tones, emotional or ironic strains, facial expressions and physical gestures that would accompany the words in speech. In more learned works, reading aloud was represented as an art which improved upon the natural speech that it reflected and imitated. John Walker, for instance, described reading aloud as "a correct and beautiful picture of speaking"; and John Rice insisted that "Reading may with Propriety be called artificial Speaking" since "the Art of Reading consists in a just and unaffected Imitation of natural Speech" and is "the Art of converting Writing into Speech."[57] "The art of reading" was thus one name given in the eighteenth century to orality as what Cavallo and Chartier call "a vocalized version of writing, oralized by the reader." Pronunciation was another name for the same thing, "the Art of Reading being simply the Art of Pronunciation in general, or that of *intelligibly* and *emphatically* repeating or rehearsing what is written in any language. . .[and] conveying to the *Hearer* the whole meaning of the Writer."[58] Reading in this sense also had a marked interpretative moment.

Reading aloud entered some letter manuals through Guides to Pronunciation, which included the following rules:

Pronounce every Word clearly and distinctly. Let the Tone of your Voice in Reading be the same as in Speaking. Do not read in a hurry. Read so loud as to be heard by those around you, but not louder. Observe your Pauses well, and never make any, where the Sense will admit none. Humour your Voice a little according to the Subject. Attend to those who read well, and endeavour to imitate their Pronunciation. Read often before good Judges, and be thankful when they correct you. Consider well the Place of the Emphases in a Sentence, and pronounce it accordingly.[59]

But the art of reading or pronunciation was represented and taught in letter manuals most consistently by means of punctuation. Unlike modern punctuation which is used to mark grammatical units, eighteenth-century punctuation points and capitalization of the first letter of words (at the beginning and anywhere in the sentence), were understood, used and taught as guides to pronunciation or reading aloud, and likened to notes in music. Compendia reinforced the punctuation modeled in their printed letters by including guides to punctuation and often rules for capitalization too.

---

57 Walker, *Elements of Elocution*, 2; Rice, *Art of Reading*, 9, 19, 194.
58 Rice, *Art of Reading*, 4.   59 Johnson, *Art of Writing Letters*, 10.

Despite postmodern attempts to construe them in terms of absence and lack because they represented "pauses" or "stops," punctuation points were not devoid of sound or meaning.[60] Used "to direct the pronunciation of the reader" by "pointing" the sentence, punctuation points showed readers how to pace and regulate the phrasing and the breath. This was especially useful in long periodic sentences where the meaning was "suspended to the end," since the colon dividing the period in half, and the semi-colons dividing each half in half again, told readers both where to pause to catch their breath, and how to modulate the voice so as to indicate that the meaning of each part of the sentence was linked to the rest. Punctuation points were signals not only for pauses or stops, but also for the rising and falling inflexions or cadences of the voice: "Every pause, of whatever kind must necessarily adopt one of these two inflexions."[61] Points inhabited a complex interdependent system of proportionally related pauses and inflexions: a parenthesis, for instance, called for a more moderate depression of the voice than a period, and for a pause greater than a comma.

Capitalized first letters (like underlines) indicated the words on which emphasis was to be placed. "Emphasis is to *Reading* a Language, what syntax is to the writing of it," Rice insisted,[62] because emphasis determined which words or groups of words within a simple sentence or within the parts of a periodic sentence, should be read together as a unit, and thus where the comma pauses should be placed. Used to "distinguish the Sense of the Author" and to draw "the line of Circumscription which bounds one object from another" by delimiting units of meaning and punctuating "weighty and important Sentiments," the pauses marked by punctuation points also provided hearers with an opportunity to "at once compose and affect the mind, and give it Time to think."[63] Paragraph breaks, double paragraph breaks, double periods, and blank lines (——) merely represented proportionately longer intervals than periods, colons, semi-colons and commas for hearers to collect their thoughts, absorb what they had heard, and prepare for what was to come.

Compendia not only followed schoolmasters and grammarians in using punctuation and capitals in their model letters to indicate where the reader should place the emphases, phrasing, pauses and inflexions in each

---

60 Fliegelman, *Declaring Independence*, Parkes, *Pause and Effect*. But see Salmon, "Orthography and Punctuation."
61 Walker, *Elements of Elocution*, 125.
62 Rice, *Art of Reading*, 6.   63 *Ibid.*, 236.

sentence; they also provided "Instructions for Punctuation" that summarized the best scholarly thinking on the subject. Manual instructions compared punctuation points to notes in music, and minimally, repeated Dilworth's recommendation that readers pause to count one at each comma, one–one at each semicolon, one–one–one at each colon, and one–one–one–one at each period. Most gave instructions about the length of pauses and character of inflexions for other punctuation points too, and explained about emphasis. Many manuals also provided a list of nine occasions on which it was proper to begin a word with a capital letter, including as number 3: "'Tis esteemed ornamental to begin every Substantive in a Sentence with a Capital, if it bears some considerable Stress of the Author's Sense upon it, to make it more remarkable and conspicuous."[64] Only secondarily, did manuals' instructions for punctuation add a statement to the effect that the use of punctuation was capable of disambiguating sentences; but this too was immediately referred back to reading and speech by reprinting without attribution John Mason's example, "*Shall you ride to Town today?*" to show that a sentence could have different meanings according to where the emphasis was placed (here: four different meanings, as the emphasis is placed on *you*, *ride*, *Town*, or *today*).[65]

Punctuation was yet another area where letter manuals sought to "improve" the letter-writing practices of educated letter-writers as well as those of their less-accomplished counterparts. Most manuscript letters that I have seen, including those by obviously educated writers, either ignored punctuation altogether, or consistently used only two forms of it – capital first letters for emphasis on almost any word anywhere, and the all-purpose dash. In 1771, printer Philip Luckombe was still expressing frustration about this:

It is impossible for a Compositor to guess at an Author's manner of expressing himself, unless he shews it in pointing his Copy; and if he would have the Reader imitate him in his emphatical delivery how can a writer intimate it better than by Pointing his Copy himself?. . But notwithstanding this essential duty, incumbent upon Authors, not all have regard to it, but point their Matter either very loosely or not at all.[66]

In practice, punctuation (or "pointing") according to the rules of grammarians and schoolmasters given in "Instructions for Punctuation"

64 *Accomplished Letter-Writer*, 36.   65 Mason, *Elocution and Pronunciation*, 25.
66 Luckombe, *History and Art of Printing*, 262, 265.

was too often left to compositors and printers. This meant that print "intimated" the writer's "emphatical delivery" far less effectively than writers did by using the "looser" practices Luckombe complains about, because the more standardized rules for punctuation borrowed from the schoolmasters excluded many of the spontaneous inflexions of speech. For instance, the schoolmasters prohibited capitalization of any word in a sentence that was not a noun – but letter-writers were constantly emphasizing (by capitalizing) words that were not nouns. Indeed, only one of the four meanings even in Mason's example ("Shall you ride to Town today?") is achieved by emphasizing the noun.

Printers' use of an increasingly standard and predictable system of punctuation did, however, make it easier to read a letter competently from a printed than from a manuscript text, as Cockin pointed out with some wonder:

As from the fairness of printed types; the well known pauses of punctuation; and a long acquaintance with the phraseology and construction of our language, experience tells us it is *possible* to comprehend the sense at first reading, a previous perusal of what is to be read does not seem necessary.[67]

When sentences in a handwritten letter might have to be pored over to decipher illegible words, and reread several times to recapture the breaks and cadences of speech that made their meaning intelligible, a person performed a real service for others by perusing it first and reading it aloud in such a way as to make its meaning immediately comprehensible. But the legibility of type and printers' use of punctuation made it quite amazingly "*possible* to comprehend the sense at first reading," obviating any need for prior preparation on the part of the reader aloud, and ultimately, the need for the reader himself. Cockin attributes any "preference due to a silent perusal" of a printed text in 1775 to the fact that silent readers did not always find that oral readings accorded with the way they pronounced the words and phrases in their heads, rather than to any difference between these "two methods of reading. . .with regard to the pleasure they yield, or their effects upon the understanding."[68]

For much of the eighteenth century, print was expressive too, not merely on title-pages which are what are generally regarded now, but also in the body of the text. Compositors used italics, capitalization of first letters, different fonts or sizes of print in the body of the book, the lay-out of letters and the lay-out of pages not only in aesthetic, but also in

67 Cockin, *Art of Delivering Written Language*, 42.   68 *Ibid.*, 232.

interpretative ways. The 1764 edition of *The Young Secretary's Guide*, for instance, italicizes key words within each letter not for emphasis, but to highlight commonplaces and make the sections within each letter easier to find when one is referring back to the book. Beyond whatever limitations there might have been in available type, each compositor seems to have related to print in a personal interpretative way, as the producer of a play might do today. As a result, no two editions of the "same" manual by different compositors look or read or even mean quite the same. The Ffoulis "reform," which consisted of eliminating capitals except for proper names and after full stops and of printing everything in the same light and "clean" roman font, has been much admired for its beautifully "classical" and "modern" appearance. But it silenced compositors and letter-writers both. Regarded from the point of view of the letter, it represented the death both of voice and of expressivity in print.

IMITATION FOR READER-WRITERS

Compendia and Letter-Miscellanies generally juxtaposed model letters with little or no explanation, because it was believed that "arts may be learned by imitation only, without precept,"[69] and that "models in art are certainly more instructive than rules; as examples in life are more efficacious than precepts."[70] Teaching by offering epistolary models for the reader to see, transcribe and imitate aligned letter manuals not only with the practice of the classroom, but also with the way in which people expected to learn during apprenticeships, and with the ways in which learning was thought to occur in life. In schools, writing was learned both by transcribing and by imitating (i.e. restating, varying and rewriting) the sentiments and words of others. Indeed, some schoolmasters made students copy out letters again after they had been corrected, to fix the corrections in their memories. In mercantile apprenticeships, clerks were thought to acquire "experiential knowledge" of business practices and of epistolary forms by endlessly copying out letters of business and "other mercantile Precedents" for their masters. Similarly, in artisanal or domestic apprenticeships, people learned to make or do things by watching and imitating what others did. This is still the way many of us learn to garden or cook. The practice of

---

69 Priestley, *Theory of Language*, 4.   70 Knox, *Elegant Epistles*, vi.

imitation therefore linked the letter manual's ideological, generic, rhetorical, grammatical and compositional teachings, and connected it to practices outside the world of the book.

John Rice complained in 1765 that learning to write letters by imitating models produced a situation where "almost all write in the same Manner; their common Letters on Business or Pleasure running all in the same Strain; being composed of Phrases and Turns of Expression taken from popular writers or those generally in Use." He bemoaned the fact that "comparatively but few persons," even among the learned, possessed "a Stile or Method of expressing themselves on any Subject with Ease, and *in their own Way.*"[71] He was complaining, in other words, that too few produced "fine letters" by expressing common sentiments in "uncommon ways." As we have seen, the ubiquity of conventional epistolary forms, phrasing and sentiments meant that letters were written and read, decoded, enjoyed and admired (or not, as here), against the norms and conventions of what Roland Barthes called "the already seen, the already said and the already written." Elegance and originality in epistolary writing, grace and ease in execution, sincerity and spontaneity of style – even meaning, as we have seen – could be appreciated as such only in relation to this "already."

Before leaving this point, it is important to understand that in the eighteenth century the "already seen" and "already said" extended to model letters, whether written in the vernacular or translated from the classics, which both the letter-writer and the letter's readers would already have read, transcribed and imitated at home or at school, or which they would have encountered in letter-collection after letter-collection. It is said that a few hundred common words are basic to speaking and understanding a language. One might likewise say that in the eighteenth century a hundred letters or less constituted a basic vocabulary of epistolary models. Like awareness of the commonplaces for different classes of letters, familiarity with this vocabulary of basic model letters has to be assumed in informed contemporary readings of eighteenth-century epistolary writing. Affinities between recurrent model letters and real letters can turn up in unexpected places, as the following example will show.

In each of the following letters, a daughter is trying to persuade her father not to force her to marry an old but wealthy suitor. The first two

---

71 Rice, *Art of Reading*, II, note.

letters come from manuals, and are variations on one another. I have
included two (only two, there are more of the same) to try to re-create the
sense of what it feels like to read the third letter when one has read a
model and variations on that model before. The third letter is a letter by a
young woman who is actually writing to her father. The young woman is
Eliza Lucas, later Pinckney, from South Carolina, who was by no means
either a foolish or an uneducated woman, and her letter has been much
praised.

1. Honored Sir,
   I am sensible of the obligations which both nature and gratitude lay me under
to obey your commands; and am willing to do so at all events, if what I have to
offer be not thought sufficient to excuse my compliance.
   Mr. Rowe is, I believe, possessed of all the merit you ascribe to him. But be
not displeas'd, dear sir, when I say, that he seems not so proper a husband for
me, as for a woman of more years and experience.
   His *advanced years*, give me leave to say, will be far from being agreeable to *me*,
and will not my *youth*, or at least the *effects of it*, in some particulars be distasteful
to *him*? Will not that *innocent levity*, which is almost inseparable from my time
of life, appear to him in a more despiseable light, than perhaps it deserves? For,
sir, is not a likeness of years attended with likeness of humors, an agreement in
diversions and pleasures, and thinking too? And can such likeness, such
agreements, be naturally expected, where the years on one side *double* the
number of the other? Besides, sir, is not this defect, if I may so call it, a defect
that will be far from mending by time?
   Your great goodness, and the tenderness I have always experienced from you,
have embolden'd me to speak thus freely upon a concern that is of the highest
importance to my future welfare, which I know you have in view from more
solid motives than I am capable of entertaining. And if you still insist upon my
obedience, I will only take the liberty to observe, that if I do marry Mr. Rowe, it
will be entirely an effect of my *duty* for the best of fathers, and not an *Affection*
for a Gentleman that I respect in every other light but that you propose him for.
And, dear good Sir, consider then, what misunderstandings and evil
consequences may possibly arise from hence, and render unhappy the future
life of,

Your most dutiful Daughter.[72]

2. Honoured Sir,
   Though your Injunctions should prove diametrically opposite to my own
secret Inclinations, yet I am not insensible, that the Duty which I owe you binds
me to comply with them. Besides, I should be very ungrateful, should I presume,
in any Point whatever, considering your numberless Acts of parental Indulgences

---

72 Richardson, *Familiar Letters*, 117–18.

towards me, to contest your Will and Pleasure. Though the Consequences thereof should prove ever so fatal, I am determined to be all Obedience, in Case what I have to offer in my own Defence should have no Influence over you, or be thought an insufficient Plea for my Aversion to a Match, which, unhappily for me, you seem to approve of. 'Tis very possible, Sir, the Gentleman you recommend to my Choice may be possessed of all that Substance, and all these good Qualities, that bias you so strongly in his Favour, but be not angry, dear Sir, when I remind you, that there is a vast Disproportion in our Years. A Lady, of more Experience, and of a more advanced Age, would, in my humble opinion, be a much fitter Help-Mate for him. To be ingenuous (permit me, good Sir, to speak the Sentiments of my heart without reserve for once) a Man, almost in his grand Climackterick, can never be an agreeable Companion for me; nor can the natural Gaiety of my Temper, which has hitherto been indulged by yourself in every innocent Amusement, be over-agreeable to him. Tho' his Fondness at first may connive at the little Freedoms I shall be apt to take, yet as soon as the Edge of his Appetite shall be abated, he'll grow jealous, and for ever torment me without Cause. I shall be debarr'd every Diversion suitable to my Years, tho' never so harmless and inoffensive, permitted to see no new Company; hurried down perhaps to some melancholy rural Recess; and there, like my Lady Grace in the Play, sit pensive and alone, under a green Tree. Your long experienced Goodness, and that tender Regard, which you have always expressed for my Ease and Satisfaction, encourage me thus freely to expostulate with you on an Affair of so great Importance. If, however, after all, you shall judge the Inequality of our Age an insufficient Plea in my Favour, and that Want of Affection for a Husband is but a Trifle, where there is a large Fortune and a Coach and Six to throw into the Scale; if, in short, you shall lay your peremptory Commands upon me to resign up all my real Happiness and Peace of Mind to the Vanity of living in Pomp and Grandeur, I am very willing to submit to your Superior Judgement. Give me leave, however, to observe, that it is impossible for me ever to love the Man into whose Arms I am to be thrown, and that my Compliance with so detested a Proposition, is nothing more than the Result of the most inviolable Duty to a Father, who never made the least Attempt before to thwart the Inclinations of,

Your ever obedient Daughter[73]

3. Hond. Sir

Your Letter by way of Philadelphia which I duly received was an additional proof of that paternal tenderness which I have always Experienced from the most Indulgent of Parents from my Cradle to this time, and the subject of it is of the utmost importance to my peace and happiness.

As you propose Mr. L. to me I am sorry I can't have Sentiments favourable enough of him to take time to think on the Subject, as your Indulgence to me

---

73 *The Complete Letter-Writer or Polite English Secretary* (1768), 100–1.

will ever add weight to the duty that obliges me to consult what best pleases you, for so much Generosity on your Part claims all my Obedience, but as I know 'tis my Happiness you consult must beg the favour of you to pay my thanks to the old Gentleman for his Generosity and favourable Sentiments of me and let him know my thoughts on the affair in such civil terms as you know better than any I can dictate, and beg leave to say to you that the riches of Peru and Chili if he had them put together could not purchase sufficient Esteem for him to make him my Husband.

As to the other Gentleman you mention, Mr. Walsh, you know, Sir, I have so slight a Knowledge of him I can form no judgement of him, and a Case of such consiquence requires the Nicest distinction of humours and Sentiments. But give me leave to assure you, my dear Sir, that a single Life is my only Choice and if it were not as I am yet but Eighteen, hope you will [put] aside the thoughts of my marrying yet these 2 or 3 years.

You are so good as to say you have too great an opinion of my prudence to think I would entertain an indiscreet passion for anyone, and I hope heaven shall always direct me that I may never disappoint you; and what indeed could induce me to make a secret of my inclination to my best friend, as I am well aware you would not disapprove it to make me a Sacrifice to Wealth, and I am as certain I would indulge no passion that had not your Approbation, as I truly am,

Dr. Sir, Your most dutiful and affecte. Daughter
Eliza Lucas[74]

When she wrote this letter, Eliza Lucas was successfully running her father's American plantations while he was in the West Indies. She was therefore being extremely useful to him, and it would no doubt have been inconvenient for him to see her married just then. But Eliza Lucas's letter makes no reference to this. Instead, it reproduces the same forms and expressions as the model letters, and the same cultural assumptions too: that this is an occasion that must be constructed in relation to a father in terms of love and duty, obedience and indulgence, and in relation to a suitor in terms of the alternative between wealth and sexual attraction, unhappiness and shared humor and sentiments. In later ages, wealth and the power it brings would be construed as an aphrodisiac, and the December–May marriage as the young woman's unconscious desire for her father. These letters belong to a particular cultural nexus. At the same time, though they are all versions of one another, the model letters are far more didactic; they elaborate the arguments against December–May marriages in ways that Eliza sees no need to do. Indeed, Eliza can run rapidly and almost breathlessly through the proper forms and objections

74 Pinckney, *Letterbook*, 5.

because she knows that she and her father are both familiar with these other fuller arguments – that other letters resembling these models and other writings like this – exist. The same "occasion" and petition condensed into the model letters above and represented in Eliza's life-writing had also been amplified numerous times in fiction and in drama. Considered as a writing, this occasion and this petition crossed boundaries between fact and fiction, and circulated in different media and literary forms. Because they did, Eliza could use allusion to the fuller arguments ("old gentleman," "humours and Sentiments"), and rely on her father not only to fill in the formulae and ellipses, but also to imagine the possible consequences of any lack of "indulgence" on his part in equally familiar literary and cultural terms. Indeed, she forestalls and uses the literary expectation that desperation might make her elope, to strike a bargain with him.

Rice's objection to letters that reproduced phrases and turns of expression from the "writers generally in use" was not an objection to imitation *per se*, but an objection to imitation of an elementary sort, which consisted of merely copying out phrases and expressions. There were different levels of proficiency in imitation, and at the higher levels, imitation *was* a "Method" of expressing oneself with ease and in one's own way. It involved the selection and variation of models, their inversion, amplification, adaptation or reinterpretation, and at best, their creative transformation into something that was really quite different.[75] Though one might blame epistolary models in manuals and schoolbooks for creating a situation in which everyone's "Letters of Business or Pleasure run in the same Strain," Rice does not, for letter manuals' collections of model letters were designed to be imitated in different ways by reader-writers with different levels of proficiency. They offered a *combinatoire* that was capable of being used differently by writers with different levels of education and accomplishment, as well as of generating a large variety of different letters.

For the least skilled, the least confident in their social skills or in their ability to indite, and the most impatient, situated fictional models provided practical solutions to a variety of social and writerly problems, that did indeed only have to be copied: just how did a man write to his wife's father to inform him that his daughter, far away from home, was

---

75 See White, *Plagiarism and Imitation*, and Rollin, *Belles Lettres*. For the distinction between imitation and emulation, see Weinbrot, *Britannia's Issue*.

dangerously ill? Or to her best friend? What were the proper things to say
to get a recalcitrant debtor, who was one's social superior, to pay what he
owed without losing his future trade or good will? Or a fellow tradesman?
What did one say to a son, a daughter, a friend, on the other side of
Britain or of the Atlantic who wanted to marry a person one had never
seen? And when it could take from six months to a year to receive an
answer to a transatlantic letter, how did one so construct a letter of
business as to ensure that nothing that one's trading partner needed to
know had been forgotten? Transcription, which was also the first step in
learning to write a letter, was an easy way of solving these problems. The
least educated, the least confident or the laziest reader-writers had only to
insert different names, perhaps vary a phrase here and there, as they
copied out the manual's modeled solutions.

For the better educated and more adept, displaying series of letters of
the same kind to different addressees offered the possibility of a more
complex *combinatoire*. Transpositions of the same classes of letter to
different occasions and to addressees of different ranks in manuals themselves indicated to users how they too might mix and match. One way to
do this was to borrow the style of address from one model letter (for
instance, to an acquaintance), to join it to the substance of another letter
(for instance, informing a parent that a marriage or a death had taken
place), and to resituate both in the framework offered by yet another
model letter (for instance, a "Letter to a Friend Beyond the Sea inquiring
after his Health and Welfare"). Another way to mix and match was by
patching together a letter from models of different classes of letter and
write what was known as "a mixed letter."

Patching together a missive in this way was a common practice among
educated letter-writers. Writing to Sir John Halkett, his closest friend in
Scotland, from the "the middle of a wood bit to death with all kinds of
Flyes" in America, William Erskine – sometime quartermaster general to
Howe's army in America during the Revolutionary War, and long-time
Scottish farmer who had gone into the army to pay the debts on his farm
– literally patched letters of business onto letters of news. He simply
added to his pages of narrative about the progress of the American
campaign, pages of instruction to his friend about what crops to plant
on his farm, which of his young horses to break in, how to discharge his
farming debts with the bills of exchange he sent back, and what to do for
his wife ("Go to my wife poor woman make as light of war as you can").
While relying on his friend to "manage for me as I would for you,"

Erskine clearly felt that sending news at every opportunity was what Halkett's friendship demanded in return, and apologized on the one occasion when he had to "trouble you with a long Letter without containing newes."[76]

William Ellis, on the other hand, was an impoverished petty clerk from England, who went out to Maryland under the patronage of Governor Robert Eden, to work in the land office and prosper for the first (and last) time in his life. Upon his return to England, he was obliged to supplement his income by publishing letters about Maryland in the 1770s that he had written to a correspondent in Britain during his time abroad.[77] Ellis, who is characterized by his modern editor as a "born letter-writer in a great age of letter-writing," wrote quite competent letters as patchworks of set pieces from different classes of letter. His second *Letter from America*, for instance, opens by responding to news just received from his British correspondent that actor William Powell had died in Britain during his absence, with a letter of praise and commendation ("He was the valued friend of my early youth") – complete with a vivid and moving description of Powell's death-bed scene which Ellis had not, of course, been present in Britain to witness. Subsequent paragraphs are patched together from the topoi prescribed for descriptions in travel letters, one topos per paragraph: civil institutions, political situation, situation of the town of Annapolis, and so on.

Finally, for more advanced and educated learners, manuals frequently offered, in addition to the fictionally situated letters written for the express purpose of illustrating kinds and styles of address, a variety of "more elegant letters for Examples and Improvement of Style." Most of these had been written to real addressees in the course of their real lives, by "eminent persons" and by "the best modern authors" – invariably either men and women of letters or men and women of rank. These generally obey the injunction to "follow Horace's advice to 'express common Things and Subjects as if they are not,'" and are what we now think of "literary familiar letters." One of the functions of these letters, as we have seen, was to demonstrate to more advanced and educated learners how commonplaces could be disguised or transformed,

---

76 Sir William Erskine to Sir John Halkett, Bart., September 17, 1776; November 29, 1776; May 20, 1777. National Library of Scotland, MS 5083, fols. 15, 16 and 35.
77 Eddis, *Letters from America*, 10.

and how classes of letter could be combined in the same missive more "elegantly" or seamlessly than those above. Improving the style of already accomplished letter-writers was the stated purpose of some letter-miscellanies too.

The chapters in the next section, which show how writer-compilers produced new letters from old, as well as how American and Scottish provincial printers produced new manuals from old, will demonstrate more advanced techniques of imitation, and familiarize us with at least part of the eighteenth century's vocabulary of models.

PART II

Letter manuals in Britain and America

Introduction

Imitation and compilation were the means by which producers of letter manuals in London and in the American provinces translated letters and letter-collections from one culture to another, or between ranks and registers within a given culture. They served different purposes in different hands, and neither necessarily produced likeness. John Hill's manual, *The Young Secretary's Guide, Or Speedy Help to Learning,* for instance, used imitation to fashion a rejoinder and corrective to Puget de la Serre's influential French letter manuals, *Le Secretaire de la cour* (1634) and *Le Secretaire à la mode* (1640), which were combined and translated into English by John Massinger as *The Secretary in Fashion* (1640).[1] Through Serre, as we will see, Hill struck at the seventeenth-century vogue in Britain for *Academies of Complement, Mirrors of Complement* and *Wit's Cabinets* which were based, as Roger Chartier has pointed out, on translations and imitations of the Frenchman's manual.[2] In Hill's hands, imitation not only created differences between English and French letters both in terms of manner and of matter; imitation also underlined national difference by encouraging comparison and recognition of what Locke called "the agreement and disagreement of ideas" between the two styles of letter. Thomas Goodman's *Experienc'd Secretary,* by contrast, used imitative rewriting to place a courtly complemental language at the disposal of a broader non-courtly public, and to model methods of extending courtly forms to heterosexual courtship and to the common occasions of social and domestic life.

The Boston and Philadelphia printers who produced compilations based on one or both of these manuals between 1703 and 1737 made no secret of the fact that their goal was to offer their customers versions of

---

1 An enlarged edition was printed in 1654; I am quoting from the 5th edition of this (1673).
2 Chartier, "Secretaires of the People," in *Correspondence.* Chartier includes *The Young Secretary's Guide* among manuals based on translations of Serre; I am disagreeing with him on that particular point. For French epistolary manuals, see also Cook, *Epistolary Bodies.*

these manuals that were "more suited to New England," and thus to mark a local, regional or proto-national difference. For these printer-compilers, "anglicization" and "exceptionalism" were not mutually exclusive alternatives, but simultaneous affirmations that grew out of their understanding of local needs and tastes. Using letters borrowed from London manuals, American colonial printers created compilations that offered ideological, moral and religious messages differing from those in the London manuals, which their local readerships could more readily recognize, even while enabling them to communicate creditably in a transatlantic market. They created compilations whose projected audience was invariably narrower in rank and purpose than that of London manuals, though most of the American manuals we will be looking at went through multiple editions, and clearly enjoyed quite a large provincial buying public. American compilations also differed from their London originals by associating the ornamental, complemental style with education and gentility in ways that English manuals, and the English buying public, did not. One reason for this may be the similarity between some versions of this style and the language of Puritan sermons or Harvard disquisitions. Another may be Americans' continued exposure to unusually large numbers of courtly seventeenth-century plays and books – these figure hugely both in library and booksellers' catalogues to very late in the eighteenth century. Another reason may be a difference in attitudes to French culture. But whatever the reason, the result does appear to be that the "Frenchified" complemental style was "marked" differently in English and American manuals, and had a different history in each place.

The construction of compendia and letter-collections from the work of other writers and other texts, many of which were themselves letter manuals of one sort or another, adds another level of "reader" or reader-user of pre-printed letters. By publishing the fruits of their reading and collecting (and of their correction and rewriting too) in a genre that admitted alteration from edition to edition, printers and compilers provide enduring evidence of successive acts of reading and of successive judgments of what they read. At the same time, reading as a collector and compiler of the writings of others was something more than copying, borrowing or mere plagiarizing. As Vincent Kaufman has put it, compilation "removes texts from their original contexts, breaks them up, reassembles and reorders them"; it "makes new parts out of old wholes" and "new wholes out of old parts"; and it uses common materials and commonplaces to "perform an act of interception and ventriloquism."[3] *Compilatio* has long been understood as a meaningful way of giving a different signifying order to culled materials. As M. B. Parkes explains: "the compiler adds no matter of his own by way of exposition (unlike the commentator) but compared to the scribe he is free to rearrange (*mutando*). What he imposed was a new *ordinatio* on the materials he extracted from others. . . The *compilatio* derives its value from the authenticity of the *auctoritates* employed, but it derives its usefulness from the *ordo* in which the *auctoritates* were arranged."[4] Or as Charles Hallifax put it in 1765, his role as editor or compiler was to "throw [letters] out of that Method" in which he found them, and to "distribute them" anew in a way "which will be useful to all Persons. . ."[5]

In compilations, order is a signifier that we must learn to read. One of the important ways in which compilers expressed their judgments about the letters they read and fashioned new manuals with new thematic foci from their copy texts was by controlling and altering the sequence in which letters appeared. By reordering carefully selected letters, by abridgment,[6] by careful choice of their opening or "anchoring" letter, and by "clustering" letters together in different ways,[7] successive American, English and Scottish compilers changed the tenor, emphasis and ideological bias of their collections and even of their own successive editions.

As a result, eighteenth-century British and American letter manuals behaved more like medieval and early modern manuscript and print miscellanies than like "organic" modern books. With the notable exception of a few single-authored letter-miscellanies, they were unstable and changing compilations of pre-printed materials. Each manual title must therefore be considered as representing a variable "series" of versions rather than the label for a fixed book, and we must bear in mind that each manual series opened intertextually onto other manuals through fragments of shared, adapted or purloined contents. In the case of letter manuals, print was not a fixing and reifying technology.

Though sometimes confusing in bibliographical terms, the fundamental instability and potentially serial character of letter manuals created positive opportunities for local printers or compilers, which would be

---

3 Kaufman, *Postscripts*, 128.   4 Parkes, *Scribes*, 59.
5 Hallifax, *Familiar Letters*, 5th ed. (1765), vii.
6 The conventional attitude to American abridgments is that they showed that American printers and publishers "were little concerned about the integrity of the texts they published; they simply wished to produce cheaper books in easy to sell formats." Remer, *Printers and Men of Capital*. But see Tennenhouse, "Americanization of *Clarissa*."
7 For "anchoring" and "clustering" in poetry anthologies, see Benedict, *Making the Modern Reader*.

inconceivable for the fixed organic book. They made letter manuals flexible and adaptable to local conditions, and made it possible for London manuals to be reinvented in Edinburgh, Glasgow, Philadelphia, Boston, Worcester and New York. Even reprints can be unexpectedly interesting. Boston printer Thomas Fleet, for instance, made his otherwise accurate 1750 reprint of John Hill's popular English classic, *The Young Secretary's Guide, or a Speedy Help to Learning* (1687) "suitable to the People of New England" in an unusual way. He inserted, almost unnoticed among the usual "forms of Bills, Bonds etc.," a short tract on "The Advantages *Englishmen* enjoy by the Trial by Juries, above any other nation under Heaven," and another arguing against Lord Mansfield and the English government, "That Juries are Judges of Law in some respect as well as of Fact." These tracts educated Boston manual users on issues that were to become prominent during the revolutionary years.

Chapter 2 showed the importance of repetition and difference in the writing and interpretation of letters. Repetition of the same conventional thoughts and sentiments on the same occasions over long periods reassuringly reinforced the conviction that human nature was fundamentally the same at all times and in all places, and that people on different sides of the Atlantic participated in the same British culture. It also accommodated the design of facilitating commerce across ranks and regions by inculcating the same polite commonplaces and epistolary forms in everyone. Yet, repetition of conventional commonplaces and of familiar models also highlighted the signifying force of even minor differences in idea, expression or style. For the modern reader and interpreter both of eighteenth-century letters and of manual series, it is essential to be able to recognize epistolary models, commonplaces and conventions and to develop an eye and an ear for expressive and stylistic difference. Throughout Part II, there is therefore extensive quotation, analysis and comparison of entire letters that were included in different manuals, and discussion of implicit dialogues amongst them.

The analyses of London manuals in these chapters serve as baselines against which the changes introduced by American, and later by Scottish, provincial printers, can be measured. They also describe values, sentiments and styles of writing that had currency in the provinces as well as in London. The presence or potential presence everywhere of these London "originals" alongside any provincial or regional adaptations, must be assumed throughout. London booksellers, who were linked to provincial retailers and colonial importers, disseminated London versions of the epistolary culture throughout the English, Scottish and American provinces. Provincials frequently ordered books from London directly from booksellers or through agents or friends, and the same provincial booksellers who sold or produced their own local adaptations of London manuals, would also often import the London "originals." Refitted versions of British manuals did not necessarily replace the import and the reprint in America; different versions of a manual were in use simultaneously. Thus while some British letter manuals were never taken up in America, all versions of a letter manual that made the crossing are relevant to letter-writing, letter-reading and printing practices there. As Hugh Amory has pointed out, "the 'colonial book' was what colonists bought and read, as well as what they printed and reprinted."[8]

The following chapters display an interesting rhythm in American compilations. American printers produced numerous adaptations of London manuals during the first decades of the eighteenth century, before London booksellers developed a bulk trade in books to America.[9] William and Andrew Bradford suggested why, when they presented production of their own adaptation of English manuals, *The Secretary's Guide, Or Young Man's Companion*, as a public service because "in these *American* Parts. . . books of this Nature are not frequently to be got." The fact that so many Boston and Philadelphia printers also fashioned their own adaptations of London manuals before 1740, when most colonial printing consisted of sermons, almanacs, newspapers and assembly work, together with the fact that most of their adaptations went through several editions, suggests that other printers also found it profitable to address the shortage of such books in America before the bulk trade with Britain took off. Scottish printers began to reprint and adapt London manuals only in the 1760s. When American adaptations of English letter manuals began to multiply again during the early Republic after a hiatus of several decades at mid-century, American printers worked from Scottish rather English versions of these books. Irish "pirates" (who reprinted everything else that London produced before the printers' ink was dry) rarely touched letter manuals before the end of the eighteenth century, when Union with England was almost upon them, and do not significantly figure in the story outlined in the next three chapters, which for the most part moves back and forth along the three sides of a triangle formed by London, Edinburgh or Glasgow and Philadelphia, Boston or New York.

8 Amory, "Reinventing the Colonial Book," in *History of the Book in America*, 28.
9 Botein, "Anglo-American Book Trade"; Barber, "Books from the Old World"; Raven, "Commodification and Value."

CHAPTER 3

"Secretaries" at the turn of the eighteenth century

With its introductory chapter on the matter and forms proper to different classes of letter and its sections of letters of complement, consolation and love, *The Secretary in Fashion* provided Hill with a framework and point of reference for contrapunctal imitative rewriting. Hill replaced Serre's abstract, masculine world, where men courted one another through letters of extravagant complement and where letters of complement did the business of the court, with a more socially diverse social world, where business meant government, trade or domestic service, where family relations were valorized, and where work was emphasized, theorized and moralized. He did so not only by extending the occasions for writing different classes of letters into different ranks and areas of culture, but also by answering Serre letter by letter, class by class, and section by section, as the following examples will show:

Serre: *Congratulatory Letters to a Person of Eminent Quality, no. 63*

My Lord,

    I could not be silent to the Acclamations of such an universal gladness, being forced to join my voyce to other Mens, in Publishing our Commune contentment touching the *Marshalship of France*, wherewith the King has been graciously pleased to honour you: This action of Justice is so Highly approved by every Person, that your Enemies are constrained to condemn themselves to an everlasting silence, being notable to open their mouths but to their own confusion. Live then happily with this part of good fortune which your merit first made you aspire to, and believe assuredly that in the whole train of your Excellencies' servants, there shall be very few able to intimate me, in the resolution which I have taken to carry to my grave the quality of,

My Lord,

                    Your most humble and obedient Servant (27–8)

Hill: *A Letter of Congratulation*

Sir,

The News of your Advancement no sooner reach'd my Ear, but I found a Spark of Joy shoot through my Soul; which kindled in me such a flame of Love and true Affection, that I could no longer contain my self but was constrained to let you know it. I hear, Sir, by undoubted report, that you are raised to the Dignity of ——— And that you, notwithstanding, like one, in whose Soul true Generosity reigns, scorning to be puffed up with Pride, or towering Ambition, are still, as far as the Character you bear will permit, the same in kind respect and condescending goodness to your Friends, amongst which Number I beg the Honour ever to be continued, as knowing a great part of my happiness consists therein, especially when I consider your Affability and Condescending Meekness, from which I may be bold to presage, that the Honour to which you are advanc'd, will be rather graced by being possessed by you, than you by possessing it. But, Sir, not to trouble you in the midst of your great Affairs with a tedious Epistle, I shall only say, That I could not have heard anything on Earth, that could have administered greater Satisfaction to my mind: that it shall be my continual wish, That you may still rise high as your Merit and that Peace and Prosperity may never be strangers to your Dwelling, and so humbly assuming the liberty to acknowledge my self the Honourer of your Vertues, I remain,

Sir,

Your most Obliged, and most Devoted Servant,
S. K.

An Answer to a Letter of Congratulation

Sir,

After having told you, that the Expression with which you accosted me, proceeded more from your Generosity, than any Merit in me, I cannot but pardon that in you, which I should have taken in another as too much favouring of Flattery; because I am convinced that through the Vehemency of your Affection, it proceeded from your good meaning. It is true, Sir, as to what you have heard of my Advancement; for which I must, with all submission, pay my due Acknowledgment to the Fountain of Honour from whence it proceeded; ascribing it solely to the innate goodness of the Royal Favour, as not desiring so much as to imagine that any Service I am capable of doing, can merit so great a Trust, though my Endeavours shall never be wanting in anything that is Just and Honest. And if it raises any Joy in me, it is, to think, that in the station I am, it may at one time or another, lie in my power to serve my Friends, and more especially your self: and so, Sir, desiring your mutual Friendship may continue, I subscribe my self,

Your faithful Friend, whilst I am,
T. G.

Serre's letter is yet another variation on the basic theme of all his letters of complement: "Sir, It would be very hard for me to express how strictly I am yours. . .[or] but one part of the passion which I have to your service" (51). The writer is reminding the new marshal of France that he forms, or would like to form, part of the great man's train of servants and admirers, and that he is willing to advance on his coat-tails, so to speak. The writer seeks to ingratiate himself with the new marshal by flattering his pride through allusions to the absoluteness of his victory over his enemies, the number of his supporters and the universal gladness. He treats the position of marshal of France as his addressee's personal honor and triumph; issues of justice and merit appear only in passing in connection with the new marshal's ambition.

Hill's letter of congratulation has a similar purpose – it is designed to ensure that the addressee remembers the writer when there are posts or favors to be handed out. But it rapidly moves beyond the sweetmeats in the exordium to indicate the incompatibility of "Pride, or towering Ambition" with true "Generosity of Soul," and the importance of gracing any government or administrative position with affability, modesty and merit. In the writer's "continual wish, That you may still rise high as your Merit," there is the intimation that a man should rise no higher than his abilities and deserts, as well as the more flattering implication that his correspondent's merits are such as to promise further advancement. Hill reinforces this message by adding an "Answer" which demonstrates the writer's modesty, affability and recognition of his duty to help his friends, while stressing that a government or administrative post is a "Trust" – a word pregnant with responsibilities between governors and governed – that must be performed honestly and justly. The capital letters used to emphasize "Fountain of Honour" and "Royal Favour" highlight the writer's modesty, while those emphasizing "Trust," "Just," "Honest," and "Friendship" indicate his recognition of the importance of these qualities for the task upon which he is to embark. Hill generalizes these points to all parts of the administrative hierarchy by not specifying which level of government the correspondents are talking about, by omitting the word "eminent" from the letter's title, and by replacing Serre's "My Lord" with "Sir," which was used in England for men of various rank. Above all, Hill's "Answer" demonstrates that the proper way to read letters of complement is with the awareness that they are full of baseless flattery, and with skepticism about the writer's sincerity. Only in the context of a continuing and mutual friendship in which the first writer is performing a friend's office by indirectly warning his newly promoted correspondent of the moral dangers before him, is such "Vehemency" acceptable to its English recipient. And even then, it is treated as an error, and quietly corrected by the Answer's gentlemanly good sense, simplicity of expression and elegance of style.

Serre represented "Letters of Advice, Counsel, Remonstrance, Command, Intreaty, Recommendation, offering of Assistance, Complaint, Reproof, Excuse and the like" as letters of business, as they would be at court. But Hill described business letters more substantially, as we saw, both as missives bearing on substantive matters of state and as "Trustees of the Trading part of Mankind." He therefore created parallel letters addressing the virtues that men ought to bring to commerce and trade, this time by means of letters of advice and letters of reproof from fathers, uncles and elder brothers, which both spelled out the requisite virtues and reinforced them by repetition:

Hill: *A Letter of Advice from a Father to a Son*

Son,

   It is now so long since you departed from me that I cannot but judge you, by this time, to be at Years of Discretion, sufficient to take upon you the management of some Affairs in the World; in order to which, for your better Ability, I have sent you, by the hands of your Uncle, —— ——, Twenty Pounds, and as I find you improve them, you may expect a greater Summ. And the better to confirm you in your Undertakings, let me give you a word or two of Advice: First, when you settle your self in the World, beware of being enticed or drawn away by Flatterers, or debauched Persons: nor is there any better way to shun it, than to decline and avoid them. In the next place, be diligent in your Affairs: mind your Employment, and deal uprightly with all Men, whereby you may not only gain an honest Repute, but expect a Blessing upon your endeavours: But above all, preferr the Service of your Maker, and pray to him for his Support and Assistance, and in so doing, you will not fail of living happy, and more especially of obliging him whose Joy it will be to see or hear that you do well: And so at present taking my leave, I remain,

Your Careful and Affectionate Father,

P. D. (62–3)

To the young beginner in trade or commerce, Hill was advocating the Protestant ethic, with its combination of diligent industry, moral conduct, ascetic mores and religious faith. The importance of dealing "uprightly" to gain "an honest Repute" in the trading community is reinforced by the promise of divine reward in the form of success and happiness. The distrust of flatterers and emphasis on honesty recur, but otherwise the values here are significantly different from those recommended to gentlemen in government or administration in the letter of congratulation. The inflexibly hierarchical character of the relationship between father and adult son is expressed both in the superscription's naming of the relationship between the parties (the son's answer begins "Honoured Sir" and ends "Your obedient Son") and in the direct and peremptory style of a letter of advice that is virtually a letter of command. Yet this is a letter that instructs fathers as well as sons. It teaches that the paternal role requires a man to help a son in trade or commerce with capital and advice long after the latter has reached maturity and gone into business for himself – with the caveat (expressed in that emphatic "Careful" in the subscription and in the promise of more funding only as he finds his son "improves" the twenty pounds) that money should never be wasted by being lavished upon the undeserving. However "affectionate" he may say he is, the father is thus constructed as a lifelong spectator and judge. The letter also portrays a situation in which the father and his brother cooperate in helping and supervising the adult son – the money will be transmitted through the uncle, who will also be in a position to report back. In Britain, family cooperation and backing were considered great advantages in commerce and trade. The son is careful to indicate that he is worthy of both in his answering Letter of Thanks by assuring his father that he has "since receiving your bounty, procur'd me such things and necessaries as are suitable to my Trade and Employment, and find such Encouragement, that I doubt not but my Proceedings will rebound to your Satisfaction, and my Advantage" (63). The familial character of commercial success is also emphasized in a "Letter from an older brother to a younger Brother exhorting him to good Behaviour and seemly Carriage" which points out that his brother's performance (or lack thereof) will reflect on the family as a whole (below, p. 126).

Hill also offers a whole series of helpful commercial letters, which have the immediately practical purpose of showing reader-users what such letters should say. These include a letter from a factor telling his correspondent what goods to send, a letter requiring payment for goods sent, a letter to accompany the shipping of goods, a letter acknowledging receipt of money and goods, various letters of introduction and recommendation, and the following Letter of Advice:

Sir,

Understanding you have left Town, I thought it convenient to inform you how things are carried on; especially in relation to Trade, a particular account of which I have included in this Paper. I would indeed have communicated it to you in writing, but I found it done to my hand. Our Friends are in perfect Fruition of Health, and kindly present (especially such as I have had lately the opportunity to converse withal) their Love and kind Respects to you and your good Lady. As for your Affairs in *London*, as far as I can see, or enquire into them, they go on prosperously: and for News, we have none of moment: Wherefore, not to trouble you with a tedious Epistle, I only make it my Request that a good Correspondency may be maintain'd between us as heretofore; and that I may still be ranked in the number of your Friends, desiring always to be, whilst my own,

Your's in all Friendship and Respect,
W. T. (22)

Here only the bare bones of the letter's structure are indicated. Nothing is actually said about the topics alluded to. The letter only indicates that a letter of advice between commercial correspondents should contain news about trade, news about mutual friends and their greetings, local news, and news of the addressee's affairs. The next letter in the collection fills this out by informing the addressee that one of his trading partners has died with an unexpectedly encumbered estate. Since this man's bankruptcy would most likely put the addressee's own solvency at risk, this would be valuable, if unwelcome, "advice." Other letters in the collection, from a "Prentice" and from a Clerk to their master who is out of town, show that Letters of Advice like the above are the proper form for their letters too, with this difference that they would also be expected to give news of the master's family and of any new orders or payments received. Like Hill's letter of congratulation above, this letter makes the point that long ("tedious") letters should be avoided, and brevity preferred.

The purpose of the above letter of advice, thin as it is, is the same as that of Serre's courtly, and Hill's more down to earth, letter of congratulation: to ensure that his correspondent remembers the writer next time there is trade to be done (viz. his request at the end that a good Correspondency be maintain'd between them). The strategy is different. Where Serre's courtier offers himself as a mirror of compliments, and Hill's gentleman offers the moral concern of a friend, the commercial correspondent offers his usefulness as a source of news and information in the interstices of useful and mutually beneficial trade. The personal quality of business of all kinds is blatant, and so is the way in which the seemingly more democratic word "friend" has supplied the place of the word "servant," at least in the body of letters, without altering the assumption that "Friends" are those who are able and willing to be of service, and that serving each others' interests is the function of friends.

In each of these different cultural registers, Hill's letters not only demonstrated the Enlightenment truth that man as a social being was dependent on others for all his needs and wants; they made satisfying needs and wants the subject, demonstrating and preserving mutual dependence the function, of epistolary exchange. The formulae modeled expressed the desire to create "bonds of union" with other men and set the terms of those bonds. They also made letters the vehicle and instrument of bonding, in a process that laid bare the verbal character and mechanics of social alliances. Though Serre and Hill agreed that social relations, and the letters that gave suitably graceful expression to them, were at base utilitarian, an important part of Hill's critique and rewriting of Serre had to do with whether the language of Serre's letters, and the social code it represented, were capable of cementing social alliances and of preserving social harmony. In the examples that follow, Hill addressed issues of speech as well as of writing, and modeled different forms of conflict resolution, to broach a constant theme in his collection: the importance of conciliation to maintain "correspondence" in the word's other eighteenth-century sense of harmony and accord:

Serre: *Letters to clear our selves of a false report, no. 98*

Sir,

I need not much Eloquence to perswade my innocency touching the report which was made to you of late, since I will oblige my self to make them confess the truth publickly, that have been too shameless to maintain the contrary in private. 'Tis a Malice so ill contrived (though black as Hell) that I am perswaded it will deceive itself. For what appearance is there, that having received an infinity of favour from your goodness, I should so irreverently contemn a thousand other noble qualities that elevate your esteem above the common? I beseech you believe that I shall be of your admirers all my life, and a continual flail to the approachers of this imposture. I have no respect of persons when my Honour is questioned; I bear a Sword to defend it with the hazard of my life, which I esteem far less. But if this cannot give you satisfaction, let me know the name of the reporter, and I will make you sport in laying open the particulars of his knavery, and the sincerity of my innocency, which shall give you sufficient cause never to make doubt of the Passion I have to serve you, as being,

Sir,

Your most humble and most obedient servant (43–4)

In Serre's world, a gentleman, courtier or noble asserted his innocence with his sword, or used his readiness to do so as evidence that he viewed a malicious report as an insult to his honor. His letter illustrates "the principal rules of honor" as Montesquieu describes them, which "are that we are indeed to give importance to our fortune but that we are sovereignly forbidden to give any to our life" and "that when we have once been placed in rank, we should do or suffer nothing that might show that we consider ourselves inferior to the rank itself."[1] At the same time, the writer is dissimulating his real situation of dependence with blustering and sabre-rattling bravura. While reminding his addressee that his rank is such that it would be dangerous to treat him as one of no account, and asserting that it is beneath him to defend himself verbally, he repeatedly protests his innocence, his recognition of the favors granted him by his addressee, his admiration for the latter and his undying passion to serve him, in an attempt to ensure that the favors continue to flow. For Hill, attempting to mend fences with one "friend" or patron, by completely destroying any possible future relation with the other party involved, foolishly rends the social fabric; and resorting to violence or to fighting language merely deepens the divisions caused by slanderous speech. His response and corrective has two parts.

First, Hill approaches the situation outlined in Serre's letter from the point of view of Serre's addressee, the man who has been told that the writer has slandered or traduced him. Rather than "complaining to others" and creating a divisive public drama as Serre's addressee has done, Hill's gentleman prefers to proceed "softly and in silence" by writing a gently worded Letter of Complaint to the man who has "abused my kindness." Reluctant to "slightly shake off, on my part, the Bonds of Amity," he offers his addressee a face-saving way out by suggesting that the words reported to him had proceeded from "Rashness or some misunderstanding created by false report." He also indicates that he would be willing to forgive the offence if it were acknowledged and repented (37–8). The Answer is a Letter of Apology which begins: "Sir, Your mild way of proceeding, has entirely conquered and subdued my rough Nature, so that I find myself constrained to an acknowledgment of my Rashness, and therefore, with Blushes for what I have done, have sent this Letter to entreat your Pardon. . ." (38). The carefully placed commas in this sentence give the reader time to focus on the effectiveness of wielding that disarming "mildness" against rough natures; on the rashness over which it triumphed; on the embarrassment that the slanderer has brought upon himself; and on the pardon which resolves the conflict. Capitalization of Nature, Rashness, Blushes and Pardon draws

---

1 Montesquieu, *Spirit of the Laws*, 34.

attention to the process of consciousness and self-correction, and to the distance between rashly disrupting relationships by speaking ill of others and seeking reconciliation to preserve or restore "the Bonds of Amity" between men. Moreover, a letter, which itself represents and bridges physical distance, is used to introduce a temporal distance during which anger can be dissipated and conciliation can occur. The message here, which is reiterated in other letters, is that speech, which characterizes man as a social being, should not be used rashly, slanderously and without restraint, and that letters, which extend sociality to those at a distance, can be interjected at moments of conflict to preserve and restore "good Correspondency" and social concord.

The second part of Hill's response to Serre's letters to clear ourselves of a false report, which address mischievous gossip and backbiting at court, is to give such letters to sons whose conduct at school or in apprenticeships has been misrepresented to their fathers, and to a maidservant who has been traduced to her mistress:

Hill: *A Letter from a Maid-Servant to her Mistress, excusing some Fault whereof she has been accused*

Madam,
    I take this leave (though with Submission and humble regard to the distance between us) to write to you, that if it be possible, I might hereby make you sensible of my Innocence, in relation to the things wherewith I stand charged before you the which could you, Madam, but read the Sincerity of my Soul, you would plainly discern. My Accusers, indeed, have laid their Accusations with no small Aggravation: but believe it, Madam, upon the solemn Protestation of her that would lay down her Life to do you Service, what they have said against me, proceeds from Malice and hopes of Revenge, because they could not corrupt my Fidelity to your Detriment and Damage, as I am able to make appear, whenever your Ladyship shall, laying your Anger aside, give me leave to speak for my self: however, in these and all other Affairs submitting my self to your Ladyship's Goodness, and wise Discretion, I remain,

Madam,
                                        Your most humble and obedient Servant (72)

By transposing to a maidservant Serre's efforts to persuade his addressee of "my innocency, touching the report which was made to you of late" and of "the passion I have to serve you," Hill exposes the dependence that Serre's letter seeks to disguise, while implying that such servility is beneath the dignity of a supposedly independent English gentleman. In demonstrating that the proper stance for a servant or dependent child is a conciliatory submissiveness and humble acknowledgment of the power that another holds over his or her fate, Hill also transposes to children and dependents in the domestic sphere the conduct that the anonymous author of *The Art of Complaisance*, a seventeenth-century courtesy book, recommended for ambitious nobles and aspiring gentlemen at the Stuart court. In dealing with the powerful, *The Art of Complaisance* explained, "the first and greatest caution that is to be observed is that [our] language be not only full of submission and humility, but of such a difference [deference] as approacheth to the abasing of ourselves." To "prevent the effects of their enmity," he continues, the best strategy is "to dissemble with patience the resentment that we have," always remembering that "we act not safely or wisely to present ourselves with defiance in our mouth, or casting out menaces in quarrels so disproportionate, the power of those who have done us wrong without cause, excusing in this our dissimulation."[2]

Hill turns this cynical but pacific piece of worldly wisdom into an empowering strategy for repairing the "Detriment and Damage" to a relationship of dependence caused by malice and false report, by using to the maidservant's advantage the very social distance that is at once represented and bridged by the letter. The maidservant marks her recognition of the distance separating her from "her Ladyship" by the terms of address in her super- and subscriptions, by using the written speech of her letter to beg permission to speak, and by repositioning her Ladyship as a judge between herself and her accusers. If anything, she increases the distance that daily familiarity between mistress and maid might have blunted, to redefine the situation in such a way as to force her mistress back into the position of unchallenged superiority, where kind condescension to inferiors constitutes the aristocracy's duty to society. At the same time, by making her mistress "read the Sincerity of my Soul" in her written words, where everything conveys unflinching loyalty and submission, rather than in her face or speech, the maidservant reinforces social distance with a temporal distance designed to give her Ladyship the opportunity to "lay aside your Anger," absorb a different characterization of the situation, and adopt the "wise discretion" of a superior and judge. The language used in Hill's other letters from maidservants, and strident complaints about the conduct of servants throughout the long eighteenth century, do not suggest that Hill seriously expected an English maidservant to write that she would "lay down her life to do you Service."

2 *Art of Complaisance*, 139, 142.

This is the language of the court. Like other authors of manuals and conduct books, he did think that deference and self-abasement were appropriate to children, dependents and inferiors in their dealings with their superiors. But unlike them, he showed that submission, acknowledgment of another's power, and appeal to their goodness could be empowering instruments for the weak, if used to place parents or superiors in the awkward position of having to publish their goodness or malice, justice or folly. Transposing the occasion for Serre's letter and the courtier's fearful submission to this household environment also had the benefit of re-marking the boasted difference, at least for men of a certain rank, between French servility and English freedom.

Restraint is the recurrent motif in Hill's rewrites of Serre's Letters of Consolation. Serre's letters abound in expressions of inconsolable grief. The writer of a letter of consolation to a grieving widower tells him: "I would not have you Dream of anything so much as following her." Answers to letters of consolation pronounce all comfort vain: "my affliction is of such a Nature that Death only is able to give me Satisfaction" (54); "I cannot employ my Spirit without Violence in any Thoughts but those of my misfortune" (58). By contrast, Hill's letter to a grieving widower condemns "immoderate grief" (32). His letter to a friend who has lost his father urges "Manly force. . .to moderate the unruly Passion" (31). His letter to a mother on the loss of her son tells her: "Be more moderate in your Lamentation, than to afflict yourself for what is past recovery"(31). Hill placed several such letters of consolation in a sequence to drive home the injunction: keep a stiff upper lip. Hill also omitted answers to Letters of Consolation, presumably to avoid expressions of those "natural Affections. . .that are prevalent" at such times.

The one exception occurs in a Letter of Consolation to a Sister upon the loss of a Brother. In response to the usual bracing consolation, the sister replies: "[I] must crave leave to lament the loss of one, who was so dear to me, that he was even the Support and Stay of my Life, upon whom my Parents, being before deceased, depended the Strength and Joy of a helpless Virgin: Wherefore blame me not if Sorrow gains the upper hand. . ." (41). Hill was using this opportunity, as he used others in his collection, to strengthen brother–sister relations by portraying an ideal of brotherly concern and involvement, and stressing the value to a sister of a brother's good offices. For an unmarried and "unprotected" woman of a certain rank, unable to support herself and helpless in law, a brother's aid and concern could be vital. This point about the importance of brotherly intervention, and its extension to married women's lives, was a theme that would recur in women's novels to the end of the eighteenth century – for instance, in Haywood's *Betsy Thoughtless*, Charlotte Smith's *Montalbert*, or Austen's *Sense and Sensibility*, where the point is made negatively through a brother's failure to support his mother and sisters.

Where Serre collected all but one of his courtiers' letters to and from women into a slim section at the back called "Love Letters upon all Sorts of Subjects," Hill scattered women's letters throughout his collection, offering examples of women writing virtually every kind of letter. Hill encouraged maidservants to write letters as a matter of course, by including a letter from a maidservant to her friends back home, "desiring to continue our former Friendship, by a mutual Correspondency of Letters" (70). He also encouraged women to get an education, for instance in a "Letter from an Aunt counseling her Niece to Study" to enable her "to obtain, when [she] came to years of more maturity, both Credit and Advantage" (78). Eliza Haywood would rewrite this letter in what was to become its most reprinted form, by giving far more specificity to the subjects young women should be taught.[3] But Hill made the importance of education a theme for subsequent letter manuals, and sought to extend education to women at a time when women's education was becoming a prime feminist issue. He was also comparatively egalitarian on this issue. Alongside a son's "Letter of thanks to a Parent for a good Education," for instance, there is a comparable "Daughter's return of Thanks for her good education." Alongside a "Letter of thanks from a Scholar to his Master," and a "Letter from A Scholar inviting a cousin to betake himself to learning," there is a letter from a young gentlewoman in school asking to be allowed to learn to dance – later manuals would give this letter to a schoolboy. Hill also included a gender-neutral letter of advice from one friend to another, "to persuade him to give his children a good Education" which argues that education provides "a better and surer Estate than Lands or Possessions," which can easily be lost (62).

There are no love letters or letters of courtship in Hill's collection. Hill was interested in the household and in marriage, not in love. One of the few letters he transposed more or less intact from Serre is a "Congratulatory letter to a new Married Man." But he also multiplied the number of letters relating to marriage which would become standard occasions for model letters in subsequent letter manuals.

3 See Chapter 4.

The final point I want to make about Hill's manual has to do with its treatment of absence. A large number of Serre's letters to male patrons and fellow courtiers elaborate on standard complemental themes which are, in a sense, merely the inversions of their protestations of love and service: they complain of absence or neglect, or express fears that a coldness has set into the relationship or that they will be forgotten. Such letters flattered their male addressees by showing them how much they were missed or how much their friendship was valued, while keeping their memory of the writer alive. Serre extended these themes quite cursorily to men's letters to women in his brief section of love letters. Hill, by contrast, transposed such letters wholesale into the context of the household-family. But here letters complaining of the absence of a husband, wife, sister, brother or friend, and their answers invariably underline the necessity of continuing absence for the purposes of business, or the impossibility of leaving the household in which the absentee is being entertained without appearing rude. In Hill's manual, absence and travel are actively promoted at all social levels. A "Letter from a Maidservant to another encouraging going to work in London" informs her country cousin that the stories she has heard about the dangers of London are only designed to prevent "Pursuit of our better Fortunes and Advantages" and offers to help her find suitable London employment. The fairly large number of "beyond the Sea" letters that Hill added to his collection include a Letter from a Wife to her Husband in Foreign Parts; a Letter from one at Sea to his Friend on Shore; a Letter from one at Sea to his Wife; A Letter from one who is traveling to see the Rarities; a Letter of Consolation to a Wife who supposes her Husband, by reason of his long Absence, to be dead; a Letter of Congratulation to a Party upon overcoming a Danger; and a Letter to congratulate a Person upon his Return from Foreign Parts. The tenor of these letters can be seen from the following:

Dear Love,

Since my Departure from you, we have made way through many dangerous Seas, and weather'd, as often heretofore we have done, many rough Storms and Tempests: so that at the writing of this, our Ship was within sight of our intended Port; yet, by cross Winds, we were obliged to stand off at Sea, for some time, before we could enter it: yet the danger of the Passage being, as we well hope, altogether over, I sent this Letter to certifie you as much, that you need not perplex yourself with needless Fears; and do assure you, I, and my fellow-Sailors, are not only in Health, but in hopes to gain no small Advantages by this Voyage. Pray let not the thoughts of our returning the same way we came, nor the fear of encountering the same Dangers oppress your Mind; for I assure you, it will be far otherwise, considering the difference of the Season, as to its Calmness; yet let me, however, have the benefit of your Prayers, and the unalterable Continuation of your Love and Constancy, though absent; and so with my kind Love and Respects to all our Friends and Relations, I conclude, yet continue to be,

Your ever loving Husband,
C. R.

Though Hill's invention fails him when it comes to descriptions of places and events, this letter, like his other letters from foreign parts, indicates that some account of the absent person's experiences and some description of his or her environment are needful, as is the regular use of letters to assure those at home that the traveler is still alive and well. The dangers of travel, especially at sea, are never played down, but the message is that dangers are worth braving in pursuit of "no small Advantages," and that rather than perplex themselves with fears, wives and family or friends should remain constant and loving, and cheerfully support the adventurer's endeavors by taking care of business at home. Such attitudes on the part of men of business and women at all ranks were the *sine qua non* for empire and for extension of Britain's trade into the New World. And it may be that they were nowhere so explicitly, or so widely, inculcated as in letter manuals of this kind.

Henry Rhodes, the bookseller in Fleet Street who published Hill's *Guide*, generally shared copy in the practical, historical and religious books he favored with a variety of other London booksellers. Hill's *Young Secretary's Guide* was one rare exception. Another was *The Wit's Cabinet*, which taught "the whole art of wooing and making love with the best complemental Letters, elegant Epistles, Amorous Addresses and Answers." The fact that Rhodes was willing to assume the entire risk for publishing both indicates his sense of the size and importance of the market for manuals teaching the proper conduct of epistolary writing. It also suggests that in England, the choice between complemental letters modeled on Serre and Hill's more substantive missives, or between *Academies of Complement* and *Secretaries*, was made, not by booksellers, but by the consuming public. Rhodes published *The Wit's Cabinet* for the first time in 1685, just before the first edition of Hill's letter manual (1687); but he tried to relaunch it in 1703 and 1705 to little avail, while skyrocketing demand for Hill's *Secretary* justified reprintings in 1689, 1691, 1696, 1697, 1698, 1699, 1701 (twelfth edition), 1706, 1712, 1719 and 1724. The same pattern recurred after Rhodes' death, when Allington Wilde and John Clarke bought

Rhodes' quires, copies and shares of copies at an auction in September 1730,[4] and William Johnson ("one of the foremost booksellers and publishers in London" between 1748 and 1773[5]) bought Clarke's share. The books they acquired included *The Wit's Cabinet*. They too tried to reprint it in 1737 – as Charles Gildon cynically put it, "the Bookseller, instructed by interest, [is] zealous for his Property."[6] They owned it and wanted to turn it into profit if they could. But like Rhodes, they found that they did far better from Hill's *Young Secretary's Guide*, which they reissued in 1734, 1741 (22nd edition), 1749, 1752 and 1760. The last British printing of Hill's *Guide*, now in its twenty-seventh edition, was published in 1764. In Britain, this preference for *Secretaries* and later for *Complete Letter-Writers* remained the trend. As we will see in the next chapter, the few remaining London editions of the *Academy of Complements* that were printed at mid-century changed their contents, formats and titles to accommodate the shift to *Secretaries*. In England, if the genre did not entirely go away, it significantly moderated its forms to compete for the buying public. In America, letters of complement had more success.

BOSTON: BARTHOLOMEW GREEN'S YOUNG SECRETARY'S GUIDE (1707)

Bartholomew Green, Boston printer and heir to a notable family of printers, made it clear on his title-page and in his prefatory letter to the reader, that his edition of Hill's *Young Secretary's Guide* was designed to produce a version "more suited to New England than any yet Published." It contained only "such Presidents [precedents] as are most in Use among us here in New England," and "fit them to the Circumstances of this Country, and Terms used in our Writings."[7] This was an adaptation of Hill's manual to a different environment, for a different public. Green adapted Hill to New England as a compiler – by excision, by selection and by clever reordering of Hill's letters, rather than by materially changing their wording, beyond putting Boston in place of London wherever it occurred. The fact that American printers frequently abridged English

---

4 Plomer writes that Rhodes died before 1725, but there is a *Catalogue of the quires, copies and shares of copies belong to the Stock of the late Mr. Richard Sayre, Mr. Henry Rhodes, Mr. Thomas Speed, to be sold at Auction in Westminster, September 1730.* His name is first replaced on imprints by "Executors of Henry Rhodes" in 1730.
5 Plomer, *Dictionary of Printers and Booksellers*, 142.
6 *Postboy Robb'd of his Mail,* 2nd ed. (1706), 15.
7 Green, *Young Secretary's Guide,* title-page and "To the Reader."

books is a familiar fact, which is often attributed to the need to keep costs down or to the perennial scarcity of paper. But Green also used it as one of the several instruments of cultural adaptation and ideological refashioning that *compilatio* put at his disposal.

Green described his target audience as "men of ordinary Learning and Capacity," who merely needed a little help to "make [a Letter] when needs so requires."[8] The fact that he assumed a fairly literate and resourceful readership is clear from the reason he gave for omitting Hill's introductory chapter about letter classes as well as other matter bearing on epistolary form: "It is an easy matter for a Person of Ingenuity to frame or indite any Letter, on any occasion whatsoever; if they know but how to begin and conclude handsomely, for which the foregoing Examples may be sufficient Direction" (35). Where he expected to find these men of ordinary learning is demonstrated by the *dramatis personae* he selected. In cutting Hill's 120 "Examples never before published" down to less than fifty, Green excised all letters referring to posts in government or administration and to social relations among gentlemen, with the exception of one fairly abject "Letter of Acknowledgment to a Person of Note for a Benefit receiv'd." He also excised all letters from apprentices and maidservants, as well as all letters of recommendation for servants or government posts. By eliminating both the top and the bottom of Hill's social hierarchy, and removing such estate letters as Hill's "Letter of Excuse from a tenant to his Landlord" for not paying his rent on time, Green produced a manual geared exclusively to an urban, trading and mercantile buying public. He also made society appear to be virtually without ranks.

Green included Hill's list of the proper forms of address for everyone from the king and princes down to Esquires and Gentlemen, and informed users that "Would you write to any Person, to good Acceptation, you must consider their Title, Degree or Alliance, and frame your Complement, Superscription and Subscription accordingly" (35). But he clearly did not expect his fellow colonists to have much occasion to write to English lords, ladies, esquires, gentlemen, or even to their social superiors, for there are no examples of such letters in his manual. This is surprising, since Green himself was printer to a succession of noble English governors, as well as to the Governor's Council, and communication with and among such gentlemen was part of Boston life.

---

8 *Ibid.*, "To the Reader." Page references to this edition will subsequently be in the text.

Green reprinted all Hill's letters of trade and commerce, even adding two from elsewhere, to provide what is in effect a tradesman's complete business-letter writing kit. Even more significantly perhaps, given the brevity of the collection, Green included three letters of advice to young merchants and tradesmen – including the letter recommending the Protestant ethic and paternal support and supervision, transcribed above on p. 113. Both the relative proportion of these letters, and their positions in Green's collection, substantially changed their import and effect. Green moved Hill's letter "From an older Brother to younger Brother exhorting him to good Behaviour and a seemly Carriage" from the very back of Hill's collection to the very front of his. It is the first letter a reader-user encounters when opening Hill's book, replacing Hill's letter of intreaty from a schoolboy to his father, which is pushed back to number 3:

Dear Brother,
   I Thought fit, seeing you are arrived at sufficient years of discretion, to put you in mind, that your Childish affairs ought now to be laid aside, and instead of them more serious thoughts and matters take place, that you may add to the Reputation of our Family, and gain to your self a good Esteem, which is of great value, and ought to be prized at no common rate, as being the chief adornment of Youth and Age: nor would I have you take this admonition amiss, or altogether out of humour, and consequently tearm [sic] it out of season; but as the true sense and cordial desire of him that loves you, and wishes your advancement and welfare equal with his own, coveting nothing more than to see you thrive both in Wealth and Reputation: And so hoping this Advice will not be taken amiss, nor create any wrong understanding between us, I take my leave and am,

Your ever loving Brother,
N. W. Salem,
Sept 4th, 1707

Green's choice of opening or "anchoring" letter may have been designed in part to immediately reassure Puritan Boston that his book was safe to buy. But together with several letters from sons apologizing to their fathers for their misdeeds, and Green's placement of the following letter of reproof directly after the letters of trade and commerce, it helped to give Green's version a far sterner and more monitory character than Hill's original:

Letter of Reproof from an Uncle to his Nephew

Cousin [sic]
   I am sorry to have occasion to Write unto you in this Dialect but really, the Care I have of your welfare, being daily Disturbed, together with my own quiet,

thro' the loud clamours and complaints that are frequently brought against you, arising from the effects, as I understand of your Extravagancies and Debaucheries: I can do no less than deal plainly with you, and let you know how heinously I resent it; and further since you are left my ward, I consider my self in part answerable to Heaven, if I do not use my endeavours to Depress the Youthful folly that reigns in you, which I share take care to do with all diligence, if this Friendly Reproof turn to no account; however, till I hear farther, I shall subscribe my self,

Your careful and Loving Uncle,
A. D. (12–13)

The overall goal to which Green's selection from Hill's letters tends is set out in that first, anchoring letter from the older brother, when he tells his younger brother that he wishes "to see you thrive both in Wealth and reputation" and "add to the Reputation of our Family" (1–2). The alternative to thriving in this manner is demonstrated in the second and fourth letters in Green's sequence: one imposes on a friend's good nature to ask for a loan; in the other, a son writes to his father "as a beggar who having often received Alms, is yet imboldened by Necessity to intrude upon your charity and good nature...being in a strange Place, Destitute of Imployment and my Money failing," with no other source of relief or support (3–4). Flanked by these two letters, the schoolboy's letter of entreaty for books and clothes, which Hill had used as an opener, indicates the inappropriateness of a man having to ask others to supply his needs and wants after childhood, and reinforces the older brother's injunction that "your Childish affairs ought now to be laid aside" (1). The alternative presented to the reader by the sequence in which Green placed these letters is wealth or alms, reputation and esteem or shame and destitution, adding to the reputation of one's family or diminishing it, remaining a child or being a man. Green immediately follows this sequence with five letters pulled together from different places in Hill's manual in which sons give thanks to fathers or to masters for a good education, and a father commands his son to continue his studies. Arranged in a cluster, these letters have a far more insistent effect than they did dispersed throughout Hill's collection. Indeed, here they suggest that in order to obtain Wealth and Reputation, a good education is essential. The place of the letter of advice recommending the Protestant ethic and of the uncle's letter of reproof in this overall schema should be clear. While offering such letters of advice as overt pointers, Green used both the juxtaposition and the clustering of judiciously selected letters from Hill's collection to ventriloquize through Hill and construct what is in effect a wholly different text. By omitting any table of contents, Green also forced anyone wishing to use his manual to read through all the letters, just to see what is there.

Green omitted all letters referring to women's education. Indeed, he represented his projected audience as "*men* of ordinary learning and capacity." In Hill's manual, as we saw, girls go to school, are encouraged to pursue their education, and thank parents for a good education, as do boys. Women give counsel, address business matters in letters to their husbands, and write letters of recommendation for servants, as well as letters of invitation to their sisters and friends. But in Green's manual, women only write to inform a father when they have married against his will, to complain to a husband that he is unnecessarily delaying his return home, to excuse themselves for not paying a visit, to extend one they are making with their children, or to inquire about a sister's health and welfare. For women considered as individuals, this is a step back. On the other hand, while there are no "gentlemen" in Green's collection, the term "gentlewoman" does appear; and it may be that his selection implied that the wives and daughters of provincial tradesmen who were achieving wealth and reputation ought to adopt a more genteel and leisured life-style.

Moreover, in the broader context of Green's manual, these letters from women further strengthen Hill's focus on the family, which now dominates virtually all letters but letters of trade. In the first half of Green's manual, where matters of work and education are brought to the fore, sons' relations to their fathers and uncles are particularly stressed. But later, there are also letters from young men to their mothers and sisters, letters between husbands and wives, and a letter between sisters. In other words, almost all the letters in this manual other than letters of commerce and letters requesting loans from "friends," are depicted as passing between members of the nuclear family, which here includes uncles acting *in loco parentis*. Despite the absences which immediately occasion these letters, therefore, the nuclear family is portrayed as the individual's primary source of sociality and support. The solidity and permanence of the nuclear family, despite absences, is underlined by Green's exclusion of all but one of Hill's "beyond the Sea" letters. The one he includes is that from a husband seeking "no small Advantage" from his dangerous journey abroad (above, p. 122). Where the reader of Hill's manual is positively encouraged to travel abroad in pursuit of empire and trade, Green's reader is, on the whole, expected to concentrate on his family and trade in New England.

In its obituary in 1723, *The Boston Newsletter* characterized Green as "a very humble and exemplary Christian, one who had much of that primitive Christianity in him which has always been the distinguishing glory of New England." *The Boston Newsletter* also described him as "caut[ious] of publishing anything offensive or hurtful" and as keeping "close and diligent to the work of his calling."[9] Green was sometime deacon of the Old South Church in Boston, as well as printer to Harvard College, official printer to the governor and counsel, and a highly successful tradesman. Yet the tradesman "close and diligent to the work of his calling" is the only dimension of his Boston experience that is represented in this manual. Was he being cautious of publishing anything offensive when he fitted Hill's manual to the circumstances of New England by centering it on non-sectarian issues of family and trade? Was he seeking "no small Advantage" by identifying his most promising market? Or did his choice among these different dimensions of his experience and of Boston life cautiously express and reinforce, as early as 1707, a certain dissociation of tradesmen and mechanics like himself from "primitive Christianity," from Harvard's more than "ordinary" learning, and from the gentlemen who governed New England?

LONDON: THOMAS GOODMAN'S EXPERIENC'D SECRETARY

The Experienc'd Secretary, Or Citizen and Country Man's Companion was published in London in 1699, when *The Young Secretary's Guide* was going into its tenth edition. Not surprisingly, therefore, Goodman's manual engaged Hill's both on the level of the collection's overall design and on the level of individual letters. Goodman's answer to Hill was only a modest success in Britain, which saw three further printings, in 1703, 1706 and 1716. But adaptation of Goodman's manual between 1703[10] and 1730 by Boston printers Bartholomew Green, John Allen and Thomas Fleet were both popular and influential in the American provinces, producing seven editions and multiple runs for two generations of booksellers. *The Experienc'd Secretary* has been described as "closely related to *The Young Secretary's Guide* in spirit and content."[11] In fact, they were, ideologically and stylistically, poles apart.

---

9 January 4, 1733. Quoted in Thomas, *History of Printing in America*, 91.
10 This is called the second edition; there is no extant copy of an earlier edition.
11 Quoted in the ESTC from Hornbeak, "Complete Letter-Writer in English."

Where Hill's *Secretary* theorized and moralized work and the "Service-ableness" of letters for a variety of practical household and imperial pur-poses, Goodman's *Secretary* valorized the letter's role in sustaining sociality and maintaining networks for the sake of potential benefits. Of the seventy-three letters in Goodman's collection, only four deal directly with work: there is a letter of excuse from that tenant who is unable to pay his landlord's rent on time; a letter from a country chapman to his city dealer asking for a list of prices; a letter urging a friend to enter into some employment so that society might benefit from his "Parts and Merits"; and one from a master giving his servant work to do while he is out of town. The latter more or less sums up this manual's attitude to labor: everyone out to lunch. The majority of letters in Goodman's collection relate to peoples' leisure hours, when they are free to enquire after, congratulate, console, invite, advise, solicit favors from and excuse themselves to their family and neighbors, and pay court to ladies and to their friends. What is at issue in this manual is not the diligence, industry or responsibility a person might bring to his or her workaday employments, but the manner in which his or her familial and social relations might be embellished and refined.

Consequently, where Hill critiqued the style of Serre's complemental letters and the courtly French culture they expressed, Goodman trans-posed the complemental genre into the domain of the family and of its social life. The tone is set by the collection's opening or "anchoring" Letter from a Nephew to his Uncle:

Honoured Sir,

The Distance of Place interposing between us has caused me to commit that to Paper, which in all Respect and Duty, as many Obligations compel me, I ought with low Submission to have verbally delivered, which is my entire and hearty Thanks for the many Kindnesses and Favours your Goodness has heaped upon me: How shall I retaliate your Bounty and Tenderness towards one you have such a providential Care over, must be the Business of my Study; and be assured I shall omit nothing that a grateful Mind is capable of, to oblige and serve you in every respect, as far as my mean Capacity will permit; though to my no little sensible Sorrow, I foresee my Actions will come far short of making any suitable Returns: therefore, let me beg, that my willingness, more than Words can express, may make some Attonement for my other Deficiencies. And so not to be tedious, however, imploring the continuance of your Esteem, I crave leave to subscribe my self, in all Love and Respect,

Your obedient Nephew and Servant,
P. G.[12]

12 Goodman, *Experienc'd Secretary* (1699), 1–2.

Read this without its title, and you have a general letter of complement that might be written to any hierarchically superior male who is capable of conferring benefits, to express the usual flattering gratitude and respect, and the usual love and passion to serve him. Read it with the subscription, "Your obedient Nephew and Servant," and you will see exactly what Goodman has done. Using the language and syntax deriving from bad translations and imitations of the French, this letter re-presents the commonplace that letters supply the place of speech, to show how it can do so during the sort of social-ceremonial visits that were paid to keep social connections alive. Implicit in the letter is the suggestion that those who take the trouble to show such flattering attentions when they have no immediate need for "Bounty and Tenderness" will have a resource to turn to when "Necessity" or "crazy Fortunes" impel them to seek aid. This point is developed in the "Letter of Request from a Niece to her Aunt" which follows. The opening letter's topos of "distance of place," with its implicit danger of neglect, forgetting and estrangement, is then fleshed out in the third letter, a "Letter of Friendship from one to another to tax him with Neglect of Writing to him." I quote only a part:

Dear Friend,
    Though Distance of Place Separates our Bodies, which gives me no small Pain, till we hold a closer Community, I find no reason that our Minds, ever be alienated or estranged from each other, who can actuate and unite in kinder Thoughts and Wishes, without regard to Space; the active Soul in its airy Motion out tracks the Sun, and puts a Girdle around the immense Globe of Earth, even with a Thought Scales the crystal Arch and mingles with the Stars; and if it can do such Wonders, I must chide you (though I dare not lay Lukewarmer Friendship to your charge) for a Neglect, I do not think Forgetfulness, in not oftener communicating your Mind to me. . .(3)

The idea that letters permitted minds to meet when bodies were apart had been commonplace at least since the Renaissance,[13] but here Goodman joins it to the complemental letter's recurrent theme of fear of neglect or coldness in friendship in an almost parodically heightened rhetorical style. Goodman explains that he has "scattered through the whole series of. . . Letters" what he calls "a Prospect" of the "Flowers of Rhetorick," to show readers how they may be "mixed with your Dis-course, gracefully to set it off" (74). *The Experienc'd Secretary* is perhaps the only manual in the eighteenth century still to include a section on

13 Goldberg, *Writing Matter.*

"Tropes and Figures in Scheme of Rhetoric and Oratory" and to stress Eloquence, and the importance of using rhetorical figures and methods of expression to "take the Fancy and strike the Imagination with Pleasure and Delectation" (76). Goodman's heightened language, elaborate figures, and concealing circumlocutions were an important part of his contemporary appeal in America, as we will see.

Like Hill, Goodman included quite a large number of "beyond the Sea" letters; but the attitude of most of them follows from the complemental letter's bemoaning of absence and separation. Rather than preaching the value of travel for a commercial empire, and the need for courage and a stiff upper lip in the quest for some "Advantage" as Hill had done, Goodman includes letters like the "Letter to a Brother, dissuading him from a dangerous Voyage," an "Affectionate Letter from a Sister to a Brother, persuading his Return" and a "Letter from a Wife to her Husband" taxing him with "Unkindness, Lukewarmness or Indifferency" for delaying his return. These letters positively discourage absence, even for "weighty Affairs." Other letters, such as Goodman's rewrite of Hill's letter from a Person at Sea to his Friend on Shore, emphasize the moment of return:

Sir,

After many Tossings and Roulings in the Deep, sometimes the Topmast tilting at the Stars, and then sinking as low as from *Olympus's* Spires to the Valleys beneath, I have found the leisure to write to you these few Lines, to tell you, that, amidst so many Dangers, I am in good Health, and hope, through the Blessing of God, the continuance of it; not in the least amidst our frequent Hurries, forgetting the many Favours and Kindnesses I have received at your Hands; hoping I shall be preserved from a Winding sheet of Waves, and other Misfortunes, to return with Success; if upon no other account to return to your Love, and pay my Respects for the signal Service you have done me. . . as soon as my Foote resalutes my Native-Shore, expect me with the utmost Expedition, who am ever,

Your Friend and Servant,
B. L. (11–12)

The complemental need to hasten to the side of the friend to whom one must demonstrate one's uncommon love and gratitude accords ill with the need to pursue other advantages abroad.

What Goodman's transposition of the complemental genre into the domain of the family and its social life did add to Hill, however, was a language and set of forms for letters of courtship to women. As one of Goodman's letter-writers puts it, "Complements in wooing are required."

One of the interesting things about Goodman's collection is that it offers more examples than Serre or *Mirrors of Complement* of the extension of complemental letters' primarily homosocial language and sentiments to heterosexual relationships. Here is an extract from one example, a "Letter from a Gentleman to a Gentlewoman in her Commendation":

Good Madam,
    The long and considerate Regard by which, in deep Contemplation, I have eye'd your rare and singular Virtues, joyned with so admirable Beauty and much pleased Condition grafted in your Person, hath moved me, among a number whom I am satisfied favour you earnestly, to love you, and thereupon humbly to lay my self and Services at your Feet. . .if continual, nay, rather inexterminable Vows in all perpetuity addicted to your Service; if never ceasing and tormenting Grief, uncertainly carried by hazardous Expectation, close in the Circle of your gracious Conceit, whether to bring my Soul a Sweet Murmur of Life, or a severe Sentence of a present death; may ought prevail either to move, entreat, sue, sollicit or persuade you, I then. . .have resolv'd, whilst living to honour you, and the Days I have to live, never to serve other but you. . .Your most passionate, loyal and perpetually devoted Servant, M. Q. (44–5)

Perspicuity was not high on the list of requirements for letters such as this, which were already being mocked in England by Charles Gildon in 1699, the year Goodman's *Secretary* was published. In *The Postboy robb'd of his Mail,* Gildon's group of gentleman critics ridiculed "a Mighty Affector of Similes to his Mistress" by observing: "We were all pleased with the *Extravagance* of the Humour (though none of us knew at what the Letter aim'd)." They dismiss another letter in the same style as one in which the writer has "patch'd together a Rhapsody of bombast from some Old Academy of Complements on purpose to compound a Mishmash of Extravagancies."[14] This extravagant but sanitized style was to become the hallmark of noble gallants, libertines and rakes, and later of false suitors and would-be gentlemen, in eighteenth-century novels. Restoration gallantries were, on the whole, not so mealy-mouthed, and left their recipients in little doubt as to how their writers hoped to "die." In Goodman, such sexual realities are only hinted at, for instance as the possible reason for which a daughter has married without her father's consent. Goodman juxtaposes a "letter from a gentleman to his mistress," written in this heightened and sanitized style, with a more pedestrian "Letter from Roger to Margery, a plain country Love Letter," to stress that the heightened

14 *Postboy,* I: 56, and II: 66.

complemental style is the one to be used by anyone with pretensions to a place among the social elite.

In seeking to better Hill, Goodman offered his own complemental imitation of almost all the familial and social letters to be found in *The Young Secretary's Guide*, as we will have occasion to see. But one significant alteration deserves particular mention, since it follows in an unexpected way from the complemental style to which Goodman's male writers have been returned. In Hill, with one exception, the letters of advice and reproof that conveyed the norms of conduct expected of young men in the different ranks of society were written by fathers, uncles, older brothers and male friends. In Goodman, by contrast, with a single exception, the letters of advice or reproof that convey norms of conduct both to sons and to daughters are given to mothers. Women are made the moral censors, and morality is transferred into the mother's domain, as in the following "Letter from a Mother to a Son, extolling him to Temperance and a sober chaste way of Living":

Dear Son,
  The Pains I underwent for you, and the Care I have taken in bringing you up, not to mention the great Cost bestowed in Education, should methinks lay a strict Obligation on you to hearken to my Advice above all others, considering you must needs be sensible a Mother's Admonishments can have no other tendency than to the Happiness and Welfare of her Child: you are now arrived at those Years of Discretion: be cautious then in all your Ways and Actions, fixing your Mind on Vertue as its center; shun bad Company as you would fly the approach of some dismal Ghost, that comes to terrifie and affright you; let not Wine inflame you to commit Folly, nor lewd Women, by their betwitching Inchantments lay Snares to entrap and bring you to Misery and Disgrace; let no Spot sully your good Name, but in all things so wisely demean yourself, that my Rejoycings may be dated with my Life, in having a Son whose Vertues may be an Ornament to his Family: But if my Advice be neglected and Vice get the upper hand, clouded with Sorrow, I shall go down to my Grave; a fatal Misfortune will, as a just judgement of Heaven, pursue you to the gloomy Regions of Dust, to lye in oblivion without a Name or Memory. Ponder well what I have said and keep to the right-hand, that you may be happy and she have no cause at any time to repent of all that she has done for you, who is,
  Your tender and loving Mother,
  E. B.

Since the male writers in this manual were writing flattering complemental letters to engage or seduce their correspondents, or inviting male friends to share a bottle in a tavern, it was left to mothers to preach chastity and temperance. As the above letter shows, the result was a dissociation of virtue and morality from the working world of government and trade, and a recommendation of virtue for individual happiness or salvation that elides or obfuscates its applicability to Britain's conduct of her domestic and foreign commercial empire. Perhaps this was one reason for Goodman's lack of success in Britain.

BOSTON: THE YOUNG SECRETARY'S GUIDE OR EXPERIENC'D SECRETARY BY "THOMAS HILL" (1703)

All seven American editions of this manual, whether printed by Bartholomew Green, John Allen or Thomas Fleet, used the title-page of Hill's *Young Secretary's Guide, Or Speedy Help to Learning*, and Goodman's full title, *The Experienc'd Secretary, or Citizen and Country-Man's Companion* as the running title on the pages inside. This combination is echoed by the pseudonym the printers gave the author of their adaptation, which likewise joins Thomas [Goodman] to [John] Hill, but in reverse order. These devices indicated the strategy that was used to abridge and adapt Goodman's *Secretary*. This was to reprint for the most part Goodman rewrites of Hill's letters, and thus to import Hill's concerns with Goodman's style. This combination proved so successful in the province that, as Thomas Fleet pointed out in the fourth edition that he printed for Samuel Gerrish in 1713, "the Sale of three large Impressions, all of which were sold in a short Time. . .were found too few to furnish this large and daily increasing Country." With the exception of this edition of 1713, the manual was therefore reprinted with minor alterations by a succession of printers for a large number of different booksellers, mostly in Boston, until 1730.

One way of profiling the distinctive character of this adaptation of Goodman's collection is to trace the line of its exclusions. This is relatively easy to do, since the Boston printers faithfully followed the order of the letters as they appeared in Goodman's *Secretary*, merely skipping letters as they went to reduce the collection by half and give it the design they desired. The Boston printers excluded almost all of Goodman's complemental letters between male friends, and most of his letters of courtship to women. Significantly, they retained the relatively simple and slightly clumsy "Letter from Roger to Margery, a plain country Love Letter" but dropped the "Letter from a Gentleman to his Mistress," that had been designed in the London edition to show up rustic ineptitude and showcase the eloquent style of gentlemen. The Boston printers also eliminated all letters bemoaning friends' absences, dissuading brothers from dangerous voyages and persuading husbands and brothers to return home. There was therefore in their adaptation no suggestion that travel "beyond the Sea" should be eschewed. They also eliminated the letter from a master telling his servant what work to do while he was out of town and that suggesting that a gentlemen would benefit society by seeking some employment. Thus while their adaptation remains primarily focused on times of leisure, there is no suggestion in their version of this manual that leisure has supplanted work. Indeed, Fleet's somewhat anomalous edition of 1713 clustered all the letters bearing on work or travel or requesting financial aid together at the beginning, as if to emphasize that the work-a-day world has not gone away.

One important effect of the Boston printers' excisions was to increase the relative proportion of family letters to about two-thirds of the thirty-five missives in Green and Allen's edition of 1703, which was the basis of all subsequent editions but Fleet's of 1713. They began, as Goodman did, with the complemental letter from a Nephew to an Uncle (above, p. 130) and the Letter of Request from a Niece to her Aunt, but completely changed their tenor by using the niece's distress to lead into a series of letters on that subject. The niece's letter begging for aid is followed by a Letter of Consolation to a Friend in Adversity, which urges him to show manly fortitude and courage in the face of a sudden fall from prosperity, and assures him that though flatterers have abandoned him, he still has friends who are willing to help him. A letter of reproof from a father to an ungracious son, and a letter from a daughter who has married without her parents' consent then demonstrate how sons and daughters could, through their own misconduct, alienate their parents and bring misfortune down upon themselves. The theme of misfortune and distress is picked up in other letters scattered throughout the first half of the volume: there is a letter recounting misfortunes and petitioning a friend to help relieve them; a letter from that tenant who cannot pay his rent; a letter from a son begging his father not to "blast me with your Frowns" (14), and a letter addressing an unfortunate quarrel. These serve as the backdrop for the short collection's three letters of advice from mothers, which include the Letter to a Son exhorting him to Temperance and a sober Way of living (above, p. 134) and the following letter from a mother to a daughter:

My dear Daughter,

Since your Absence, my Thoughts have not been unemployed to study for your good: you cannot be insensible how careful and tender I have been over you, with all the reasonable Indulgence of an affectionate Parent, to cultivate your sprouting Years in Ways of Vertue: now you are in the Bloom of your Age, be wise and careful in what you undertake; let no vain Imaginations wander your Mind; let Pride be a Stranger to you, and look on Flattery with Detestation, lest they prove Snares to entrap your Virtues, and then a world of Misfortunes will, like a Torrent, break in upon you not to be stayed; keep your Eyes from alluring Objects, lest they prove Inlets to betray your Heart and lead you beyond the Guidance of Reason, and so you stumble on your Ruine. In all your Words and Actions be modest and sober, courteous and humble; shun all affected Ways, and let Vanity have no Place in you: Let your Conversation be grave and serious; shut your Ears to what is obscene or prophane, let them not be conveyers of anything to your Soul that may fix the least blemish or Stain on it, but in all things so order your Affairs and behave your self, that the most censorious may have nothing to fasten upon you to your prejudice. If you are disposed to alter your Condition, let nothing be done in it without mature Deliberation; let no hasty Passion surprise you; rather make your Choice by the Beauty of the Mind, than Comeliness of the Body; and in so weighty an Affair, trust not too fondly to your own Judgement, but be advised by more knowing than your self, always making Passion subordinate to sound Judgement and Reason. Much more I might intimate to you, but not to be over tedious, this at present may serve to direct to what may further you in Degrees of Vertue, that growing up in them to a height, you may entail to your self and your Posterity a good Name, which will embalm your Memories more lasting than Beauties, Riches or Honour; which may it succeed, is the cordial Wish of,

Your affectionate Mother,
A. D.

The Boston printers' preference for Goodman's style over Hill's can in part be explained, it seems to me, by letters such as this. For here, the conventional tropes and schemes of Goodman's "flowers of rhetoric" – the metaphors (eyes as inlets, misfortunes as torrents), the personifications of pride and flattery, the rhythms and pauses produced by the *anaphora* or repetition of "let. . .let. . .let" – not only add dignity and vividness to the message; they are also reminiscent of sermons that would have been heard in Boston, which Green and Allen were accustomed to printing for the Mathers and others. One can also imagine this letter, with its warnings against the wages of sin and its recommendations of modesty and obedience, being read in Boston as an exemplum of the conduct recommended to parents as well as to daughters in sermons such as Benjamin Wadsworth's "The Well-Ordered Family" (1712). This enjoined parents to "follow your children with wholesome counsels, tho' they are grown up," to teach them "a civil, respectful, courteous behaviour," to see that they are instructed "in the things of God," to "restrain, reprove and correct them" and to "warn them particularly against those Sins you see them most particularly prone to and in danger of."[15] Comparing Goodman's best rewrites to

---

15 Wadsworth, "The Well-Ordered Family" (1712), in Smith, *Theories of Education*, 49–52.

Hill's original letters also makes it plain why these printers might have thought that Goodman's complemental style added grace, dignity and distinction to the commerce of everyday life:

Hill: *A Letter from a Youth to his Sister*

Most loving Sister,

   Our Absence so long from each other, has occasion'd my writing to you, that I might be inform'd of your Health and Welfare, of which I am as sollicitous and tender as my own; not forgetting you in my Prayers, nor neglecting to do you all the good Offices I can, with our Parents, Friends and Acquaintance. In requittal of which, let it be your part to return me an Answer, that I may be satisfied in what I have required, which will render me no small contentment of Mind; in expectation whereof, I rest,

Your ever loving brother,
AP (Hill, p. 57)

   Goodman, and Green and Allen (p. 11 and p. 8, respectively):

A Brother's Letter to a Sister, enquiring of her Welfare

Loving Sister,

   My long Absence from you, though I have not wanted good Conversation, has however made the Time seem tedious; my natural Affection inclines me always to have you in Remembrance, tendering your Health and Welfare in all Respects as dear as mine own, and there is nothing in my Power that can be reasonably granted, but you may request it, and call that Request your Command: I intend shortly to pay you a Visit, and had done it long since, had not urgent Business, contrary to my expectation, fallen upon the neck of another to hinder it. I pray give my humble Respects to all our Friends; and so, in expectation, to find you, and all the rest in Health and Prosperity upon my Arrival, which shall be suddain, God permitting,

I remain your affectionate loving brother,
DC

   In comparison to Goodman's rewrite, Hill's letter is well meaning but peremptory. There is an implicit reproach to the sister for not having written to so tender and solicitous a brother to set his mind at rest as to her health and welfare. There is also a demand that his good offices be repaid by a prompt answer, with the implication that a prompt answer is the least he can – and does – expect in return for them. The brother writes as a kindly superior in an unequal relationship, and his letter borders on a letter of complaint or reproach. Goodman's letter, by contrast, uses the language of complement to invert the relationship Hill portrays. Here it is the sister whose commands must weigh with her brother, while the latter both tenders his services to her and apologizes for business that has prevented him from coming to pay his respects in person. The letter's gallantry is underlined by its placement by Green and Allen in proximity to the complemental Letter from a Nephew to his Uncle, which makes a similar point. Goodman's version of Hill's letter includes the flattery demanded by the complemental style – the brother indicates, for instance, in his first sentence, that he misses his sister's conversation despite the "good Conversation" he enjoys among his friends. Goodman's version of Hill's letter therefore demonstrates that it is graceful and proper for a man in relation to any woman, including the women of his own family, to politely conceal the real inequalities in such relationships by gallantly deferring to the weaker party, offering his services, and inviting her "commands."

Another interesting inclusion in the 1703 Boston adaptation of Goodman's collection was the latter's rewrite of Hill's Letter of Congratulation to a Friend on his Advancement (above, p. 111), now transformed into a generalized letter of joy at some unspecified good fortune: "Sir, If you could any way sensibly conceive how acceptable the News of your good Fortune is to me you would, past all peradventure conclude, that the Joy which surprizes me for the same is equal to yours; for to be plain, nothing can be added to it to render it more sublime, since it proceeds from the lasting Friendship I have vowed to you, which is not common, since your Merit is the Object. . ." (24). There is no critical or mitigating answer, as there was in Hill, so the letter stands as a model of its kind. The purpose of such letters in this Boston adaptation is made clear by Green and Allen's choice of closing letter. This is a Letter of Thanks from a Daughter to her Mother for her Good Breeding (Goodman's rewrite of Hill's letter from a daughter thanking her mother for her good education). Good breeding is thus identified with the complemental style in the preceding letters, where it has been used both inside and outside the family.

These two letters were cut out of the adaptation of this adaptation performed by Thomas Fleet in 1718, and in subsequent editions. By cutting out these letters, as well as letters of petition to family and friends and letters of recommendation, these later editions downplayed both the hierarchical character of their epistolary world, and the importance of complement as a signifier of good breeding. These later collections generally conclude with the Mother's Letter to a Son, exhorting him to Temperance and a sober chaste way of Living (above, p. 134) and with a letter from a country chapman to a city dealer inquiring about his health and affairs. They thus return the reader to uncompromising virtue and to the workaday world.

NEW YORK AND PHILADELPHIA: THE BRADFORDS'
SECRETARY'S GUIDE, OR YOUNG MAN'S COMPANION

In their efforts to provide a manual that would be "Useful and Necessary in these American Parts, where books of this Nature are not frequently to be got," William and Andrew Bradford, printers in New York and Philadelphia, selectively melded together Hill's *Young Secretary's Guide*, Goodman's *Experienc'd Secretary* and William Mather's *Young Man's Companion* – a fact they eventually reflected in their title.[16] In the epistolary section which concerns us here, where Hill was from the first the dominant influence, the Bradfords produced what was in effect a new manual, not only by excising, selecting and reordering preprinted letters as the Boston printers had done, but also by "collecting and compiling out of several large volumes" one "small" but very efficient one.[17] Between 1710 and 1737, they also revised their selection of letters several times, by repeatedly dipping back into the same sources for other letters, and by replacing or rewriting letters to suit the changing times.

The Bradfords identified the principles governing successive selections on their title-pages, and increased the number of letters they offered from thirty-five in the 1710 edition to over sixty in the fifth edition of 1737, to accommodate their changing goals. The editions of 1710 and 1718, which appeared in New York and Philadelphia respectively, sought to model "the Method of Writing Letters upon most Subjects, whether Trade,

16 "To the Reader" (no page numbers). The earliest extant edition is the second edition of 1710. In this and the third edition of 1718, the manual's title was *The Young Man's Companion*, which was also the title of William Mather's revised *vade mecum*. The Bradfords drew on Hill from the first, because Mather's section on letters was both extremely thin, and itself partly borrowed from Goodman or Hill. Mather's *vade mecum* was also constantly being revised. The earliest edition of 1681 contained no letters and was entitled *A Very Useful Manual*; by 1710, it had changed its format, moderated its excessively religious tone, and included fourteen letters. By 1727 there were sixteen letters, mostly new. The Bradfords drew heavily on the letters in Mather's 1727 edition for their major revision of their manual in 1737. Mather's influence dominates the arithmetical, book-keeping, geographical and other practical sections of the Bradfords' manual. This justified their preserving Mather's title as part of theirs when the increasing number of letters from Hill and Goodman in their collection also justified their calling their manual a Secretary's Guide.

17 It is not clear whether William or Andrew or both were responsible for the compilations and revisions of their manual. Andrew was William's son, and the first two editions of this manual were produced when they were working together in New York. There is also a later joint edition. But once Andrew set up on his own in Philadelphia, father and son generally produced separate printings under separate imprints – there are slight differences, for instance in the order of letters in their printings of the same editions. In the earliest, joint New York editions, the prefatory Letter to the Reader is signed by Andrew, but he speaks of "us" when discussing the compiler. Thereafter, the signatory initials used at the bottom of the same Letter to the Reader were WB in New York printings and AB in Philadelphia ones.

Traffick or otherwise." The fourth edition of 1728 and 1729, however, offered models for "Writing Letters on most Subjects as one Friend to another, as well as Trade, Traffic or otherwise." The fifth edition of 1737 promised to show readers "How to write Letters of Complement, Friendship or Business, with proper Directions for external and internal Subscriptions and other things necessary to be understood in that Affair." If these successive goals are viewed as a measure of social change in New York and Philadelphia during the intervening years, they suggest a marked increase in the importance of sociality, and in the value placed on ceremony and civility. However, the last edition also contained a heavily moralizing strain that was absent in earlier editions.

Like the Boston printers, the Bradfords omitted the bulk of Hill's discursive and explanatory material; but unlike them, they cleverly replaced it with two pieces of doggerel, which recurred in all editions, one immediately before, the other immediately after, the letter collection. The first outlines the letter's proper structure:

> All Letters should begin with a Declaration
> Of friendly Titles, as a Preparation;
> Saluting them with Love and Commendation,
> As they are in Esteem, or in Relation;
> Then to the matter needful, short and plain
> They should proceed in, as being the main.
> And wind up all with words of love and peace,
> Concluding as unto their Friends they stand,
> In humbleness theirs when they them command,
> Subscribing those their Letters with their hand,
> And for their Superscription on the side,
> The Name and Place where now their Friends abide.

Besides indicating the unvarying features of epistolary form in verse to make it easier to memorize, this rhyme had the virtue of alerting inexperienced readers to pay close attention to the opening and closing phrases and to the super- and subscriptions of the letters that followed. If readers thought to jump straight to "the main," and skim it because it was only "short and plain," they would miss much of what the letters were modeling and how they were going about it.

At the end of the collection, another piece of doggerel explained how the reader could use the collection to generate new letters:

> 'Twould swell this Volume too too large
> And make this Book of too much charge
> To put down Copies in all things

> That Trade and Friendship daily brings
> Therefore a little take and see,
>   And strive for ingenuity.
>   'Tis matter that will thee and I,
>   Both Mind and Heart and Head imploy.
>   And when engaged with all our Might
>   Our Business will teach to endite,
>   The form being design'd only
>   To give a sample to write by.

Once again, as in Green's Boston adaptations of Hill, the colonists' ingenuity was called upon to make up for the scarcity of local resources. Offering only thirty-five letters might keep down the cost, but it did not provide copy for all the most common occasions of life. Readers would have to use whatever letter came closest to what they needed as "a sample to write by," take a little from it and a little from other letters where they could, and rely on their own knowledge of their own business to supply the words for the "main." What is modestly passed over in silence, is that the Bradfords also showed considerable ingenuity in selecting a small number of letters that could be combined and varied in this way.

One way the Bradfords multiplied what they had was by making many passages do double duty. In the long introductory paragraph to their letter section, which recurs in all editions, they highlighted and elaborated two points that Hill had made about the value of letters: their "Serviceableness in negotiating and managing important Affairs throughout the habitable World"; and their role as "Maintainers of Love, Amity and Correspondency." They then selected for their opening/anchoring letter, a paired unit apparently of their own composition, which they described as "A Letter from one at School to his Father and another to his Friend," which demonstrated the advantages to the individual of obtaining an epistolary education:

Honoured Father,
    My humble duty unto you presented, giving you all hearty thanks for all your love and kindness manifested to me. I make bold at this time to present you with a few lines, being the fruits of my Labour and do hope in time to be better accomplished to give you an account of my proceedings. In the meantime crave your acceptance of this as coming from
                                        Your Obedient Son,
                                            AB

Worthy Sir,
    Having gained some skill in this Art of Writing, since my being trained therein, I think it my duty to present you with some Fruits thereof, as an humble

gratulation and thankful remembrance of your great Love and Respect shewed me from time to time; hoping it may gain esteem, and acceptation with you, do with brevity, yet all humility rest, subscribing my self,

Your obliged Friend and Humble Servant

Contextualized by the introductory paragraph, these letters suggest that education is the gateway to managing affairs throughout the habitable world and to maintaining love, amity and correspondency with people like that worthy Sir, as well as with one's family. They demonstrate, with every indication of hope and pride, that letter-writing is the fruit of labor and training, while indicating that only a gradual process of improvement can be expected. There is also some small improvement between these two letters, especially marked in the vocabulary and punctuation. Moreover, while the first letter conveys Locke's point that a man cannot but "show himself" in his letters, the second letter implies that the ability to demonstrate the fruits of labor and learning in his epistolary writing will earn a young man all the "esteem and acceptation" he could desire.

Another way in which the Bradfords made the most of their small collection of letters was through the principle of selection they chose. In his brief introduction to his own section of letters, John Hill had claimed that he was going to start with letters suitable to the capacities and affairs of "the Younger Sort of either Sex" and then, "by degrees rise" to matters of greater Moment (Hill, 14–15). But ordering letters was not his forte, and arguing with Serre was distracting. Hill could never quite make up his mind whether he was moving from youth to age, or following his nemesis, Serre's, practice of grouping letters together by class (letters of entreaty, letters of thanks, letters of congratulation, etc.). In the event, he did neither consistently. The Bradfords, by contrast, worked their way simply and economically through the ages of man and woman, using Hill's own letters to construct what was almost a trajectory for men's and women's lives. In the 1710 edition, the above letters from the young man at school, are followed by a son at school asking his father for books and clothes. A daughter then asks her mother for permission to return home, while the son requests to be allowed to continue abroad. The daughter thanks her mother for kindnesses received, while the son thanks a patron for advancement. Now at work, the son writes a commercial Letter of Advice (above, pp. 114–15) and its sequel informing his correspondent that one of his trading partners died bankrupt. But he has not forgotten his father, for he writes him a letter of congratulation upon his recovery from sickness. While the daughter, still at school, asks to be allowed to learn some additional subjects, the son writes apprentice letters to his father and to his master, and then a "Letter from a young Man newly out of his Time" in which he tries to make trading connections for himself to start up in business on his own. The young man and the young woman each write a letter to a parent informing them that they have married, and the brother writes the sister to congratulate her on her choice of husband. Then there are letters between a husband and wife, who now have children of their own. The young woman writes to enquire after her sister's health and welfare, while the young man writes a series of letters of trade and commerce, which conclude with a father's warning to his son against youthful extravagance. The whole culminates in a "Letter to Congratulate a Person for his Return out of Foreign Parts or from a long Journey," which both suggests that the son's trade is flourishing, and takes us back to the notion of managing affairs throughout the habitable world with which the collection began.

The ideological subtext of this sequence is that family relations in trading, mercantile and perhaps artisanal families can be amicably sustained if family members both virtuously perform their relative duties and keep in touch by letter, as children grow up, daughters marry, and sons proceed from school to apprenticeship, from apprenticeship to trade, from trade at home to trade abroad, and from trade abroad back home. In the process, the collection has modeled letters of entreaty, reproach, congratulation and thanks, letters of trade and commerce, and letters of advice of various kinds, which could fairly easily be adapted – for instance the letter congratulating a sister on her marriage or that inquiring about a sister's health would not have to be altered much to be readdressed to friends.

The Bradfords preserved this framework in the 1718 and 1729/9 editions of their manual by adding most of their revisions after the original thirty-five letters, and by inserting into the sequence they had created only such letters as did not disturb the design: for instance, they added some more letters of trade, a letter of excuse to a father, and a response to the father's imputation of youthful extravagance to his son defending him from the charge. Two of the letters that were tagged on to the end of the collection in the revised edition of 1718 continued the theme of conducting business at a distance while keeping in touch with one's friends at home. But the other six introduced a non-business related "genteel" social life for the first time, by means of letters of complement largely taken from Goodman. The Letter from a Gentleman to a Gentlewoman to beg Pardon for an Offence, and the Letter to a Lady desiring Admittance to her Presence and their answers provided examples of his heightened, complemental style.

The Bradfords also included the following letter in that style, "from one Lady to another," which has the virtue, especially in such a short collection, of highlighting the possibilities and pleasures of friendships between women, and the role that letters can play in women's friendships:

Madam,

If to be forcibly deprived of what we most delight in, is to be justly reckoned amongst the Misfortunes of Life; then such I may esteem your absence from me; whose Conversation was so extreemly agreeable, that I find the Loss of it to be a very sensible Affliction. For the Honour you did me of taking me into more than ordinary Intimacy, the Effect of which was the unbosoming of our Thoughts to each other, did as it were twist our very Souls together, so that they could not be parted without Violence. The only way left, madam, to make up this Separation, is to hasten your Return, which like the Sun's breaking forth after having been a considerable time enveloped in Clouds and Darkness, can only revive the drooping Spirits of,

Madam,

Your Friend and Servant,
MF

The flowery figures and superfluous verbiage contained in this letter contrast sharply with the comparatively spare and perspicuous style of most of the letters the Bradfords borrowed from Quaker William Mather, as well as from Hill's far more moderate transports. The collection in this incarnation also rounds off its series of complemental letters with a letter of consolation to a widow on the death of her husband which rapidly turns into a merriment, for it both advises the widow to "Dry up your Tears, and prepare to follow him" and shows the writer offering himself as a potential second husband.

This collection was reprinted with few alterations until 1737 when it was given a new, heavily monitory and moralizing cast. The Bradfords took many more letters from Mather, whose *vade mecum* had also undergone some sea changes in later editions, and they changed or rewrote some of the letters they had taken from Hill. Since Mather had also borrowed some letters from Hill, there are letters common to all three collections.

In the Bradfords' edition of 1737, the two letters suggesting that an epistolary education was the gateway to the world which opened earlier editions (above, p. 142) were replaced by five letters on the virtues of education taken from Hill and Goodman which were clustered together at the beginning to reinforce the point: A son returns thanks for his good education, a scholar writes to his cousin to tell him to betake himself to learning, a scholar writes to his parents a letter of thanks and another of excuse. The last letter in this cluster demonstrates both what has happened to the theme of defending oneself against slanderous talk (above, pp. 116, 118) and the difference in Mather's "Quaker" style:

Honoured Father and Mother,

The ill Report that you have heard of me, I suppose comes from some of my School-Fellows, who either envy my Happiness, or by aggravating my Faults, would be thought to seem less Criminal themselves; but when I consider the Time and Credit I have lost thereby, the first being irrecoverable, my double Diligence for the future, I hope, will regain the last, that I may still subscribe my self,

Your dutiful Son,
James Love.

There is no abject submission here, and the language and syntax are simpler and more colloquial than any cited so far. This letter also virtually dismisses the problem of false reports carried by malicious people to those in power, and shrugs off the importance of reputation ("credit" can be recovered), in favor of issues of individual conduct and conscience. The important question for "James Love" is whether there is a kernel of truth in the ill report his parents have heard, and how he can correct his faults. What he finds he has really lost, and must work diligently to regain, is his own time. The moral tone of this letter is reinforced in short order by the Letter from an Elder Brother to a younger Brother exhorting him to Good Behaviour (above, p. 126), which Mather had reprinted and to which he had added his own commentary. The Bradfords printed the letter with Mather's commentary, which follows:

Observe: Young Men, when they first appear in the world, ought to have a Care what Company they keep: their future Happiness depends very much upon the Qualifications of those they converse with.

Though such may have received good Principles in their Education, yet they want Practice to confirm their Habits of Virtue, and Courage to resist the Allurements of Vice and Error.

They are apt to catch at any Thing, that indulges and countenances their youthful Fancies. The Misfortune is, when they want Prudence most, they have then least of it. 'Tis happy when they listen to the Advice of their Parents or some experienc'd Relation, who may be able to direct them in an Affair of such Consequence.[18]

18 In Andrew Bradford's Philadelphia edition of 1737, 54.

The "Letter to reclaim Youthful Extravagance" which was the only monitory letter in previous editions now figured as part of an ongoing theme, which was reinforced by other new borrowings from Mather. These add "some experienc'd relation" by including a letter of apology from a nephew to his uncle, with the uncle's stern reply requiring him to show "more substantial Proof" of his repentance and warning him that "if you should lapse into your former follies, you must expect a much severer treatment." In this edition, only two of the six complemental letters remain: a letter to a lady desiring admittance to her presence and its response. Any worldly effect they may have is blunted by the new letters which now precede and follow them: a "Letter to a Friend desiring him to end a Difference" and a sermonizing letter of consolation to a lady on the death of her husband which tells her that "God is an inexhaustible and overflowing Fountain: and what wise Person grieves so much because the Stream is dried up, when there is a Living Fountain to repair to?" By eliminating six letters and adding ten, the Bradfords entirely altered the tenor and focus of their collection.

The Bradfords not only replaced and added letters; they also appear to have rewritten some of them in the simpler and more modern style which they had, from the first, preferred for letters of trade or commerce. Here, for instance, is their substitution for Hill's and Goodman's Letters of Congratulation to a man upon his Advancement and their answers (pp. III and 139, above):

Sir,

The news of your Promotion into that Charge which you wish'd for so long, hath added such Contentment and Satisfaction to my Thoughts, that I am able to express one part of the Joy which reigns in me. I trouble not my self, to persuade you to it by a long Discourse; your own Merit and our reciprocal Friendship (supplying the defect of my Eloquence) will give a far better Testimony than my Pen is able, which has in Charge at this present, only to put you in Mind that I am always,

Sir,

Your very humble Servant,
J. G.

Answer:

Sir,

I always believed you were so generous, as to take Part in whatever should concern me, having begun so strict a Commerce of so reciprocal Friendship. I persuade myself likewise, that you make no doubt of the Passion which I have to do you Service; whereof you may be as confident, as of the most assured thing in the world, since I am in Heart and Soul,

Sir,

Your most humble Servant,
J. W. (55–6, 1737)

As the reference to "the defect of my Eloquence" underlines, there is no longer any need for the writer to rack his brains for recondite ways of saying what the occasion demands. Hill's phrase that the writer will "not trouble you in the midst of your great Affairs with a tedious Epistle" is here actualized by paring Hill's letter of congratulation down to its bare bones: the writer's expression of joy at the promotion and sense of the addressee's merit. The letter's real purpose, to ensure that the writer is a friend who is remembered when it counts, is then stated fairly directly in the lead up to the subscription. In the answer, modest disclaimer, thanks and acknowledgment of longstanding mutual friendship are taken care of in the first sentence, while the second sentence provides the assurance that the first writer was seeking. A man in the midst of great affairs now has no need – and no time – for more. While reducing congratulation and thanks for congratulations to a merely formal exchange of civilities, this rewrite of Hill also heightens its utilitarian function.

We are looking here, in 1737, at a rewrite of Hill's rewrite of Serre's letter of congratulation to the Marshal of France (above, p. 110), which was first translated into English by John Massinger in 1640, almost a hundred years earlier, and at a formula for epistolary exchange that has "erred" or wandered from France to England to Philadelphia and New York, while both admitting cultural and historical differences, and remaining in many respects the same. In 1737 different versions of the same letters and their different styles of expression continued to circulate on both sides of the Atlantic. Similitude of sentiments and formulae in different versions of the same letters circulating simultaneously high-lighted the importance of style as a means of self-representation (or self-betrayal). For it was style that differentiated letters which said the same proper things on the same occasions; style bearing cultural content which could in principle be freely chosen from a range of options; thus style which made the man. The fact that not all styles were necessarily available to particular readers or buyers was turned into a differentiating and thus characterizing feature by contemporaries too, and treated in some quarters as evidence of rusticity, ignorance, pretension, affectation, provinciality or old-fashioned old-worldliness. To read a letter as an informed and cultured person therefore meant developing an ear for written epistolary style as acute as that which twentieth-century Britons developed for varieties of accent, and using it in the same sorts of ways, to "place" the writer by education, class and region.

The Bradfords represented themselves from the first as patriotic bene-factors of their country and as "real well wishers" to their fellow provin-cials. Their prefatory "Letter to the Reader," which appears in all editions but the last, stressed that the printers sought to profit others, "Elder people as well as Youth," to be "Advantageous to the Country in Gen-eral," and to "better furnish and enable the diligent to perform the several Callings, Professions, Imployments or Exercises, which Providence may allot to everyone." The edition of 1710 concluded with a poem which boasted that the printer had offered his readers a "fragrant Garland" of roses and lilies, "Such as in *America* were ne'er found." How far their collection was useful to people in all callings, professions, employments or exercises is open to debate; but their brilliance certainly lay in understand-ing that they could best serve their fellow provincials by offering a garland of different styles, and models of different available modes of expression, in one "small book."

The various American compilations from English manuals that have been examined in this chapter married "anglicization" to "exceptional-ism" in some of the same ways. Their projected audience was almost invariably primarily a trading and mercantile clientele, which they envi-sioned as wishing to add gentility and refinement to their social, domestic or leisured moments. Beyond their differences of style, Hill and Goodman treated politeness as the *lingua franca* for people at all ranks. By contrast, these American printer-compilers almost invariably represented Goodman's complemental style as the signifier of gentility for a far narrower audience, which is represented in their manuals as the whole of society. One might say that most of the "condescensions" and "humiliations" modeled in Hill's and Goodman's collections fall away because everyone, except children in relation to their parents, has more or less the same rank; or that issues of rank are elided by this focus on the epistolary needs of a social group that is represented in isolation from all others. But this does give provincial American collections a more egalitar-ian and universalizing appearance than London manuals. It also increased the importance of the heightened gentility and refinement that they modeled in domestic and social matters as a differentiating cultural marker both within this group and between this group and others. A number of Americanists have described this use of politeness to mark elite status and distinguish the genteel from everyone else as characteristic of the upper ranks in America.[19]

The careful ordering of letters in these American compilations also contrasts with Hill's and Goodman's collections of "miscellaneous letters," which promiscuously combined heterogeneous business and household letters of different classes. These colonial American printer-compilers added letters of genteel complement onto compilations that reordered the letters they selected from English manuals in implicitly narrativized ways, which offered in outline familiar moral and religious lessons about virtue and vice, success and failure, punishment and salvation. American printer-compilers seemed to think that New England's particular needs could best be satisfied by manuals compiled according to a formula that combined in various proportions *useful* bread-and-butter letters of a commercial and domestic character with insistent *moral* teaching and some complement of *gentility*. The sales seem to bear them out.

There were, as we saw, differences between the different London and the different Boston and Philadelphia manuals, and between different manuals in manual series. But identifying resemblances not only underlines the fact that compilation can register and/or construct marked cultural differences; it also indicates how different the functions of manuals were on different sides of the Atlantic. Whether we look at Hill's concern with conciliating different people and different ranks within a broad imperial vision, or at Goodman's efforts to give a broad public access to the eloquence of the orator and the graces of the court, we are looking at manuals which promoted integration within a hierarchical society that had a recognized elite at the top, and which facilitated the geographical movement outwards and/or the upward professional and social movement of almost all its members. Far more inward looking both geographically and socially, and representing foreign trade, if at all, only at the periphery of their collections, these colonial American compilations acknowledged no elite above merchants and tradesmen, and paid little attention to the colonial administrative hierarchy. While facilitating transatlantic trade and communication by offering English epistolary models whose codes were recognized and understood, they included letters whose heightened ornamental language distinguished areas of gentility from areas of trade, and constructed certain forms of politeness as the gentility of a particular group.

---

19 Bushman argues that gentry culture began to flourish around 1706. "American High Style and Vernacular Cultures." For elite markings of politeness in America, see Shields, *Civil Tongues*; Bushman, *Refinement of America*; Wood, *Radicalism of the American Revolution*.

CHAPTER 4

The "Complete Letter-Writers" of the middle years

A marked cultural shift took place during the 1750s both in the style of letters and in the treatment of issues. The letter-collections in *Complete Letter-Writers* continued to address the same "occasions," to model the same classes of letter, and to represent the same cast of generic characters as *Secretaries* had done. But the themes we have been exploring – "friendship" between men, trade and commerce, the household, apprenticeship and domestic service, education, the role of women, marriage, travel and absence, and written and oral conversation – are expressed and addressed in significantly different ways. Three issues are also given far greater prominence: relations between the elder brother (who now frequently supplies the place of the father or uncle) and his younger brother or sister; the conduct of courtship; and bankruptcy.

The two most influential and widely reprinted British letter manuals of the second half of the eighteenth century were both compilations: Crowder's *Complete Letter-Writer, or Polite English Secretary* (1755) and Dilworth's *Complete Letter-Writer, or Young Secretary's Instructor* (1783). The *Eminence grise* behind them was Charles Hallifax's *Familiar Letters on Various Subjects of Business and Amusement* (1754). This had a respectable run in London – it was in its fifth edition in 1758, and was reprinted in Britain until 1764 – but its success did not compare to the huge popularity of the Crowder and Dilworth manuals. Hallifax, who presented himself as a compiler of "genuine letters" who had added "many Letters of his own Writing from supposed Persons, and upon imaginary Occasions," produced a collection of letters representative of the epistolary needs of a wide range of different ranks, as Hill and Goodman had done. But socially, he went higher: he introduced the aristocracy in letters such as "To a Person of Quality, requesting a Place," "To a Duke to Request his Favour and Interest," to offer men in administration examples of "Letters written to the greatest Persons, and from those in different Stations" so that they could "see in what Manner this form is to be conducted."[1] There were also social letters, of invitation, of thanks and such, suitable for use in the upper ranks. Hallifax's letters of trade and household letters were commensurably more up-market, and geared to the upper strata of the mercantile and trading community. Crowder and Dilworth both eliminated the aristocratic upper reaches of Hallifax's manual, and supplemented the letters they selected from him with a solid infusion of household, courtship and business letters culled from *Secretaries* and from Samuel Richardson's *Letters Written to and For Particular Friends* (1741).

From the 1740s, when England's bulk-trade in books took off, the American provinces appear to have relied almost exclusively on imported English letter manuals. Crowder's *Complete Letter-Writer* figures on several American booksellers lists of imported books, along with London editions of Hill's *Young Secretary's Guide*, Dodsley's *Preceptor*, Fisher's *Young Man's Best Companion*, Haywood's *Epistles for the Ladies* and Rollin's *Belles Lettres*.[2] American printers got back into the business of compiling their own versions of British manuals only in the 1790s, when they used Scottish editions of these two London compilations as their copy-text. In America, the influence of Crowder's *Letter-Writer* and of the Scottish Dilworth continued well into the early nineteenth century, as American printers continued to cull letters from both for their own manuals.

LONDON: CROWDER'S COMPLETE LETTER-WRITER, OR POLITE ENGLISH SECRETARY

The Complete Letter-Writer, or Polite English Secretary (1755) came as close to becoming a standard, universally available, compendium during the second half of the eighteenth century as any letter manual managed to get.

The book history is instructive here. Crowder's *Complete Letter-Writer* acquired the reach and influence it had in England, in Scotland and in America after Independence, not only because its popularity justified nineteen English editions before 1800, but also because it was so frequently "pirated" (in the view of its English publishers) by Scottish and American printers, who reprinted it with comparatively minor variations.

---

1 Hallifax, *Familiar Letters* (1765), ix, viii, xi.
2 For instance: in Philadelphia, William Bradford's Catalogues of 1760 and 1769, John Rivington's Catalogue of 1762, David Hall's Catalogue of 1769; in New York, Hugh Gaine's Catalogue of 1761, and Noel & Hazard's Catalogue of 1771.

Crowder's "original" compilation of 1755 was itself repeatedly altered, revised and corrected from 1756 until the twelfth edition of 1768, after which the collection remained fairly stable.[3] Scottish printers began to pirate the compendium in 1768, producing at least twelve different runs before 1796.[4] Since the Scots were not "English," Edinburgh printers made the manual's title more inclusive by dropping "Polite English Secretary" and simply calling it *The Complete Letter-Writer* (or as library catalogues now have it, *The Complete Letter-Writer, Containing Familiar Letters*. . . .). Scottish editions also tended to differ from Crowder's by adding back into their 1768 version some letters from Crowder's earlier London editions that had been excised in the process of revision, as well as by introducing a prominently placed and well-organized set of rules for reading aloud. During the 1790s, American printers in Boston, New York, Philadelphia, Hartford and Salem who printed their own versions of this manual, adopted the Scots' truncated title which also suited them better after Independence. The changes they introduced were generally limited to adding or removing letters in the two final sections. Though Crowder's *Letter-Writer* was rarely identical with itself in any two editions, therefore, it did circulate with the bulk of its contents and most of its sequencing more or less intact after 1768, which meant that for the rest of the century, users of this manual in different parts of Britain and America were exposed to mostly the same letters in the same contexts, despite America's political break with England.

One reason for its success was certainly this Letter-Writer's "completeness": it was a compilation, and in some cases rewriting, of letters from earlier manuals and letter-miscellanies that presented all their different styles and preoccupations in one convenient volume. The collection of letters had four sections. The first, consisting of "Miscellaneous Letters on the most useful and common Occasions," combined letters selected from Hill, Goodman and Mather with letters taken, likewise without attribution, from Richardson's *Letters written to and for particular Friends* (1741), Hallifax's *Familiar Letters* (1754) and Haywood's *Epistles for the Ladies* (1749), to fashion a collection which, like the *Secretaries* of earlier years,

---

3 Perhaps because Stanley Crowder was now publishing the manual in partnership with Benjamin Collins in Salisbury, rather than with Henry Woodgate around the corner in London, and long-distance coordination was less easy. The major change after 1768 consisted of adding some letters by Sterne, Sancho and Lord Chesterfield at the end.

4 Edinburgh printers and publishers included David Paterson, John Reid, William Darling, T. Ross, Alexander Donaldson, and P. Anderson. The last Edinburgh edition appears to be T. Ross's in 1796.

addressed the domestic and business needs of the household-family. The second section consisted of "Letters of Courtship and Marriage" taken from Richardson and Hallifax, again without attribution, and generally addressed to the same clientele. In the early editions, the third section coopted *Lettres gallantes* and *Academies of Complement*, by offering love letters written in the complemental style as well as exempla of real love letters from Frenchmen and Restoration rakes. By 1759, however, these had been replaced by a far more improving collection of "Familiar Letters of Advice and Instruction," which never fully distinguished itself from the final section of "Elegant letters on various Subjects to improve the Stile and entertain the Mind." Both sections contained letters by "eminent authors" culled from letter-miscellanies, most of which were "real" letters, and some of which were fictional.

In this way, Crowder's *Letter-Writer* gave expression to the continuity contemporaries assumed between ordinary, everyday and business letters written specifically for manuals, "real" letters to and from distinguished people, and letters written for or adapted from fictional works by the "best writers." Though they might demonstrate different levels of proficiency, all drew on the same letter classes and on similar epistolographical skills, as William Milns explained:

Composition is not only the most elegant, but the most useful vehicle in the literary world – without it Poetry, History and Science would be unknown, and the arts would die with the inventors of them; nor is it less valuable in social and commercial life; it is the faithful and sacred medium through which the reciprocal exchange of sentiments is effected between distant friends; and there is nothing perhaps upon which the character of the merchant so much depends as the language of his letters.[5]

Milns saw a continuity between poetic, historical and scientific letters and everyday epistolary exchanges, and between literature and mercantile correspondence, where modernism saw only diverse binary oppositions, because he understood all epistolary compositions as applications of the same epistolary and rhetorical practices. This is also why real and fictional "literary" familiar letters by eminent authors proliferated in mid-century London manuals. As John Newbery put it, "Proficiency in this Art" is "best obtained by Imitating very frequently and with due Attention, the Letters of those who have been most celebrated and distinguished for this Species of Writing."[6] At the same time, once included in Crowder's

---

5 Milns, *Plan*, 4–5.
6 Newbery, *Letters on the most common as well as important Occasion of Life*, iii.

manual (or anyone else's), whether "real" or fictional, pedestrian or "literary," all the letters selected became equally subject to the taxonomies examined in Chapter 2, and to the laws of *compilatio* which recontextualized them and gave them new thematic meanings and stylistic functions within the letter collection as a whole. These meanings and functions are those which primarily concern us here.

Crowder updated the household letters and courtship letters that occupied the first two sections of his manual both in sentiment and in style. Some of his methods of updating *Secretaries* will become evident from the way he imitated and superceded Hill's "Letter from an Elder Brother to a Younger Brother exhorting him to good Behaviour and a Seemly Carriage" (above, p. 126) to introduce ideological and stylistic changes characteristic of the collection as a whole:

From an elder Brother to a Younger

Dear Brother,

As you are now gone from Home, and are arrived at Years of some Discretion, I thought it not amiss to put you in mind, that your childish Affairs ought now to be entirely laid aside, and instead of them more serious Thoughts, and Things of more Consequence should take Place; whereby we may add to the Reputation of our Family, and gain to ourselves the good Esteem of being virtuous and diligent in Life, which is of great Value, and ought to be studied beyond any trifling Amusements whatsoever, for 'twill be an Ornament in Youth, and a Comfort in Old Age.

You have too much Good Nature to be offended at my Advice, especially when I assure you, that as I sincerely wish your Happiness and Advancement in Life as I do my own. We are all, thank God, very well, and desire to be remembered to you: Pray write as often as Opportunity and Leisure will permit; and be assured a Letter from you will always give great Pleasure to all your Friends here, but to none more than,

Your most affectionate Brother,
And sincere humble Servant,
Edward Stanley[7] (76)

Crowder's *Letter-Writer* uses many of the same words and phrases as Hill, but he makes small stylistic changes that give the letter a simpler and more modern, colloquial style and easy, mellifluous tone. If one were not actually comparing the two, one might even think it was the same letter. But Hill's central points have been quietly left out. Where Hill's elder brother wishes his sibling to "thrive both in Wealth and Reputation," and to "add to the Reputation of our Family, and gain to yourself a

---

7 Quotations are from the 1768 edition.

good Esteem," Crowder's elder brother only recommends that he seek "the good Esteem of being virtuous and diligent." Where wealth in Hill's letter suggested success in trade, here the goal of the young man's diligence is left obscure. Praise is given instead to good nature (emphasized by the paragraphing and capitals), which had begun to replace what Maria Edgeworth would call "humbling himself in all the hypocrisy of politeness"[8] as the key virtue in eighteenth-century representations of masculine good-breeding.

Crowder's *Letter-Writer* does not get more specific about work-a-day goals in the "Letter from a Father to his a Son just beginning in the World," which follows two pages later. Crowder substitutes the following letter of Richardson's for Hill's "Letter of Advice from a Father to a Son" which recommended the Protestant ethic and paternal help and supervision (above, p. 113):

Dear Billy,

As you are now beginning Life, as it were, and will probably have considerable Dealings in your Business, the frequent Occasions you will have for Advice from others, will make you desirous of singling out among your most intimate Acquaintance one or two whom you would view in the Light of Friends.

In the Choice of these, your utmost Care and Caution will be necessary; for by a Mistake here, you can scarcely conceive the fatal Effects you may hereafter experience. Wherefore it will be proper for you to make a Judgment of those who are fit to be your Advisers by the Conduct they have observed in their *own Affairs*, and the *Reputation* they bear in the World. For he who has by his own Indiscretions undone himself, is much fitter to be set up as a Landmark for a prudent Mariner who shuns his Courses, than an Example to follow . . .

Let your Endeavours therefore be, at all Adventures, to consort yourself with Men of Sobriety, good Sense and Virtue; for the Proverb is an unerring one, that says *A Man is known by the Company he keeps*. If such men you can single out, while you improve by their Conversation, you will benefit by their Advice; and be sure to remember one Thing, that tho' you must be frank and unreserved in delivering your Sentiments when Occasions offer, yet that you be much readier to hear than to speak; for to this Purpose it has been significantly observed that Nature has given a Man two Ears, and but one Tongue. Lay in therefore by Observation and a modest Silence, such a Store of Ideas, that you may, at their Time of Life, make no worse Figure than they do; and endeavour to benefit yourself rather by other People's Ills than your own. How must those young Men expose themselves to the Contempt and Ridicule of their Seniors, who, having seen little or nothing of the World, are continually shutting out by open Mouths

8 Edgeworth, *Patronage*, 8.

and closed Ears, all Possibility of instruction, and making vain the principal End of Conversation, which is Improvement! A silent young Man makes generally a wise old one, and never fails of being respected by the best and most prudent Men. When therefore you come among Strangers, hear everyone speak before you deliver your own Sentiments; by this Means you will judge of the Merit and Capacities of your Company, and avoid exposing yourself. . . .

I have thrown together, as they occurred, a few Thoughts, which may suffice for the present, to shew my Care and Concern for your Welfare. I hope you will constantly, from Time to Time, communicate to me whatever you may think worthy of my Notice, or in which my Advice may be of Use to you; for I have no Pleasure in this Life equal to that which the Happiness of my Children gives me. And of this you may be assured; for I am and ever must be,

Your affectionate father. (81–2)

This letter shows what Crowder meant in the elder brother letter above by adding the phrase: "As you are now gone from home." For it tells the young man to look to older, successful men *outside* his own family for advice, instruction and aid. This is a function of Crowder's recontextualization, and not representative of Richardson's Letter-Miscellany as a whole, which portrayed fathers and uncles not only as the advisors and instructors of young men, but also as their supervisors, rebukers, punishers and necessary backers long after they had left home, just as Hill had done. Denuded of Richardson's context of letters of advice from fathers and uncles, the above letter suggests that for a young man, leaving home means leaving the tutelage and control of his father, whose role is reduced to "throw[ing] together" a few thoughts in a letter to demonstrate his "Care," and to wishing to hear (in letters) of the happiness of his children.

Richardson's "Letter from a Father to a Young Beginner in the World" also shifts men's courtship of other men into yet another cultural register. Rather than using eloquence to flatter and capture the benevolence of men who could be useful or dangerous to him with professions of love, admiration and service, the young man is told to use a respectful and attentive silence to achieve the same end. Rather than seeking favor and proximity to power, he is told to seek information, the means of improving himself, and reputation through the social status of the company he keeps. The character of conversation has shifted too. The idea, which was still important in Steele's characterization of the "man of conversation" in *The Tatler*, that polite conversation requires everyone to speak and contribute to the information and entertainment of the company, and that only boors and bores hold the floor for long, is replaced here by the idea that the goal of conversation is to improve oneself and to benefit from what others say, while saying as little as possible oneself. The young man is also told to be as guarded as possible when he does speak to avoid ridicule, embarrassment, shame or contempt.

The idea of leaving home and the tutelage of fathers or uncles, and of learning to please other older men in order to achieve success and higher social status, is reinforced in Crowder's *Letter-Writer* by yet another rewrite of the elder brother letter, by Charles Hallifax this time, which appears within a page or two of the father's letter of advice:

From an elder Brother in the Country to his younger Brother put Apprentice in London

Dear Brother,

I am very glad to hear you are pleased with the new Situation into which the Care of your Friends has put to you; but I would have you pleased not with the Novelty of it, but with the real Advantage. It is natural for you to be glad that you are under less Restraint than you were, for a Master neither has occasion nor Inclination to watch a Youth, so much as his Parents: but if you are not careful, this, although it now gives you a childish Satisfaction, may, in the End, betray you into Mischief; nay, to your Ruin. Though your father is not in Sight, dear Brother, act always as if you were in his Presence; and be assured that what would not offend him, will never displease any Body. . .

I would have your Reason as well as your Fancy pleased with your new Situation, and then you will act as becomes you. Consider, Brother, that the State of Life that charms you so at this Time, will bring you to Independence and Affluence; that you will, by behaving as you ought now, become Master of a House and Family, and have every Thing about you at your Command, and have Apprentices as well as Servants to wait upon you. The Master with whom you are placed was some Years ago in your Situation: and what should hinder you from being hereafter in his? All that is required, is Patience and Industry; and these, Brother, are very cheap Articles, with which to purchase so comfortable a Condition.

Your Master, I am told, had nothing to begin the World withal: In that he was worse than you; for if you behave well, there are those who will set you up in a handsome Manner. So you have sufficient Inducements to be good, and a Reward always follows it. Brother, farewell! Obey your Master, and be civil to all Persons; keep out of Company, for Boys have no Occasion for it, and most that you will meet with is very bad. Be careful and honest, and God will bless you. If ever you commit a Fault confess it at once; for the Lie in denying it is worse than the Thing itself. Go to Church constantly; and write to us often. I think I need not say more to so good a Lad as you, to induce you to continue so.

I am your affectionate Brother. (79–80)

By the middle of the eighteenth century, complaints were rife that masters were no longer doing their duty by their apprentices, either in teaching them their trade or in treating them as part of their families, and that apprentices were impudent, idle, careless and apt to run away. There is therefore an element of bribery, as well as a plea to consider his long term "advantage," in the injunction to this apprenticed brother to be civil, careful, honest, obedient to his Master and restrained in his use of his new-found freedom from his Father, in order to gain what his Master and his Father already have: independence, affluence, and a household-family in which to have "everything about [him] at [his] Command, and apprentices and servants to wait on [him]." But along with the carrot of supplanting fathers and masters in the household for the pleasure of rotating into the place of power, comes a notion of a man's movement towards independence and freedom from his family of origin that is new in manual representations of the household-family. This is reinforced by using the brother, rather than the father, uncle or master, to advise, instruct and rebuke his sibling. The increased focus on the elder brother here, and again in Dilworth's *Complete Letter-Writer*, derives from the influence of Hallifax on both. Hallifax banished the father and the uncle, to begin his *Familiar Letters* with a long correspondence about letter-writing and conduct, in which a mother tells a younger brother to follow his elder brother's advice and example in all things. This move recalls the revolutionary shift to fraternal relations discussed in Jay Fliegelman's *Prodigals and Pilgrims*.

Crowder made self-reflexive meditation on epistolary styles and practices an ongoing theme of the entire manual and added a new concern with descriptive and narrative letters of news or intelligence.

The elder brother launches *The Complete Letter-Writer*'s self-reflexive letter-writing theme in Crowder's opening or anchoring letter. This letter was Hallifax's rewrite of Hill's letter from a youth to his sister (above, p. 138), now openly represented as a letter of complaint or rebuke:

From a Brother at Home, to his Sister, Abroad on a Visit, complaining of her not writing

Dear Sister,

    I must acquaint you how unkind 'tis taken by every Body here, that we so seldom hear from you; my Mother in particular, is not a little displeased, and says, you are a very idle Girl; my Aunt is of the same Opinion, and none but myself endeavour to find Excuses for you; but I beg you will give me that Trouble no more, and, for the future, take Care to deserve no Rebuke, which you may easily do by writing soon and often. You are very sensible how dear you are to us all, think then with yourself, whether it be right to omit giving us the only Satisfaction that Absence affords to real Friends, which is often to hear from one another.

    Our best Respects to Mr. and Mrs. Herbert, and Compliments to all Friends,
From your very affectionate Brother, T. C.

The sister's answer describes writing letters as her "duty" to her family and promises to "write to Mamma by the next post," in the first of several references to this institution. This letter opens onto letters dispersed throughout the collection about the style of letters and conduct of correspondence. Most of these are likewise addressed to the sister since they occur in women's correspondences and/or deal with women's epistolary style. The few that are not by, to or about women's epistolary writing, are addressed to boys at school or university.

The schoolboy letters stress the importance of education for gentility.[9] Schoolboys are told that "Boys who do not mind their Learning, will never become Gentlemen, and will be laughed at for their Ignorance, though they have ever so much Money" (52) or that "Learning, properly cultivated and applied, is what truly makes the Gentleman" (53). Here again, shame and fear of ridicule are invoked to motivate boys to learn to be gentlemen, and to prescribe the proper attitude towards those who, despite their wealth, are "ignorant" of gentlemen's books and conduct. The elimination of all business letters except those bearing on loans or payments in later editions, together with excision of Hill's goal of seeking "Wealth and Reputation," supports the emphasis in this *Polite* English Letter-Writer on learning norms of polite conduct in order to ingratiate oneself with others.

To develop this theme with specific reference to epistolary practice, there is a letter from a talking and letter-writing bird, "Robin Redbreast in the Garden, to Master Billy Careless, abroad at School," expressing horror at a carelessly written letter Master Billy sent home, and informing the boy that:

No one should ever write to his Pappa, or Mamma without beginning his Letter with *Honoured Sir*, or *Honoured Madam*, and at the same Time not forget to observe, through his whole Epistle, the most perfect Obedience, in a very obliging, respectful Manner. By these Means, you may not only increase your

---

9 In the earliest versions of Crowder's *Letter-Writer*, schoolboy and apprentice letters, maidservant and young lady letters, were repeatedly paired as the collection moved from school and service or apprenticeships to business, courtship and marriage, and thence to adult concerns. By 1768, however, most of the business letters had been cut out, and the maidservant and apprentice letters severely trimmed.

Pappa's Affection, but obtain almost any Thing from him, that you can reasonably ask, provided it be proper and in his Power to grant; what can any good Boy desire more? (69)

Recommending that a boy write letters that profess the most perfect obedience and respect to his parents for the purpose of getting what he wants, is a cynically utilitarian approach to politeness. It is reinforced by the recommendation that the boy never foolishly neglect his mamma, since she has "so gained the Ascendant of your Pappa, that he does nothing relating to any of you without her Consent and Approbation; so that in gaining her Esteem, you are almost certain of his" (69). In this strange *reprise* of the maidservant's strategy with the mistress to whom she had been maligned in Hill's collection (above, p. 118), the weaker party is empowered not only by assuming a feigned and exaggerated posture of submission and respect, but also by correctly assessing the dynamics of power among those who have power over him before making any epistolary moves. There are also echoes here of the courtly practice of approaching the king's mistress to obtain a benefit or post from him.

A course of education for girls from the age of fourteen is laid out by means of a mother's letter of advice culled from Eliza Haywood's *Epistles*, which instructs her to read books of history, geography and science (at home, alone and without a tutor) every day and to reflect carefully upon them. A large part of this letter is devoted to teaching girls how to read and reflect upon such texts. When young women are then shown in this collection writing to each other "on the present Letter-Writers," and on their "Opinion of a well-wrote Letter" or "on the Expressions and Compliments commonly made Use of in Letters," they are shown reflecting upon their reading, and improving each other by their reflections. "Miss J's" letter to "Miss L" about letter-writing is about her reading of Pope and Wycherley, whose letters were frequently used as models in English letter manuals and in collections of letters by eminent persons at mid-century. These letters between Miss J[ones] and Miss L[ovelace] were real letters culled from *Select Collection of the most Original Letters written by eminent Persons* (1755):[10]

... But the most universal Complaint among Scribblers of my Rank, is, Want of Sense. These [Letters] generally begin with an Apology for their long Silence, and end with that moving Petition, Excuse this Nonsense. This is modest, indeed;

---

10 Vol. II: 231ff.

but though I'm excessive good-natur'd, I'm resolved for the future not to pardon it entirely in any one but myself.

I have often thought there never was a Letter wrote well, but what was wrote easily; and if I had not some private Reasons for being of a contrary Opinion at this Time, should conclude this to be a Master Piece of the Kind, both in Easiness of Thought and Facility of Expression. And in this Easiness of Writing (which Mr Wycherley says, is easily wrote) methinks I excel even Mr. Pope himself; who is often too elaborate and ornamental, even in some of his best Letters. . .(85)

Facility of expression is here identified not with eloquence or practiced rhetorical skill but, on the contrary, with prose that demonstrates its colloquial character through its rhythms, its use of idiomatic phrases ("excessive good-natur'd" "there never was a Letter wrote well, but what was wrote"), its contractions ("I'm. . .I'm"), its merriment, and its directness. Despite some falling off in the second paragraph, this is a letter seeking to become "silent speech" by representing on the page through its "easiness of writing" the way the writer might speak to her addressee if she were present. Miss J's condemnation of the elaborate and ornamental style of epistolary writing is taken up again in another letter to "Miss L" which ridicules the way "We Geniuses are forced to vary our Expressions and invent new Terms" to show "our great Command of Language" (88). The writer mocks this practice by offering absurd alternatives to everyday expressions and showing that the complimentary "Forms, which most People are sick of, and yet surfeit their Friends with" at the end or peroration of their letters, scarcely admit of variation (88). Declaring herself "sick of saying for ever, I beg my Compliments to such a one," she boasts of varying this expression by sometimes *communicating* her compliments, sometimes *desiring they may be made known,* and sometimes employing "the laconic Stile of – *my Deferences as usual*" (89).

In the context of the collection as a whole, these letters are negative examples. They are later mocked in a "Letter in the Style of a Lady by Mr. Pope," which ridicules what could happen to letters in the hands of a self-educated young girl, who had perhaps pursued Eliza Haywood's course of education, and who took literally the injunction to write as she would talk:

Pray what is your Opinion of Fate? For I must confess, I am one of those that believe in Fate and Predestination–No, I can't go so far as that; but, I own, I am of Opinion one's Stars may incline, tho' not compel one; and that is a Sort of Freewill; for we may be able to resist Inclination, but not Compulsion.

Don't you think they have got into the most preposterous Fashion this Winter that ever was of flouncing the Petticoat so very deep, that it looks like an entire Coat of Lutestring? It is a little cool indeed for this Time of the Year, but then, my Dear, you'll allow it has an extream clean pretty Look. . .

Well, now I'll swear Child you have put me in mind of a very pretty Dress; let me die if I don't think a Muslin Flounce made very full, would give one a very agreeable Flirtatious Air. Well I swear it would be charming!. . .Do you think there are any such things as Spirits? Do you believe there is such Place as the Elysian Fields? O Gad that would be charming! I wish I were to go to the Elysian Fields when I die. . .(186)

This farrago of non-sequiturs and colloquialisms, and of flighty fashion mixed with half digested learning, brings a young lady no credit. The female reader would clearly do better to pay close attention to the "useful Hints in regard to writing Letters" which appear in a Letter from Bishop Atterbury to his Son that begins the letters of advice in the manual's third section.[11] Atterbury, who is returning a letter his son sent him from Oxford with critical comments about his epistolary style, instructs his son to "consider what you write, and to whom, and let nothing tho' of a trifling Nature, pass through your Pen negligently." His detailed criticism, designed to help the boy "get in the Way of writing correctly and justly," demonstrates that the way to ensure that "the Turn of them" is always "natural and easy" enough to make them appear "an Image of private and familiar Conversation," is to reread and rewrite one's letters with a critical eye, rather than to emit private and familiar conversation spontaneously onto the page as the young lady in Pope's letter has done (151). The patriarchal sub-text here appears to be that a girl should learn to write letters not from her friend or her mother, but from men like Bishop Atterbury, and her epistolary older brother in Crowder's *Letter-Writer*. But the function of this letter in the collection is clearly to encourage careful rereading of the letters for the improvement of style which follow.

Crowder's *Letter-Writer* dealt with the problem of "Want of Sense" in letters not only as earlier manuals had done, by supplying "Samples to write by" that showed what one should say on each occasion, but also by indicating the kinds of *subjects* writers could write about in a species of letter that had barely featured in earlier *Secretaries* and *Companions*: letters of advice, news or intelligence that were neither purely personal nor

---

11 This was a popular and much reprinted letter, despite or perhaps because of, the fact that Atterbury was banished from England as a convicted Jacobite.

commercial in nature. Descriptive and narrative letters of news or intelligence were designed to give "the only Satisfaction that Absence affords real Friends, which is often to hear from one another," as the elder brother put it in Crowder's opening letter (50). Here absence is neither something to be encouraged for the purposes of work or mercantile advantage, nor something to be bemoaned as flattering evidence of one's love or eternal friendship, nor even something to be cheerfully endured by those left at home. It is something to be filled with letters that convey the writer's conversation about his or her perceptions, thoughts or experiences elsewhere, in order to give family and friends back home the satisfaction of hearing him or her converse on paper.

A letter "To Mr.——," removed from the London edition of 1768 but put back in the manual's Scottish and American versions, demonstrates how letters of news were designed to supply the want of sense in letters of Complement, while playing many of the same roles in friendships between men:[12]

To Mr.——

Tunbridge, August 4, 1758

I think I promised you a Letter from this Place; yet I have nothing more material to write than I got safe hither. To any other Man I should make an Apology for troubling him with an Information so trivial; but among true Friends there is nothing indifferent, and what would seem of no Consequence to others, has, in Intercourse of this Nature, its Weight and Value. . . . I have often wondered what odd Whim could first induce the Healthy to follow the Sick into Places of this Sort, and lay the Scene of their Diversions amidst the most wretched Part of our Species: One should imagine an Hospital the last Spot in the World, to which those in Pursuit of Pleasure would think of resorting. However, so it is; and by these Means the Company here furnish out a Tragi-Comedy of the most singular Kind. While some are literally dying, others are expiring in Metaphor: and in one Scene you are presented with the real, and in another with the fantastical Pains of Mankind. An ignorant Spectator might be apt to suspect that each Party was endeavouring to qualify itself for acting in the opposite Character: For the Infirm cannot labour more earnestly to recover the Strength they have lost, than the Robust to destroy that which they possess. Thus the Diseased pass not more anxious Nights in their Beds, than the Healthy at the Hazard Tables; and I frequently see a Game at Quadrille occasion as severe Disquietudes as a Fit of the Gout. As for myself, I perform a Sort of middle Part in this motley Drama, and am sometimes disposed to join with the Invalids in envying the Healthy, and sometimes have Spirits enough to mix with the Gay in pitying the Splenetic. The

---

12 Culled from Newbery's *Letters*, 102, apparently by Dr. Garth.

Truth is, I have found some Benefit by the Waters; but I shall not be so sanguine as to pronounce with Certainty of their Effects, 'till I seee how they enable me to pass thro' the approaching Winter. That Season, you know, is the Time of Trial with me. . .

But let Time and Seasons operate as they may, there is one Part of me, over which they will have no Power; and in all the Changes of this uncertain Constitution, my Heart will ever continue fixed and firmly yours.

I am etc. (71–2)

This letter preserves the traces of its complemental origins in its exordium and peroration. The exordium indicates the letter's complemental function by turning the very writing and reception of the letter into a reminder and reenactment of the two men's exceptional friendship. While demonstrating the writer's politeness, the apology about the trivial information that it will contain, compliments and flatters his addressee: the latter is constructed as the privileged recipient of such information, because he has the character and delicacy to appreciate the nature of the offering, and to understand that the writer is in reality writing only to be able to write to his friend. The apology is thus a graceful variation on a standard opening to complemental letters: "I honour you more than all the rest of the world." The peroration in the last paragraph is likewise a variation of the complemental letter's assurance that "I am unfeignedly in heart and soul. . .yours" and of its expression of "the Resolution which I have taken to be all my life, Your most humble Servant."[13]

At the same time, this letter adds sense to the empty and repetitive complemental forms by introducing something new, informative, entertaining or amusing in the body of the letter, to remind the addressee of the pleasure he has taken in the writer's conversation. Despite the apparent colloquialism of such expressions as "I think I promised you" or "The Truth is," and the "Image of private and familiar Conversation" that is created, there is nothing idiomatic, no contraction, and little of the rhythms of everyday speech in this prose. The body of the letter consists of an extended figure (the spa as a tragi-comical theatrical scene with the writer as its spectator) which is developed and amplified by means of the eighteenth century's favorite schemes of antithesis and paradox (the healthy as opposed to the sick, and the sick who pretend to be well, as opposed to the well who make themselves sick). This is therefore not a letter that could have been written without rhetorical schooling, or in which "Things tho' of a trifling nature" have passed "negligently through

13 *Secretary in Fashion*, 2, 3, 12.

the pen." It may sound as if the writer were simply conversing with his friend, but he does so in the manner that John Constable praised when he observed that "the greatest art of expression consists in the judicious choice and application of the most ordinary terms" and that "Art is never greater than when you cannot distinguish it from Nature."[14]

Letters demonstrating the proper descriptive and narrative techniques for conveying perceptions and experiences in letters of news or intelligence were clustered in the last section of "Letters for the Improvement of Style." These more literary letters demonstrated how to tell a local anecdote; describe and reflect upon manners in foreign places or in the country; narrate battles, an execution at Tyburn, or a failed romantic encounter; describe a woman's dress and conduct at a ball; or compare the entertainments available in town and in the country. As one young lady points out, such "News [was] the Life of Correspondence" (210). Particularly interesting from a transatlantic perspective is Eliza Haywood's letter "From a Young Lady in one of the Canary islands, to her sister in England, whom she had never seen; containing a pressing Invitation to her to come over, and describing the Beauties of the Place in order to prevail on her." This "mixed letter" marries the letter of advice and letter of invitation to a descriptive letter of news from "beyond the sea," while transforming the latter into a political meditation and justification for migrating to the New World. Since it is long, I will cut part of the complemental exordium and peroration, and some of the rhetorical amplification:

Must we for ever, my dear Sister, converse only at this unhappy Distance? – Are we born of the same parents, to be eternal Aliens to each other – I have been told Wonders of your Wit, Ingenuity and Good-Nature – Must Strangers, or at least very distant Kindred, reap all the Benefit of these amiable Qualities, while those who are nearest, and ought, methinks, to be dearest mourn the Want of it. . . . What can withhold you from coming to a Place where your Presence is so ardently desired? – What can you find so pleasing to you in a Kingdom rent with internal Divisions? – Where Father against Son, and Brother against Brother, maintain an unnatural Contest! – A Kingdom, where Pride, Injustice, Luxury and Profaneness, are almost universal, and Religion become a Reproach to the Profession! – A Kingdom sinking by swift Degrees into Misery and Contempt, yet infatuated so far as to doat on the Cause of their Undoing – At least this is the Account we have of it . . . O, my dearest sister, listen to the Dictates of Reason, of Duty, and of Nature, all join to call you from that worse than *Egypt* into the Land of *Canaan* – Here Peace and Innocence go Hand in Hand, and all

---

14　Constable, *Reflections upon Accuracy of Style*, 55.

the Graces, all the Pleasures, wait upon their Steps – No foreign Wars, no home-bred Jars, no Envy, no Distrust, disturb the soft Serenity of these blissful Seats, but all is Harmony and Love – Eternal Zephyrs watch our Morning Wakings, bringing ten thousand Odours on their Wings, and tempt us to the Groves from whence they spring – In Troops we wander through the *Jessamine* Lands, or sit in *Orange Bowers,* where Fruits, ripe and in Blossom charm our smell and Taste. . . . But there is no describing Half the various Sweets which Nature, with a lavish Hand, pours on these Isles, which justly have the name of *Fortunate!* Nor (I flatter myself) will there be any Need of farther Arguments, to bring you to us: – my Father has just now informed me, that Captain——carries his positive Orders for your coming, and I may now rest in an assured Hope of enjoying the Happiness I so long, and so earnestly have wished. . .(152–4)

One can imagine this letter being heard in Britain as an echo of emigration tracts, and of the real and fictitious letters from settlers beyond the sea inviting their families to join them that were frequently printed in eighteenth-century newspapers. One can also imagine it being heard in the American provinces during the 1760s and 1770s as a confirmation of the view of Britain as a corrupt, unjust and divided country, that was increasingly promulgated as revolution approached. There is irony in Haywood's contrast between the freedom the writer promises her sister to roam at will among the sweets of the *fortunate* isles and the letter written to try to reconcile her to a father's "positive Orders for your coming." Clearly, being bound to obey their father against their will, follows daughters from Egypt into Canaan.

Crowder's *Letter-Writer* was more geared to women's interests and concerns than earlier *Secretaries* and *Companions* overall, and it offered what amounted to a conduct book on courtship and marriage in its second section. But this combined letters from Richardson and Hallifax to construct ideals of courtship and marriage that were sternly patriarchal. In these letters, young ladies do not permit their heads to be turned by young men who entertain them with complemental letters and address them as goddesses. With monotonous regularity, they refer their suitors to their fathers for decisions about courtship and marriage (or if they are orphans, to their aunts). They demonstrate their obedience to paternal commands regardless of their own wishes. Men ask women's fathers for permission to court them, or write to aunts to intercede for them. If a man writes directly to a woman, she refers him to her father or to a relation. In one instance where a woman is shown actually answering a suitor herself, she demonstrates her good sense by forcing him to declare that marriage is his goal before she will even consider meeting him. Women are repeatedly told to suspect men of trying to deceive them, while fathers, mothers and aunts inquire into the character, credit and financial situation of young men before agreeing to allow them to approach their charges. Young men are also careful to allude to their finances in proposing themselves as suitors. For men, courtship and marriage are therefore presented as rewards for success and reputation in the world of men, and for approaching a woman as he ought. A "discrete man" declares his "passion" in the following prudent style:

Dear Madam,

Now I have the Hope of being not more despised for my acknowledged Affection, I declare to you with all the Sincerity of a Man of Honour, that I have long had a most sincere Passion for you; but I have seen Gentlemen led such Dances, when they have given up their Affections to the lovely Tyrants of their Hearts, and could not help themselves, that I had no Courage to begin an Address in the usual Forms, even to you, of whose good Sense and Generosity I nevertheless had a good Opinion. You have favoured me with a few Lines, which I most kindly thank you for. And I do assure you, Madam, if you will be pleased to encourage my honourable Suit, you shall have so just an Account of my Circumstances and Pretensions, as I hope will intitle me to your Favour in the honourable Light in which I profess myself, dear Madam,

Your most obliged and faithful Admirer

Be so good as to favour me with one Line more to encourage my personal Attendance, if not disagreeable. (114–15)

In answer, the woman demonstrates her good sense (but perhaps not her generosity) by referring him to her man of business, to get a "just Account of [his] Circumstances and Pretensions" before she will consider encouraging his suit.

These letters condemn coquetry as well as the use of letters of complement in wooing. Courtship is practical, earnest and absolutely no fun: a young woman who complains about a solemn suitor who insists on sermonizing at every opportunity and on holding forth about his good works, is severely reproved for levity by her aunt. A young woman who has inadvertently made her fiancé jealous by talking to another man in company one day, apologizes to him for "the gaiety of my Temper" and promises to "get the better of it." Another young woman who has done the same receives a letter from her fiancé accusing her of inconstancy and terminating the engagement. Courtship is therefore not represented, as it often was by women novelists, as the one time in a woman's life when she could enjoy some power, have a multitude of men at her feet, and select among her suitors. On the contrary. "Coquetry" – here meaning any conversation with another man even in an innocent social situation – is severely proscribed; and "propriety of character" precludes a young woman from seeking any pleasures or diversions in mixed company at all.

Significantly after the Marriage Act of 1753, what Crowder offered in place of the fashionable English marriage of convenience in which each partner was permitted to go their own way and seek their own diversions, is a highly idyllic representation of married togetherness in a pastoral surround.[15] Using letters taken from Haywood and Lady Mary Wortley Montagu, Crowder's compilation offers a vision of hymen in which, as Lady Mary puts it, "Marriage is not like those of Ambition and Interest: it is two Lovers who live together. . .and have the Pleasure of forming the entire Happiness of the Object beloved. . ."(130). Between such a husband and wife, power and duty have no place, for each seeks only to serve and delight the other, she by carefully preparing repasts for his reception, he by distinguishing himself in the public sphere for her sake. Lady Mary admits that such "married lovers" scarcely exist in English life; but in the context provided by the manual, the remark is overshadowed by her extensive, poetic portrayal of the idyll.

Crowder edited and almost completely reworded Lady Mary's letter,[16] as he reworded and altered letters borrowed from Hill and others, to give it his preferred style and clarify the meaning he wished it to have. This did not prevent him from attributing the letter to Lady Mary, and using her name to further his goals by allowing the context created by his choice and sequence of letters in the compilation to create for this letter a meaning that it might not otherwise have. For instance, an actual friend and correspondent of Lady Mary's, who knew that Lady Mary had eloped in quest of the marital idyll she describes only to bitterly discover that it had eluded her, might read this letter as seeking reasons in the mores and morals of her society to explain her own failure to achieve the dream of her youth. In Crowder's compilation, however, Lady Mary's idyll of married lovers appears quite insidiously as the backdrop to a letter from a husband, entitled "To Lucinda, on the happiness of a Domestic Life." This man tells his wife that he could have been a good husband to any number of different women; he is happy he chose her only because she has remained in the country well away from other men and from the temptations of the town for over

15 Bannet, "Marriage Act."
16 Lady Mary's letter, "Concerning M. De la Rochefoucault's Maxim. . .," appears in *An Additional Volume*, 79.

twenty years, has invariably demonstrated an "amiable Disposition," and has proved her virtue by devoting herself exclusively to him and to their children. Turning wives into a convenience for husbands is not what Lady Mary had in mind. But the presence of her letter, and the affectionate tone of Lucinda's husband's letter, suggest that these too may be "married Lovers" in the privacy of their country home, and that a woman conducting herself as Lucinda has done might be able to live Lady Mary's dream.

Only two letters in Crowder's compilation disrupt the portrait of courtship and marriage I have described, and they are designed as humorous or ironical polar opposites. One is a lively letter from a young woman advising her friend to marry an old man for his money and the access to high life marriage to him would afford, the other a representation of the matriarchal feminist position about women's proper place in the household, called *Domestic Rule the Province of the Wife.*[17] Scottish and American printers prudently left this out, even after the American War of Independence had proved women's abilities to govern households (and farms, plantations or estates) when men had gone to war.

GLASGOW: DILWORTH'S COMPLETE LETTER-WRITER, OR YOUNG SECRETARY'S INSTRUCTOR

Dilworth's manual was an abridgement of Charles Hallifax's *Familiar Letters on Various Subjects of Business and Amusement* (1754) to which were added some letters from Richardson's Letter-Miscellany, and a few letters from Goodman and Hill. Dilworth's manual was printed only once in London, in 1758, under the title *The Familiar Letter Writer or Young Secretary's Instructor.* Peter Tait's Scottish abridgement apparently relaunched it in 1783. After that, its history became entirely provincial, with several editions of the manual appearing under its new Scottish title, *The Complete Letter-Writer, or Young Secretary's Instructor,* in Glasgow after 1783 and in New York during the mid-1790s. There was also a short New York edition in 1775 and a late New Haven edition in 1809. If this manual had a history between 1758 and 1775, it is now lost to us. The New York editions of the 1790s all worked from the Glasgow version of 1783, usually adapting it to American needs by adding letters at the end. Because Dilworth's compilation had no impact in England,

17 Bannet, *Domestic Revolution.*

but was a fairly important influence in the provinces, the focus in this section and the next will be on the Scottish and American versions of Dilworth's manual. I will be calling Peter Tait's Glasgow abridgement "Dilworth."

Dilworth's and Crowder's *Letter-Writers* shared some of the same letters, because the initial compilers of both manuals selected letters from Hallifax and Richardson, and because American printers seeking to supplement Dilworth's lacks often borrowed additional letters from Crowder's *Letter-Writer*. The two manuals have sometimes been mistaken for one another as a result. The change of title in the provinces suggests that provincial printers saw Dilworth's *Letter-Writer* as an alternative or rival to Crowder's. In their hands, it certainly met different needs. The provincial Dilworth was more focused on the world of work and less concerned with issues of politeness than Crowder. Nor did it emulate Crowder's manual in emphasizing self-consciousness about letter-writing and the improvement of style. Dilworth had no subject sections, and folded letters of morality into household-family and courtship letters in the guise of letters of advice, as the older *Secretaries* had done. It also explicitly included a lower-class audience.

Tait's Glasgow edition of Dilworth's *Letter-Writer* cut out all letters relating to the nobility, to placement in government or court posts, and to the social life of the leisured classes, to produce a manual that was directed, as Boston versions of English *Secretaries* had been during the earlier eighteenth century, essentially to the urban trading and commercial classes. However, it also explicitly addressed the mechanic, artisanal and manufacturing classes in some letters. Upward social mobility was a preoccupation in all versions of this manual, but there are differences between different provincial versions, which largely relate to their printers' different sense of what kind of guidance in commercial writing, how much instruction on gentility, and how many courtship letters their local markets required. The Glasgow version generally offered fewer business letters, fewer courtship letters, and less focus on gentility than American ones did, but included letters of recommendation for servants, and letters on the subject of local elections that American versions often cut out.

The Glasgow Dilworth opened with schoolboy letters borrowed from Hill and Goodman, followed by a new letter from a schoolboy beyond the sea to his father in England, which begins, as many real transatlantic letters at the time did, by noting that this was the sixth letter the boy had sent by diverse ships without evidence that any of them had reached their destination.[18] The importance of sending children away to a school, rather than training them at home in a father's mechanick or artisanal trade in the old-fashioned way (or, by extension, apprenticing them to an artisan without formal schooling), is explained in a "Letter to a Father on his Neglect of his Children's Education." This letter stresses that illiterate young men will now "only be fit for mean and sordid employments" and be confined throughout their life "to the drudgery of their own servile station, . . .entitled to neither honour and respect" (93). Fathers are advised to give their sons formal schooling in penmanship, accounts and letter-writing because this would teach them to "converse or correspond with those whose acquaintance is most worth their while to cultivate," and was now absolutely requisite in London to get "a comfortable and genteel support in some mercantile compting house or in some one of the several offices about this great metropolis, as book-keepers, clerks, accomptants etc" (93). Schooling – or rather the "English" school – is therefore presented to fathers and their sons as the way to rise out of the mechanick and artisanal classes into the more genteel and respected ranks of traders and merchants or even into the lower reaches of government bureaucracy.

Consonant with this destination for young people and manual buyers, Dilworth included large numbers of letters of advice bearing on the conduct of apprentices and even larger numbers of letters of advice bearing on the proper conduct of a business. Dilworth reprinted Hallifax's letter "From an elder Brother in the Country to his Younger Brother put Apprentice in London" and Richardson's "Letter from a Father to a young Beginner what Company to chuse, and how to behave in it" (above, pp. 158 and 156). But return to the *Secretary* tradition of teaching proper conduct through letters of rebuke and reproof from fathers, uncles and even masters, dominates the collection. Here too, the issue of rank is paramount. Dilworth included Richardson's letter "From a Father to a Son on his Negligence in his Affairs," which warns the son against "suffering himself to go backward in the world" and describes the "indignities he is likely to suffer from those whose money he has unthinkingly squandered" (26). He reinforced this with Hallifax's correspondence between an apprentice whose inability to pay for his wife's lying-in obliges him to inform his uncle that he has married without his consent. His uncle's discouraging reply calls his marriage "the only act of disobedience

---

18 See Part III.

that cannot be forgiven" and refuses to have any more to do with him (58). He also reiterates Richardson's warning about the evils of becoming impoverished and losing rank, by telling his nephew that the fact that he has "imprudently" married a woman without family or fortune precludes him from being received amongst them upon his old footing, because "it would be impossible to receive into our families and acquaintance a mean person" (59). The young apprentice's imprudent marriage thus prevents him from rising in the world. One might also say that here snobbery and class consciousness are being, if not created, at least propagated and rammed home, and that they are used to supply the place of morality and religion in other collections as motivating forces for industry, prudence and sexual restraint.

The bulk of the letters of business in this collection develop themes of impoverishment and indignity by addressing issues of debt and failure. There are no letters of advice containing information about trade, no letters ordering goods, no keeping in touch with potential trading partners, in this Glasgow edition – only letters asking for loans, deferring payment of rents, and dealing with the accommodations that had to be made when a trader went bankrupt. Glasgow, which had grown to prominence and wealth on the tobacco trade, had suffered after Britain's loss of America; and this 1783 version of the manual seems to be addressing these losses, not only by presenting a grim scene of business, rife with commercial difficulties, but also by seeking to disseminate methods of mitigating the evils the letters describe.

To this end, the Glasgow compiler included letters insisting on the importance of paying debts on time – "trade is so dependent a thing, that it cannot be carried on without mutual punctuality" (38). He included letters that argued the folly of having bankrupts arrested and thrown into prison, where they would never be in a position to repay what they owed, and the folly of going to law, which cost both time and money and offered no assurance of obtaining material satisfaction. He reprinted letters preaching the virtues of informal accommodations between creditors and debtors, and the advisability of making financial arrangements through an adjustor in which the bankrupt's remaining moving property and outstanding credit was divided up among his creditors at so many shillings a pound. The collection also provided exemplars of all the letters that would have to be written if this course of action were pursued. Another way of responding to bankruptcies is exemplified in a letter in which one trader offers financial assistance to another who "had received great Losses by a Person's Failure." This was a popular letter, which appeared in Hill and in numerous *vade mecums*, because in the interconnected world of eighteenth-century credit, one trader's failure could easily have the domino effect of bringing others, and eventually the whole commercial system of financial interdependence, down. Proffering assistance to a trader whose business was incapable of absorbing the effects of another's bankruptcy, in order to prevent him from failing too, was a sensible way of containing the damage. The compiler also included epistolary exchanges in which a young person in trade requests guidance on debt-related issues from the master to whom he had been apprenticed. The master recommends method in book-keeping, and gives extensive advice about how to avoid getting involved in bad debts in the first place: "Never lend money to your customers," to dubious people, or to those already in your debt, because "one bad debt runs away with the profit of many good ones" (78); but if you have got bad debts on your books, keep on asking for the money you are owed, and be ready to accept it in small payments over time if your debtor is unable to pay what he owes all at once. Here again the emphasis is on keeping people afloat and on keeping the money and credit circulating.

Conciliation is an important theme in this collection, as it was in Hill's *Young Secretary's Guide*, but Dilworth went further than Hill in dismissing the importance of honor in relations between men. Using letters from Hallifax, which reproduce and redefine the triangular situation explored by Serre and Hill, where one man has been insulted by another and honor calls for revenging the insult in a duel (above, pp. 116–17), Dilworth's *Letter-Writer* refashioned the proper manifestation of friendship between men in ways that recall the role of the adjustor in negotiations between bankrupt debtors and their creditors. He included two sequences of letters in which the friend plays the role of a neutral party who prevents a duel or a court case by negotiating a reconciliation between insulter and insulted. Reconciliation is recommended even when the insulting party has spoken the truth about a bad man. In one letter, the friend acknowledges that his addressee's insult was no more than the truth, and observes sympathetically that "People are always nicest about their Characters who have no Characters at all" (83); but he advises him that he would do better to ask the bad man's pardon, even in public, than "be plagued with a law suit that will take up all your time, and cost you heaven knows what into the bargain" (83). This point about staying out of it, or staying in the middle of opposing parties when that fails, is reinforced by a father's letter to a son in trade at the approach of an election, which advises him stay neutral and avoid offending either side.

The fact that Dilworth borrowed so many letters from Hallifax also added to the provincial world of letter manuals some marked differences in style. First, Halifax contributed a new sentimental and lachrymose note to family letters, as well as to letters recommending philanthropy or demonstrating charity. In a letter "To a Mother to thank her for her Care and Tenderness," for instance, a son writes that "the pain with which I saw you part from me on the road has made an impression on my heart, which time will never wear out" (11). His mother replies that "the fullness of my heart prevents my informing you of its sensations," adding that "if you see more blots than this, which is just now made in my writing, do not wonder, or be uneasy. I will not dissemble to you that they are made by tears" (11–12). We are eventually informed that her transports are due to her happiness at having such good sons. Family feeling is expressed in pain and joy, both of which generate tears. In another letter, a boy at school called Billy, who is saved from drowning at the last moment, sends a letter home narrating the event. Unfortunately, his letter arrives after a letter from his schoolmaster informing his parents that he has drowned. In his answer to his son, his father describes how the family read and reacted to the master's letter: "I will not say how much I was affected at opening Mr. Thomson's Letter. Your mother and sister were present, and seeing me lay it down to wipe my eyes, eagerly cast a look upon it, and immediately burst into tears, and the most affecting lamentations" (17). Nothing daunted, Billy shows himself to be as much a man of feeling as his father by informing the latter that he read this account of his family's response to the master's letter "with many Tears" and much concern for the grief he had caused them (18). The uncle mentioned above, who washed his hands of his apprenticed nephew on account of his imprudent marriage, does not cry; but he does speak of his grief, charitably send fifteen guineas to help his nephew pay for his wife's lying-in because "I pity the person you have married," and say "I would not write cruelly to you, for I am inclined to love you tenderly" – before casting him off (58–9). This curious juxtaposition of tenderness and ruthlessness is echoed in the Dilworth compilation as a whole by the juxtaposition of excessive expenditure of emotion in family relations with calculated neutrality or non-involvement in dealings with fellow traders, customers and male friends. This is a new element, and one which novels that focus on sentimental feeling rarely expose; for rather than distinguishing between people according to whether they are "sensible" or unfeeling, this collection suggests that the same people's lives and psyches are split into areas of sensibility and insensibility.

The second stylistic shift that Dilworth's manual absorbed consists of Hallifax's attempts to create an "easy and natural" style that more closely approximated the tones and rhythms of real conversation. Equating rhetorical turns with old-fashioned manuals (i.e. every manual but his own) and eloquence with affectation, Hallifax announced that neither had any place in epistolary writing. In his rewrite of one of Hallifax's letters on letter-writing, which appears in Dilworth as a letter from a mother to her son, Dilworth summed up Hallifax's position thus: "Dear child, take care of your heart, and you may be less uneasy about your expression; let your thoughts be good, and never be uneasy about the words you put them in. . .nor is it a pin matter in the affairs of life, whether you put every word where it should be" (11). What Hallifax considered "a natural and easy manner" of epistolary writing can be seen by contrasting Hallifax's letter of news to a male friend who has gone into the country for the summer, as it appears in Dilworth's *Letter-Writer*, with that which appeared in Crowder's *Complete Letter-Writer* (above, p. 164):

Dear Sir,
   You left me your commands, when you took your leave of us, to write to you once in a fortnight, and give you the news of the town; but you that make the news are gone; and what is there worth your attention among the inconsiderable people that remain here? Shall I write you word the King is gone to Kensington: you know he resolved it before you went; or that the duke is at Windsor; you are as well acquainted with that as I am. Shall I describe to you the new equipage of the princess of Wales; the newspapers have done it already: or if I were inclined to give you the scandal of the people that are left in this desolate place, the pamphleteers have spread that also. The French parliament had bribed Madam de Pompadour on their side; but the king discovered the conspiracy, and he forbade the one his sight, and turned the other out of doors. The clergy were a match for the lay antagonist on this occasion. If only a mistress was to affect the matter, the holy panders did not scruple to do the office; and his most Christian Majesty is at this moment probably, for it is morning though I am writing to you, at rest in the arms of the daughter of an Irish shoemaker. . .
   Mr. Sullen is more than ever out of humour with his wife; but he cannot be more eager to get rid of her than her lover is to get her. The lady will not be long without a protector. It is expected that it will come to this, but when, no mortal can tell. She is agreeable, though she is a baggage; and the husband is in the condition of Prior's thief, who often took leave, but was loth to depart.
   I do not know that there is anything else here to tell you of. As to your friends, you have most of them with you, and the rest are not here. What remains in Grosvenor Street are well. . . .I am apt to believe that we are as much in love with green trees as you are tired of them. With all your boast of ease, and solitude, and retirement, and contemplation, I fancy you would be very glad to change the

scene for bustle and business. . .Dear Sir, I have written, as you will perceive, rather because it was proper I should write, than that I had anything to say. But there is merit in obedience; and when it is your commands, there will always be pleasure also in it, to Your most obedient and humble Servant. (51)

It was clearly difficult for any man who had been brought up on oratory and classical texts to write "easily and naturally" without such traces of eloquence as the series of rhetorical questions linked by *anaphora* or repetition of the same first words that appear in the first paragraph, the "indirect comparison" worked into the literary allusion in the second paragraph,[19] or the antithesis between town and country in the third. Moreover, the complementary conventions remain in force: the graceful variations on "I honour you more than the rest of the world" at the beginning, and on "I am unfeignedly in heart and soul. . .yours" at the end; the bemoaning of the friend's absence in the second half of the first sentence; and in the sentence before last, the variation on the polite apology for writing about trivial matters and on the claim that one is doing so only to be able to write one's friend.

Nevertheless, this letter is somewhat less stylized in structure and expression than the version used in Crowder's *Letter-Writer*. Rather than amplifying a theatrical figure, the body of the letter is organized quite straightforwardly by topics of news – English court, French court, town gossip about Mr. Sullen's *ménage à trois*, news of mutual friends. There are no long periodic sentences, or balanced repetitions of the same thought. Clauses are kept short and snappy, and include fairly colloquial phrases ("you left me your commands," "write to you once a fortnight," "give you the news of the town," etc.). Despite the fact that much of the news given here is court news, it is possible to see this letter being used as a framework for writing other quite ordinary letters of news.

Several of the letters to and from women in Dilworth's *Letter-Writer* come from Richardson, and also appeared in Crowder's *Letter-Writer*. The Glasgow version contained mostly maidservant letters: the maidservant describes her initial homesickness in her new post, receives her mother's advice on the conduct she should adopt there, writes to tell her mother that following her advice has enabled her to settle in very well, and finally asks her father's permission to wed. Also included was Richardson's letter warning maidservants coming up from the country

---

19 An "indirect comparison was a simile" without "like" or "as" that was worked into the sentence without drawing attention to itself as a figure; considered a way of making style appear more natural.

about the dangers of being scooped up on arrival in London by one of the procuresses who haunted the coaching inns; and letters requesting and giving a recommendation for a maidservant who wanted to change her post.

Tait cut out most of the courtship letters in Dilworth's "original" compilation, and this was to prove a significant problem in America. As a group, the few courtship letters that Tait selected – a letter from an exemplarily respectful lover who is too modest to do any courting, that by the prudent young man who shows his wariness of coquettes (above, p. 168), and the letter from the young woman who complains about her sermonizing suitor and is reproved by her aunt for levity – conveyed in a nutshell the same message as Crowder's *Letter-Writer*: seriously negotiating a marriage is a good thing; courtship, with its attendant compliments, flirtation and focus on the power of a woman's beauty, is a bad thing. Tait also included a letter from a young woman jilted for a wealthier prospect, and one from a daughter to a father protesting his decision that she must marry an old man which, upon consideration, make the sermonizing suitor and the one too modest to do any courting look pretty good.

NEW YORK: DILWORTH'S COMPLETE LETTER-WRITER, OR YOUNG SECRETARY'S INSTRUCTOR

American editions of Dilworth's *Letter-Writer* printed in New York for Benjamin Gomez in 1793 and by T. Allen in 1794 reprinted the Glasgow version, but sought to supply its lacks by adding letters at the end.[20] Though not identical with one another, the Gomez and Allen versions both added to the maidservant letters a number of model letters that would be useful to young ladies, such as letters inviting friends to a party or to the country for the summer, or congratulating a friend on her marriage. They also added to the letters of courtship letters culled from Crowder's *Letter-Writer*: the letter from a man withdrawing his suit, and a protracted epistolary negotiation between a young woman trying to rid herself of a suitor her parents commanded her to receive by representing to him all the evils of a marriage without love. The suitor stubbornly

---

20 The earliest extant American edition of Dilworth's *Letter-Writer* printed by Samuel Campbell in 1775 was even more sparing of letters on courtship and marriage than the Glasgow edition would be, Evert Duyckinck's New York version of 1795 almost equally so: Duyckinck added fourteen letters to the Glasgow version, but only one bore on courtship or marriage.

refuses to make himself scarce unless she assures him she is in love with someone else. Most interesting, perhaps, all three American editions of the 1790s added the following ambiguous letter, "From a Lady on the Point of Marriage." This is a heavily edited version of Letter XXIII, in Mary Collyer's *Letters from Felicia to Charlotte* (1755).

Dear Madam,

    Tell me (for you know) if there can be greater pleasure than that which results from the reflection of pleasing a person dearer, infinitely dearer to us, than ourselves. The grateful look, the kindling glance, the expressive glow of tender fondness silently shot from the thankful eye. O can there be a greater reward, to soften the charming toil, if that can be called a toil, that will gladden the heart we love? For this I will read and study to enrich my mind, for this I will dress, for this I will plot new arts to please, while virtue, innocence, and truth shall lead the way, and mark my path to lasting bliss. What delight the distant prospect beams upon my soul! my husband! my friend! dear epithets! – enchanting sounds! – sounds swelling with every thrilling joy – O all gracious Being! May my abilities be equal to the ardor of my soul! may the wife be lost in the friend; the soft, the tender, the generous friend!

    The pleasure I may be supposed to receive from these resolutions, is extremely damped by abundance of intruding fears, that dash my joys, with a mixture of bitterness; I tremble, lest in the unguarded moments of life I should drop the regard I resolve to keep over my temper; lest I should forget to please, or lose the power of doing it. Tho'ts that are always attended with pain.

    You see what a fond unfashionable creature I am grown; but, as your ladyship has given me some reason to believe that you are not less weak than myself, I boldly brave your satire; so that if you make merry with me on this occasion, I shall freely join in the laugh.

    My happiness is now so great, that there seems nothing wanting but the consideration of its being perpetual, to render it complete: nor does my sister's appear less exquisite than mine; we are surrounded with every laughing delight, every social endearment. The congratulations of our friends, the caresses of our parents, the tenderness of our lovers, and the pleasing sympathy in each other's felicity, all heighten to contribute our joy; while rapture itself grows more pleasing, by settling into a serene and most charming tranquility. Everything is preparing for the ceremony that is to unite us for ever to the dearest person on earth; and next Thursday, my sister and I are to be hailed under the title of brides, and initiated into the dignified state of venerable matrons. And, between you and I, Madam, we both heartily which these solemn doings over, for really they have something terrible in them that frightens at a distance.

I am your Ladyship's sincere Friend,
Felicia.

Decontextualized from Collyer's story, this letter performs the same function in these American collections as Lady Mary Wortley Montagu's letter did in Crowder's *Letter-Writer*: it offers an idyll of married happiness, and after letters proscribing the pleasures of coquetry and courtship, suggests that married bliss is the goal to be preferred. But unlike Lady Mary's vision of "married lovers" mutually working to please each other, this letter places the entire burden of achieving "lasting bliss" upon the young bride. She is the one who expects to read and study, to dress, and to plot new arts to please her husband, for the pleasure of a grateful or kindling glance from him; her fear is only that by losing her temper, she will lose him. Read in one way, therefore, this letter lays the foundation for years of effort and guilt, should the bride's "abilities" to attach her husband not be "equal to the ardour of [her] soul." Where Lady Mary's letter projects blame for an unhappy marriage outwards, onto the mores of her society which neither permitted nor promoted marital togetherness, Felicia sees success or failure exclusively as a result of her own performance, and teaches girls who read her letter as exemplary to do the same.

The timing of this letter just before the wedding, together with the reference to her addressee's satirical laughter, also open this letter to a more distanced and cynical reading, which also in some sense represents an answer to Lady Mary's letter. Read through the eyes of her ladyship – the letter's addressee, who is represented as laughing at Felicia's romantic visions of perpetual happiness – the point of the letter is that the highpoint in a young woman's life, her moment of greatest bliss and supreme power, is neither courtship nor marriage, but the moment when she is poised between – after the courtship and before the wedding, when she is the center of attention for family, friends and husband-to-be, and praised and caressed by all. While understanding her unfashionable desire for perpetual bliss in marriage because she has shared it, her Ladyship laughs because can see it for what it is – an innocent young girl's charming, idealistic, but naive dream of love.

These American editions of the 1790s also supplied lacks in the Glasgow Dilworth by adding some letters between siblings, and making substantial additions to the letters of business between men. They suppressed the rather bleak outlook of the Glasgow collection and made issues related to failure less prominent in the collection as a whole, by overshadowing them with letters of trade for thriving businesses, letters thanking friends for kindnesses, and letters congratulating friends on their success. They also retraced some of the outlines of the household-family by representing men in business as having strong supportive relationships with a brother, and being in a position to help their sister.

For many of the business and household letters that they added here, the New York printers turned back to Hill's *Young Secretary's Guide* – for instance, the Letter of Advice to a fellow tradesman who is out of town, and its sequel reappear (above, pp. 114–15), and so does the letter of complaint to a man who maligned him behind his back (above, p. 117). Most significant perhaps in terms of changes in American society since the American manuals of the teens, twenties and thirties is the inclusion after Independence of two letters that colonial American printers had carefully excluded: Hill's still fairly flowery letter of congratulation to a friend on his advancement, written in answer to Serre, and its gentlemanly reply (above, p. 111).

The New York printers of the 1790s tried to supply the Glasgow edition's shortage of models for young ladies, its failure to provide a sufficient number of business letters for thriving or ongoing businesses, and the comparative paucity of letters among members of the household-family. Around the same time, a printer in Philadelphia identified the same lacks in the Glasgow Dilworth; but because he went about supplying them in a different way, he called his version of Dilworth, *The American Letter-Writer*.

PHILADELPHIA: McCULLOCH'S AMERICAN LETTER-WRITER (1793)

The American Letter-Writer, printed by John McCulloch in Philadelphia in 1793, also used Dilworth's *Letter-Writer* as its basic framework. But he turned it into a new compilation with a clear new orientation, by cutting out quite a large number of Dilworth's letters, by reordering letters to create a sequence with a different logic, by clustering letters first by generic character and then by topic, and by liberally adding letters from Crowder's *Complete Letter-Writer* throughout.

McCulloch had no patience with Hallifax's sentimental representations of family feeling, or with his view of what was "natural and easy" in letter-writing. He threw out the "Letter to a Mother to thank her for her Care and Tenderness," the mother's weeping reply, and almost-drowned Billy's multiple lachrymose exchanges with his family, as well as the pitiful letter from the apprentice who had married against his uncle's wishes. Instead of reproducing the idea that epistolary writing did not require anyone to mind too much where they put their words, McCulloch reprinted from Crowder the "useful hints in regard to letter-writing" provided in Bishop Atterbury's letter to his son. McCulloch also clearly approved the Dilworth letter recommending method in business, because he not only reprinted it, but himself set about introducing method and – like his colonial American forbears – implied narrativization, into the letters he chose.

McCulloch clustered schoolboy letters, apprentice letters, schoolgirl letters and maidservant letters in that order. He opened with Dilworth's letters from schoolboys to their parents, but cut them down to three, proceeding to apprenticeships and to advice about how a young man should conduct himself in the world. Changing place names, McCulloch reprinted both the "Letter from the elder Brother in the Country to his younger Brother put Apprentice in *Philadelphia*" and the "Advice from a Father to a young Beginner, what Company to chuse and how to behave in it," that the Dilworth and Crowder shared (above, pp. 158 and 156), but he presented them as answers to an apprentice's "how I go on" letter to his family in the country. McCulloch then turned to young gentlemen and young ladies who were still at school, clustering the letters for each, and using his clusters to create parallel but contrasting structures. He allowed the young gentleman to explain that "boys who do not mind their learning will never become gentlemen" and young ladies to ask favors of their mothers and aunts, to ask permission to invite a schoolfriend home, and to correspond with their girlfriends. While the young gentleman wrote a letter of excuse to his uncle for his immoral frailties, the young lady wrote a letter of excuse to her mother for her shortcomings in piety. McCulloch also balanced the advice to a young man about what company to choose with a letter to a young lady cautioning her against keeping company with a gentleman of bad character. The cluster of maidservant letters which follow balance the apprentice letters by offering maternal advice about how a daughter should conduct herself in service, and they take her to the point of marriage.

From the beginning of *The American Letter-Writer*, we are therefore once more squarely back in the framework of the household-family; but this time, for the first time, not only is the difference in gender roles clearly marked, but there is also epistolary segregation between men and women in the family. With the exception of the maidservant's letter asking permission to marry which is addressed to both parents, mothers and aunts educate and monitor their daughters, who correspond exclusively with them, while fathers, uncles and brothers deal with boys.

Issues of class, as well as gender, are addressed indirectly by clustering letters around these generic characters, for clustering juxtaposes the different advice given to apprentices, young gentlemen, young ladies and maidservants, the different virtues demanded of each, and the different faults for which each is reproached. None of the letters that McCulloch used was new. Each contained injunctions that had already been in circulation in more or less the same language in multiple manuals for fifty years – or in the case of apprentices, for a hundred years. But McCulloch's clusters of letters for each kind of young person fore-grounded what was never as apparent in manuals where these letters were simply scattered among miscellaneous household and business corres-pondence: that character, even more than conduct, was to be viewed as a function of rank, and that to educate a child for the position that he or she was to occupy in life, as pedagogical theory demanded, meant social engineering in the sense of instilling in that child the character traits considered desirable in his or her destined place in society. The young lady is taught to be pious, modest and chaste, affable, good natured and closely attached to her family and friends; and she is told to guard her reputation (and thus her "future happiness and welfare") by not allowing herself to be seen with immoral men. But the young serving maid is taught that she must detach herself from her family and friends, and that in whatever household she finds herself,

If you continue virtuous and obliging, all the family will love and esteem you. Keep yourself employed as much as you can, and be always ready to assist your fellow servants. Never speak ill of any body, but when you hear a bad story, try to soften it as much as you can; don't repeat it again, but let it slip out of your mind as soon as possible. . .If you have any time to spare from your business, I hope you will spend some part of it in reading your Bible and other books of instruction. . . Remember that the more faithful you are in the discharge of your duty as a servant, the better you will prosper if you live to have a family of your own. (37)

The maidservant must be consistent, loyal, obliging and diligent, mind her tongue, ingratiate herself with all members of the household-family with whom she is living, and spend her spare time in self-improvement. American manuals in the colonial period did not, as we saw, generally represent maidservants. It is significant that McCulloch does include them, and also that he culled letters that represented them in these terms. The significance becomes evident when we compare this representation to Haywood's *Present for a Serving Maid*, which takes the form of a long letter. Haywood made no distinctions between the virtues of the mistress and those of the maid; her representation of maidservant virtue consisted of adapting what she considered virtue in all ranks of women to the particular circumstances of her situation.[21] But letter manuals throughout the century, including McCulloch's, contributed to the conduct literature for servants in such a way as to inscribe and reinforce the differences between the conduct expected in different ranks.

In McCulloch's sequence of letters, the young apprentice has become a tradesman entering into business for himself. After showing that (unlike the maidservant) he ought not to marry yet, but instead demand letters from his sister, and write letters of condolence to his friends, McCulloch's manual launches into thirty-six letters of business. This constitutes just over a third of the entire collection of 106 letters, an exceptionally large proportion. The letters of business include all Dilworth's business letters, followed by almost every other kind of letter of business that eighteenth-century manuals had ever modeled, including letters taken from Hill's *Young Secretary's Guide*, which had been drafted over a hundred years before. The letters of business are intelligently framed, at the beginning, by Dilworth's letter recommending method in business and, at the end, by the letter to a father in the mechanic or artisanal trades that explains why formal schooling is essential if his son is to climb out of the artisanal ranks into the more genteel ranks of traders and merchants.

This last letter also forms a kind of bridge to the issues of gentility that dominate the last third of the collection. McCulloch moves on through letters of invitation to a party, letters of thanks, and Bishop Atterbury's advice about polite letter-writing, to a sequence of nineteen letters of courtship, about half the number in Crowder's *Letter-Writer*. The respectful lover who is too modest to court, the prudent lover who is wary of coquettes, the lover who withdraws his suit and the lady trying to persuade a suitor whom her parents favor to leave her alone, all reappear; as do the suitors applying to fathers and aunts for permission to court their charges, the suitor who complains of ill success, and the aunt who informs him that he cannot expect the lady to simply fall into his lap, and the ubiquitous letter from a young woman acquainting her father with a proposal of marriage. But there are in McCulloch's manual no letters complaining of sermonizing lovers or criticizing girls who dislike them for levity; no letters about jealousy and inconstancy; and no letters conveying idealized views of marriage, or indeed any views of marriage at all. In fact, the courtship sequence concludes, quite wittily I think, with Gay's much

---

21 Bannet, "Female Spectator."

reprinted letter about two perfect country lovers who are killed by lightening just before their wedding.

Other than a couple of letters advising women not to build their entire identities on their beauty, the major piece of advice for adult women that McCulloch adds argues that "simplicity" is the mark of a lady:

From a Lady to her Niece, on the Subject of Dress

Dear Bibby,

I am much of your opinion, that the make of a woman's mind, greatly contributes to the ornament of her body. Behold Mrs. Vicars! She has the largest share of simplicity of manners, perhaps, of her whole sex. This makes every thing look native about her; and her clothes are so exactly fitted, that they appear, as it were, part of her person. Every one that sees her, knows her to be a lady; but her distinction is owing to her manner, and not to her habit. Her beauty is full of attraction, but not of allurement. There is such a composure in her looks, and propriety in her dress, that you would think it impossible she could change the garb you one day see her in, for anything so becoming, till the next day you see her in another. There is no mystery about this, but that however she is appareled, she is herself the same; for there is so immediate a relation between our thoughts and gestures, that a woman must think well to look well: this I have no doubt of your endeavouring to do, my dear: which will give the utmost satisfaction to

Your affectionate and tender aunt,
Letitia. (83)

This letter, which does not appear in the Glasgow edition and appears in only one of the New York versions of Dilworth, equates the lady's simplicity of manners with transparency and unchangeableness: the lady's mind can be faithfully read in her body. Despite all her different garbs and all the different circumstances in which she might be seen, she is always the same perfect, proper, composed and tranquil creature. Because the body has to manifest what is in the mind, to be a lady is not merely to demonstrate this passionless simplicity outwardly in one's dress and manners, but also to ensure that one's thoughts are suitably stilled and tranquilized. McCulloch then concludes his manual with Judge Hale's letter on serious observance of the Lord's Day.

INSTRUCTORS AND ACADEMIES OF COMPLIMENTS

Instructors and *Academies of Compliments* both offered very short collections of letters that traveled the Atlantic unchanged, despite local reprintings. Though the volumes that contained each type of collection had different histories and served different functions, the letters within both had currency on both sides of the Atlantic. In style and in content, they represented two extremes that were mediated by the *Complete Letter-Writers* discussed above. For these reasons, the letters they contained are usefully discussed in the same section.

Overshadowed though they were by *Secretaries* and *Complete Letter-Writers*, the persistence of *Academies of Complement* into the early nineteenth century is a noteworthy fact, which prevents us from concluding too rapidly that "style" was developing teleologically from the ornamental and courtly to the plain and colloquial. Seventeenth-century *Academies of Complement* taught both oral and written conversation: they offered models of what readers should say when inviting someone to dinner, conversing at table, introducing themselves to a stranger, or trying to court a woman, as well as models of complemental letters; but the oral dominated the written and the number of letters was small. Seventeenth-century *Academies of Complement* also generally included songs, straightforward expository information about good breeding and the conduct expected of parents, young men, and young women, and practical advice about such things as how to carve at table.

There were two attempts to update the seventeenth-century's *New Academy of Compliments* in the British Isles during the eighteenth century. Both continued to model oral conversation, to include songs, and to teach good breeding in an expository manner; but they introduced interesting transformations into their letter-collections as they struggled to compete in a market dominated by the *Secretary* phenomenon. One of these versions of *The New Academy of Compliments*, which was published in Dublin in 1743 and supposedly reached its seventeenth edition in London in 1784, was subtitled "the lover's secretary." It merely added to its reprints of letters selected from Serre's *Secretary in Fashion* (still in Massinger's translation of 1640) a few slightly more down-to-earth letters between family members such as might appear in a *Secretary*. The other version of *The New Academy of Compliments* was produced in London in 1748, and reprinted in Glasgow in 1789. This version was subtitled "the Compleat English Secretary" and described its letter-collection as "relating to familiar Conversation between Friends and Acquaintance, Husband and Wife, Children and Parents, Masters and Apprentices, Brothers and Sisters, and Kindred in general; also, Love Letters on all Occasions; with others relating to Trade and Business of all Natures. . ." In other words, Serre had been completely thrown out, and the letter-collection had been turned into a regular *Secretary*. The reviser followed Goodman's practice in *The Experienc'd Secretary* (1699) of adapting complemental forms to ordinary household, business and social occasions, to produce letters for the everyday that boasted a heightened, "eloquent" style. It will be noted that his letters say essentially the same conventional things as the same letters in Goodman or Hill; what is significant is his choice of "empty" complemental language:

A Letter from a Son to his Father

By this I let you know, that my separation from you has been very tedious to me. Since the distance of place will not permit me to pay my humble duty, and just acknowledgment of your love, tender care, and regard towards me in person, I have made these lines the messenger of my willingness, in all things to deserve, as far as in me lies, such goodness as you have always shewed me. I am constrained to confess, that my deserts hitherto have not merited what you have bestowed upon me; but I shall be careful to make it the future business of my life to be doubly diligent to perform to the utmost of my power, all that shall become an obedient son, to answer the expectations of so indulgent a parent: and so, with my wishes and prayers for your long life and felicity, I remain, as by the ties of nature bound,

Your most dutiful and obedient Son, J. C.[22]

This letter from a son to his father is a variation on Goodman's letter from a nephew to an uncle (above, p. 130) and is in much the same style.

The *New Academy of Compliments, or Compleat English Secretary* was re-named *The American Academy of Compliments, or, The Complete American Secretary* when the Glasgow copy of 1789 was reprinted in Philadelphia in 1796 and in Hudson, New York, in 1804 and 1805.[23] The only changes introduced by its Philadelphia printers, Godfrey Deshong and Richard Folwell, were to the preface, to explain why on earth they thought reprinting this work could be useful to anyone at this late date. The major reason they gave accurately pointed to an important shortcoming in the Crowder and Dilworth *Letter-Writers*. This *Academy of Compliments*, they explained, "may rightly be called *The Young Lover's Academy, or, His Ready Path to his Mistress's Favours*, smooth and even, without stumbling, without running into abrupt discourses, or unpleasing language."[24]

22 *New Academy of Compliments*, 7.
23 There are slight differences in the order of letters between London and Glasgow printings, showing that American editions followed the Glasgow version. The 1804 and 1805 editions by J. Stoddard in Hudson, New York, have the same text as the Philadelphia edition but a different title: *The American Academy of Compliments*. The Philadelphia edition is called *The American Academy of Compliments, or the Complete American Secretary*. A manual with this title was also advertised in Wilmington, Delaware, according to Evans.
24 *American Academy of Compliments*, Preface to the Reader, n.p.

Complete Letter-Writers did not deal with love, or show a young man how to go about courting a woman. The suitors populating *Complete Letter-Writers* – the respectful suitor too shy to speak to his mistress, the sermonizing suitor, the suitor who complains of his ill success after a couple of visits, the suitors who have to watch their mistresses flirting with more amusing men, and those other suitors who were better at appealing to fathers and aunts than to their charges – all badly needed a book that offered a readier path to their *mistress*'s favors and advice about not stumbling on the path to winning her.

Where the letters were concerned (as opposed to the instruction about what to say to a lady), however, the American printers were not getting quite what they thought. Not only is the one example of a love letter reprinted in this American collection shown to be unsuccessful in gaining the lady's favor, but it sends an oddly ambiguous message:

A Citizen's Complaint to a Country Gentlewoman

Madam,

Were you sensible of the Fervency of my Affections, and with what intolerable Anguish I undergo the Burden of my Passion, I do not question but your Goodness will vouchsafe to consider my Distress, and quietly grant some Relief to your endeared Lover, who hath vowed to be your true and faithful Servant, even till Death shall deprive me of the Devotion due to yourself, and I am made uncapable of admiring your Beauty, which above all the World is most delectable to mine Eye. I implore you, *Dear Madam,* not to misconstrue the Time and real Meaning of my unfeigned Affection, which if your Favour please once to try, I doubt not, but that you will acquiesce with me in this Point; and conclude with me, that I am of all Lovers the most affectionate, burning with desire of Enjoyment of that, which is only left to your disposal. I mean that that inestimable gem of your affection, which if you hold at so high a rate from me your afflicted servant, I shall be bound to curse the hour I first saw your divine beauty, and doubtless pass out of this life in a Hurricane of Sighs, to that sweet Elysium, which after the Tyrant of impenetrable Beauties only gives to broken hearted Lovers, some Drams of Comfort to heal their love-wounded Souls. Therefore, if any tender Pity lodges in that snowy Breast, be pleased (by a kind Answer) to allay the Storms of my raging Passion, and for ever make him happy who subscribes himself,

Yours beyond Expression, J. B.[25] . . . (29)

---

25 In the British edition of 1748, 30; in *The American Academy of Compliments* of 1796, 29.

The Gentlewoman's Answer

Sir,

I have very often heard of that which now you have manifested sufficiently, by
the Smoothness and Sweetness of your amorous Dialect, which tho' it may seem
prevalent enough in your Mind to carry on your pretended Suit; yet it is not of
such Power as to rob me of my Virgin Liberty, or bereave me of my Senses so far
as to confide in the Shadow of your Complemental Discourse. As for the Title of
Madam, which you so freely bestow on me; did you but know how acceptable it
is to me, you would have let Mistress have served in the Room, and better had
you pleased me too; for we that live a Rural Life are not so fond of Court
Language, or Titles of your City Dames, whose Gentility consists chiefly in
Bravery and Courtship; but as to your Suit, I desire you to desist, for I am not
yet disposed to alter my Condition; but if I were I should be more difficult in my
Choice, than to suffer my Senses to be captivated by a few fair Pretences, with
which you Citizens are so frequent, that I fear many of my Sex have long e'er
this, repented their Credulity. Pray trouble me no more with your Paper
Visits. . ." (30)

The English compiler's placement of the extravagantly complemental
love letter in the hands of a "Citizen" suggests that "cits" have taken over
what was once an elite style of epistolary courtship, and that the down-to-
earth country gentlewoman is far less gullible than her town sisters about
such smooth and eloquent nonsense. Read in this way, the message to
women is: do not allow yourself to be captivated by fair pretense and
pretty words just because they seem to have the seductive flavor of Town,
Court and high life. Here, as in Hill who made the same point, the
recipient models the proper reading: complemental letters should be
viewed with suspicion and the writer's sincerity should be doubted. Read
in another way, however – especially in a republican environment where
the term "Citizen" evoked a respectable member of urban society rather
than a vulgar London cit clumsily aping his betters – it would be the
country gentlewoman who was shown up. Ignorant of town forms, and
embarrassingly unwilling to adopt the proper style of address for a woman
with pretensions to gentility (her refusal to be called "Madam" rather
than "Mistress," for instance), she has no idea how to answer such a letter
in proper form. Her rude dismissal only shows that she is out of her
depth. In this reading, the flowery and complemental language of the love
letter is re-marked as the language of the upper ranks in Town, Court and
high life, and perhaps re-re-marked as language that is both current in
such circles and intrinsically deceptive. Far from sending the complemental love letters out of fashion as both silly and ineffective, as the first
reading would do, this second reading keeps that language in circulation

as a signifier of sophisticated and seductive upper class gallantry and "love."

Even more significantly, perhaps, this flowery and complemental language remains the *only* language modeled by letter manuals in which to write of premarital love. Viewed in the context of letter manuals, the only alternative facing the woman who wants to love and be loved rather than just to become party to a business-like, negotiated marriage, and whose desire in *Complete Letter-Writers* has branded her a "coquette," is that offered by American woman novelist, Hannah Foster in her epistolary novel, *The Coquette*: the woman can choose between the language and attitudes of the *Academy of Complements* lover and those of the *Complete Letter-Writer*'s sermonizing suitor who is boring, business-like about marriage, and busy with good works. Viewed in the context of eighteenth-century letter manuals, Foster is not so much exploring a problem of character or psyche, as reflecting on the written languages and cultures of courtship available to American men, and using her heroine's depression and tragedy to show up their shortcomings. One might say that this characterization of complemental love letters was only compounded by the presence in libraries, like Philadelphia's, of manuals such as *Polite Epistolary Correspondence*, which consisted largely of flowery translations of classical and seventeenth-century French letters.

George Fisher's *Instructor or Young Man's Best Companion* (c. 1735) was a *vade mecum* teaching penmanship, grammar, arithmetic, book-keeping, elementary history and geography, and gardening or farriery as well as letter-writing. Its "sundry Examples promiscuously exhibited" contained only seventeen household and business letters, which it recommended students frequently read over and sometimes copy as "a good Introduction to a handsome Style of Sense."[26] These seventeen letters are important because Fisher's *Instructor* was so widely used. It reached its twenty-first London edition in 1772. An inscription in a copy of the seventeenth edition of 1763, places the book in Lincolnshire in 1836, as the property one George Bennet Skelton. Minor changes were introduced in the London edition after 1763, and the manual was reprinted in Edinburgh with these changes.

In America, the manual had a long and extremely curious history. It circulated in three versions, in the reverse order from what one might expect. The first version was an American adaptation called *The American Instructor or Young Man's Best Companion*, which Benjamin Franklin and

---

26 Fisher, *Instructor*, 59–60.

David Hall produced in 1748 and reprinted in 1753. This was reissued by different American printers multiple times under the same title to 1779. Arguing that "in the British Edition of this Book, there were many things of little or no Use in these Parts of the World," Franklin and Hall produced an edition that omitted what they thought useless, and "[inserted] in their Room many other Matters. . .more immediately useful to us *Americans*." These changes are especially interesting in the sections on history and geography. As far as the model letters are concerned, Franklin and Hall left Fisher's collection intact; but, noticing that Fisher had failed to include any letters of advice from fathers, uncles or older brothers on the proper conduct of business, they inserted a "Letter of Advice to a Young Tradesman, written by an old One" culled from Franklin's *Way to Wealth*.

Another version of Fischer's *Instructor* then began to circulate in 1775: it was an American reprint by Isaac Collins in Burlington of the English version of Fischer's manual, complete with its English history and geography and other matters that Franklin and Hall had pronounced "useless to us Americans." This could be dismissed as an anomaly due to wartime conditions, loyalism, or some such thing, were it not for the fact that this English *Instructor* continued to be reprinted until 1810. In some versions, a little American geography was added to this English material but without the *American Instructor*'s more useful substitutions and without its "Letter of Advice to a young Tradesman." These versions circulated under the title *The Instructor, or American Young Man's Best Companion*.

Many of Fisher's letters were just simplified and shortened versions of Goodman or Hill, as in the following Letter of Congratulation:

Sir,

If you were but sensible how much I am affected with the good and most acceptable News that I hear of your good Fortune, you would conclude that the Joy that surprizes me for the same, is equal to yours that enjoy so happy a Turn of Providence: I could express myself further on this Theme, and enlarge exceedingly on so pleasing a Subject; but let this at present suffice, till I have a more favourable Opportunity of expressing my Joy to you personally; In the Interim, I am truly,

Sir,

Your sincere Friend, and very humble Servant,
Ralph Real.

Only the very elaborate and deferential subscription indicates that this is a letter to a superior, and therefore perhaps congratulation for an advancement. With "Your Friend and humble servant," or "your loving

Nephew" for its subscription, it is generic and simple enough to serve for anyone on any occasion, including a fortunate inheritance or the birth of a healthy baby.

More interesting are the letters between father and son, and uncle and nephew with which the collection opens, both of which concretize what other collections left abstract:

A Letter from a young Man to his Uncle

Norwich, Dec. 7, 1746

Honoured Uncle,
    The many kind and courteous Things that you have done for me, oblig'd me, in Point of Gratitude, as *well* as Duty, to return you my most humble Thanks, and to offer you my poor, but real and hearty Service, in the Affair between you and Mr. A. B. of this Place: And if *you'll* please but to communicate to me your Intentions and give me your Directions therein, I shall observe and *follow* them with all Punctuality; and will from time to time give an exact Account of my Negociations in that Affair. So expecting to receive your Commands by the first convenient Opportunity, I rest and remain,

Sir,

your most obliged Nephew, and very humble Servant,
Brian Bing.

The Uncle's Answer

Nephew
London, 12 Dec. 1746

I take your Offer of Service to me in the Business between me and Mr. A. B. of your City, very kindly, and think none fitter to adjust that Affair than yourself; but I am *unwilling* to go to Law, and had rather, much rather, that you would endeavour to bring him to some reasonable Accommodation; for in such Contests the Winner is a Loser at the Upshot. So if I can bring him to any reasonable terms I *shall* be very glad: You understand the Affair, and so I *shall* commit *wholly* to your discreet and good Management, being persuaded that you'll do for me as for yourself: So I remain your Loving,

And Affectionate Uncle,
Bazil Bing.

These letters economically do double duty. On the one hand, they are what any agent might write to his principal or any tradesman to a "friend" or fellow tradesman in another town. They enable Fisher to get in the familiar point about preferring informal accommodations to the folly and expense of going to law. On the other hand, by turning the nephew into the uncle's factor or agent, Fisher gives the obligatory language of service, gratitude and duty a concrete rather than merely rhetorical mode of existence, as Brian Bing underlines by speaking of his "poor, but real and hearty Service." The letter indicates the value in trade of having diligent, capable and well-established nephews, brothers, uncles and cousins who can offer their practical aid when needed. Perhaps in eighteenth-century manuals, uncles so frequently advised and reproved their nephews to ensure that they grew up to become what Brian Bing so evidently is – a potential partner and helper to other family members. The Letter of "Advice to a young Tradesman, written by an old One, to his Friend, A. B." which Franklin and Hall added to *The American Instructor* follows directly from this, and is a good place to end inasmuch as, at the opposite end of the spectrum from *Academies of Complement*, it serves to sum up the uncles' and fathers' messages about trade and commerce in virtually all the letter manuals we have seen: "In short, the Way to Wealth, if you desire it, is as plain as the Way to market. It depends chiefly on two Words, INDUSTRY and FRUGALITY; i.e. Waste neither Time nor Money, but make the best Use of both."

CHAPTER 5

The "Art of Correspondence," 1790–1820

The turn of the nineteenth century saw another sea-change in manual styles and in the approaches taken to the same household, courtship, bonding and business issues. Most of the manuals that became popular between 1790 and 1820 were subtitled the new, whole or plain "Art of Correspondence" to indicate a more far-ranging interest in modeling ongoing epistolary exchanges. *Secretaries* included model answers when needed as we have seen, and Crowder's *Complete Letter-Writer* also experimented with some longer exchanges; but London manuals that modeled the art of correspondence consistently paired letters and answers and frequently used longer sequences to outline the proper course and conduct of an entire situation. They also stressed the conduct book functions of their model correspondences by offering thematic tables of content that do not reflect the titles (or even sometimes the subjects and sequence) of the letters within. In London at the turn of the nineteenth century, the market for 'arts of correspondence' was dominated by two populist Paternoster Row printers of the 1770s, John Cooke and Alexander Hogg. Since both generally omitted to print the date of publication on their title-pages, the sequence and relations among their several competing manuals cannot be determined with absolute certainty.

During the early 1770s, Cooke and Hogg each published a manual of "original letters" by a probably pseudonymous "Reverend" with an A. B. or A. M. Both publishers were known for puffing their authors' qualifications and for issuing books under feigned names. John Cooke's manual was unquestionably the most influential. Probably dating from late 1771 or early 1772,[1] *The Universal Letter-Writer; or New Art of Polite Correspondence* by one "Reverend Thomas Cooke, A. B.," was reprinted eleven times in the British Isles before 1798 (in London, Newcastle, York and

---

1 The ESTC suggests 1770 based on dates attached to the wills; but this edition also contains letters dated February 1771. It was not later than 1772, since there was a pirated Dublin copy that year.

Dublin). Most of the British reprintings occurred after 1788 when the manual became the property of two London congers who may be said to have successfully relaunched the manual,[2] which continued to be printed in England and Scotland until 1841.[3] While tackling many of the same subjects and occasions as Crowder's or Dilworth's *Complete Letter-Writers*, Cooke's *Universal Letter-Writer or New Art of Polite Correspondence* offered a plainer, clearer and more concise style of epistolary writing and a more kindly, moral and religious approach to social and domestic issues. This made the manual attractive to American printers in several states. Recognizing that *The Universal Letter-Writer* was an updated and restyled version of Crowder and Dilworth, Americans printed their various adaptations of Cooke's manual under the title *The New and Complete Letter-Writer, or New Art of Polite Correspondence*, and their miscellanies of letters from Crowder, Dilworth and Cooke under the title *The New Complete Letter-Writer, or Art of Correspondence*. These titles continued to circulate in America until about 1820.

In London, Cooke's rival, Alexander Hogg, likewise printed a manual of "entire new letters" by one "Reverend George Brown, A. M." Brown's manual reproduced the same distinctive subjects as Cooke's *Universal Letter-Writer*, explaining that its goal was to correct the defects of earlier manuals which lacked sufficient "reference to moral obligations."[4] In publishing Brown's manual, Alexander Hogg lived up to the reputation that Charles Timperley gave him of being one who, "when the sale of a book began to slacken. . .immediately employed some scribe to make him 'a taking title'; and the work, though not a line was altered, was brought out in a new edition."[5] For over time, Hogg issued Brown's "entire new letters" under at least three different titles: *The English Letter-Writer; or Whole Art of General Correspondence; The New English Letter-Writer or The Whole Art of General Correspondence;* and *The New and Complete English Letter-Writer or The Whole Art of General Correspondence.* Brown's letters did not "take" in any of these incarnations, in part, no doubt, because they were too sententious, sentimental and moralized to be useful

2 Andrew Millar, William Law and R. Colar, who co-published with printers in York; W. Osborne, T. Griffin and J. M. Mozeley.

3 The last surviving London edition was in 1825, but there is a Derby edition of 1832, several Edinburgh editions in the 1820s, and a Canadian edition, probably the last, in 1855.

4 *New English Letter-Writer*, Preface, n.p. Quotes are from this edition. The ESTC suggests 1770 for the earliest edition.

5 Timperley, *Encyclopedia*, p. 838. Most of Timperley's anecdotes are taken from Nichols, *Literary Anecdotes* (1812); his information about Alexander Hogg does not appear there.

as epistolary models, and in part because Brown recommended Christian resignation as the panacea for all ills and proscribed any attempt to extricate oneself from them by improving oneself or rising above one's station.

Cooke and Hogg also issued another pair of competing manuals (possibly *c.* 1790).[6] Neither seems to have had much of a following, but their titles create confusion. John Cooke published a *New and Complete Universal Letter-Writer* by the "Reverend Thomas Cooke, A. M.," which was subtitled *The Young Secretary's Instructor* because it returned to the *Secretary* format. This manual reprinted a number of letters from earlier manuals, and contains different versions of the letters it shares with Cooke's earlier *Universal Letter-Writer*. Not to be outdone, Alexander Hogg produced a *New and Complete Universal Letter-Writer*, subtitled *The Whole Art of Correspondence*, by one "Henry Hogg, A. M." While more sentimental than Cooke's, Hogg's manual again resembled Cooke's new manual in many respects. In 1800, Hogg's manual was reprinted with the addition of a substantial number of letters and attributed to Henry Hogg *and* the Reverend George Brown. Confusion arises because unconnected American manuals used similar titles. David Hogan, a Philadelphia printer, published several editions of a very popular manual called *The New Universal Letter-Writer or Complete Art of Polite Correspondence* (1800), and there was another *New Universal Letter-Writer* printed in Hallowell in 1812. These works are different both from each other and from Cooke and Hogg's respective works of the same title. Both American manuals are heavily indebted in different ways to Cooke's *Universal Letter-Writer* rather than to his *New and Complete Universal Letter-Writer*.[7]

Virtually all American printers at the turn of the nineteenth century produced adaptations of Cooke's *Universal Letter-Writer* or built on a miscellany of Dilworth, Crowder and Cooke called *The New Complete Letter-Writer or Art of Correspondence*, that was printed in Whitehaven perhaps as early as 1775, and reprinted by Isaiah Thomas in Worcester in 1791 and 1794.[8] During the early Republic, American printers were

---

6 The ESTC's conjectural date. However, Plomer says that John Cooke ceased printing in 1766. He did have a son, also John Cooke, who continued printer and died in 1810.

7 The American *New Universal Letter-Writer* by Rev. Thomas Cooke, published for Ezekiel Goodale in Hallowell in 1812, is a version of Cooke's *Universal Letter-Writer* with the sections in a different order. Hogan's manual will be discussed below.

8 Thomas shortened the Whitehaven title to *The New Complete Letter-Writer*. After Thomas, there are only two documented printings of this manual, in New York in 1800, and in Boston in 1803.

divided about how to represent their epistolary models. Some stressed the English provenance of their manuals, when in fact they were offering essentially new compilations with different ideological emphases. Other printers stressed the American provenance of their manuals, when in fact their compilations were largely or wholly composed of letters reprinted from English manuals. This difference was reflected in titles as well as in prefaces: there is *Magee's London Letter-Writer*, and there is *The Columbian Letter-Writer*, which is in fact a miscellany of Crowder and Cooke. But however they defined what they were doing, only one of the several manuals that American printers produced in these years can be described as a more or less straightforward reprint of a British manual. Thus, once again, the same was circulating differently in different places. While many of the same models of conduct and writing were being offered on both sides of the Atlantic, they were abridged, rearranged or recombined in different American states to advance different social and ideological agendas.

LONDON: COOKE'S UNIVERSAL LETTER-WRITER; OR NEW
ART OF POLITE CORRESPONDENCE

Cooke assumed that he was writing for busy and fairly letterate readers with unreliable grammar, who were "so immersed in the affairs of the world, they have seldom time" to read a variety of authors and study how best to deliver their sentiments (10). He gave them a large number of clear, colloquial, and well-focused correspondences written in "language plain, easy, sensible, elegant and suited to the nature of the subject" (18), which he thought that "the judicious, by a little variation, [would] soon be able to accommodate to their different situations" (10). Consequently he spent little time considering or expounding the art of letter-writing. There are no letters about writing letters in his collection. He assumed that "to enumerate the many advantages which society enjoys from the use of epistolary writings, would be altogether superfluous" (Pref.); and his brief directions for writing letters take it for granted that polite forms of address and epistolary practices are known. For him, the important thing to teach about considering "the different characters of persons" when one writes letters is how to assume the character proper to one's own situation and condition: writing as a father, one should use "gentle authority," writing as a son "express a filial duty" and so on. Cooke, accordingly, devoted most of his energies to the conduct book dimensions of letter manuals, reproducing many of the concerns of

Complete Letter-Writers, but also introducing important changes with far-reaching social and ideological implications. These can be summarized under four headings.

First, Cooke abandoned all pretension to address those seeking to rise in the government or administrative hierarchy, and included in his collection of epistles no fawning letters of thanks or application from inferiors to their social superiors.[9] He supplied the place of such letters with an exceptionally large number of letters to and from professional characters – army officers, sailors, attorneys at law, clergymen and teachers – who are shown interacting and intermarrying with tradesman and merchant families. Indeed, a major issue in his section of letters on courtship and marriage is the permissibility of marriage between the professional and mercantile classes, despite inequalities of fortune. Historians have found that social and marital relations between professional and mercantile groups were becoming frequent in the British provinces during the latter half of the eighteenth century, and Cooke may have been seeking to remove any lingering impediments to them.

Secondly, and perhaps in part as a consequence of this large influx of professionals, Cooke sharply separated the concerns of the household-family from matters of avocation and business. The usual cast of fathers, mothers, sons, daughters, maidservants and apprentices appears in only two of the four sections of this manual: that consisting of "Letters to and from different relations" which contains the usual letters to and from schoolchildren, apprentices and maidservants, and that consisting of letters "On Love, Courtship and Marriage." The letters of business and the letters of advice and instruction (collected in a section entitled "On Friendship etc.") pass between strangers, friends, business associates or professional advisors such as clergymen and teachers, rather than between fathers, uncles, elder brothers or aunts and their charges. Cooke explained in his Preface that he was "writing to ordinary readers" whose "necessary avocations oblige them to converse by Letters with their correspondents, and either paternal or filial duty obliges them to converse with their absent relations."[10] People were obliged to write letters in the course of their work or they were obliged to write to their relations. There was now a certain separation of spheres.

---

9 These were moved into a section called "The Complete Petitioner," added after the legal forms and cards of compliment at the end.
10 Cooke, *Universal Letter-Writer* ([London, 1770?]), 10. All quotes are from this edition.

Thirdly, unlike earlier manuals, Cooke's *Letter-Writer* was overtly, even brazenly, political. From this point of view, John Cooke's choice of pseudonymous author for his compilation was genial, for apart from its implicit reference to the volume's publisher, the name Thomas Cooke conjured up a writer now dead, who had flourished in the 1730s and 1740s and shared many of the political positions espoused in this manual. Possibly as a result of the success of this manual, he also became popular again in the 1790s as a translator of the classics. A friend of Steele, Tickell and Philips, Thomas Cooke (1703-56) had been a Whig propagandist much given to religious and epistolary (as well as dramatic) writing. He was a strong advocate of liberty, the enemy of party and faction, a foe of Popery, and a vociferous supporter of war against the Spanish and the French.

Finally, while rewriting many of Crowder and Dilworth's standard letters and reproducing many of their domestic, social and mercantile concerns, Cooke changed the way some of those concerns were resolved and introduced quite a large number of new situations and problems. Besides demonstrating the possibility of marriages across class and occupational lines, Cooke's letters showed readers how to apply to a college or school to admit one's son as a pupil; how to start up in business without patronage, family connections or money; how to refuse premature requests for payment of sums owed; how to save money by asking friends at a distance to purchase goods on one's behalf; how to complain about shoddy goods and respond to such complaints; and how to deal with eloping apprentices, eloping young women, impoverished gentry, and the sexual harassment of young companions by their mistress's sons. The fact that many of these situations were also addressed in Brown's *New English Letter-Writer*, and that the correspondences dealing with them were reproduced in American manuals, suggests that such innovations accurately reflected the changing times.

Unlike the earlier manuals we have examined, Cooke emphasized the benevolence, "tenderness," even the "indulgence" of fathers, masters and schoolmasters, in the household-family letters he grouped under "Letters to and from various Relations." This benevolent patriarch is particularly evident in Cooke's treatment of the plague of run-aways among apprentices, of which contemporaries complained. Rather than offering the usual letters of reproof and reprimand to young men for dissipation and negligence of their duty as *Secretaries* had done, or trying to bribe young men to remain in their apprenticeships as the *Complete Letter-Writers'* elder brother had done, Cooke provided a correspondence designed to show run-away apprentices how they could return to their masters and to induce fathers and masters to give them a second chance. In the first letter of the series, "a young Man, who had eloped from his Apprenticeship" writes to his father asking him to "intercede with his Master to take him again into Service." The message to young apprentices in this letter is that their father (who had to pay a large sum of money for their indenture) was the most "powerful advocate to intercede for [them]" with their master (25), and should be applied to first. In his letter, the young apprentice properly expresses his contrition and firm resolve to reform, while explaining that "vicious company" had led him to "forsake the paths of virtue, and neglect my duty in a family where I was treated with the greatest tenderness." Vicious company generally seems to have been considered a convincing reason for all kinds of misconduct. The father's answer speaks of his "resentment" on account of his son's "ingratitude," but rapidly allows "paternal affection" and "real concern for [his son's] future happiness" to "become predominant," with the result that he writes to his son's master asking him to take the errant apprentice back. The fourth and final letter in this correspondence is the master's tender answer to the father's request:

Sir,

Ever since I first considered the state of human nature, or the difference between right and wrong, I have always preferred mercy to the austere rigour of justice. However seasonable your request may appear to yourself, yet to me it was really unnecessary. I am a father, sir, and can feel at least part of what you suffer. My resentment against the young man is less than my anxiety for his happiness, and were I sure of his adhering to an uninterrupted course of virtue, I should have more real pleasure than his acquiring me the revenue of a nabob.

In the mean time, that nothing may be wanting on my part to make both you and him as happy as possible, all faults are from this moment forgotten; my house is open for his reception; and if he will return, he shall be treated with the same indulgence, as if he had never committed any fault whatever,

I am, Sir, your affectionate friend. (27)

To err is human; to forgive, divine. It was far wiser – and more beneficial both for the individuals involved and for society as a whole – for fathers and masters to demonstrate their humanity by helping young men who strayed back onto the path of virtue and duty, than to punitively give way to anger or just resentment. Cooke characteristically downplayed the economic motive for relationships, and here represents the master as one whose primary concern is the moral well-being of his charge.

The equivalent for young women was the standard letter from a mother or aunt cautioning a daughter or niece against keeping company with a gentleman of bad character. It reappears in Cooke's manual among the maidservant letters, where it is preceded by the usual exchange between a homesick young maidservant newly come to town and her mother's advice about how to conduct herself in her new household, and followed by a letter from the maidservant to her father informing him of a marriage proposal. Cooke took these letters from Crowder's *Complete Letter-Writer*, but gave them a stylistic face-lift to bring them closer to the "plain, easy, sensible and elegant" mode of epistolary writing he favored. The difference can be seen by comparing an extract from Crowder's letter cautioning a niece against keeping company with a gentleman of bad character, with Cooke's version of the same passage:

Dear Niece,
    The sincere Love and Affection which I now have for your Indulgent Father, and ever had for your virtuous Mother, not long since deceased, together with the tender regard I have for your future Happiness and Welfare, have prevailed on me to inform you, rather by Letter than by Word of Mouth, concerning what I have heard of your unguarded Conduct, and the too great Freedoms that you take with Mr. Freelove. You have been seen with him (if Fame lies not) in the Side-Boxes at both Theatres; in St. James' Park on Sunday night and afterwards at a certain Tavern, not a Mile from thence, which is a House (as I have been credibly informed) of no good Repute. You have both, moreover, been seen at Ranelagh Assembly, Vauxhall Gardens, and what is still more flagrant, at Cuper's Fire-Works. Don't imagine, Niece, that I am in the least prejudiced, or speak out of any private Pique; but let me tell you, your Familiarity with him gives me no small Concern, as his Character is none of the best, and as he has acted in the most ungenerous Manner by two or three very virtuous young Ladies of my Acquaintance, who entertained too favourable an Opinion of his Honour. . . ."[11]

Dear Niece,
    The sincere love and affection which I now have for your indulgent father, and ever had for your virtuous mother when she was alive, together with the tender regard I have for your future happiness and welfare, have prevailed upon me to inform you rather by letter than by word of mouth, concerning what I have heard of your unguarded conduct, and the too great freedoms you take with Mr. Lovelace. You have been seen with him at the Playhouses, in St. James' Park, Ranelagh, and Vauxhall. Don't imagine, niece, that I write this from a principle of ill-nature, it is on purpose to save you from ruin; for, let me tell you, your

11 Crowder's *Complete Letter-Writer*, 74–5. In Dilworth's *Complete Letter-Writer*, the gentleman's name is Mr. Trippit.

familiarity with him gives me no small concern, as his character is extremely bad, and as he has acted in the most ungenerous manner to two or three virtuous ladies of my acquaintance, who entertained too favourable an opinion of his honour. . ." (37)

Cooke shortened Crowder's letter, simplified sentences, and clarified the points it was making. To this end, he eliminated the parentheses, the unnecessary detail, commas, capitals and circumlocutions ("in the least prejudiced, or speak out of any private Pique," "his Character is none of the best"). Unlike Crowder, he directly stated the purpose of the letter: "to save you from ruin." Instead of belaboring that point, Cooke changed the name of the gentleman of bad character to Lovelace, to evoke the isolation, suffering, rape and death that befell Richardson's heroine, Clarissa, as a consequence of her poor choice of suitor. Cooke also added a grateful response from the niece, who writes that she had been "utterly ignorant of his real character," and has now broken off with him because, as she put it: "I am sensible every young woman ought to be careful of her reputation, and constantly avoid the company of libertines" (38).

The long section of letters "On Business" showed young men how they could get started on their own without patronage, family connections in trade or a family business to move into. There are letters "offering a correspondence" (opening a trading relationship) with a London merchant not only from a provincial young man whose parents have the wherewithal to set him up in trade, but also from one who unexpectedly came into a business when his master died. There are also letters "from a young man who has an opportunity to set up in business, but is destitute of money, to a gentleman of reputed benevolence" requesting a timely loan to get him started, and a letter from a sailor to his wife explaining that he has saved enough from his wages and from prize money to open a shop. In response to such letters from young beginners in trade, the London merchants stress that an apprentice who has behaved correctly during his apprenticeship has "a double advantage over a stranger, as being well acquainted with [his] master's trade and customers" (45), and that customers and suppliers would be all the more willing to deal with him because they already knew him. The benevolent gentleman loans the needy young man money to set up in business, and takes advantage of the opportunity to preach the Protestant ethic as uncles and fathers had earlier done: "while you continue to act consistently with the principles, and regulate your conduct by the practice of virtue, you will have great reason to expect the divine blessing on whatever you undertake" (57). Opportunity beckons for all.

Historians have argued that during the last decades of the eighteenth century, the economic situation both in Britain and America was such that apprentices were less likely than before to be able to become masters themselves, and that many were obliged to spend their entire lives as wandering journeymen. Cooke seems to have believed, however, that industry and ability could overcome all obstacles. He did several times refer to "the very precarious nature" of trade, and to the fact that "the Gazette [was] so often filled with the names of bankrupts" (57), and he did admit that people might sometimes fail through no fault of their own. Like Dilworth, he also offered letters showing how tradesmen could help one another out by agreeing to a delay of payment, by offering financial assistance, or by granting bankrupts "a letter of licence." A letter of licence was a document signed by all a bankrupt's creditors which permitted him to continue trading for a specified time without penalties or financial demands, while he attempted to restore his business to the point where he could pay his debts. But despite his recognition of such problems, Cooke made it clear, in a letter of advice from a retired merchant to a young merchant who was fearful because "many daily fail who have the fairest characters," that he took the position that the real causes of bank-ruptcy were lack of moral character and lack of "regularity" in business:

There are some unforeseen accidents, which even the greatest prudence cannot prevent. But these are extraordinary cases, and seldom happen. If you examine minutely into the nature of those causes which generally occasion bankruptcies, you will find them [as follows]. . .And the first is generally a careless attention to business, the not keeping regular accounts, and a more earnest desire after public entertainments, than assiduity to business on the change. . . .Assiduity always procures respect, and generally assures success. Another cause of the many failures in the mercantile world, is the vanity of those in trade, living above their circumstances. This vice is at present so predominant among the citizens, that one would almost imagine the people were labouring under some penal infatuation. . .The last cause I would mention, is naturally the effect of the others, I mean, a desperate attempt to repair a broken fortune, by engaging too deeply at gaming in the alley." (142–3)

The old merchant's advice was never to leave until tomorrow what could be done today; never to trust either a friend or a servant to do what you could do yourself; to keep an account of every day's expenses and tally one's books every week, and to be satisfied when "Trade is solid but slow" rather than risk all by striving for sudden riches (144).

Cooke firmly opened this world of slow but solid trade onto the international scene by including letters to and from officers posted to regiments which were going to war with Spain or from sailors who had just come back from giving the Spanish a "drubbing," all of which are strongly supportive of war and of the men doing their "duty" for their country. He also used the standard "Letter of Advice" from a clerk or apprentice in London to his master in the country to recommend trade with America in lieu of trade with Catholic Europe:

Sir,
   Our not hearing from you these three weeks has made us very uneasy, but still we hope you are well. The business has been carried on in the same manner in which you left it; but yesterday an order came from New York for goods to the amount of five thousand pounds and upwards. You know the American credit, and therefore I would not do any thing until I heard from yourself. If you please to write by next post I shall abide by your directions, and everything shall be conducted by your order. We would not wish you to return before your health is fully re-established, although we long to see you ever day. All the family are well, and I am,

Your obedient faithful servant,
James Thompson. (59)

   The master's response to the American order is that he is "extremely glad to hear of it, not only on my own account, but also of trade in general. Their credit to be sure is long, but I would rather trust our brethren in that part of the world two years, than those who are our natural enemies" (60). Writing before the American War of Independence, Cooke represented trade with America as a patriotic issue for British merchants. Here and in other letters, he made the case (also made by John Oldmixon and others) against those who claimed that colonies were nothing but a drain on England: that the "progress of navigation and commerce to the present time" had produced important "advantages arising from the colonies to the mother-country" (128).

   Cooke saw marriage as a primarily practical and utilitarian matter for men in the trading classes who were not in possession of comfortable fortunes. He stressed this point by including two correspondences in which a young merchant just starting in business informs his father or the woman he is courting, that he needs a wife to help him in his trade. In one of these correspondences, which is also interesting in other ways, the young merchant writes to a widow older than himself, whom he has seen on the road to Bristol, in the following terms:

Madam,
   Ever since I saw you at the wells when I was on a journey to *Bristol*, my mind has been continually ruminating on your many accomplishments. And although

it is possible this may be rejected, yet I can no longer conceal a passion which has preyed on my spirits these six weeks. I have been settled in business about three years, my success has been equal to my expectations, and is likewise increasing. My family is respectable although not rich, and as to the disparity of our ages, a few years will not make any difference, where the affections are placed on so lovely an object. I can only say madam, that I prefer you to all the young ladies I have yet seen, and if business continues to increase, I shall be greatly in want of one of your prudence, to manage my domestic affairs. Be assured madam, that whatever time I can spare from the necessary duties of my profession, shall be devoted to your company, and every endeavour used to make your life both agreeable and happy. As you have relations in London, they will give you every necessary information concerning my character and circumstances, although I have not the pleasure of being known to them. If you will favour me with an answer to this, it will be ever esteemed as a particular favour, and acknowledged with the sincerest respect, by your real admirer,

King Street, London
John Moreton (73–4)

The letter in which a man introduces himself to an unknown lady's notice is a genre that goes back to Goodman's *Secretary* and to *Academies of Complement* before that, and which had obvious occasional uses. One exemplar of this kind of letter was therefore included in many manuals. In Crowder's letter manual, however, a tradesman seeking to introduce himself to a young lady he had seen at the theater with a view to a more permanent connection is blocked by an aunt, who answers instead of her niece, to tell him that the latter already has plenty of suitors among men who are known to her family. Crowder apparently disapproved of marrying persons outside one's social circle as much as he disapproved of courtship. Cooke's answer was to use this device to bring strangers together and to launch courtships between men and women of different stations from different social circles. The young merchant in the above letter, for instance, comes from a poor but respectable family and is only just beginning to improve his fortunes; but he is introducing himself to the notice of a well-to-do widow, whose brother is a successful attorney in the Temple. He is therefore seeking to marry "up" into a polite, professional and more comfortably situated class.

Unlike Crowder or Dilworth, Cooke recognized that "love" was a necessary lubricant for such transactions, and often used it as a justification for marriages between ranks or between rich and poor. But he allowed passion to become passionate ("is not absence death to those who love?") only between a young woman and an officer whose regiment has been ordered to Minorca, where he is expected to die. Elsewhere, "love" or "passion" is little more than a euphemism for a man's calculated judgment that a woman has the moral virtues or the practical accomplishments he needs in his station in life. The "lovely object" on which the above young merchant is placing his affections is the prospect of taking a woman to wife who has the experience, abilities and prudence to help him manage his affairs. "Passion," alias practical self-interest, joins men and women across ranks and economic lines.

Unlike Dilworth's *Letter-Writer*, which stringently proscribed remarriage for widows, Cooke used the continuation of this correspondence to show that second marriages were both permissible and sensible for widowed women. In writing to consult her brother about the young merchant's proposal, the widow expresses her fears about the faithfulness of a husband who is "at least a dozen years" younger than she is; but she thinks it is a good idea to remarry not only because she is tired of rakes and coxcombs and of the "many inconveniences" of widowhood, but because she is anxious "as I advance in years to have a friend to whom I might at all times be able to open my mind with freedom, and who would treat me with that tenderness which my sex entitles me to" (75). She needs someone to take care of her as she grows older. Though different from the young merchant's, her goal in marriage is no less practical or self-interested. In his answer to her letter, her brother, the attorney, gives remarriage a patriarchal seal of approval by praising her reasons for not remaining a widow. He also approves the young merchant on the grounds that he is honest and not likely to prove an obvious social embarrassment: this suitor is, they agree, "polite without affectation" and "a very sensible young man." The brother's only reservation is that "there is nothing more precarious than commerce, and the merchant who today has unlimited credit, may be tomorrow in the Gazette [i.e. as a bankrupt]." But, as he explains, it was possible to take legal measures prior to the marriage "to secure [for her] a sufficiency against the worst" (75). With her suitor vetted and her financial security legally assured, the widow writes back to the young merchant to accept his proposal in principle and to demonstrate the prudence for which he is marrying her by insisting that, before tying the knot, they spend some time conversing with each other to see if there is any "union of minds" between them. What a thought!

Like Crowder, Cooke emphasized the importance of obtaining a parent's or a brother's consent before agreeing to a marriage, whether one was a young woman, a young man or a widow. In one correspondence, a young woman refuses to consider a young man's intentions serious until his mother has written to tell her she approves the match, and will not agree to marry him before she has traveled into the country to consult her guardian. Cooke generally made the correspondences on courtship and marriage triangular, not only to make the point that a parent's or brother's vetting and background checks were essential when marriages were contemplated between virtual strangers, but also to show that willing acceptance by the other person's family could make an otherwise impractical marriage feasible. There are instances, for example, in which a struggling young tradesman or impecunious army officer is enabled to marry the young woman he loves because her father approves of him sufficiently to take him into his business in order to enable him to support a wife.

Cooke downplayed financial motives for marriage, even among young beginners in business, by giving other practical motives more prominence. But in courtship correspondences between a rich young gentleman and a beautiful young lady with no fortune, and between a wealthy widower and a friend's sister, he positively argued that a wealthy man could afford to marry at his pleasure, for love, for companionship or to secure a woman of merit, and that he should do so rather than seek to increase his fortune. The rich young gentleman points out in his first letter to the beautiful young lady with no fortune that this was not currently the norm: "It is a general reflection against the manners of the present age, that marriage is only considered as one of those methods by which avarice may be satisfied, and property increased; that neither the character nor the accomplishments of the woman are much regarded; her merit being estimated by the thousands of her fortune" (95). The young gentleman blames the many unhappy marriages he sees around him on the fact that "merit and riches are far from being connected, and that a woman may have those qualifications, necessary to adorn her sex, though adverse fortune has denied her money" (96). In her response, young Cinderella is doubtful about the wisdom of accepting his proposal: she worries about her reception by his family and friends, fearing contempt and rejection on account of her poverty and orphaned state; but having been assured that his family approves his choice and that her "virtues entitle [her] to much more than [he] is able to give," she consults her benefactress and agrees to marry him. Her second letter to him, accepting his proposal, does not, however offer a story-book ending. Instead, it reveals her fearfulness about the consequences of this decision: "I must give myself up to you as a poor friendless orphan"; "If I must comply I shall be obliged to trust the remainder to yourself";"If you should. . .deviate from the paths of virtue. . .I have no friend to complain to. . ." (98). To marry, especially as a woman without family or fortune, was to render oneself helpless and dependent upon the "virtue" of another.

Though Cooke included a letter from a young woman describing the joys of marriage, it was this helplessness and dependence of women in marriage that he explored in his letters of instruction and advice. Two letters on marriage, supposedly from a lady in town to a friend who is unhappily married, describe the shortcomings of marriage for women, while insisting that having made the decision to marry, a woman had no choice but to make the best of it:

Since the laws of God and nature have given men supreme authority in marriage, we ought not first to accept them upon those terms, and then mutiny upon all occasions. For though some men are so kind as to make our yoke light unto us, yet we take them "for better or worse," and experience shews us that the odds are on the worse side. All this we should consider before we engage ourselves in those strict ties, which oblige us to deny our own inclinations, to comply with those of our husbands. (172)

This "lady" proscribes all the devices that she says women used to ease their situation, such as encouraging their husbands to spend as much time as possible outside the home, developing their own hectic social life, retaliating by being more unreasonable or more angry than he, or trying to leave him. And while admitting that "a husband's keeping another before one's eyes is the cruelest thing he can do," she insists that the wife must continue to appear "unmoved" even "under so great a provocation," and seek to reclaim him with tenderness (176). "It is," she observes, "a very silly thing for people to quarrel who must be friends again" (175). A woman should bear such crosses with Christian resignation, remembering that "we every day deserve God's chastisements, and that wicked and unreasonable men are a sword of his. . .to humble us, in order to draw us nearer to himself" (174).

Christian resignation to death and dissolution was a long-standing topos of letters of consolation, but Cooke used it to criticize Britain's hierarchical and political divisions:

If we examine the records of mortality we shall find the memorials of a mixed multitude resting together without any regard to rank or seniority. None are ambitious of the uppermost rooms, or chief seats in the mansions of the dead. . . Why then should we raise such a mighty stir about superiority and precedence, when the next remove will reduce us all to a state of equal meanness? Why should we exalt ourselves and debase others, since we must all one day lie upon a common level? We must all be blended together in the same common dust. Here persons of contrary interests, and different sentiments, sleep together. Death having laid his hands on the contending parties, and brought all the differences to an amicable conclusion. (148)

Cooke included several travel letters comparing Britain to her Catholic colonial rivals, Spain, Portugal and France, to argue that "the meanest subject in England, or any part of the British dominions, enjoys more real liberty than a Spanish grandee, or a peer of France" (132), and to warn his readers that the violent political dissensions shaking England would destroy English liberty (134). In one of these letters, a traveler returning to England after several years abroad pronounces himself shocked by the "animosities" subsisting "among all ranks of people" and by the party factionalism he found everywhere. He observes that "when I find no fault committed by administration except such as is inseparably connected with human nature, I consider the abettors as real incendiaries, who want to create dissensions amongst a brave united people" (192). The people should, presumably, treat government in the same humane and forgiving manner as the master did his erring apprentice.

According to Cooke, the people should be united across ranks and party by the Enlightenment recognition that man is a social being who needs society to subsist, and that it is therefore every person's duty to contribute to the public good: "Since choice, as well as necessity and conveniency, induce all men to unite and form societies, it is the indispensable duty of every individual to become a useful member, and contribute all in his power to promote the happiness of the whole" (158). Cooke also stresses the allied argument that for individuals to live happily together in society, it is essential for everyone to be virtuous. Cooke acknowledged that justice and law were too frequently perverted: "men often commit injustice because it is in their interest, and they chuse rather to satisfy themselves than others" (180). But he argued that everyone was a loser thereby, and that the cure was a massive injection of virtue. This led to a certain anti-intellectualism, for Cooke repeatedly used the authority of a clergyman in this collection to argue that "the endowments of the head deserve no admiration compared to those of the heart" (115) and that the thirst for knowledge must be kept "in a proper subordination to a thirst after moral improvement" (118). But it also led to an emphasis on philanthropy as the means of remedying the ills and injustices of society – there are several exemplary instances in these letters, besides that of the gentleman of known benevolence, of haves helping have-nots to raise or establish their children in such a way as to enable them to become useful and self-supporting members of society.

What appears most curious, however, given this emphasis on man as a social being, is Cooke's dissociation of what we would call "friendship" from social relations of all kinds. Cooke makes it clear through letters of advice and instruction which question whether friendship was possible between men, that the complementary conception of friendship as an effective, but hypocritical and often deceptive, means of forging social alliances by establishing relations of service and patronage, could no longer be called friendship. But he also indicates that no substitute was yet officially in place. Friendship, defined as a relation of affection, in which individuals who are not kin could safely "unbosom themselves" to one another, and trust that the other would be there to help in times of trouble, is presented as an ideal that is rarely realized and that still has to be sold to the public as consistent with "the prudence of man and the piety of a Christian" (107).

US BOOKSELLERS: COOK'S NEW AND COMPLETE LETTER-WRITER, OR NEW ART OF POLITE CORRESPONDENCE

The New and Complete Letter-Writer, by the Rev. Thomas Cook (without an e) was an abridged version of Cooke's *Universal Letter-Writer* that was reprinted in New York, Philadelphia, Poughskeepie, NY, Brattleborough, VT, and possibly elsewhere, between 1803 and 1818.[12] Its anonymous compiler used excision and selection to obliterate Cooke's social, commercial and political messages. Though he reproduced Cooke's four sections, he eliminated all the political letters, the travel letters, most of the letters of advice and instruction and all but two of the letters to and from professionals, sharply reducing the number of letters in Cooke's manual from 140 to fifty, and the size of the manual from 240 pages to 107. Since these excisions removed almost all Cooke's letters between mature adults other than those concerned with trade or commerce, this had the effect of reorienting the rest of the manual exclusively to young people prior to marriage. The manual's focus on young people, and especially on young women, was reinforced by the addition at the end of three long conduct book letters on female conduct, from a mother called Portia to her daughter, Sophia.

There are only six letters in *The New and Complete Letter-Writer*'s section of "Letters to and from Relations," the first of which is a version

---

12 Possibly elsewhere because the 1803 edition states that it was printed in the United States, but gives no place or publisher.

of Charles Hallifax's letter from a younger brother explaining that his mother has instructed him to look to his elder brother to supply the place of his deceased father. This letter was introduced to promote what the table of contents calls "the Respect and Obedience due to Parents." In keeping with this by now familiar focus on fraternal relations, the compiler followed up with one of Cooke's letters from an apprentice to his mother (extracted from the correspondence of which it there formed part), and Cooke's exchange of letters between a boy at school and his older brother, now apprenticed in New York rather than in London. The compiler omitted all Cooke's other schoolboy and apprentice letters, as well as all his maidservant letters, and concluded this section with the aunt's letter to her niece cautioning her against keeping company with a gentleman of bad character, and the niece's obedient reply (above, p. 201). In this context, this cautionary exchange does double duty as a letter warning young men not to be libertines if they wish to succeed in courtship. Education and training were not stressed by this compiler perhaps because apprenticeships now involved schooling as well as practical service, and he assumed that children and apprentices were now being effectively served by schools.

The New and Complete Letter-Writer devoted most of its attention to letters of business (sixteen letters) and letters of courtship (twenty-three letters), as if sharing the view of earlier *Complete Letter-Writers* that issues of courtship were important to young women, and the perception of American printers of *New Academies of Compliment*, that earlier *Letter-Writers* had left young men without a language in which to court them. What is surprising in both sections, however, given representations of America as "the best poor man's country" in the world, is the compiler's elimination of virtually all letters demonstrating upward social mobility. The letters of business focus on issues of mercantile payment and on the vexed problem of bankruptcy. But there are no letters showing a young beginner how to get started in business without family connections – the one letter opening a trading relationship with a merchant in New York is from the young man whose parents have the wherewithal to get him started. The courtship letters include Cooke's letters about elopement, the passionate letters between the young officer going to Minorca with his regiment and the girl he has to leave behind, and the long sequence in which a young woman refuses to take her suitor seriously until she receives a letter from his mother. But all but one of the letters showing marriages occurring between persons of different ages and classes have been eliminated, including that between the young tradesman and the widow. The sole exception is the correspondence between the rich young gentleman and the beautiful impoverished young orphan (above, p. 207). It might be argued that this was sufficient to make the point that marriage was conceived more democratically in the new nation; but taken by itself, it might as easily be read as a recommendation that marrying a woman without family and fortune was a good way of obtaining a beautiful, submissive and totally dependent wife.

Eliminating all the controversial political and social material in Cooke's *Universal Letter-Writer*, the compiler of this manual reduced the number of letters of advice and instruction to five. All were "politically safe" inasmuch as they related to women's conduct rather than to the conduct of government or society, and ignored Cooke's letters dealing with women's suffering in marriage. In one correspondence, a man informs a clergyman of his wife's exemplary Christian death, and the clergyman offers entirely conventional Christian sentiments of consolation. In another, a young woman informs her mistress that she left her house suddenly as a result of sexual harassment by her son, and her approving, philanthropic mistress helps her reestablish herself elsewhere. In the final letter, a lady consoles a friend whose lover has married another. This letter was Cooke's rewrite of a letter originally by Eliza Haywood, that was reprinted in Crowder's *Complete Letter-Writer*.

The bias towards women's conduct demonstrated in this compiler's highly truncated version of Cooke's section "On Friendship etc." is reinforced by the addition of a final section "On Cleanliness and Behaviour in Company" which consists of a mother's advice to her fifteen-year-old daughter. These unattributed letters between Portia and her daughter Sophia were selected and adapted from Charles Allen's *The Polite Lady* (London, 1760). One of the interesting things about the selected letters is that they constitute a more or less direct transposition to young women of the *Complete Letter-Writer*'s conventional letter to a young man advising him how to conduct himself in company. Young women are now the ones being told to listen to their elders with flattering attention, not to interrupt, not to bring shame upon themselves by speaking about subjects about which they know little, and to take every precaution not to offend. It is somehow assumed in this manual that young men will know just how to conduct themselves both in business and in society, and perhaps that it is now perfectly permissible for them to talk in company if they wish.

The other interesting thing about this correspondence between a mother and her fifteen-year-old daughter is the paradoxical relationship to England that it delineates. On the one hand, noble English ladies are used as examples of conduct that a nice young woman should avoid: a Lady Dormer is very fine but very dirty, and a Lady Danvers chatters nonsense all the time and listens to no one but herself – unlike the exemplary young miss who becomingly unites simplicity of dress with cleanliness, and knows how to be silent and when to speak. On the other hand, the daughter addressed in these letters, who is to be imitated by American readers, has been sent to her aunt in London to learn proper manners and conversational skills; and the letters from her mother which pursue her there with additional advice reiterate that she must follow her aunt's guidance on all such matters. One might say that the imperative inscribed by this paradox is the same as that implied by the compiler's selections and excisions from Cooke's English *Letter-Writer*: be English, but in a different manner.

PHILADELPHIA: HOGAN'S NEW UNIVERSAL LETTER-WRITER, OR COMPLETE ART OF POLITE CORRESPONDENCE

Like Cooke, Philadelphia printer David Hogan assumed that his audience consisted largely of people who had difficulty drafting a letter from scratch. Essentially letterate, and already "convinced of the great importance and utility of epistolary correspondence to almost every occasion of life," his readers had the ability to "make a proper application of the examples given," but lacked "a ready pen" because they "ha[d] not acquired early habits of correspondence." Hogan's goal, as he described it, was not only to offer them examples of letters for every occasion, but also to produce a collection that was "particularly suited to the circumstances of our own country." To this end, the letters in his massive and very successful *New Universal Letter-Writer* were not only "carefully selected from the most approved Epistolary Writers." As he was careful to stress, "several of the letters [were] taken from approved American writers, and were never before published in any work of this kind."[13]

Where the anonymous compiler of *The New and Complete Letter-Writer* altered the ideological contents of Cooke's *Universal Letter-Writer* principally by excision and selection, Hogan altered – and all but reversed – Cooke's ideological positions principally by combining letters from several English *Letter-Writers* and by the strategic addition and positioning of his new American materials. He added his American letters

13 *New Universal Letter-Writer* (1800), title-page, and preface, iv. Quotations are taken from this edition.

– some of which were by Benjamin Franklin, some of which he may have written himself – to a mix that he created by combining large numbers of letters from Cooke's *Universal Letter-Writer* with letters and an initial framework taken from Isaiah Thomas's *New and Complete Letter-Writer or the Art of Correspondence* (1791, 1794).[14] Thomas's manual was already a combination of letters from Crowder's and Dilworth's *Complete Letter-Writers*, with a few letters from Cooke thrown in. Hogan reversed the proportions: his is a reproduction of Cooke interspersed with considerable Crowder and a little Dilworth. But though the greater part of his collection was composed of letters from English manuals, Hogan rearranged them and recombined them with his American supplements in such a way as to produce a manual that was distinctively different from others on the market. Perhaps for that reason, it was also considerably more successful than any other American manual on the market during the same years. Where other American adaptations at best produced a few single printings in different states, Hogan printed and sold six editions of *The New Universal Letter-Writer* in Philadelphia between 1800 and 1818, with only minor changes from edition to edition.

The four sections in Hogan's manual reflected the four sections in Cooke's *Universal Letter-Writer*: "Letters of Business"; "Letters on Love, Courtship and Marriage"; "Letters of Advice, Affection etc."– which corresponds to Cooke's "Letters to and From Relations" but lacks the schoolboy letters – and "Letters on Friendship and Miscellaneous Subjects." The fact that Hogan changed the order in which Cooke's sections appeared is significant for, like *The New and Complete Letter-Writer*, the manual as a whole is dominated by business-related issues and by matters related to women's conduct.

Hogan began his collection and the section of Letters of Business with a rewrite of Dilworth's letter "To a young Trader, generally in a hurry of business, advising Method as well as Diligence" taken from Isaiah Thomas's *New Complete Letter-Writer*. Thomas's version of this letter starkly framed the alternative facing merchants and traders – method and diligence in business or bankruptcy – which Hogan's subsequent selection of letters from Cooke implicitly reinforced. Hogan also included all Cooke's letters showing young men without family connections how to set up in business for themselves, even adding one "From a young Person just out of his Apprenticeship to a Relation, requesting a loan" in

---

14 The first seven letters in Hogan's first section follow the order of letters in Thomas's Table of Contents.

order to be able to become a master rather than have to remain a journeyman. Hogan likewise included all Cooke's letters showing tradesmen how they could help each other out in hard times. But rather than leaving discussion of the moral causes of failure to the letters of instruction and advice at the end as Cooke had done, he foregrounded the moral alternative from the beginning and made it the thematic focus of his selection, in accordance with the narrativized tradition of American *Letter-Writers* like Bradfords' or Greene's.

The other major alteration that Hogan introduced in the letters of business had to do with the scope of the trade he portrayed. While including all the letters in Cooke that involved doing trade at a distance, with the exception of the exchange about trading with America, Hogan changed the place names to make it appear as if trade were occurring exclusively within the American continent, notably between the backcountry and Philadelphia or New York. Though New York and Philadelphia were major ports for transatlantic and West Indian commerce, there is no reference to such commerce in Hogan's *Letter-Writer*, and no mention of ports. Where Cooke had used his business letters and letters from officers to open a vista onto the international scene, Hogan offered the image of an independent or isolationist economy in which the American continent was sufficient unto itself. As if to reinforce this point, he concluded his section of letters of business with Benjamin Franklin's self-reliant "Letter to his Friend AB containing useful hints to young Tradesmen" about the way to wealth.

Hogan introduced his most far-reaching changes in relation to courtship and marriage. Though he reprinted many of Cooke's courtship correspondences, all of which involved the intervention of a parent, guardian or brother in the decision leading to marriage, he came out strongly against "compulsive marriages" and used the addition of new American letters to teach young women how to make good marital choices for themselves. Having represented the possibilities of marriages across differences in age, family occupation and wealth through Cooke's letters, he "corrected" their emphasis on obtaining parental or fraternal consent by introducing six American letters of advice from a father to his daughters, on how they should conduct themselves during courtship and on how best to choose a mate.

In these six long letters, the father first teaches his daughters to distinguish among their suitors. There is, he explains, "an unmeaning gallantry" which is harmless if properly handled, and offers a young woman the advantages of an escort, useful little observances, and conversation with a man (whose conversation is always "superior" to that of women). This is to be distinguished from "male coquettry," fortunately "rare in this country," where "men employed in the pursuits of business, ambition or pleasure, will give themselves the trouble to engage a woman's affections, merely from the vanity of conquest" (77). The father warns his daughters not only against marrying a rake, but also against marrying a man with hereditary diseases in his family, a man who has applied to her family or friends for their intercession, and a fool, because he is "the most intractable of all animals." The father does his best for those dull and inarticulate lovers who populated *Complete Letter-Writers* by assuring his daughters that "True love, in all its stages. . .renders a man not only respectful, but timid to the highest degree, in his behaviour to the woman he loves" and makes him "always appear to disadvantage in the company of his mistress" (73) and by advising his daughters to seek a man who has a "sense of religion." But he also opens up other possibilities by telling them not only to "examine your tempers, tastes and hearts severely before allowing your affections to be engaged," but also to decide what traits or circumstances they think essential to their happiness, and which they think may be sacrificed. The father insists that his daughters themselves eschew coquetry by undeceiving any lover who is fooling himself about their feelings for him, rather than keeping him on a string. He also insists they reject any man's attempt to make them show their feelings before he has openly and honorably made his addresses, since male coquets specialized in ambiguous courtships and in evading attempts to pin them down. This father therefore gives young women far more autonomy in relation to men than English *Letter-Writers* had done. But he insists that romantic views of marriage must be avoided by any young woman who does not wish to remain an old maid, for "without an unusual share of natural sensibility and very peculiar good fortune, a woman in this country has very little probability of marrying for love" (71).

Hogan supports this paternal American advice by a careful selection of letters from Crowder's *Complete Letter-Writer*. In this context, Crowder's letters from a lady professing aversion to the tedious formality of court-ship and insisting on a clear declaration of the gentleman's passion serve to illustrate how a young woman can go about cutting through the ambiguous smoke screens produced by rakes. In this context, too, *The Complete Letter-Writer*'s letter from an aunt reproving her niece for mocking her sober, sermonizing lover and the Lady Wortley Montagu letter describing her idyll of marriage, read as a reiteration of the father's advice to seek a man with "a sense of religion" and as confirmation that romantic views of marriage are incompatible both with extant mores and with realistic expectations. *The Complete Letter-Writer's* letters from the lover accusing his lady of inconstancy and from the lover who breaks off all relations with a lady who flirts with another, support the father's injunction against playing the coquette.

The father's letters of advice to his daughters are also adamant that women not be forced into marriage against their inclinations, and promise to ensure that his daughters are left financially independent so that they will never have to marry from necessity. In an allusion to the imperatives of republican motherhood,[15] this father asserts that "I am not enough of a patriot to wish you to marry for the good of the public" (79). To underline these injunctions against forced marriage, Hogan created a cluster of nine reprinted letters which argue against forcing a young woman to marry against her inclinations or show her rejecting a suitor she cannot like. The *Complete Letter-Writer's* letter from a daughter to a father, dutifully expostulating against a match with a man much older than herself (above, pp. 96–7) begins the cluster. The sequence in which a young woman urges a man who had obtained her family's consent to drop his suit because she could not love him also reappears, with its portrait of the misery that awaits the suitor in a marriage in which he can receive "nothing but forced civilities in return for tender endearments" (108). Hogan also adds an answer to a standard letter from a young woman informing her father of a proposal of marriage in which the father insists that he "would neither thwart nor force [his daughter's] inclination" since "the consequences, especially of the latter, have been in many instances fatal" (105). Hogan closes the cluster with Cooke's rewrite of the first letter dutifully expostulating against a match with a much older man.[16] In this rewrite, a ward explicitly writing to her guardian "against a compulsive marriages," uncompromisingly refuses to marry the much older man he has selected: "You have expressed a great desire that I should give my hand to Mr. Sturdy: herein I must disobey. . .duty, if not directed by inclination, must give way to nature" (109).

Yet despite this American father's assertion that he is "not enough of a patriot to wish you to marry for the public good," and despite his insistence that romantic views of marriage are to be eschewed, there is

---

15 Kerber, *Women of the Republic.*
16 This is one of only three or four letters Hogan took from Cooke's *New and Complete Universal Letter-Writer.*

considerable idealizing pro-marriage propaganda throughout Hogan's *Letter-Writer*. Interestingly, however, it is almost exclusively directed to men. In one letter, for instance, one male friend writes to another in the following terms:

Dear Charles,
  I am sorry to hear that you have absolutely declared against matrimony, and for no other reason, as I can learn, but because you are not acquainted with its sweets. Has not both Providence and religion enjoined this sacred union? Would we be now in existence only for it? But without confining ourselves to general reflections, let us see if you could not live more comfortably with a woman, than in the single state you are at present resolved to make choice of; for my part I must think that if you find yourself capable of regulating a family, or living upon good terms, with an honest person, and of giving good education to your children, you would find that there is nothing more agreeable than to live with a woman, who has made a tender of herself to you, and who is inclined to discharge faithfully all the duties incumbent on the union. . . ." (127–8)

  The letter goes on to offer an idyllic portrait of domestic life, in which husband and wife "never act but by agreement" and the husband can safely "leave the care of his family concerns to a frugal and good house wife" while he enjoys "uninterrupted tranquility" elsewhere. It concludes by pointing out that "there is something unnatural in a man desiring to remain a bachelor all the days of his life" and that the Romans therefore "expelled from their city those who persisted to live in a state of celibacy" (128). Marriage is a patriotic duty for men. Hogan supports the advertisement of marriage to men in anonymous letters like this by the authority of some big guns. He includes Benjamin Franklin's letter to John Alleyne which points out that "with us in America, marriages are generally in the morning of life," and argues both that "early [marriages] stand the best chance of happiness" and that "by early marriage, youth is earlier formed to a regular and useful life" (243). He also includes a long paper from *The Spectator* describing marriage as an "institution calculated for a constant scene of as much delight as our being is capable of" (129) and telling men how to adjust their minds, conduct and expectations to ensure their own happiness and satisfaction.

  Women are given a grimmer view of the institution. To ensure that the husband can safely leave his family concerns to a frugal and good housewife, there are letters instructing women on the government of servants and care of their house. Hogan includes the letter called "Domestic Rule the Province of the Wife," which here reads as a straightforward list of the wife's proper duties. But he is more interested in shaping wives' conduct towards their husbands than in household matters. To this end, he offers a rewrite of the edited letter from Felicia shortly before her marriage (above, p. 179), which states that:

The great error that women fall into about marrying, is the seeking wives instead of husbands. The fear of having it thought that they have submission enough to be governed, raises a monstrous disturbance in their breasts. To join the ideas of love and obedience is not in their power. If a woman would marry sensibly, let her choose the man whom she can obey cheerfully. To marry Florio, and then to obey him, ever appeared to me as if I was commanded, as Desdemona says upon another occasion, "To do peculiar profit/To my own person." It is a command to follow the bent of my inclinations. (126–7)

The reference to Desdemona (who is murdered by her husband) does not appear to be ironic. There is a letter from a mother advising a daughter who suspects her husband of having an affair to suppress her jealousy and "make home agreeable to him" (121); and a letter from the mistress of a boarding school instructing one of her late pupils that to avoid strife with her husband, she "must bear, with calmness, everything that the *sincerest* desire for peace can dictate; and studiously avoid every expression, and even look, which may irritate or offend" (140). Here too Hogan brings on the big guns in the form of Swift's three rather harsh letters to "a very young Lady on her Marriage." These inform the young lady, among other things, that Swift hopes her husband will use his authority to prevent her from visiting; that she must spend hours every day reading so that she can attempt to hold his interest by conversing with him; and that "after all the pains you may be at, you can never arrive, in point of learning, to the perfections of a school-boy" (99). If women are freer in Hogan's *Letter-Writer* to choose their husbands than they were in English manuals, the conduct prescribed to them after marriage is uncompromisingly harsher. It seems designed to ensure that husbands achieve "as much delight as their being is capable of," while leaving wives to experience the truth of Rochefoucauld's maxim that "marriages are convenient but never delightful."

Like *The New and Complete Letter-Writer*, Hogan excluded Cooke's political letters, whether they preached loyalty to government, the virtues of war or anti-papism, but he went further than Cooke in exploring the limits of friendship and sociality, by recontextualizing the letters containing Cooke's Enlightenment vision of man as a social being whose duty it was to be virtuous and to contribute to the public good, and reexamining the letter questioning the possibility of friendship within the context of immediate social life.

Hogan thematized issues of sociality and friendship in terms of the opposite imperatives of sincerity and secrecy. The letters from Cooke that he included argued that "Friendship obliges the parties engaged to lay open their minds to one another; there must not be any concealment" (192), that man "has a capacity, and even desire for friendship" precisely because "man is a social being" (191), and that a rational consideration of the sources of pleasure and pain must tend to promote benevolence, friendship and honesty among mankind" (205). In the household and courtship letters from Cooke that Hogan selected, it is therefore always a strong recommendation for a suitor that "an air of *sincerity* appeared in all he said" (57) or that he asks "leave to deal *sincerely*" and for a young woman that she has "an open temper" (67) or is willing to display an "inoffensive *sincerity*" (108). The word *sincerity* is regularly italicized in the text. The American father agrees: the problem with "the luxury and dissipation that prevails in genteel life," he complains, is that "as it corrupts the heart, it renders it incapable of warm, *sincere* and steady friendship" (67), for "simplicity of manners and integrity in all. . . naturally lead us to expect sincerity in those with whom we are in any way concerned" (227).

But supported by Swift and other letters in this volume, the American father also stresses the importance of secrecy, concealment and reserve. Young women are advised not only "never [to] discover the secrets of one friend to another" and to take care to "be secret in love matters" (68) but also to seek information about a suitor's character for sense, morals, family and fortune "in a secret and prudent manner" (82). They must also keep their feelings secret at all times: "If you love him, let me advise you never to discover to him the full extent of your love, no, not although you marry him. That sufficiently shows your preference, which is all he is entitled to know" (73). It goes without saying that women are also instructed to hide their feelings from their friends and nearest relations, especially where these concern love, jealousy or anger. "Reserve and delicacy ought to be kept up" at all times (84). "True love" in men likewise "seeks concealment" (73); and if it does not, there is a friend to chide the "*foolish* Lover" for keeping his love a secret from his friend, while displaying it to the young lady: "be assured, my friend, that disappointment and vexation will be the consequence of this over-passion. . .Love is such a nice matter that it requires more economy than you are aware" (124). Uneconomically "violent" feelings which show themselves are treated with suspicion whether they occur in women or in men, and are said to create "satiety" and "disgust." Given this emphasis

on secrecy, it is hardly surprising that young women should have difficulty in determining whether their suitors are deceiving them or not; for
judgment of another's character and intentions becomes a matter of
distinguishing between one kind of duplicity and another. As we will
see in the next chapter, this is also a version of the problem of reading in
the Atlantic world.

Hogan's last significant alteration of Cooke is to partially reproduce
Crowder's self-reflexive treatment of letter-writing. He includes two key
letters about letter-writing that Crowder had used: the letter "in the Stile
of a Lady by Mr. Pope" and Bishop Atterbury's letter to his son "with
hints on writing letters" (above, p. 163). But he adds Johnson's essay on
letter-writing from *The Rambler* and a letter from *The Spectator* that
includes some discourse on epistolography. These take rather different
positions. Ignoring *The Spectator,* letter manuals, the numerous collections of letters published during the eighteenth century, and the ongoing
pedagogical and rhetorical tradition of classical and vernacular epistolary
instruction in universities and schools, Johnson proclaimed in his usual
magisterial manner that "as we have few letters we have likewise few
criticisms upon the epistolary stile" (251). He insisted that "letters cannot
be properly reduced to settled rules"; that "the letter has no peculiarity
but its form"; and that "letters that have no other end than the entertainment of the correspondents, are more properly regulated by critical
precepts [than letters of business or letters of news] because the matter
and style are equally arbitrary" (251). The selection from *The Spectator*
that Hogan included reminds us of what Johnson was dismissing as
non-existent:

I have often thought, if the letters written by men of good-nature to their wives,
were to be compared with those written by men of gallantry to their mistresses,
the former notwithstanding any inequality of stile, would appear to have the
advantage. Friendship, tenderness and constancy, dressed in simplicity of
expression, recommend themselves by a more native elegance than passionate
raptures, extravagant encomiums and slavish adoration. If we were permitted to
search the cabinet of the beautiful Narcissa, among heaps of epistles from several
admirers, which are there preserved with equal care, how few should we find but
would make any one sick in the reading, except those who are flattered by them!
But in how different a stile must the wise Benevolus, who converses with that
good-sense and good humour among all his friends, write to a wife who is the
worthy object of his utmost affection! (134)

These lines in Hogan's *Letter-Writer* return us, in early nineteenth-
century America, to England at the end of the seventeenth century and

to John Hill's rewritings of Serre's Letters of Complement, with their "flattery," "passionate raptures," "extravagant encomiums" and "slavish adoration." They recall the long struggle to supplant complemental letters with letters demonstrating good sense dressed in simplicity of expression, in which, as we will see in Chapter 7, *The Spectator* played a leading and ongoing part. They also remind us of some of the rules and traditions that Johnson conveniently ignored.

Primary among these were the convictions that, far from being arbitrary, matter and style were always conjoined in epistolary writing; and that far from bearing, as Johnson claimed, on "trifles" and "affairs considerable only by their frequent occurrence," their frequent occurrence made the letters concerning them integral to the nature and construction of social life. As we have seen, rules and social conventions conjoined matter and style, inasmuch they dictated the contents and the sentiments to be expressed in different classes of letter, *including* those that were designed to entertain. As we saw too, matter and style were each construed as indices of the moral character and taste not only of individual letter-writers, but also of society as a whole. Though differing in taste and in social, moral and political philosophy, *The Spectator* and all the diverse printers and compilers of letter manuals on both sides of the Atlantic during the long eighteenth century shared the conviction that letters expressed, modeled and constructed social relations, and that to change the letters people were writing was to change the world.

PART III

Secrecy and the transatlantic culture of letters

Introduction

There is a long history of secret writing in England, which we are beginning to recover. Work has also been done on seventeenth- and eighteenth-century uses of secret writing in European political contexts – for instance in connection with the Jacobites and with France.[1] The transatlantic dimensions of this phenomenon, and its impact on the writing, reading and interpretation both of ordinary transatlantic letters and of eighteenth-century literary texts, concern us here. And here, the spread of letter-writing down the social hierarchy and across the provinces gave the issue of secret writing a whole new accent and domain.

The dissemination of letter-writing practices to the populace at large was a phenomenon that a succession of ruling elites rightly understood to be both necessary to and potentially disruptive of centralized government and authority from above. Letters might make empire work; but they also permitted lateral communication among the king's subjects independently of the London authorities, and enabled subjects all over the empire to share plans and intelligence without reference to their governors and social superiors. Development of the infrastructure that facilitated the national and transatlantic circulation of letters also facilitated intercourse capable of disturbing the peace and prosperity of the royal, governing and mercantile elites in whose interests that infrastructure had been developed in the first place. Consequently, British government was in a cleft stick: unable to suppress correspondence and unwilling to give it unlicensed freedom, ministers and parliament struggled throughout the long eighteenth century to contain the proliferation, and control the uses

---

1 Lerer, *Courtly Letters in the Age of Henry VIII*; Patterson, *Censorship and Interpretation*; Potter, *Secret Rites and Secret Writing*; Jagodzinski, *Privacy and Print*; Marshall, *Intelligence and Espionage*; Frazer, *Intelligence of the Secretaries of State*; Keeble, *Literary Culture of Nonconformity*; Pollock, "Living on the Stage of the World"; Mee, "Examples of Safe Printing"; Watson, *Form of the English Novel*; Wilson, *Sense of the People*, 45ff; Zaczek, *Censored Sentiments*; Bannet, "Secret History."

both of printed *and* of handwritten letters, by means of laws and taxes, censorship and stamps, interception, detection and punishment.

This was so much part of the culture – indeed had been for so long – that, as we will see, letter manuals, *vade mecums* and other printed books throughout the century taught evasion through secret writing along with epistolary communication skills. While the epistolary models that we have been considering so far in this book taught reader-writers the proper forms and commonplaces for what contemporaries called the "*external letter*," instruction was also publicly given in manuals and in other published books about how best to write and read for the "*internal letter*" it contained, where a correspondent's true meaning might be expressed. Along with their conduct book teachings and their models of the common forms and commonplace sentiments of different classes of letters, eighteenth-century letter manuals and *vade mecums* recommended secrecy in the conduct of oral and written conversation, and provided instruction in secret writing. To communicate "privately" by letter was often to communicate "secretly" as well.

This introduced another level of writing and reading to those we have examined to date, and one which could markedly alter the *prima facie* meaning of letters. Here the commonplaces and conventions of different classes of letter became a means of making letters look ordinary that were not in reality so. The epistolary models merely served as useful masks for politically or commercially riskier messages that correspondents wished to conceal from third parties of various sorts.

The interactions, reversals and conjunctions of external and internal, public and hidden, meanings in the same letters suggest modifications of two still influential theories about eighteenth-century discursive practices: Habermas's thesis that late seventeenth- and eighteenth-century British culture produced a democratic bourgeois public sphere that was "open to all" and "constituted by private people putting reason to use";[2] and Foucault's description of the Panoptikon – the Benthamite prison where prisoners were disciplined and controlled in their cells by the surveillance of a hidden observer – as the *summum* of the so-called classical age. The collaboration of public and hidden transcripts across Habermas's divide, which will be explored in Chapter 6, reminds us how pervasively in British culture the private has inhabited the public domain, how far public matters have shaped the expressions of private life, and that the

---

2 Habermas, *Structural Transformation*, xvii, xviii. Critiques include: Calhoun, *Habermas and the Public Sphere*; Love, *Scribal Publication*; Backscheider and Dykstal, *Intersections*.

private sphere has always already had to fashion a public face. At the same time, the reversals of public and hidden transcripts produced by the efforts made by all sides to obtain "sight" of the hidden transcripts of others indicate, contra Foucault, that in the eighteenth century, for government and governed alike, "power" resided in the exchanges occurring privately off stage, thus in what escaped surveillance, eluded punishment and remained carefully hidden from view, and in the associated ability to control what was displayed. Where power lay in concealment of what transpired off stage and in the clever management of what appeared on stage, detecting, deciphering, sharing with others and/or publishing to the world the hidden transcripts of others became, for government and governed alike, quintessentially *dis*empowering acts.

To make visible the implications of secret writing for transatlantic relationships, and the structure of the transatlantic culture of letters in which manuals' teachings about secret writing were relevant, Chapter 6 begins by returning to the post, and to Benjamin Franklin's interrogation at the bar of the House of Commons in 1766 about its transatlantic functions. Without pretending to be exhaustive, the second section builds on extant scholarship in a variety of fields to review the different threads of correspondence that linked Britain and America. The focus is on the collaboration of public and hidden epistolary transcripts in producing and transmitting "intelligence" – in the compound eighteenth-century sense of information, news, knowledge and judgment – about what was going on the other side of the water. This was an important common thread running through political, commercial, periodical, literary, personal and domestic letters of diverse sorts. The question of intelligence was a key issue both in eighteenth-century letters and in thinking about the post because in the transatlantic connection, little could be done either in public business or in private matters without obtaining information, news, knowledge and some evaluation of what was transpiring "beyond the sea." This leads, in the third section, to another major issue that Franklin's interrogation raises: the question of communication at a distance, and of how letters were written, interpreted and read. The focus here is on epistolary practices, on style, and on the way the collaboration of public and hidden transcripts in the same letters enabled ordinary letter-writers to communicate what they chose. In the terms set by Franklin's interrogation, the issue addressed here is a question of the liberty that the empire of letters left correspondents both to use and to evade government when they wished. The final section discusses the instruction in secret writing widely available in the Atlantic world in *vade mecums* like Mather's or Fisher's *Young Man's Companions*, in letter manuals, and in books on conveying "secret information" to which users were referred. Approached in this way, I hope that it will become apparent that in the eighteenth-century culture of letters, various kinds and degrees of secrecy had a place within the normative culture, and that our modern association of ciphers and other forms of secret writing exclusively with outliers, foreign agents and spies does not necessarily apply. Chapter 7 considers some of the implications both of secret writing and of the other features of epistolography examined in this book for our reading of literature through an examination of three familiar literary texts.

CHAPTER 6

Public and hidden transcripts

GOVERNMENT BY POST

In the version printed and circulated in 1766 of Benjamin Franklin's interrogation at the bar of the House of Commons about repeal of the Stamp Act, the question of Britain's proper relationship to her American colonies resolves itself into a series of differences about the cost, reach and efficacy of transatlantic letters. Identifying himself as "Deputy Postmaster General of North America," Franklin establishes the terms of his argument early on, in his response to the question: "What was the temper of America towards Great Britain before the year 1763?"

The best in the world. . . Numerous as the people are in the several old provinces, they cost you nothing in forts, citadels, garrisons or armies, to keep them in subjection. They were governed by this country only at the expense of a little pen, ink and paper. They were led by a thread. They had not only respect, but an affection for Great Britain, for its laws, its customs and manners, and even a fondness for its fashions, that greatly increased the commerce.[1]

Franklin uses his contrast between the instruments of force and the instruments of writing to contrast the cost and efficacy of government by compulsion and government by consent, and to discuss different kinds of proximity and distance. He begins by warning the House that the costs of what he calls "the stamping of America," with its connotations of violence done and violence provoked, would far exceed the direct costs of deploying the instruments of war – forts, garrisons, armies. There would also be the indirect costs of cutting the customary threads of intercourse between America and Britain on a variety of levels – legal, commercial, cultural, social and material – and of driving Americans to prefer their own fashions, spin their own thread and manufacture their

---

[1] "Examination of Doctor Benjamin Franklin," in *Pamphlets*, 3.

own dress. There were no such costs, he insisted, to governing America in the usual way through the instruments of writing:

Q. What is the usual constitutional manner of calling on the colonies for aids?
A. A letter from the Secretary of State.
Q. Is this all you mean, a letter from the Secretary of State?
A. I mean the usual way of requisition, in a circular letter from the Secretary of State, by his Majesty's command, reciting the occasion, and recommending it to the colonies to grant such aids as became their loyalty, and were suitable to their abilities. . .
Q. Would they grant money alone, if called on?
A. In my opinion they would, money as well as men, when they have money or can make it. (14–15)

Empire by letter was both cheaper and more effective. Letters brought Britain pure profit in the balance of trade, both in money and in men, because they treated Americans as "part of the British Empire and as having a common interest with it" (12).

Franklin's explanation of how letters situated America as part of the empire turned on the proper distances that correspondence established and maintained. His representation of the Secretary of State's letter courteously recommending an occasion of common interest to the attention of his American correspondents, and politely inviting a favorable response, invoked formulaic phrases from commercial letters, like those that Henry Laurens regularly wrote to his transatlantic correspondents: "I shall endeavour to make our correspondence mutually advantageous, and doubt not you will contribute to the same."[2] For Franklin was arguing that the proper way for Britain to treat America was as a commercial correspondent – a British factor or agent on the American continent, who was left to manage the commerce within that country and to act for his principals on the other side of the water in the best interests of both. Such a correspondent remained linked to Britain by mutual advantage, by a common language and culture, and by exchanges of letters, goods and bills. Government by correspondence such as this preserved the proper distances between their authors "within the realm" in England and their recipients "within their country" in America, whether these distances were construed in terms of "customs and manners," and thus of the usual forms of politeness and respect, or in terms of the distance imposed by the geographical terrain. For in spatial terms, commercial correspondents construed the sea as an interval between, across which they desired the

---

2 Letter from Henry Laurens to Samuel Wilson, July 8, 1747, in *Papers of Henry Laurens.*

threads of mercantile and epistolary commerce to be securely knit, and thus as a space that they had a common interest in safeguarding with money and with men: "You maintain by your fleets, the safety of navigation in it; and keep it clear of pirates; you may have therefore a natural and equitable right to some toll or duty on the merchandise carried through that part of your dominions, towards defraying the expenses you are at in ships to maintain the safety of that carriage" (9).

The stamping of America failed to respect either these polite or these geographical distances. For on the one hand, the Stamp Act brought Britain too close by rudely intruding taxes on the colonists "within their country": it "says we shall have no commerce, make no exchange of property with each other, neither purchase, nor grant, nor recover debts; we shall neither marry, nor make our will, unless we pay such and such sums. . ." (6). And on the other hand, it set the colonists too far from native Britons, by treating them as foreigners to be conquered and subjected by garrisons and armies. Americans "may be looked on here as foreigners, but they do not consider themselves as such" (12). Both by excessive proximity and by excessive distance, the "stamping of America" eliminated the proper distance between "internal" and "external" that empire required and correspondence preserved.

The questioner, Q., expressed skepticism about Franklin's representation of government by the instruments of writing through the tenor of his questions. One set of questions politely points out that, in reality, letters crossed the boundaries that Franklin was trying to establish between what was "within their country" and what was external to it: "Do not letters often come to the post offices in America, directed to some inland town. . .?" "Can the postmaster answer delivering the letter without being payed such additional postage?" "Is not the post office, which they [Americans] have long received, a tax as well as a regulation?" "Is not the post office rate an internal tax laid by Act of Parliament?" These questions also subverted Franklin's argument about excessive proximity by reminding him that the post office was an arm of British government which had its citadels in post offices throughout the colonies and its army in postmasters who, like Franklin, were servants of the Crown. The post office was regulated from London and paid for by Americans, without complaint, by means of stamps on letters. Q. was suggesting that since Americans had long accepted that letters they received from Britain brought them regulations and internal taxes from Parliament, like the rate for postage, stamps were surely the usual, sensible way of paying for an empire ruled and linked by letters.

Franklin's rebuttal was ingenious and from the point of view of Americans, politically correct; but it inadvertently belied his contention that empire by letter was effective and free of cost. Stamps on letters were not a tax, he maintained, but money voluntarily paid for a service rendered: "No person is compellable to pay the money, if he does not choose to receive the service. A man may still, as before the act, send his letter by a servant, a special messenger, or a friend, if he thinks it cheaper and safer" (8). Voluntary consent was reasserted, but with the admission that a man who could choose to send his letter by messenger might deprive the Crown of needed revenue, just as an Assembly might, which could choose how to answer a letter of requisition from the Secretary of State. Letters left correspondents at liberty to evade government if they chose.

A second series of questions attacked Franklin's argument that correspondence preserved the proper distances between Britain and America, by returning again and again to the difficulties it caused. Q. sought to establish that what Franklin considered a proper distance was in reality excessive distance, by indicating how tenuous letters made the threads that linked Britain and America:

Q. Are all parts of the Colonies equally able to pay taxes?
A. No, certainly: the frontier parts which have been ravaged by the enemy, are greatly disabled by that means, and therefore, in such cases are usually favoured in our tax laws.
Q. Can we, at this distance, be competent judges of what favours are necessary?
A. The parliament have supposed it, by claiming to make tax laws for America; I think it impossible.
Q. If the stamp act should be repealed, would not the Americans think they could oblige the parliament to repeal every external tax law now in force?
A. It is hard to answer questions of what people at such a distance will think.
Q. Does the distinction between internal and external taxes exist in the words of the Charter?
A. No. I believe not.
Q. Then may they not, by the same interpretation, object to the parliament's right of external taxation?
A. They never have hitherto. . .
Q. Do not the resolutions of the Pennsylvania assembly say all taxes?
A. If they do, they mean only internal taxes; the same words have not always the same meaning here and in the Colonies. (11, 15, 16)

The questions come back again and again to Franklin's point that Americans should not be subjected to internal taxes "by persons at a distance unacquainted with their circumstances and abilities" (9).

Franklin had used this point to support his contention that Americans should be treated as commercial correspondents who knew their own business and could be left to run it in their country; but Q. endeavors to undercut this contention by getting Franklin to repeat that Britons who remained at what he claimed was the proper distance from America, and who relied on letters to obtain information and to communicate their meaning across the water, could have no acquaintance with what was going on in America or with what people at such a distance would think, and could thus have no control over how the meaning of their letters patent or regulatory would be interpreted. Q. was showing that far from representing a mark of respect, the distance introduced by correspondence was the distance that lack of acquaintance with America, the ambiguities of letters, and the different interpretations of words, had produced. The upshot of arguing that Britain should keep her proper distance, he was suggesting, was to make it impossible for Britain to govern America at all.

As it happens, both sides were right about the empire of letters – at least up to a point. But in England in 1766, which side was right could not have mattered less. The year before, the leading colonial agents in London had privately informed colonial assemblies by letter that Lord Hillsborough at the Board of Trade had called them in to tell them – quite informally, of course – that Rockingham's government had decided to have the Stamp Act repealed when Parliament reconvened. The outcome had already been decided. What mattered in England in 1766, when Parliament did reconvene, was to put on a creditable show. Edmund Burke described the process at the beginning of one of Parliament's Christmas recesses: "Our first scene in this third act of our seven years piece is concluded; our fiddles are playing, and we are here snug in the green room, to prepare, by a little leisure, laughing and chat, to walk out again with grave faces and solemn speeches upon the old stage."[3] The examination staged in Parliament with grave faces and solemn speeches in 1766 was carefully rehearsed with Rockingham's people in advance of the event; for the work of repeal had been done long since in the green room, or as Goffman would say, "off stage," in conversations among members of the government, leading London merchants in the American trade, colonial agents, influential Quakers, and members of parliament, some of which have left their traces in the letters they wrote.

3 Edmund Burke to Charles O'Hara, Dec. 31, 1770, in *Edmund Burke*, 480–1.

In its way, the printed version of the event that was cited above, *Examination of Dr. Benjamin Franklin before an August Assembly, relating to Repeal of the Stamp Act*, was a public performance too. Based on illegally pirated copy of the proceedings in Parliament, circulated in manuscript and ultimately published by Franklin's partner, David Hall, in Philadelphia in 1766 – just before an election for the Assembly that Joseph Galloway feared would go against his party due to its identification with Franklin – the *Examination* redirected the first performance in Parliament towards an American audience that believed Franklin had supported the Stamp Act (which he had) and condemned him for it. The *Examination* sought to change Franklin's public image in America by reenacting the performance in Parliament as the redemptive spectacle of Franklin single-handedly championing colonial interests before the highest powers in Britain. To this end, the scene in Parliament was pared down to a spare dialogue, without comment or stage directions to impugn its apparent objectivity. It was represented as a dialogue between Franklin and what appears to be a single, anonymous questioner – though in reality there had been several different questioners. It was pruned of all the deferential formulae of language and courtesies of address (Sir, my Lord, Dr. Franklin) that would have been used in speech, to make the sides seem more equal than they were. And it was denuded of all context – including that provided by the prior and far longer examinations of Barlow Trecothick, Capel Hanbury and David Mildred – to make the scene of Franklin standing up to Parliament seem more decisive in the decision for repeal than it was. Re-presented in this way, Franklin's performance in Parliament could be used publicly to substantiate the private letters that were hastily being sent to America by Franklin's friends in London, to reassure Philadelphians about Franklin's dedication and effectiveness as a colonial agent in order to keep him in the job.

James Scott's historical appropriation of Goffman's work is a useful place to begin considering the topography and dynamics of the discursive practices indicated here. Scott distinguishes the "open," "staged" interactions between subordinates and governing elites in hierarchical societies like eighteenth-century Britain and British-America, where superiority and subordination, power and deference, had to be properly coded and ceremonially displayed, from the very different oral, written or material exchanges taking place "off stage" both within the elite and within subordinate ranks, that those within each group "hid" from those without. Scott describes this distinction as one between "the public transcript" and the "hidden transcripts" of "restricted publics." He argues that the latter could be expressed in the public transcript only in properly muted or disguised forms. Scott shows that in dominating regimes that demanded deference and consent from powerless subordinates like slaves, colonized peoples and the working class, the latter expressed their frustration, anger or critique by deploying deference as tactic and mask (the pulled forelock), by perpetrating anonymous acts of subversion (pilfering, poaching, slow or shoddy work), and by developing hidden subcultures (jokes, songs, stories, rumor, gossip, folktale, rite).[4]

In the transatlantic culture of letters, however, the dynamic of public and hidden transcripts was not the property of powerless subordinates alone. Among the more empowered ranks of society in the transatlantic world, it was evident to all participants that both public and hidden transcripts were necessary to make the British colonial system work, and that they had to deploy both simultaneously to get anything done. The primary meaning of the word "private" in the eighteenth century was still "secret"; and in this age obsessed with the secrets hidden behind the display of ceremonious, violent or graceful masks, there were many forms and levels of secrecy, the potential presence of which was known to all.

In the above parliamentary *Examination of Doctor Franklin*, for instance, the awareness of everyone present that the Secretary of State had been opening the mail and using the post office as a central arm of his secret intelligence network for over a century was implicit in the discussion of using the instruments of writing to govern or evade government control, as well as in discussion of the different ways in which written words could be meant and understood by government and people. Implicit in the stamping of America, likewise, was the awareness of everyone present that the stamp tax was a way of limiting communication by increasing its costs, which government had used in Britain from the beginning of the eighteenth century. Interception of mail by the Post Office's "Secret Office" on the orders of the Secretary of State, and the stamping of paper were both part of ongoing government efforts to stamp out potentially destabilizing dissent.

As we will see in the next section, this dynamic of public and hidden transcripts shaped the transatlantic culture of letters across domains – political, commercial, periodical, legal, literary and personal or domestic.

4 Scott, *Domination and the Arts of Resistance.*

It was deeply ingrained in the culture for habitual and social as well as legal reasons, all of which taught people who wished to communicate privately to hide their meanings within the proper epistolary forms.

THE TRANSATLANTIC SCENE OF WRITING

The British Board of Trade and Plantations, London's central clearing house for colonial affairs, is a good place to begin reviewing the threads of correspondence linking Britain and America because the Board's very existence underlines the importance of letters in making empire work. Established in 1695 to support the mercantile interests which drove and largely funded colonization and to keep control of the colonies in the hands of the king, the Board of Trade's primary duty throughout its eighty years of activity was to correspond with royal officials in the colonies and to receive, process and respond to colonists' letters of petition and complaint. Filled with placemen like John Locke, Joseph Addison and Matthew Prior as well as with the relations of the great, the Board sought, inquired into, and collated information about what was transpiring in distant territories and about the effects of government measures and laws. It also made recommendations to the king and Privy Council on the basis of its findings, and transmitted their instructions back to royal officials and to petitioners in epistolary form. The extent to which the Board actually controlled British colonial policy varied widely over time, but one thing remained constant throughout the Board's checkered history: the importance attached by contemporaries to controlling colonial correspondence and to interpreting, doling out, and re-presenting the often conflicting intelligence it contained. This was manifest, for instance, in the efforts made by various Secretaries of State to wrest the prerogative of corresponding with Royal Governors from the Board of Trade, and in attempts by a succession of Presidents of the Board to acquire the prerogative of delivering its representations directly to the king. Letters brought an official intelligence, and intelligence bought him power and influence. Nor was the importance that con-temporaries attached to the Board's "secretarial" functions misplaced; for by the first decades of the eighteenth century, the Board had become the chief source and framer of intelligence on colonial matters not only for the king and Privy Council, but also for the Admiralty, the Treasury, the Commissioners of Customs, and Parliament. All colonial laws, whether originating in British-American Assemblies or in Parliament, as well as all treaties, boundary disputes, petitions and complaints on matters of government, religion, property or trade, were passing through its hands.[5]

By the first decades of the eighteenth century, British-American assemblies were also regularly appointing London agents – with whom they of course corresponded – to counteract the interpretations of events transmitted by royal officials in their letters home and to represent their interests to the Board. As time passed while laws and petitions moldered, even agents who were sent over from America, like Charles Pinckney, Benjamin Franklin or Henry Laurens, had to rely on their private communications with correspondents in their home colonies for intelligence about sentiment, opinion and the "reasons, circumstances and views" behind provincial acts. Since it often took between six months and a year to receive an answer to a letter one had sent across the Atlantic, it was easy even for them to lose touch. William Franklin was obliged to tell his father in 1766, in a letter from New Jersey where he was serving as Governor: "It is impossible for you at so great a distance to be acquainted with every Circumstance necessary to form a right Judgement of the Expediency or Inexpediency of particular Transactions."[6] Colonial agents in London, like Edward Montagu, Richard Jackson or Edmund Burke, who lacked any direct exposure to colonial life beyond that offered in epistolary communiqués by their colonial employers, were even more hard pressed, as Burke's letters to the Gentlemen of the Committee of Correspondence at New York repeatedly tried to get them to understand: "I must entreat that you may add to my zeal for your service the ability of serving you with effect, by sending me such materials of fact and argument as may enable me in all disputed cases to answer objections and instruct counsel"; "Nobody has attended to give me any light on the subject; and proper instructions to counsel are no less necessary to them than their fees."[7]

The eight-man Board performed most of its work orally, generally leaving its Secretary and his cohort of clerks to draft, write up, copy, store – and for a surreptitious fee, unofficially "share" with outsiders – its confidential correspondence. But the Board's trial-like hearings imbricated epistolary scripts with speech: the Board would "hear" the letters

5 Dickerson, *American Colonial Government*; Basye, *Lords Commissioners*; Steele, *Colonial Policy.*
6 Letter from William Franklin to Benjamin Franklin, April 30, 1766, in *Papers of Benjamin Franklin*, XIII: 256.
7 Letter to the Gentlemen of the Committee of Correspondence at New York, Aug. 20, 1772, and to William Wickham Esqr. at New York, Aug. 19, 1772; in *Edmund Burke*, 218, 212.

that it had received on a particular issue read out loud; and it would "hear" the oral representations of British lawyers speaking to the issues the letters raised on behalf of the parties concerned. Since counsel was briefed (directly or indirectly via colonial agents) by a different set of letters issuing from colonial correspondents, the Board's hearings might be described as oral rehearsals and defenses of competing epistolary intelligence about what was occurring, or might occur, unseen by anyone present, on the other side of the Atlantic. Colonial assemblies and later revolutionary committees of correspondence did their business in a similar way: they too "heard" the letters addressed to them read out loud and heard debate about the issues the letters raised, before arriving at a collective response and delegating some of their number to give it written epistolary form. In some cases, the whole group then heard the draft of the letter that had been prepared and made corrections to its language and style.[8] Such imbrications of orality and script, of presence and absence, and of surrogation and re-presentation, were characteristic of eighteenth-century epistolary practices and, as we saw, accompanied letters of all kinds.

Although it reached a fairly restricted public, the Board's printed *Journals* may be said to represent its "public transcript," the official record of letters received, arguments presented and recommendations arrived at in the course of ceremonious hearings, that were reviewed and repeated on a higher level in the Privy Council. The formality of proceedings, the multiplication of administrative levels of review, and the interposition of legal counsel at every level, signaled not only the legitimacy of British rule, but also the hierarchical distance separating colonial petitioners from the highest reaches of central government, where decisions were made. Because British elites held stubbornly to the conviction that it was their prerogative to conceal the whole business of government from the governed (including the debates of their representatives in Parliament) and preferred to settle matters offstage, the "hidden transcript" included the communications between the Board and the government and between the Board and royal officials on the one hand, and the communications between agents and their principals in the colonies and between agents and pro-American interest groups in London, on the other – each of which was, in principle, hidden from the other side. It also included negotiations between the two sides in accordance with their

8 Brown, *Revolutionary Politics in Massachusetts*; St. George, "Massacred Language," in *Possible Pasts*.

"instructions" in advance of hearings of the Board. On the colonial side, these hidden negotiations included colonial agents' practice of oiling the wheels of government by leaving vails (tips) for servants and remuneration for officials in the different government offices to ensure that colonial business was attended to, and that of privately lobbying influential members of the administration. Speaking of the Attorney to the Board of Trade, whose written addresses to the Board determined whether approval of any colonial law would contravene the laws of England or infringe on the Prerogative, for instance, a North Carolinian explained the importance of the colonial agent's work offstage in these terms:

The fate of the act depends in great measure on this gentleman's report; which report must again entirely depend upon the idea, the information he receives of the reasons, circumstances and views with which the act was passed in the provincial assembly. Here is the heavy and useful part of the duty of an agent; to attend the reporting counsel, to explain circumstances and lead his opinion to a report favorable to the wishes of the province for which he acts; as a person in the reporting counsel's situation must be unacquainted with a thousand things an agent can explain, and consequently without his information be liable to many mistakes.[9]

To have any hope of affecting decisions made in London about their lives, liberty or property, British-American colonists had not only to arrange to have their case presented privately, as well as formally, to the Board. They had also to represent their interests and concerns persuasively off stage in missives to a variety of possible proxies in Britain (agents, counsels, merchants, co-religionists, MPs, family members, friends), each of whom might be able to use his influence privately with some member of administration to get approval of a particular colonial law or bounty on a particular colonial export, and to obtain for their colonial correspondents government posts, lucrative government contracts and other personal or commercial benefits.[10] Establishing personal relations and private alliances off stage was crucial to functioning effectively within the British-American patronage system.[11]

Through hints and lacunae, the printed *Journal*'s transcript of the Board's acts and decisions profiles this unsaid, even while demonstrating some of the deficiencies of governing at a distance "only at the expense

9 *North Carolina Colonial Records*, V: 747; Dickerson, *American Colonial Government*, 266, n. 627.
10 Olson, "Board of Trade," in Marshall and Williams (eds.), *British Atlantic Empire*; Sosin, *Agents and Merchants*, Chapter 1.
11 Cannon, *Aristocratic Century*; Griffin, *Literary Patronage*.

of a little pen, ink and paper." Consider the *Journal*'s record of the
Board's dealings with the complaints against Governor Nicholson that
were brought by six members of the Virginia council in 1704. Between
April 10 and June 7, 1704, a constantly changing combination of three to
six of the Board's eight members repeatedly listened to oral statements
and to readings of various documents that it ordered prepared: the
Virginians' complaints against the Governor, a summary thereof, the
"affidavits of such persons as may be in town, upon the same subject,"
an "Abstract of the Chief articles for Nicholson's mal-administration
in Virginia, with proofs noted in the margin," a written request from
one of Governor Nicholson's representatives before the Board, that "he
may have copies of such papers as are or shall be exhibited against
Col. Nicholson, in order to make his reply thereunto."[12] On June 7 and
8 and 9, 1704, the Board ordered copies of the complaints and affidavits to
be sent to a variety of people for comment, agreed on a draft of its own
representation of the complaints, and ordered that a letter be written to
Governor Nicholson's representative in London desiring him to "bring
any letters he may have received from Colonel Nicholson relating to his
defense." On June 22, the Board ordered that "a letter to Colonel
Nicholson to transmit to him copies of all the complaints that have been
exhibited against him" be sent to him via Lord Cornbury, Governor of
New York, on "a New Yorke ship that goes along with the Newfoundland
convoy." So far, the Board followed its policy of dealing with the
complaints against Governor Nicholson and with complaints it had
received at about the same time from "several gentlemen of Barbados"
against their governor Sir Beville Granville, in the same way. But the
matter of Barbados came to a formal legal hearing before the Board once
all the written evidence for both sides had been collected, the matter of
Virginia did not. Nor is there any evidence in this official transcript that
the Board ever did find out what was really going on in Virginia.

Instead, on April 2, 1705, a letter was received from Mr. Secretary
Hedges "directing the Board to prepare a commission and instruction
for Colonel Edward Nott to be Governor of Virginia." In subsequent
meetings, the Board agreed on a draft of a letter for Her Majesty's
signature revoking Colonel Nicholson's Governorship and heard a letter
to Colonel Nicholson from Mr. Secretary Hedges "signifying that
Her Majesty did not recall him from his government of Virginia on

12 *Journal of the Commissioners for Trade and Plantations*, April 10, 19, 26 and 28; May 1, 4, 17, 24, 29
and 31.

account of any information against him or any displeasure Her Majesty has taken against him." Why then was Nicholson recalled? What happened off stage can be inferred in the record only from the fact that immediately before and after Nott's appointment, a Virginia council member, who had come over in the interim to speak for the complainants and do the necessary work off stage, was granted large sums of money by the Board "out of Her Majesty's Revenue arising in Virginia, over and above the summe of 100 £ advanced to him by the governor for this service," while efforts at "distributing money to several persons on Governor Nicholson's behalf" were stymied. There was also the unfortunate fact that on February 12, 1705, the Board received a letter enclosing a certificate from the captain of *The Indian Queen* attesting that he "had thrown most of the packets he had received from the governors of Virginia and Maryland overboard" just before his ship was taken by French privateers. Governor Nicholson's defense appears to have been sunk on its way back from America, sinking him with it about a month before the decision about Colonel Nott was taken. When a copy of Nicholson's letter did finally arrive before the Board on May 31, 1705, complete with enclosed "remonstrances" and "certificates" from the Virginia clergy and trustees of the College of Virginia in his favor, Colonel Nott had officially been Her Majesty's Governor of Virginia for about three months, and there was nothing left to do but record that Colonel Nicholson's sad packet with each of its useless enclosures had been laid before the Board.

For British officials and British-American colonists alike, therefore, getting essential political, commercial, legal and personal business done resembled nothing so much as a game of cards in which each of the players tried to keep the hand that he and his partner of the moment were playing hidden close to his chest, while trying to determine from the cards publicly and ceremoniously laid upon the table how the game was going and what card to play next.[13] As this analogy implies in an age obsessed with card games, the Board's and the colonists' simultaneously public and hidden manner of conducting imperial and personal political business was characteristic of all aspects of the so-called

---

13 Scholarly publications of eighteenth-century letters and documents tend to flatten out for the unwary the difference between what was open and known to all sides, and what was designed to be hidden for a restricted public, by printing both in the same format, often in the same volume, side by side. This is worth underlining because, unlike the book, computer hypertext offers the possibility of presenting this material in a way that would make it easier to see who knew what, and how the interplay of the hidden and the open influenced the course of events.

public sphere in the transatlantic culture that produced and was produced by it.

Transatlantic trade depended on the collaboration of public and hidden transcripts too. On the one hand, as David Hancock has shown, for merchants, "the explosion and dissemination of information and the development of empire were closely linked," since the profitability of transatlantic trade depended on obtaining intelligence of various kinds: about prices in the different colonial ports, the exchange rates of the provinces' different currencies, the movements and fate of ships at sea, goods available for shipping or available in port for sale, commercial matters before Parliament or provincial assemblies, changes in laws and regulations, bankruptcies and the creation or dissolution of partnerships. Newspapers and gazettes on both sides of the Atlantic soon began to carry such items of news, to provide a public transcript that significantly reduced the transaction costs of transatlantic trade.[14] But on the other hand, in the volatile Atlantic world where demand and prices changed rapidly with the approach of peace or war and with the unexpected availability of particular goods, there was also a commercial advantage to be gained from receiving "advices" about what was going on on the other side of the Atlantic that were still "hidden" from competitors. As Boston merchant Thomas Fitch irritably pointed out in a letter to his London correspondents in 1709: "my Advices come too often late. . .and those of my Neighbours that have later letters and advices of all materiall occurrences get a start of me here, which is very irksome and also disadvantageous."[15] Factors in America were repeatedly advised by their employers that "Secrecy in all our transactions of business, even the most simple, is what I would strongly recommend." As Toby Ditz has shown, "the tension between candor and what amounted to a counter ethic of secrecy as standards for good character and conduct and for good letter-writing itself" permeated trading and mercantile letters.[16] The timely "Advices" merchants obtained from their transatlantic correspondents made their epistolary networks useful sources of intelligence for government officials – and not merely because merchants frequently got wind of political and military developments before government did. Merchants seem to have drawn the line between public and hidden transcripts

---

14 North, "Institutions," in Tracy (ed.), *Merchant Empires*.
15 Hancock, *Citizen of the World*, 36; Letter of Thomas Fitch to John Crouch and Samuel Arnold, Nov. 15, 1709, in Steele, *English Atlantic*, 214.
16 Devine, *Scottish Firm*, 48 and Ditz, "Secret Selves and Credible Personas," 222.

in their "private" commercial correspondence in a distinctive way. When they were not coordinating specific commercial transactions, they seem to have had fewer inhibitions about using letters to transmit what might be considered sensitive political and military intelligence, than about trusting them with information about their own trade. Writing at length to his business partner on July 27, 1745, for instance, William Lynde was perfectly willing to describe the military measures about to be taken in New England against the French, the size, strength and disposition of British-American military expeditions, the location of enemy fleets in neighboring waters, the damage done to settlers by the Indians and the morale in New England; but all he was willing to put on paper about the state of their own commercial affairs was: "The season is hopeful and trade brisk. Some particulars I could give verbatim, which I cannot write."[17] At around the same time, when Boston merchant Thomas Hancock was using his vessels to trade in smuggled goods, his letters of instruction to the captains of his ships dealt with the issue of discussing his business in letters in an even more decisive way: "Nor let any of your men write to their wives. . ."; "Neither bring so much as a Letter for anybody here, but what shall come under Cover to me, and be careful that your people bring no Letters neither for anybody else."[18]

The newspapers or "public prints" were open and "public" not only, or so much, in the sense of "publishing to the world" the intelligence they contained, as by virtue of their participation in a "culture of per-formance" that ruled in the streets as much as in state institutions. In the seventeenth and eighteenth centuries, even absolutist kings like Charles II and stubborn, blinkered kings like George III understood that they must seek some degree of popular consent to their measures, given the ubiquity of what Ned Ward called the British "mobocracy," with its inconvenient, democratic forms of public self-expression – charivari, riot, fire, violence – and its propensity for joining rebel armies. Charles II had operated in a traditional Tudor and Stuart manner with what Paula Backscheider has characterized as a "spectacular politics" – public display through pageant, emblem and performance in the streets of London – in a bid to gain the acquiescence and loyalty of the populace. His successors followed suit. Charivari, riot, fire and popular violence persisted throughout the eighteenth century on both sides of the Atlantic; but as Linda Colley and Kathleen Wilson have shown for Britain and

17 *Journal and Letters of Samuel Curwen*, 15–16; quoted in Hancock, *Citizen of the World*, 103.
18 Letters of Nov. 24, 1736, and April 12, 1742; quoted in Baxter, *House of Hancock*, 54, 85–6.

David Shields has shown for America, so did the spectacular politics of patriotic ceremony, performance and pageantry in town and village streets – for instance, on the king's birthday, on the occasion of a British victory at war, or later, on the anniversary of the Boston Tea Party.[19]

Imitating his royal French cousin, Charles II had extended his politics of display into the new world of print by publishing the first official *London Gazette* in 1666, to counter and replace the controversial news-books that proliferated at his accession. Here too his successors followed suit. Controlled, censored and carefully edited, the *Gazette* displayed before the gaze of the people His Majesty's declarations and appointments to places or pensions, and carefully selected foreign intelligence that his ministers had collected from their correspondence with British diplomats and residents abroad. As scholars have observed, foreign news was of particular moment to merchants trading overseas, whose cargoes and commerce were materially affected by the wars that Britain fought throughout the eighteenth century against her European rivals for control of the seas and of new-found lands. But Richard Steele, who wrote and compiled *The London Gazette* for the government in the first decade of the eighteenth century, and Joseph Addison who supervised *The London Gazette* while he served as Undersecretary of State, also put their finger on the *Gazette*'s wider import: it turned the gentlemen, merchants, soldiers, lawyers, shopkeepers and apprentices who gathered in the coffee houses of London or in the taverns of provincial cities into spectators of "the theater of the world." By displaying the king and his capital, London, at the heart of an imperial system of patronage and as the source of all proclamations and acts, *The London Gazette* extended the spectacle of royal government across the empire and turned the gaze of provincials everywhere towards the metropolis. While accentuating by their very names the distances to be run to bring their readers the latest news, the *Gazette*'s rivals – the *Couriers*, *Mercuries* and *Posts* that began to proliferate in Britain with the lapse of the Licensing Act in 1695 and in America about twenty years later – reinforced this effect. By imitating London *Gazettes* in format and style, and by reprinting much of their copy (hence *copy*) from the London papers, provincial newspapers both in Britain and in America kept the eyes of provincials fixed firmly on Britain's metropolitan center while they "engaged American readers in the affairs of the mother country and of Europe as seen through the

19 Ward, *London Spy*; Backscheider, *Spectacular Politics*; Colley, *Britons*; Wilson, *Sense of the People*.

eyes of London and Westminster."[20] By focusing predominantly on foreign news and placing London at the hub of an international network of intelligence and of global political and economic affairs, *The London Gazette* and its later rivals also expanded the sight of native Britons beyond their narrow localities and accustomed them to perceive Britain as a player on a world stage. As Horace Walpole put it, with some irony, in a letter to his friend Sir Horace Mann, the English Resident in Tuscany: "We are citizens of the world; and battles and revolutions are the common incidents of our neighborhood."[21]

At the same time, as Harold Love has shown, both in the press and at sites of reading ranging from the royal Court to the coffee house and from the Inns of Court to the country house, "there was knowledge to be shared and knowledge to be reserved" for "power resided in data remaining private – if available. . .it would deprive the owner and his allies of a vital advantage."[22] In the seventeenth and eighteenth centuries, the enduring appeal of newsletters over the "Public Prints" lay precisely here. Newsletters "opened" to a "restricted public" – consisting of a couple of hundred officials, merchants and country gentlemen – intelligence that was deliberately withheld from *Gazettes* and hidden from the wider public, even when newsletters and *Gazettes* were written and published by the same men. Especially while they were still under the control of the Secretary of State – or in America, of the Postmaster – newsletters offered reliable insider, political and commercial, foreign news, as well as "the proceedings of Parliament, which were not permitted to be printed and would not have been allowed to be disseminated even in manuscript, by private persons."[23] Newsletter writers and their official patrons made small personal fortunes by selling their subscribers the "power" and "advantage" to be derived from intelligence that was allowed to circulate only among a small and restricted public. From the seventeenth-century beginnings of commercial news, there was thus, simultaneously, both an "open" and a "hidden," both a public and a private, "public sphere."[24]

---

20 Clark, "Early American Journalism" in Amory and Hall (eds.), *Book in America*, 360.
21 Walpole, *Selected Correspondence*, 113.
22 Love, *Scribal Publication*, 201. Love uses this binary to distinguish seventeenth-century scribal publication from print. Later, when newsletters were also issued in printed form, the distinction between knowledge to be shared and knowledge to be reserved was no longer identical in all cases with the distinction between scribal publication and print.
23 Fraser, *Intelligence of the Secretaries of State*, 28.   24 Sommerville, *News Revolution*, 5ff.

The intelligence openly displayed in the public prints was constrained not only by this economy of knowledge, but also by the law. Habermas has argued that the lapse of the Licensing Act in 1695 eliminated the institution of censorship in Britain, to make the press "an instrument with whose aid political decisions could be brought before the new forum of the public." But this is somewhat misleading, for in Britain after 1695, the goals of the Licensing Act were simply pursued in other ways: by invoking the laws of criminal or seditious libel; by limiting the role of juries in libel cases; by the Secretary of State's often ruinous, administrative harassment of printers through arrests, seizures and fines or imprisonment for months when no evidence against them could be found; and from 1712, by a series of Stamp Acts that were designed to "effectively fetter," where they did not succeed in eliminating, the periodical and pamphlet press.[25] The official British position for most of the eighteenth century was that expressed by Lord Mansfield and by Blackstone: "To be free is to live under a government of law; the liberty of the press consists in printing without any previous license, subject to the consequences of the law." For "to punish (as the law does at present) any dangerous or offensive writing. . .is necessary for the preservation of peace and good order, of government and religion, the only solid foundations of civil liberty."[26] This representation of liberty justified laws designed to suppress free and open debate of the government's acts, in order to prevent "disaffection" among the people and to avoid offending the great. In eighteenth-century Britain, it was not democratic principle, but party and the patronage of powerful lords that created and sponsored the opposition press. And while great lords were safe in voicing criticism until it could be proved that they had crossed the line to treason, their printers and writers were not. This reproduced the collaboration of public and hidden transcripts in yet another form. For though they did not entirely succeed in their aims, whatever faction of the elite was in power did make it sufficiently dangerous for an opposition writer to "lay his claim openly" in the public sphere to create a print culture in which printers and publishers protected their trade by concealing the identity of their authors. It was "very usual" in this culture for writers to leave copy at the printers "without making themselves known"; printers undertook to keep the identity of their writers and correspondents secret and published their promises to that effect; and the whole trade would combine to

25 Habermas, *Structural Transformation*, 58; Siebert, *Freedom of the Press*, 322.
26 Quoted in Hanson, *Government and the Press*, 14.

withhold business from anyone who betrayed the identity of his fellows during judicial examination.[27]

Colonial America differed from the mother country only in that the Governor's instructions required him to maintain the licensing system well after it had lapsed at home. A colonial printer was therefore in principle subject to punishment for unlicensed publication, as well as for publishing writers whose opinions offended the great. Franklin's report that, when one of the pieces in *The New England Courant* "gave Offence to the Assembly," his brother was "taken up, censur'd and imprisoned for a Month by the Speaker's Warrant because he would not discover his Author" testifies that James had imported the ethos of British printers from his training in London, along with *The Spectator's* style. As opposition to royal governors and British policies grew, Assemblies in America – or powerful patriot factions within them – played the role of opposition peers in Britain in creating, writing and sponsoring the opposition press. However, once American patriots were in the saddle during the Revolution and early Republic, they not only squeezed out the loyalist (hence opposition) press, but also returned to the old British policy of censoring and penalizing criticism of government. As Richard D. Brown has put it: "Americans declared both their undying commitment to the freedom of the press and, when their own sensibilities were challenged, their readiness to put a stop to those printers who would "abuse" that liberty."[28] During the seventeenth and eighteenth centuries, therefore, the press was "open," untrammeled and uncensored only where government had temporarily collapsed. The display of intelligence and the possibility of political debate in the public prints were predicated, on both sides of the Atlantic, on a policy of suppression and a culture of concealment.

Shaftesbury's Advice to Authors to "secretly advise and give instruction" through personated epistles therefore became one of "various devices" that eighteenth-century writers for the public prints "adopted to evade the attention of the law."[29] Throughout the century on both sides of the Atlantic, epistolary debates in the public newspapers which "brought political decisions before the new forum of the public" were conducted by personated fictions, because the concealment offered by

---

27 *Ibid.*, 51ff. For America, Rice, *Transformation of Authorship*; Brown, *Idea of an Informed Citizenry.*
28 Brown, "Shifting Freedoms of the Press," in Amory and Hall (eds.), *Book in America*, 376; Buel, "Freedom of the Press," in Bailyn and Hench (eds.), *Press and the American Revolution.*
29 Hanson, *Government and the Press*, 25. Personation is not one of the devices he explores.

what Habermas calls "literary journalism" was the condition for public, political debate. To read a newspaper was to read letters from "Humphrey Ploughjogger" arguing with "Philanthrop," "A Briton" taking issue with "Pacificus," "U" insulting "J," "Obadia Plainman" responding to "Tom Truman" or Mr. Spectator making comments about Jack Lightfoot. Writers put reason to use in the public prints, as they put it to use in the epistolary novel – by feigning characters to create the illusion of openness. Personation was not, as has been argued, a way for writers like Addison or Steele to identify negatively with a "disembodied public subject" in order to "elaborate republican assumptions about the citizen's exercise of virtue," though Steele was considered by contemporaries to be sympathetic to the republican cause.[30] Mr. Spectator teased his readers with the invisibility of his person not only to mock Society for trying to guess at the real identity of authors masquerading under feigned names, but also to re-mark the conditions for "printing myself out." When he finally named himself and the other authors who had written pseudonymously for *The Spectator* in no. 555, Steele reminded his readers of just why "it is much more difficult to converse with the World in a real than a personated Character" and why it was so important for "the Praises or Censures of himself to fall only upon the Creature of his Imagination" by alluding to Anaxarchus, who was "pommeled to death with iron pestles after offending a despotic ruler." Even for the more empowered ranks of society in the Atlantic world, it was best to stage one's sentiments in the public transcript in disguised and personated forms.[31]

In reading eighteenth-century letters, it is important to remember that this dyad of public and hidden transcripts pervaded sociability and personality, as much as transatlantic politics, journalism and trade. This is particularly worth stressing with regard to the taverns and coffee houses where, in port towns on both sides of the Atlantic, merchants, their factors or agents, ships' captains, colonial agents, printers and politicians met to exchange intelligence, do business and pick up their letters, and where gentlemen, shopkeepers, artisans and writers congregated to read and discuss the latest news. As sites of business, sociability, reading and conversation, these masculine haunts are now frequently identified with a burgeoning bourgeois or democratic public sphere. However, both in Britain and in the American colonies, taverns and coffee houses generally contained two kinds of spaces: a public space, promiscuously open to

30 Warner, "Mass Public," 380–1.   31 Griffin, *Faces of Anonymity,* esp. James Raven's essay.

all comers; and a private room behind or above where "restricted publics," such as clubs and secret societies, could dine, drink and talk of matters that they preferred to keep "hidden" from those without. Curiously, there was relatively little secrecy either about the existence of even the most secret societies and clubs or about the days and times of their meetings in those private public rooms. Announcements of club activities and attacks on them by their enemies would feature in the newspapers. In England, members of the Kit-Cat Club or the Freemasons would attend plays in the public theater en masse, as a visible and self-identified group. In colonial Philadelphia, Freemasons marched ceremoniously through the streets in full regalia, held well-publicized banquets, and delivered speeches and sermons to spectators that they later printed and dissemin-ated. Yet the same secret societies and clubs also successfully kept hidden from the wider public both the meanings of their symbols, ceremonies and practices, and what transpired during their meetings. It was secrecy, rather than participation in some "open" and "rational" democratic public sphere, that enabled such societies to constitute themselves as loci of freethinking, "sedition" or disaffection. And one might say that like a playing card, an eighteenth-century secret society or club had two faces glued back to back: one open and published to the world, the other carefully hidden from it.

The playing cards' dyadic structure also impressed itself on forums of polite sociability, such as the dining room, drawing room, assembly and ball, thanks to the rules of civility imported into Britain from France during the late seventeenth century and exported to America during the eighteenth. Civility required that in public, a gentleman's countenance remain impassive and composed and his posture graceful and controlled, while he accommodated himself to the pleasure and wishes of his company, avoided giving offense, and displayed all the deference, familiarity or condescension due to interlocutors of different positions, genders and ranks. But as Ann Bryson and Michele Cohen have shown, conduct books made it clear that display of the graceful and controlled outward demeanor essential to the performance of gentility required concealment of unsociable sentiments, disagreeable ideas, and spontaneous feelings of desire, annoyance, boredom, hostility or con-tempt, as well as suppression of all the involuntary bodily motions that human beings share with animals, which were said to "disgust." These included laughing, frowning, yawning, scowling, gaping, hiccupping, burping, breathing on others, wrinkling the nose, blowing the nose, showing the tongue, grinding the teeth, scratching, fidgeting, crouching, slouching and shuffling the feet. Civility required concealment of thoughts, feelings and body language, but it also required penetration of that concealment, since a man could not please or accommodate himself to others who was incapable of discerning the physical discomfort, the need, the desire, the preference, the boredom or displeasure, that his company politely hid.[32] Here too, then, as participants well understood, public and hidden transcripts worked in tandem to fashion the social text.

The ubiquity and collaboration of public and hidden transcripts in all aspects of political, social and commercial life – and not just at Court – helps to explain the fascination of eighteenth-century readers with letters that were "private" in the primary eighteenth-century meaning of that word – "secret," "hidden," and *not* made to be "published to the world." For booksellers and publishers, there was money to be made from printing true or fictional letters bearing the marks of their origin as a "hidden transcript" confidentially addressed to a restricted public of some sort. At the beginning of the eighteenth century, publishers like Edmund Curll were infamous for publishing the stolen private letters of prominent people. When Thomas Brown and Charles Gildon published *Familiar Letters: Written by the Right Hon. John, Late Earl of Rochester, and several other Persons of Honour and Quality* in 1697, they were careful to point out that most of the letters were written "upon private occasions. . .with no intention of ever being made publick." But Curll shrewdly said it all in the imaginative title he gave his English edition of Mme de Sevigne's social and domestic letters in 1727: *Court Secrets; or, the Lady's Chronicle Historical and Gallant . . . Extracted from the Letters of Mme de Sevigne, which have been Suppressed at Paris.* From the middle of the eighteenth century, there was a similar vogue for "sentimental" letters that laid bare the sentiments, feelings and uncontrolled (or "abandoned") physical postures suppressed, and newly hidden, behind masks of civility that were spreading inexorably across genteel and would-be genteel faces and bodies on both sides of the Atlantic.

From Behn's *Letters from a Nobleman to his Sister*, through Richardson's *Clarissa* and Rousseau's *Eloise* to Eliza Fenwick's *Secresy*, epistolary novels also constructed themselves as a stage on which hidden epistolary transcripts could be paraded before the eyes of the world and the often unpredictable effects of the interplay between public and hidden transcripts explored.[33] *Clarissa*, for instance, which was as popular in the

32 Bryson, *From Courtesy to Civility*; Cohen, *Fashioning Masculinity*. See also Spacks, *Privacy*.
33 Zaczek, *Censored Sentiments*, 15, 17.

American provinces as in Britain, opens with a move very much like Gildon's or Curll's: Anna Howe's request that Clarissa recount "the disturbances that have happened in your family" to "satisfy those who know not so much of your affairs as I do" and who have made the Harlowes "the subject of the public talk." As Christina Gillis has pointed out, the "paradox of privacy" in *Clarissa* was that, from the first, she was "speaking privately for the public."[34] For his own immediate public of readers, who did make *Clarissa's* letters "the subject of the public talk," Richardson sustained the titillation of being privy to letters that would normally *not* be published to "all the world" by the device of having the Harlowes and Lovelace try throughout the novel to stifle and suppress Clarissa's correspondence (by imprisoning her, removing her writing materials, intercepting her letters, etc.) in their attempts to keep what was transpiring within Harlowe Place or within Mrs. Sinclair's establishment hidden from those without. At the same time, the novel's plot – and much of the substance of the letters – depended on what Richardson described as the "double yet separate correspondence" of the two women and the two men to hide Lovelace's "secret purposes" from Clarissa and Clarissa's secret "preference" from Lovelace, and to provide endless opportunity for each pair of letter-writers to speculate about what Clarissa's "punctilio" and Lovelace's aristocratic manners properly or politely hid.

Though naturalized by literary history, such real or fictional exposures of hidden epistolary transcripts re-present the more threatening aspect of epistolography in a British-American culture where awareness that all the public aspects of political, economic, social and domestic life involved a hidden transcript led to attempts by all sides to buy, steal, intercept, capture or get "sight" of the hidden epistolary transcripts of others. While the British government regularly intercepted and copied letters passing between British-American agents and their home colonies, colonial agents arranged with clerks, for a surreptitious fee, to give them "sight" of confidential correspondence that the government expected to hide from them. In their attempts to control lateral communication among the king's subjects independent of the authorities, Hanoverian governments not only reserved and regularly used the right to intercept, open, read and copy letters sent privately by the Post; they also developed, refined and expanded the mechanisms their predecessors had used for doing so.

34 Gillis, *Paradox of Privacy*, 3.

This turned the empire into a complex of epistolary intelligence and counter-intelligence networks. It became the job of regional and provincial postmasters, of agents at the outports, and of some ships' captains, both to collect and transmit any intelligence they could and to intercept the letters of foreign diplomats, agents, opposition leaders in Parliament, private persons who were thought to oppose government, criminals, foreigners and assorted persons whose names had been put on lists prepared by the Secretary of State, as well as any otherwise suspicious foreign or domestic mail. This would be opened and examined by the Postmaster in Ireland or Scotland, by the "Private Office" or "Secret Office" in London, or by the Private Office in Hanover, where teams of openers, decipherers, translators and transcribers processed the mail. America, too, had its epistolary networks and Committees of Secret Correspondence.[35]

The vulnerability of letters traveling by the common post was not a secret. One suspects, indeed, that on occasion, warning shots were designedly sent to correspondents. In 1766, for instance, Franklin in London informed his friend Joseph Galloway in Philadelphia:

I recollect several of my Friends Letters, and yours particularly, sent to me at several Times by the North of Ireland, appear'd to me to have been very clumsily open'd and dabb'd up again, as if done with a hot Poker, all Impression of the Sealbeing destroy'd, and a great deal of coarser Wax added. For which Reason I would wish you to write no more to me by that course, as I apprehend some Scoundrel may be employ'd there in the scandalous office of prying into, and perhaps making bad or false Copies of our Correspondence.[36]

Of more concern was the safety of coffee houses where Americans congregated in London, and where letters waiting to be sent and letters waiting to be picked up by their addressees were hung in sacks on the wall. Franklin had been told that "one Williamson of Pensilvania who is here, reads Letters at the Coffee House, said to be from you to me, or me to you. . .". Some of the letters Williamson read and copied later turned up, in print, in the *Pennsylvania Journal*.[37] Copies of intercepted private letters found their way into print on both sides of the Atlantic whenever there was personal or public political capital to be made. The best-studied examples are still the capture of Charles I's "secretary" (his secret, locked letter cabinet) and the ensuing publication of his private

35 Ellis, *Post Office.*
36 Letter to Joseph Galloway, Sept. 27, 1766, in *Papers of Benjamin Franklin*, XIII: 426.
37 *Ibid.*, 425–6; also 425, n. 7.

correspondence with Henrietta Maria during the English Civil War; and the publication, during the lead-up to the War for America, of Governor Thomas Hutchinson's confidential letters to Thomas Whately in Britain, describing the treatment of customs officers in Boston and recommending the use of military might to put down the insurgency.[38] But these were far from the only instances where this occurred – colonists, for instance, rid themselves of other Governors (Andros, Barnard) in the same way. To detect and publish to the world what was hidden from it was to *dis*empower even the most powerful. Publication of genuine letters by prominent people in their own name by those who disagreed with them was not only an embarrassment and a violation, or an act of betrayal and of war; it was a symbolic display of the other's impotence to bring his schemes quietly to fruition behind the scenes, as well as of his vulnerability once denuded of protective cover. To force what transpired in the green room onto the stage, and make a spectacle of a person in his own name, was to make him stick out like Alice among the fictions with grave or satiric faces that tread the printed boards.

Far more daunting for less prominent letter-writers, however, was the conjunction of attempts to get sight of letters with laws of treason and of criminal or seditious libel which extended, in the seventeenth and eighteenth centuries, not only to the public prints, but also to people's private manuscript letters or papers, even when these were not circulated through some form of scribal publication. Whatever unknown readers determined was what Blackstone called "dangerous or offensive writing," whether found in a person's home or desk or intercepted in transit, could be used against them in a court of law, as well as in less formal and more unpleasant venues. Algernon Sidney's execution at the beginning of our period, not for anything that he had published, but for some arguments found among his private papers, remained a *cause célèbre*. Towards the end of the eighteenth century, a letter from Thomas Attwood Digges, an American from Maryland who spent the war years in England smuggling musket locks and munitions to America, vividly described what the consequences might prove to be not only of corresponding with Americans and of what he called "keeping papers by him," but also of carrying the wrong letters or of being "mentioned" in other peoples' correspondence:

---

38 For Charles II's letters, Jagodzinski, *Privacy and Print*; Patterson, *Censorship and Interpretation*; Maclean, "Re-Siting the Subject," in *Epistolary Histories*; for Hutchinson's letters, Bailyn, *Ordeal*, and Sosin, *Agents and Merchants*.

You will by this time have read that Captn Hutchins was taken up last Sunday at a friends' house near Leatherhead, his papers all seized, has had three or four close examinations as to accomplices and himself a close prisoner in New Prison, Clerkenwell. His accusation is treasonable correspondencies with Dr. Franklin, Mr. S. Wharton and other Americans – a Mr. Beasley and a Mr. Bundy are said to be his accomplices – it appears the former has been a carrier for him and it looks as if he had betrayed H—S. Since these examinations others have been taken up and their papers seized and examined, particularly a Miss Stafford, and a Clerk of Mr. Neaves who is lately come from Paris; all Neaves books and papers have been searchd and they seem to be going on to the seizure of all papers of persons who appear in the above correspondences to have any connexion or intercourse with the partys, so that every person may suffer whose names have been imprudently used. Two friends of S. W. in Wimpole and Marylebone Street may have their papers searchd, from meerly having their names (I mean the former) imprudently mentioned in these correspondences, which I suppose will turn out to be a meer friendly correspondence between Captain H. and Mr. W as countrymen; for in these times I cannot suppose any person imprudent enough to enter into politics or to be mentioning the sailing of fleets, movement of armies or panicks given at the apprehension of invasion, thereby be supposed to be giving information.[39]

Quite apart from any legitimate or illegitimate fears of conspiracy, for instance among Jacobites against the House of Hanover, the importance of intelligence for making empire work could make any sharing of news and information in private letters seem "dangerous and offensive writing," especially in those times of internal and external, real or potential, political, ideological or military conflict in which the eighteenth century abounded. But if the law, together with publicized arrests and examinations and shots across the bows of correspondents in the form of evidently opened letters, were designed to halt the flow of epistolary intelligence by making people "the principle of their own subjection," on the whole, they missed their mark. As we will see below, people simply found "prudent" ways of evading government and of transmitting their public and private intelligence in epistolary form.

TRANSATLANTIC EPISTOLARY PRACTICES

For individual writers in the transatlantic world, the risks of interception and the danger of pirated publication of hidden epistolary transcripts for political or commercial gain were not the only dangers to be braved.

---

39 Letter to Benjamin Franklin, Sept. 4, 1779, in *Letters of Thomas Attwood Digges*, 79.

The sociable practice of reading letters aloud to family, neighbors, visitors and friends, inevitably made private letters public. Eliza Lucas Pinckney described the process when she wrote to thank Mrs. King for a private letter describing George III's coronation and wedding to the new Queen:

You can't think how many people you have gratified by your obliging me with so particular a discription of the Queen. We had no picture of her Majesty nor discription that could be depended upon till I received your favour. . .Lady Ann Atkin happened to be with me when I received your favour. I told her as she was a woman of Quality, she should be first treated with a discription of her Majesty and accordingly had that honour, but not a Plebean out of my own family should hear a word of the matter that day. In half an hour after I was favoured with a vizet from our new Gov., Mr. B[oone], lately arrived here from his former Government in the Jerseys, who I found (tho' he has an extensive good acquaintance in England) knew as little of the New Queen as we did here. I had the pleasure to read him also the discription. And the next day numbers received the same sort of pleasure.

The pleasure of receiving a letter was doubled by the favor of receiving news that was still unknown to everyone else in one's locality; doubled again by the pleasure of giving one's friends pleasure by reading to them the letter containing that news; increased by the small power of deciding who among one's friends and acquaintance should hear the letter first; and multiplied by the number of people one could read the letter to. Paul Jacob observed in 1656 that the "Lettre de nouvelle" or "Letter of intelligence" was "the original and most agreeable kind" of familiar letter, because everyone was pleased to receive news and information from their friends and acquaintance. Writing from South Carolina a century later, Eliza Pinckney contended that the pleasure grew exponentially for Britons with their distance from the metropolis:

If, Madam, you have ever been witness to the impatience of the people of England about a hundred mile from London to be made acquainted with what passes there, you may guess a little at what our impatience is here when I inform you that the curiosity increases with the distance from the Center of affairs; and our impatience is not to be equalled with any peoples within four thousand miles.[40]

The "familiar letter" was not primarily a private letter in the modern sense; it was a letter bringing intelligence from afar, that was designed to be shared and discussed. Even at the end of the eighteenth century, as

---

40 *Letterbook of Eliza Lucas Pinckney*, 175. For Paul Jacob, Goldsmith, *Exclusive Conversations*, 87.

Alan McKenzie's and Susan Whealler's studies of Lord Chesterfield's and Jane Austen's letters have shown, a letter-writer who desired to transmit a message "privately" had to take quite radical measures to evade the practices of showing letters and reading them aloud to members of the recipient's conversational circle.[41] These practices were so prevalent that conduct book writers thought it useful to describe the etiquette for receiving letters in company when one did *not* wish to make them public.

Nevertheless, accidents did happen. And Thomas Cushing, Speaker of the Massachusetts Assembly, appears to have been exceptionally accident-prone. In 1769, while he was entertaining a company that included their political opponents, Speaker Cushing received a private and confidential letter from De Berndt, a colonial agent in London, which he convivially began to read aloud for the entertainment of his company. Only the rapid intervention of John Adams prevented him from giving the whole letter away. Hearing of the incident, De Berndt observed in a missive to Richard Cary, "I must be a little cautious what I write to him, for my first letter relating to Governor Bernard, Mr. Cushon opened in public Company and a creature of Lord Hillsboroughs being present took a Copy of a Parigraph or two which suited his Purposes and sent it to his Lordship." Two years later, Benjamin Franklin felt obliged to point out to Cushing – this time in a letter from London heavily marked "PRIVATE" – that: "It is extreemly embarrassing to an Agent to write Letters concerning his Transactions with ministers, which Letters he knows are to be read in the House, where there may be Governors' Spies, who carry away Parts or perhaps take Copies, that are echoed back hither privately." Cushing let this particular letter fall into the hands of Governor Hutchinson, who promptly dispatched it back to Lord Dartmouth, then Secretary of State for the Colonies in London. Nothing daunted, six months later, Cushing affably loaned a confidential letter from Arthur Lee, another colonial agent in London, to the same person who had given Hutchinson Benjamin Franklin's letter.[42]

Cushing was not entirely to be blamed, for the binary of "private" and "public" was also constantly being destabilized by the overlap in the same correspondences of private and public concerns. For Britain's or

---

41 McKenzie, "Chesterfield," and Whealler, "Austen," in McKenzie (ed.), *Sent as a Gift*. Austen would intersperse private messages to her sister Cassandra in such a way that Cassandra could skip over them when reading Jane's letters aloud to the family; Chesterfield would wrap a private letter in another which could be shown or read aloud.

42 Letter from De Berndt to Richard Cary, March 29, 1769; Letter from Benjamin Franklin to Thomas Cushing, July 7, 1773. The story is told more fully in Kammen, *Rope of Sand*, 178ff.

America's social and political elites, personal friendships, family connections, commercial dealings, political alliances and personal advancement were not yet definitively separated out. For transatlantic correspondents, who depended on distant friends to act as their agents, and on distant agents to act as their friends, they were, if anything, even less distinct. Transatlantic merchants, for instance, tried to ensure a stable market for their goods by performing a variety of personal services for their clients, from acting as their bankers and buying them wigs or china, to boarding and educating their children in their own homes. They tried to safeguard their money, in a situation where large amounts of credit had to be extended over long periods of time, by doing business with merchants or agents who were, if not actual family members, at least familiars of their family or friends. They sought to subvert government regulations or taxes by alerting all their transatlantic correspondents to the damage being done to trade and asking them to take political action. Even business letters, therefore, often drifted into a genre that *The Young Secretary's Guide* classified as "mixt" and described as "containing things of different subjects, as many things at once, depending upon both Love and Business."[43]

There was also a strong expectation on the part of transatlantic correspondents that even personal letters from family or friends would bring them public intelligence that they would find of interest or of use, as well as intelligence about such private matters as births or the death of friends. Letters were often represented by letter-writers as an intrusion or imposition on the addressee's patience, attention or time, that could be justified only by the care taken in selecting items of news and in composing letters that would be useful, interesting or pleasing to their recipient. By the same token, letters received were often represented by recipients as a "favor" in acknowledgment of the attention, time and care that had been taken over them, as well as of their value to their recipients. Implicit here too, no doubt, was the consideration that postage was paid by the recipient, not the sender, and that sending letters that were not worth paying for was unlikely to keep one on good terms with one's family or friends for long.

Together with the legal and institutional obstacles to open correspondence described above, this made writing letters a demanding art. Transatlantic correspondents had, after all, to write letters intermixing personal,

---

43 In the twenty-seventh edition, London, 1764, 13.

commercial and political matters to correspondents anxious for news, in what was for most of the eighteenth century a highly contentious political environment, while realizing perfectly well that – even aside from the constant danger of ships being captured at sea by pirates, privateers or enemy vessels – the practices of intercepting, stealing, showing, lending, copying and reading letters *viva voce* meant that neither the number nor the nature of their missive's potential readers was under their control.

Transatlantic correspondents sent multiple copies of important letters to ensure that at least one got through. They begged their correspondents to write, and thankfully described the letters they received as "cordial" for their minds and hearts. But at the same time, they tried to guard the privacy of their letters by sending them with travelers or friends rather than by the public post or by sending them under "cover" to someone other than their intended addressees. They used initials to identify the persons of whom they spoke, or affixed pseudonymous superscriptions and subscriptions to personal letters that effectively masked the identity of their writers and recipients from those outside their immediate circle. It is hard to tell whether private letters were imitating letters in the public prints in these respects, or whether letters in the public prints were imitating them. Correspondents also expressed their sense of the instabilities of privateness in the text of their letters by reminding their correspondents to be cautious in what they wrote; by indicating where they would say more if they could; and by asking their correspondents not to expose certain letters to others. The injunction to transatlantic correspondence was thus an injunction at once to write and not to write.

In 1760, for instance, when Eliza Pinckney alerted Mrs. Evance, who took charge of her sons in England, that she had received a letter from her "with the seal open," she tried to reassure and guide as well as warn her:

Whether accationed by accident or curiosity, I cant say, but as I love to think the best I can of people, I will sopose the former; however 'tis of no great consiquence if 'tis the other. It may teach them the art of writing prettily and obligingly and show how capable women are both of friendship and business, and I am sure to find my account in what ever raises the reputation of my particular friends or my sex in general by the pleasure it gives me; thus I make my self amends for the impertinance of the over curious.[44]

Judging by the letters she took the trouble to copy into her letter-book, in her later years Mrs. Pinckney herself wisely confined her own

44 Letter to Mrs. Evance, June 19, 1760, *Eliza Lucas Pinckney's Letterbook*, 152.

transatlantic letters to elaborate expressions of friendship and to specific matters of business (like the conveyance of seeds, turtles or bills of exchange to her correspondents). When something more was called for, she fell back on non-sectarian expressions of Christian sentiment. Mrs. Pinckney made sure that, should anyone have the curiosity to "open" any of her letters, including the rare ones in which she mentioned politics, they would find nothing too private and nothing to which anyone would take exception.

Writers took other precautions too. Transatlantic letters almost invariably contained a description of how they were being sent, for apparently innocuous information about whether the letter was being carried by a trusted friend, by an acquaintance, by a named ship's captain, or by the public post, signaled to the letter's recipient how open the writer had permitted himself or herself to be, what could and could not be said, how much had been conveyed by hints or allusions or just left out, and thus how the letter was to be interpreted and how closely it needed to be read. Letters of introduction sent with acquaintances who were carrying private letters with them to friends or associates across the ocean served a similar purpose. By their warmth or reserve, by their account of how and how well the messenger was known to the writer, and by whether or not the writer was asking the recipient to offer the messenger lodging, credit or further introductions, letters of introduction indicated how candid their writers felt letters sent by the bearer could be.

Transatlantic letters also almost invariably contained a list of the letters received from their correspondent and of the letters sent to their correspondent, with their dates of writing and the names of the ships by which they had been sent. Sometimes, they also contained a statement about how long the ship's passage had taken and when a particular letter had reached its recipient. This, of course, allowed correspondents to preserve continuity of communication by repeating information in a subsequent letter that had earlier been sent in a letter that had not reached its addressee. But it also enabled correspondents to work out whether letters had failed to get through because the ships carrying them had been captured or sunk, or had thrown the mail they carried overboard before engaging an enemy ship; whether the time taken for the letter to reach the recipient beyond the time taken by the ship's passage indicated a reliable captain or a possible detour via covert readers; and whether the frequency and number of letters lost or delayed suggested that they were on the list of those whose correspondence was regularly intercepted and copied. Being able to refer back to see what information to repeat, and being able to refer back to see which letters might have been intercepted, were both good reasons for the pervasive practice of keeping letterbook copies of the familiar, as well as of the business or diplomatic, letters one wrote.

The conflicts between Britain and America after 1765 progressively aggravated peoples' sense of the risks attached to letters. As John Fothergill wrote William Logan in Philadelphia, the challenge became to write a letter that "will not be deemed treasonable either on this side of the water or yours" and to "hope it will get safe to thy hands."[45] Writing from London to William Browne in Boston in December of 1775, loyalist Samuel Curwen squarely informed his correspondent:

Uncertain what may be the fate of this, I am restrained from writing what might prove amusing, perhaps informative; should it fall short of its intended destination, and get into the hands of the provincials. . .the most innocent expressions, by the force of party prejudice, might be construed into a sense entirely foreign to one's intention, and render one obnoxious or ridiculous.

William Browne confirmed Curwen's sense of things by writing back that he would be unable to forward Curwen's letters to his wife, who had remained behind in the colony, unless "you will suffer them to be inspected at headquarters on both sides of the line." Browne felt no constraint, however, about attaching to his letter a list of officers in the American army which had been found in the pocket of a rebel sergeant killed at Charleston; nor did Samuel Curwen have any reservations about forwarding the list to his friend Dr. Charles Russell in Antigua.[46] Curwen's caution about what he wrote as opposed to what he said ("as conversation admits less restraint than writing"[47]) paid off; for despite spending the Revolutionary War in London in the company of Governor Hutchinson, Jonathan Sewell and other proscribed loyalists and receiving economic "relief" from the British government during his stay, Curwen was permitted to return to America after Independence.

Anne Hulton, sister of one of the British Customs Commissioners in Massachusetts, was more ingenious. Writing from the village of Brookline near Boston in May 1770, Anne first told her friend, "Mrs. L.", in Liverpool: "there is more risque in giving a true Account of Matters & Events, than ones friends in England can easily imagine," and resorted to writing the shortest, blandest and least informative letter she could

45 Letter to William Logan, Oct. 4, 1775, in *Chains of Friendship*, 460.
46 *Journal and Letters of the Late Samuel Curwen*, 41, 48.
47 *Ibid.*, 236.

contrive.[48] But then fearing that Mrs. L. would be hurt or offended, she used her next to deliver a more complex message. Anne recounts how delivery of a letter had endangered her brother's life:

Between 12 & 1 o'Clock he was wake'd by a knocking at the Door, he got up, enquired the person's name and business, who said he had a letter to deliver to him, wch came Express from New York. My Bro. puts on his Cloaths, takes his drawn Sword in one hand, & open'd the Parlor window wth the other. The Man ask'd for a Lodging – said he, I'll not open my door, but give me the letter. The man then put his hand, attempting to push up the window, upon wch my Bro. hastily clap'd it down, instantly wth a bludgeon several blows were struck wch broke the Sash, Glass and frame to pieces. The first blow aimed at my Bro Head he Providentially escaped, by its resting on the middle frame, being double, at the same time (tho' before then, no noise or appearance of more Persons than one) the lower windows, all round the House (excepting two) were broke in like manner. My Bro. stood in amazement for a Mint or 2, & having no doubt that a number of Men had broke in on several sides of the House, he retired Upstairs. You will believe the whole Family was soon alarm'd, but the horrible Noises from without, & the terrible shrieks within the House from Mrs. H: & Servants wch struck my Ears on awaking, I can't describe, & shall never forget.[49]

The incident was carefully chosen. On one level, it indicated why Anne Hulton wanted her friend to "make favorable allowance for a delay in writing" until she felt she could send letters suitable to her "candid disposition," by making her friend *see* and feel that letters could be harbingers of terror and death. But on another level, the incident served as the fulcrum for "a hint" of a completely different situation. The fact that the letter in the anecdote supposedly "came Express from New York" indicated the motive for the attack: "the New Yorkers having broke thro' their nonimportation agreemt, is a heavy Stroke, &. . .90 out of a 100 of the Mercts & traders here, want to do the same." Since merchants could not resume importation without paying customs, a "Party of Men" had ridden all the way from Boston on a dark and snowy night to display, by "a heavy Stroke" to the head of the Commissioner of Customs, what they thought of Boston merchants following the example of merchants in New York. On the other hand, in the township of Brookline, where the inhabitants had befriended, visited and protected them and were "tak [ing] up the affair very warmly" on the Hultons' behalf, people were saying that "this outrage against Mr. H: will hurt their Country more than anything wch has been done yet." It was to protect the Hultons'

---

48 Letter to Mrs. Lightbody, May 29, 1970, in *Letters of a Loyalist Lady*, 20.
49 Letter to Mrs. Lightbody, July 25, 1770, *ibid.*, 22–3.

relationship with the people of Brookline, and from loyalty to them, that Anne was reluctant to send anyone in England any "true Account of Matters & Events" that her Brookline friends and neighbors could consider hurtful to their Country. But she was equally reluctant to hurt or offend Mrs. L. by writing her again, as she had done before, the sort of bland, uninformative and un-candid letters one wrote to strangers. The last paragraph of her letter conveyed her solution to this dilemma:

I've wrote more freely to you than I sho'd have done; but as I have that confidence in my friend that my letter will not be exposed. I wod not have my name or my Bros mentioned in a Sea Port Town as sending any news from hence, you may not know, tho'I do the risque of [it] therefore I gi[ve you] the hint.[50]

Anne's willingness to share the secret, and Mrs. L.'s ability to decipher the hint, reaffirmed the closeness of their friendship; and by asking Mrs. L. to keep both the Hultons' secret and that of her neighbors in Brookline, Anne made her friend, Mrs. L., both the guardian of her safety and the friend of her American friends.

Correspondents' perennial fears of exposure inevitably had their effect on the style and content of letters. Abigail Adams correctly observed that for most of the eighteenth century "all the specimens, which have been handed down to us as models for letter-writing, teach us that natural ease is the greatest beauty of it."[51] But as we have seen, "natural ease" was the art of concealing and naturalizing the well-elaborated social, conversational and rhetorical arts that produced agreeable letters, rather than a signifier of spontaneity or sincerity. Correspondents had what Esther Burr and Sarah Prince called their "privacies"[52] – letters to be burnt to ensure that the contents remained hidden from the eyes of a wider public, and/or letters they burned before their death to fashion the figure they wanted to cut for posterity. "I believe I have burnt this week an hundred of your letters," Mary Granville Delaney informed her sister in 1744:

how unwillingly did I commit to the flames those testimonies of your tender friendship!. . .[But] I thought it prudent to destroy letters that mentioned particular affairs, or particular people, or family business.[53]

There were subjects on which letter-writers agreed they could not write, and sentiments they were willing to convey in letters only by obscure

50 *Ibid.*, 27.
51 Letter to Lucy Cranch, London, 27 August, 1985, in *Adams Family Correspondence*, VI: 312.
52 *Journal of Esther Edwards Burr*, 52.
53 Mrs. Delaney to Mrs. Dewes, April 3, 1744, in *Autobiography and Correspondence*, I: 275.

allusions, indirection or lacunae. Some letter-writers resorted to cyphers and codes; others wrote letters "double-voiced" to lead different publics to interpret them in different ways. So widespread did such practices become that in one of her letters to her daughter, Lady Mary Wortley Montagu recounted with amusement that a little Italian priest had informed her that "Cyphers are only us'd by Novices in Politics, and it was very easy to write intelligibly under feign'd names of persons and places to a correspondent in such a manner as should be almost impossible to understand by any body else."[54] Crevecoeur even had a simple farmer's wife inform her husband when he received a letter from England, "thee must read this letter over again, paragraph by paragraph, and warily observe whether thee canst perceive. . .something that hath more than one meaning." She warned him, by the same token, to conceal his own epistolary responses from the authorities, for:

if it were once known abroad that thee writest to a great and rich man over at London, there would be no end of the talk of the people. . .Who would wish to become the subject of public talk?. . .Our colonel would be often coming here to know what it is that thee canst write so much about. Some would imagine that thee. . .art telling the king's men abundance of things. . .Therefore, as I have said before, let it be as great a secret as if it was some heineous crime.[55]

Lady Mary expected her daughter to share her amusement at the image of an insignificant little priest solemnly explaining to a woman as well versed in the ways of the world as she, a device that had been familiar to political and social elites since Cicero and Quintilian:

You can speak as openly as you like against. . .tyrants as long as you can be understood differently, because you are not trying to avoid giving offence, only its dangerous repercussions. If danger can be avoided by some ambiguity of expression, everyone will admire its cunning.[56]

Crevecoeur, likewise, would have expected his classically educated British readers – never mind the *Letters'* internal addressee, the scholarly and erudite Mr. F. B. at Cambridge – to be amused by the "simple" American farmer's wife who paraphrased Quintilian in Quaker English, and by the incongruity between her urgent injunctions to secrecy and the representation of America as a country where "cultivation is unrestrained"

---

54 Lowenthal, *Lady Mary Wortley Montagu*, 18–19.
55 Crevecoeur, *Letter from an American Farmer*, 41, 48.
56 Quintilian, *Institutio*. For methods seventeenth-century letter writers used to circumvent censorship, see Patterson, *Censorship and Interpretation*.

that the minister was citing from a century of puffing promotional emigration tracts.

Named after Cicero's letters *Ad Familiares*, which were admired throughout the century both as a model of "natural ease" in epistolary writing and as an exemplum of letters written with all due caution under a tyrannical regime, the so-called "familiar letter" had always already embraced the art of writing and not writing. And whether they had the education to realize it or not, eighteenth-century transatlantic correspondents up and down the social hierarchy were epistolizing in a long and illustrious tradition when they gave every appearance of "natural ease" to letters in which they took care what they wrote and used a variety of stylistic devices to combine, in the text of the same letter, both a public and a hidden transcript.

SECRET WRITING

As conduct books for oral and written conversation, letter manuals made no secret of the importance of secrecy. *The British Letter-Writer*, for instance, devoted a letter to explaining why "the Talent of Secrecy is of so great importance to Society" and why "the necessary Commerce between individuals cannot be securely carried on without it." *The New Letter-Writer* (1775) made it a cultural imperative by insisting that "Secrecy is a characteristic of Good-Breeding".[57] *The Art of Letter-Writing* (1762) warned that: "it is not advisable to confide a secret to Paper, which may be lost and fall into other Hands. . . .Letters of Advice are for letting our Friends know what passes, as well in our own Affairs as theirs, or those of another. . .yet with this Reserve of not writing inconsiderately any Thing that may give Offence, or may prejudice ourselves or our Friends, if it come to be known; we should be particularly on our Guard in speaking of the Great and of State Affairs."[58] Most manuals also contained a paragraph warning writers to protect themselves against interception and/or misuse of their letters by abandoning the polite custom of leaving a large vacant space between the body of the letter and their signature as a mark of respect, "because 'tis putting it in the Power of any one who has your Letter, to write what he pleases over your Name, and to make you in all Appearance have signed a Writing that you would by no means have set your Hand to."[59] The hermeneutics of

57 *British Letter-Writer*, 82.   58 *New Art of Letter-Writing*, 20.
59 *Crowder's Complete Letter-Writer* (1768), 57.

suspicion were therefore built into the writing, as well as the reading, of letters.

Recognizing that information or intelligence did sometimes have to be conveyed despite the risks, *vade mecums* with large circulations on both sides of the Atlantic included recipes for invisible inks and instructions on how to use them. William Mather's *Young Man's Companion,* for instance, instructed readers to "write your Mind on one side of the Paper with common Ink, and on the other side with Milk, that which you would have Secret, and when you would make the same Legible, hold that side which is written with Ink to the Fire, and the Milky Letters will shew Blewish, on the other side, and easy to read." Alternatively, one could write invisibly between the lines of a letter using gall water, and recover the secret writing by rubbing the space between the lines with a fine pencil dipped in copperas water.[60] Fisher's *Instructor or Young Man's Best Companion* recommended these methods of secret writing too, but added that dipping a pen in the juice of a lemon or an onion, or in your own urine or in spirits of vitriol, would also produce a writing that was indiscernible until the paper was held up to the fire. For conveying "news and other secrets" in a correspondence with a friend, Mather's manual also taught a transposition cypher, "which is but the changing of five or six Letters of the Alphabet, as for *o u d m* Read *e a r n,* and the contrary, and for *w, a a.*"[61]

More interesting, however, is the fact that both *vade mecums* nudged their readers away from such obvious and easily discernible methods of secret writing. One way they did this was by suggesting a method of communicating secret information in what would appear an ordinary letter to any third party who happened to read it. The method they suggested used two pieces of paper. One cut irregularly placed square holes in the first, laid it over the second, and wrote one's secret message in the holes. One then removed the upper paper, and "fill[ed] up the spaces with other Words, which ought to hang together in good Sense to prevent suspicion." As Mather pointed out, "each person to whom you write, must have one of the cut Papers to read your Letters" but "this way of Writing cannot be read by anyone else."[62] This method of secret writing was also used by governments and armies in America during the Revolutionary War.[63]

60 Mather, *Young Man's Companion* (1727), 82, 83.   61 *Ibid.,* 92.
62 *Ibid.,* 82–3.   63 Bakeless, *Turncoats,* 90ff.

The second way in which Mather and Fisher pointed readers away from obvious cyphers and towards inserting secret writing in what would appear to be an ordinary letter was by referring readers to printed books on secret writing, such as that by Bishop Wilkins.[64]

John Wilkins, who was chaplain to George, Lord Berkeley and later Bishop of Chester under Charles II, had published an influential book on secret writing in 1641, called *Mercury; or the Secret and Swift Messenger* which was still being reprinted in 1708 with the subtitle: "shewing how a Man may with *Privacy* and *Speed* communicate his *Thoughts* to a Friend at a distance."[65] In this book, Wilkins not only showed that secret writing had a long history going back to classical times and that treatises about secret writing abounded in the Latin scholarly literature of Europe; he also constructed from this tradition an exhaustive taxonomy of known forms of secret writing, sign languages and methods of secret conveyance for written messages. The paradox of what he seemed to be doing in this book, especially by writing it in English, was highlighted in a poetic encomium that served as part of its introductory materials: "Secrecie's now Publish'd; you reveal / By Demonstration how we may Conceal." And indeed, what was the point of publishing and making known these methods of concealment? Was Wilkins trying to facilitate the transmission of secret information, or to prevent it, by offering all and sundry the keys?

As later seventeenth- and eighteenth-century writers on cryptography understood him, Wilkins's point was that most of the methods of concealment he described were no longer safe. Wilkins claimed in his opening paragraphs that there were two qualifications for a writing to be secret: "that it should be difficult to be unfolded, if it should be doubted or examined," and "that it be (if possible) altogether devoid of suspicion. . .since what is once suspected, is exposed to the danger of examination, and in a ready way to be discovered."[66] He went on to say that most of the longstanding methods and examples he was going to describe failed to satisfy both tests.

With a respectful bow in his direction, Bishop Wilkins's successors during the long eighteenth century essentially began from this point. In his *Cryptomanysis Patefacta* (1685), for instance, John Falconer gave an account of "the Discoveries made of the Late Conspiracies against His Majesty's government" in Scotland to show that even powerful men like

---

64 Fisher, *Instructor* (1735), 72.   65 There is another edition of 1802!
66 *Mercury* (1641), 14.

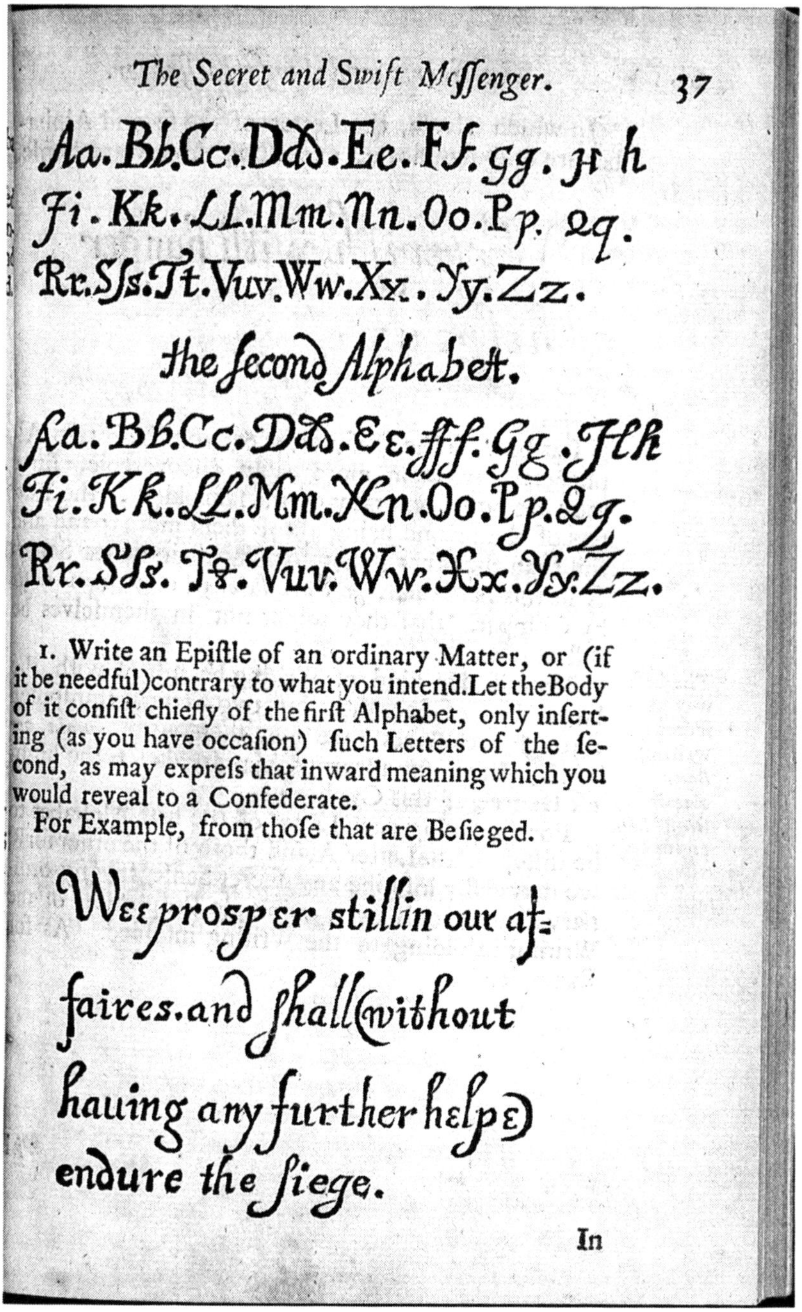
The Secret and Swift Messenger. 37

Aa. Bb. Cc. Dd. Ee. Ff. Gg. Hh

Ii. Kk. Ll. Mm. Nn. Oo. Pp. Qq.

Rr. Ss. Tt. Vuv. Ww. Xx. Yy. Zz.

the second Alphabet.

Aa. Bb. Cc. Dd. Ee. Ff. Gg. Hh

Ii. Kk. Ll. Mm. Nn. Oo. Pp. Qq.

Rr. Ss. Tt. Vuv. Ww. Xx. Yy. Zz.

1. Write an Epiftle of an ordinary Matter, or (if it be needful) contrary to what you intend. Let the Body of it confift chiefly of the firft Alphabet, only infert-ing (as you have occafion) fuch Letters of the fe-cond, as may exprefs that inward meaning which you would reveal to a Confederate.

For Example, from thofe that are Befieged.

Wee prosper still in our af-faires. and shall (without hauing any further helpe) endure the siege.

In

Figure 6.1. Two pages from John Wilkins, *Mercury; or the Secret Swift Messenger* (1708), reproduced by permission of The Huntington Library, San Marino, California.

38   *The Secret and Swift Messenger.*

In which Claufe, the Letters of the fecond Alphabet are only fignificant, expreffing this inward Senfe.

Weeperifh with hunger helpe us.

But becaufe the Differences betwixt thefe two Al-
phabets may feem more eafily difcoverable, fince
they are both generally of the fame kind , the Letters of the fecond being all of them more round and
full than the other ; therefore for their better Secrefy in this particular, it were fafer to mix them both
by Compact, that they might not in themfelves be
diftinguifhable.

The beft
way of
fecret
writing.
Bacon.
Augment.
fcient. l. 6.
c. 8.

Now if this kind of Writing be mixed with the
latter Way of Secrefy , by two Letters tranfpofed
through five Places , we may then write *omnia per*
omnia, which (as a learned Man fpeaks) is the high-
eft Degree of this Cyphering.

For fuppofing each Letter of the firft Alphabet to
be inftead of the Letter A, and thofe of the other for B,
we may eafily infcribe any fecret Senfe in any ordinary Letter, only by a quintuple Proportion of the
Writing infolding to the Writing infolded. As for
Example.

Figure 6.1. (cont.)

the Duke of Argyle, who used the most sophisticated of cyphers, had been captured and destroyed by breaking their codes. His argument was therefore that the *first* requisite for secret writing is "That it be void of Suspicion if possible." The best way to "*remove* Suspicion," he insisted, was not to use cyphers or invisible inks at all. Instead, the epistle should be "so contrived, as to outward appearance, it may appear to have nothing in it but some Trivial things, as news etc. or a private Concern, as borrowing of Money, paying of Bills etc."[67] By 1772, this had become the accepted wisdom: "The first and chief art of secret intimation in these days, is, to prevent suspicion, as scarce any kind of correspondence can be carried on by cypher but what may be unfolded without the key."[68]

One longstanding way in which secret information could be conveyed in ways that avoided suspicion (or at least that could not be proved against one), was by using methods that we think of as literary: the use of coded words, such as "the rose" for the pope and "the garden" for Rome, or of the language of trade goods for nations and the movement of armies; the ambiguous or allegorical use of stories, anecdotes and histories which manuals anyway recommended as a method of indirect communication; the use of pseudonyms for superscriptions and subscriptions in private letters. Secret information was also conveyed by using a wide variety of methods that we now associate with fictional spies, such as dead letter drops or clandestine exchanges of letters sent to false names at the address of intermediaries, which had their equivalence in print culture in the false imprints on published books.[69]

But books on secret writing also offered more technical ways of inserting a secret communication in what would appear to be an ordinary letter. One was disseminated, as we saw, by Mather's and Fisher's *vade mecums* – as they pointed out, writing a secret message in chequered holes or squares which highlighted particular words in an ordinary letter was a good method to "avoid suspicion," and produced a letter that was "not capable of being read, to any purpose of Intelligence" by anyone who did not have a sheet with the identical holes or squares.[70] But there were also other ways of avoiding suspicion that anyone could learn who took up their hints for further reading. One, which occurred in Wilkins as well as in his successors, was to write an "exterior letter" and an "interior letter"

---

67 *Cryptomenysis Patefacta* (1685), 1, 70–1.
68 *Art of Decyphering* (1772), 36. He also refers the reader back to Bishop Wilkins.
69 Treadwell, "On False and Misleading Imprints," in Myers and Harris (eds.), *Fakes and Frauds.*
70 Fisher, *Instructor* (1735), 72.

simultaneously in the same missive by adapting Bacon's idea of writing in two different handwritings simultaneously (roman and italic fonts below), one of which contained the secret message.

Exterior Letter:

We pros*per* still *in* our affairs and *sh*all *with*out *h*aving any furth*er help* end*ur*e the *s*iege

Interior Letter:

We perish with hinger [hunger] help us

The effect in handwriting is merely the impression of reading a some-what untidily written letter, but this could be mitigated if the difference between the two handwritings bore on the fatness or flourishes of letters rather than on their direction, as here. The same basic principle of indicating within an ordinary missive individual characters which to-gether spelled out a secret "interior" letter, could also be implemented in other ways in letters that used only one handwriting: by placing tiny dots under the letters of the internal missive (in visible or invisible ink), by agreeing that the first or last letter of every fourth or sixth word would be the signifiers of the secret message, or by an acrostic in a poem. Another method for achieving this result was to agree that only the words *following* some animate being (or thing or city or whatever) and the pronouns relating to it would be bearers of the secret message, as in the following example: "Let every Man *fly* to his Duty. Gentlemen, *you* now see what People *are*, and may do in their Madness: But we *discovered* long since their Folly." The inner message is "Fly you are discovered." In each case one was indicating which particular words or characters within a larger ordinary seeming letter were to be used to reconstitute the secret message.

Another recommended method of inserting a secret letter into what appeared to be an ordinary letter was to write one's internal letter on one half of the page as follows:

The design is not
Secret there is now no
safety but by flight
do not fail to meet me
half an hour hence
let the next meeting be
just without the Gate
if my senses are sound
we may conclude to have
infallible Evidence

> the snare is prepared
> effectually to entrap
> you and
> Your, etc.
> Postcript
> Prethee
> expose not thy self to
> imminent danger.

One then obscured the secret sense of this internal letter by supplying something "foreign to the design" in the empty half of each line, and then by punctuating according to the "seeming Sense" of the external letter thereby created:

> *The design is not in danger, to all it is as yet*
> *Secret; There is now nothing in view to threaten our*
> *safety, but by flight we should ruin all our designs.*
> *Do not fail to meet me by six in the old manner*
> *in half an hour hence, I intend to be at the Consult,*
> *let the next meeting be where they will, I'll have notice*
> *just without the Gate, was the Governor this Morning*
> *(if my Sense are sound) secure as we could wish him,*
> *we may conclude to have hit right on the means, and more*
> *infallible Evidence is not on this side Conjuration,*
> *the Snare is prepared they are misled, and see not that 'tis*
> *effectually to entrap them and on their Ruine to raise*
> *you and*
> *Your, etc.*
> *Postcript*
> *Prethee throw off those vain fears,*
> *expose not thy self to scorn, when there's not any*
> *imminent danger*

This is a version of the square-holes device. It is more convenient in that it does not require all correspondents to be sent identical cut-outs to lay down on top of the letter; but it is also more readily discernible if it occurs to anyone to look – one has only to slide a vertical ruler or piece of paper from left to right along the middle of the page until the sentences on the left become visible. More limited, but almost impossible to break without a key, was the use of predetermined abbreviations, as when one included in a sentence somewhere in the letter the word "fop" to signify "fly or perish."[71] The exterior letter could say whatever it wished about a

---

71 Taken from *Cryptomenysis Patefacta*, 73, 75, 84, 125. Most recur in other books.

fop; the mere presence of the word in the letter would signal the secret message.

John Mee has pointed out that the "functional ambiguities" used to circumvent censorship and danger that Annabel Patterson found in sixteenth- and seventeenth-century writings – including in letters – were still operative in the 1790s, by which time people of very various ranks had learned to write and read in an "allusive and elusive" manner that "frustrate[d] the prosecution's legal need to fix determinate meanings on a libel."[72] As we saw in the previous section, the possibility of double writing and of functional ambiguity was familiar and pervasive enough by the second half of the eighteenth century to be treated with humor. Manual instructions about the importance of secrecy and caution in letter-writing tended to encourage allusive and evasive tactics, and their modeling of commonplaces provided a baseline for such functional ambiguities. As John Falconer pointed out, nothing could be better than to use familiar classes of letters, about borrowing money, paying bills, or family news, which would not arouse suspicion, as masks for a secret meaning or "internal letter."[73] What *vade mecums* and tracts on secret writing added to literary methods of communicating a disguised meaning through functional ambiguity was a series of almost technical devices that operated through the very materiality of the letter – in the play of inks, the disposition of words and formatting of the page, through the concurrent shapes of different handwritings, or through the order and manner in which certain words were inscribed. In these regards, the secret or "internal letter" paralleled and doubled the overt polite signals of respect and relative rank through the semiology of spacing, choice of paper and forms of address that we examined in Chapter 2. Emphasizing these more material signifiers of public and hidden transcripts also reminds us just how carefully eighteenth-century letters might be read, and of how closely meaning and medium could be linked. This may enable us to replace our image of Enlightenment language as a transparent window on the world with the image of that window as it appeared in contemporary portraits: here the window gave onto the square painted sheet of paper that it delineated within the tableaux as a whole, which represented the meaning of the world in such

---

72 Mee, "Examples of Safe Printing," 86.
73 Traister, "Criminal Correspondence" discusses late eighteenth-century uses of Tory family letters by American loyalist spies.

a way as to insistently and emblematically present *itself* rather than its referents to the reader or spectator's eye.

This is not an entirely adequate metaphor. For in the eighteenth-century culture of letters, as this chapter has shown, there were diverse layers, levels and modes of secrecy. There was the *restricted secrecy* of the public business conducted "off stage" and in green rooms; of the public debates in Parliament and in government circles that were withheld from the people; of mercantile letters and of the published private newsletters that circulated among limited publics. There was the *evident secrecy* of card games, of good breeding and polite conversation which everyone knew were designed to hide what interlocutors thought, held or felt; the evident secrecy of the face that clubs and secret societies turned towards the world; and that of shorthands, cyphers and codes. There was the *published secrecy* of sealed interpersonal letters of news that were shared with family and friends or, more unwillingly, with the interceptor and secret office of the post, as well as of the intercepted letters that appeared in the public prints. There was the *semi-secrecy* of letters of introduction that signaled how open or secret the letter the carrier carried could be, and the semi-secrecy of pseudonymous subscriptions and functionally ambiguous communications both in interpersonal letters and in print. There was also the *hidden secrecy* of invisible writing and of letters which concealed the fact that they were communicating secret information without seeming to. Postmodernism has directed scholarly attention to acts, masks, masquerades, spectacles and merely performative identities. One might say, however, that the long history of acts, masks, masquerades, public spectacles and performative public identities in French, English and American culture and letters merely finds unconscious expression in the postmodern claim that there is nothing behind the masks or beyond the surfaces of language. To argue that there is nothing beyond surfaces is merely to accept the pretense, and to take Western culture, naively, at its word. This leaves a great deal of work to be done on the transatlantic cultivation of secrecy during the long eighteenth century, and on the layering, levels, forms, languages, imaginary and codings of secrecy in use.

CHAPTER 7

From Crevecoeur to Franklin
and Mr. Spectator

The pleasure and excitement people felt at gaining access to epistolary exchange is evident everywhere in contemporary arts and letters. The material accouterments of epistolography (as paper, quills, penknives, inkhorns, sanding and sealing equipment), the furnishing of writing spaces, the post and the regularity and safety of transatlantic shipping were as much a consequence and symbol of empire as sugar, chocolate, tea or *chintzes*, and were celebrated as such. Propertied people on both sides of the Atlantic had themselves painted with a desk and a globe, by a window on the world, holding a letter or a quill and surrounded by ocular evidence of their letteracy. Letter-writers turned paper, pen, ink, inkhorn, sand, seal, cover, packet, desk, secretary, closet – and even the amount of space left on the page as they wrote – into epistolary text. They reflected on hands, blots and characters, on the fact of writing, and on the position and places in which they or their correspondents wrote, copied, read, reread or preserved their correspondence. They discussed or bemoaned the timing, availability and circuits of posts, messengers and ships; the direction, misdirection, arrival, loss, interception, delay, dumping or retrieval of their letters on land and on sea; how they were sending, or arranging to receive, a letter; and why they had been prevented from doing so. Everything about being able to correspond was still new, interesting and worthy of display; and every aspect of letter-writing signified.

At the same time, and perhaps not entirely coincidentally, letters became not only "the basic structural component of many of the most widely read novels of the eighteenth century," but also the "all-purpose literary omnibus" form for "almost any kind of prose composition."[1] There were epistolary reports on travel to foreign lands, epistolary

---

1 Howland, *Letter Form*, 2.

accounts of scientific observations and discoveries, and epistolary addresses on political, philosophical and religious subjects. There were epistolary histories, conduct books, pamphlets and periodicals; and epistolary essays, satires, critiques and tracts. There were circular epistolary addresses to the freemen of England and America, and epistolary petitions to government for bounty or redress. There were collections of real, fictional and model letters, and even some flourishing manufactories in Augustan verse epistles. Letters were produced in manuscript and in print, for consumption at home and abroad, by individuals, collaborators and committees, on occasions of all kinds. As Charles Bazerman has pointed out, even bills of exchange, paper money and legal documents took the form of letters.[2]

As we saw, the eighteenth century assumed a continuity and connection between letters in these different areas of culture, as well as between everyday familiar letters and letters we consider literary. This was expressed and reinforced by letter manuals' use of the latter as models for the improvement of style. To show that awareness of manual teachings also flowed into literary texts in ways which change our reading of them, I conclude by turning to three now canonical, transatlantic and self-reflexively epistolographical, writings. These also address, review and illustrate the three parts of this book.

Each of the following texts partakes in different ways of the fragmentary structure characteristic of manuals and of the so-called "ephemeral" forms of print (newsletter, newspaper, pamphlet, novel), all of which were heavily dependent on the letter form. Each reflects too on the relations between conversation, manuscript and print and, like manuals, exploits the facility of the letter to act like a word and take on different meanings and emphases in different epistolary or narrative contexts.

CREVECOEUR'S FIRST LETTER

Crevecoeur's first *Letter from an American Farmer* is a letter about writing and reading transatlantic letters. Crevecoeur uses the device of teaching James to read and write a letter "over sea" to re-present and reenact the most commonplace and oft-repeated Enlightenment topoi about epistolography, and to ironically reproduce standard models of letters from

---

2 Bazerman, "Letters," in Barton and Hall (eds.), *Letter-Writing*.

America. The distance he creates between the untutored American farmer and his better schooled teachers – Mr. F. B. in Britain, who imbibed "worldly learning" at Cambridge; the minister who graduated from Yale, and the wife who was sent as a girl "to the very best master in the precinct"[3]– enables him to treat familiar matter with such elaborate naiveté and new world wonder that it becomes clear that the wife's warning to "warily observe where thee canst perceive some words of jesting, something that hath more than one meaning" (41) also bears on the letter in which it appears. This was a point that was not lost on Crevecoeur's British reviewers, who understood the *Letters* as a "hoax" when they were first published in London in 1782. Teaching James, the simple American farmer, to write a letter, allowed Crevecoeur to reflect, with some irony, on the migration of letter-writing down the social hierarchy in the transatlantic world, and on the ways in which the migration of epistolary models promoted the migration of men. Fearing that the unlettered were likely to take his letter *à la lettre*, British reviewers therefore also gloomily predicted that Crevecoeur's *Letters* would encourage emigration to America among the "credulous" English and Irish poor.[4]

Crevecoeur introduces letter manuals' most repeated cliché about letter-writing – together with his letter's central figure – with James's observation to his British correspondent, Mr. F. B.: "You assert that writing letters is nothing more than talking on paper, which, I must confess, appears to me quite a new thought" (41). James then transcribes the minister's elucidation of Mr. F. B.'s assertion:

"Well, then," observed our minister, "neighbour James, as you can talk well, I am sure that you must write tolerably well also; imagine then, that Mr. F. B. is still here and simply write down what you would say to him. Suppose the questions he will put to you in his future letters to be asked by his *viva voce*, as we used to call it at college; then let your answers be conceived and expressed in exactly the same language as if he was present. . .What he requires of you is but simple – what we speak amongst ourselves we call conversation, and a letter is only conversation put down in black and white. (41, 44)

---

3 *Letters from an American Farmer*, 41.
4 Rice, "Crevecoeur and the Politics of Authorship"; Allen and Asselineau, *Crevecoeur*; Crevecoeur's first letter sits uncomfortably with interpretations of *Letters* as "an American artefact. . .the voice of our national consciousness" and as a "formulation of major items of the national faith." (Stone's Introduction to *Letters*, 7; Philbrick, *Crevecoeur*, 70.) It is frequently ignored, or dismissed with a cursory summary as a result. For *Letters* as a hoax, see Mohr, "Calculated Disillusionment," 358. For the *Letters*' ambiguities, see Manning's "Introduction" to *Letters*.

This representation of letter-writing as "written conversation" was, as we saw, a commonplace that went all the way back to Cicero, and that had been tirelessly repeated ever since. The rest of the minister's elucidation was a collage of associated commonplaces from letter manuals and courtesy books. Mr. F. B. and the minister were "simply" re-presenting a long, learned and by the late eighteenth century, thoroughly popularized tradition, that related handwritten letters to everyday conversation and told people to write as they would speak.

The "jest" was that James took the minister, literally, at his word. The minister told him that "what we speak amongst ourselves we call conversation, and a letter is only conversation put down in black and white." So James wrote a letter to Mr. F. B. in which he put down in black and white the conversation about Mr. F. B.'s letter that he, the minister and his wife had amongst themselves. James points this out to Mr. F. B. with some satisfaction: "Thus, sir, I have given you an unaffected and candid detail of the conversation which determined me to accept your invitation [to write]" (49). Crevecoeur was giving a novel twist to the close relationship in eighteenth-century thinking between conversation and correspondence, and illustrating some of the ways in which letters both stimulated conversation and issued from it. But James's misunderstanding also demonstrated how the classical doctrine encouraged the perhaps unwanted proliferation of letter-writing down the social hierarchy by deluding the common people into believing that what a correspondence "requires is but simple," namely the ability to write down exactly what they would say. Crevecoeur's witty *reductio ad absurdum* of the letter as "written conversation" instructs epistolographically challenged readers in recognizable ways, while flattering and amusing his educated readers by underlining the distance separating literacy from letteracy.

For, as we have seen, letter-writing was not merely a matter of "know[ing] what sort of materials thee hast within thy own self" and of "dish[ing] them up" on paper, as the wife contended (45). However "natural" they sounded, letters were not, in reality, the spontaneous expression of Rousseau's natural man – as James points out Mr. F. B. has been careful to explain:

"Dost not thee observe what Mr. F. B. says besides; he tells me that the art of writing is just like unto every other art of man that is acquired by habit and by perseverance." "That is singularly true," said our minister, "he that shall write a letter every day of the week will on Saturday perceive the sixth flowing from his pen much more readily than the first. I observed when I first entered into the ministry and began to preach the word, I felt perplexed and dry, my mind like unto parched soil, which produced nothing, not even weeds. By the blessing of heaven and my perseverance in study, I grew richer in thoughts, phrases and words." (45)

Like the cultivation of the soil in which James and the minister were both engaged, letter-writing was an art to be cultivated by industry, study and practice. The minister's analogy between letter-writing and sermon-writing reminded educated readers that, considered as individual speech acts rather than as written conversation, letters were akin to sermons in several ways. The learned rhetorical tradition had long since addressed what James called "the difficulty" of letter-writing, namely "how to collect, digest and arrange what I know," by transposing the process of composing an oration, and by adapting the "parts" of a classical oration to the composition and structuring both of letters and of sermons. The difference between them lay in style and content more than in process or form; both were offshoots of classical rhetoric.[5] Both were also written talks, and addresses that were restored to speech as a script by the individual reader who "heard" the words she saw on the page, or more frequently, by a reader who read the words aloud to a company of listeners, as the minister read his sermons and as the wife proceeds to read Mr. F. B.'s letter to the minister and to James.

The practice of reading letters and sermons to what Franklin called an "auditory" in a manner approximating the tones, cadences, expressions and gestures of speech, made Crevecoeur's introduction into this letter of a multiplicity of different conversational voices doubly significant. While demonstrating the virtuosity of the accomplished letter-writer, whose excellence was thought to consist in his "protean" ability to adopt a multiplicity of different styles of writing, Crevecoeur's deployment of a wide range of voices, tones and styles in the letter's "written conversation" between James, the wife, the Minister, and Mr. F. B. invited the reader schooled in the "new eloquence" to display equal virtuosity in pronouncing and reenacting them. Crevecoeur was offering accomplished and educated readers a wonderful party piece.

One of the ways in which printed letters strove to carve a place for themselves in the everyday was by inviting readers to read and discuss them as they would a handwritten letter. In the Roger de Coverley papers, for instance, Mr. Spectator identifies the reception of popular printed

---

5 Kennedy, *Classical Rhetoric*; Howell, *Eighteenth-Century British Logic and Rhetoric*.

newsletters like *Dyer's*, which imitated the look and format of handwritten letters, with that of packets of manuscript letters, and brings both into line with the reading he sought for his own printed "Letters of News":

> It is our custom at Sir Roger's, upon the coming in of the Post, to sit about a Pot of Coffee, and hear the old knight read *Dyer's Letter*, which he does with his Spectacles on his Nose, and in an audible Voice, smiling very often at those little Strokes of Satyr which are so frequent in the Writings of that Author. I afterwards communicate to the knight such Packets as I receive under the Quality of Spectator. (No. 127)

Mr. Spectator was modeling a scene in which commercial newsletters are read out loud to one's company as handwritten letters were, to indicate that print and manuscript were both to be treated as a script and vocalized in the same ways. Mr. Spectator desired, likewise, that his own printed "Letters of News" (and the printed letters they contained) be "served up" to "all well-regulated Families" who "set apart an hour every morning for tea and bread and butter"; and that they be brought in again with "the Tea Equipage" in the afternoon, to provide "Tea Table Talk" by giving the "blanks of society" who had nothing else to think about matter for conversation and speculation (No. 10). Mr. Spectator was therefore representing printed letters as inserting themselves – or as being capable of inserting themselves – into a collective social and domestic space already occupied by conversation as well as by personal letters carrying news from friends and acquaintances, that were read aloud to family, friends and neighbors, and regarded as objects of curiosity and as food for general conversation and speculation. By inviting readers to treat printed letters like manuscript letters, writers and printers sought access to vocalized reading, and to the oral discourse that customarily surrounded it.[6]

Crevecoeur's first letter recycles such attempts to integrate the reception of printed and manuscript letters through James's description of the reading of Mr. F. B.'s letter in his household:

---

6 At the end of the eighteenth century, the anonymous author of "Meditation on a Newspaper" was still trying to counter the way "newspapers are undervalued" by representing them as something to be consumed in households daily, like tea and toast, for the practical purpose of stimulating conversation: "A family met together [at breakfast] would drink the tea of Lethe and eat the toast of taciturnity, were they not happily relieved from torpor of thought and immoveability of tongue, by the entrance of a newspaper. . .a newspaper supplies that dear and exquisite food, news, the daily bread of curiosity, and the panacea of all the evils arising from dullness and silence." in [Anon.], *An Historical Miscellany of the Curiosities and Rarities in Nature and Art*, 5 vols. (London, 1794–1800),: IV: 206, 207.

I wish thee would'st let me see his letter; though I am but a woman, as thee mayest say, yet I understand the purport of words in good measure. . . .She then read it herself very attentively; our minister was present, we listened to and weighed every syllable; we all unanimously concluded that you must have been in a sober earnest intention, as my wife calls it. . .Our minister took the letter from my wife and read it to himself; he made us observe the two last phrases and we weighed the contents to the best of our abilities. The conclusion we all drew made me resolve at last to write. (41)

Crevecoeur's *Letters* first came before the public in printed form. But the reader perusing this passage is carried from the printed letters she holds in her hand to manuscript, vocalized writing and the oral discourse surrounding it by James's comic description of a domestic scene that links print to voice and produces both the occasion and the content for further epistolary writing and printing. This scene of reading promotes vocalized writing and conversation by underlining the way the meaning of Mr. F. B.'s letter (Mr. F. B. as "jeering" or "in a sober earnest intention") emerges from the interplay between the script of his letter, its three readers' many whole and partial, oral and silent re-readings of it, their rewordings of parts of his letter, and the discussion and interactions amongst them about it. The conversation and interactions of these provincial readers also demonstrates the ambiguity or indeterminacy inhering in the distance between the social setting in which the letter was written and that in which it was read, and the difficulty of interpreting a letter from afar without the assistance of one's conversational circle. Janet Gurkin Altman has found a similar preoccupation with, and representation of, the different readings, re-readings, allusions, citations and interpretations of letters by their intended and unintended recipients in epistolary novels, where she construes it as a constant feature of epistolarity.[7]

William Dowling has argued in his recent study of the poetics of verse epistles that the reader of printed epistles was positioned in relation to the letter's internal addressee as "something like a reader over another reader's shoulder," or like "an audience overhearing this address from one friend to another as they converse within the boundaries of their common world . . .". This was not, as he suggests, a merely poetic literary device that Augustan poets (or indeed epistolary novelists) somehow had the genius to invent.[8] It was a citation of social practice. The practice of giving one's personal letters to others to read, either to themselves as the

7 Altman, *Epistolarity*, 88, 111.   8 Howling, *Epistolary Moment*, 3, 7.

minister does, or aloud to the assembled company as the wife does, made overhearing the correspondence of others and reading letters addressed to others, subject-positions that were familiar from everyday life. This could certainly multiply the possibilities of interpretation in interesting and "literary" ways. The extradiegetic reader of Crevecoeur's first letter, for instance, can interpret it through the eyes of Mr. F. B., the classically educated and well-informed British gentleman; through those of the minister, an American man of God with a European education; through those of James, the simple British-American farmer; or through those of his shrewd and skeptical wife. But here too, print was exploiting options that readers and auditors of letters would have encountered in their everyday lives to make the experience of printed letters resemble more closely that of reading a handwritten correspondence that one had been shown by a friend, or of listening to one's family, friends or acquaintance read aloud and discuss in company letters that had been addressed to them. A letter could communicate several messages at once, some more consciously than others, because even a relatively straightforward letter depended for its interpretation on the judgment, context and degree of familiarity with the writer that different readers brought to it.

Since, as we saw, no one was in reality expected to write a letter without a model, James's letter-writing instructions include the offer of suitable potential models, both by Mr. F. B. and by the minister. The conventional model for travel letters is invoked by the formula that Mr. F. B. provided on his visit, and by James's resolution to imitate it in "describ[ing] our American modes of farming, our manners, and peculiar customs" :

You conducted me, on the map, from one European country to another; told me many extraordinary things of our famed mother country, of which I knew very little, of its internal navigation, agriculture, arts, manufactures, and trade; you guided me through an extensive maze, and I abundantly profited from the journey. (39)

This is a fair summary of the topics for travel letters established by the Royal Society's *Catalogue of Directions to Travelers* at the end of the seventeenth century, and by Count Berchtold's *Essay to Direct and Extend the Inquiries of Patriotic Travellers* at the end of the eighteenth. Even the most casual travelers were advised to inquire not only into the education, manners and customs of the countries they visited, but also into the agriculture, flora and fauna, mines, manufactures, naval installations, inland and foreign trade, navigation, sea ports, law and civil administration. They were told to describe these in some detail, together with anything else they saw that could contribute to "the prosperity of the traveler's native land" or provide "ornamental knowledge" of other countries.[9] This turned every traveler into a spy – a charge also leveled against Crevecoeur, who had to smuggle his *Letters* out of America in the concealed bottom of a suitcase. At the same time, as Cynthia Richards has observed, it was a model which created "conquest narratives" that differed from their Renaissance predecessors only in the register they chose: they "remain acquisitive, with knowledge easily substituted for gold"; and "possession – here figured as that of a new experience rather than a new world – remains their ultimate goal."[10]

The minister offered James the model of an allied, and equally imperial form of epistle – that of the promotional letter or emigration tract. In advising him to "exhibit through these thirteen provinces so singular a display of easy subsistence and political felicity" (41) and "the spectacle afforded by these pleasing scenes. . .the new and unexpected aspect of our extensive settlements, of our fine rivers; that great field of action everywhere visible; that ease, that peace in which so many people live together" (43), the minister was suggesting that James give Mr. F. B. the appealing spectacle that Britons had come to expect from letters promoting America. Like the pamphlet that Scotus Americanus addressed to Scottish farmers in 1773, for instance, the minister described America as "a land of liberty and plenty" where "unmolested by Egyptian taskmasters. . . each may sit safe and at ease under his own fig tree, indulging himself in the natural bent of his genius"; "where the settlers are the most hospitable and charitable"; and "the poorest man, if he can but work, procures at once plenty and subsistence, which grows yearly upon his hands, until, by gentle and agreeable labour, he arrives at last at a state of affluence and ease."[11] It was the "pleasing" spectacle of America portrayed in such tracts that contemporary reviewers were recognizing when they predicted that Crevecoeur's *Letters* would promote emigration among the poor and ignorant, and prove "pernicious. . .to Great Britain."

The promotional tract had emerged at a moment during the first British empire, when British governments, British mercantile interests and British-American colonists were still more or less aligned in their desire to promote migration to America's mainland colonies in order to

---

9 Batten, *Pleasurable Instruction*, Chapter 3; Adams, *Travel Literature*, 78.
10 Richards, "Fair Trade," 74.   11 Scotus Americanus, *Informations*, 433, 434, 442, 450.

supply needed labor, expand Britain's trade, help secure British possessions in the new world against the Spanish and the French, and enrich land speculators in the new provinces. The challenge then had been to persuade Britons to agree to hazard their lives and fortunes to sustain a century of almost continuous expansionist wars and to colonize newly conquered lands. It had been met by a host of letters – letters from real migrants written to their epistolary networks in Britain and subsequently disseminated in the public prints, and epistolary promotional tracts written at the behest of land speculators in America who sought to populate their properties. The promotional letter or tract was the very model of a letter that moved men and their goods across the sea, and created wealth on both sides of the Atlantic.

James's no-nonsense wife therefore places this model of letter-writing, and the profit to be gained from it, in a series of letters that includes bank notes, bills of lading, bills of exchange and paper money, all of which created wealth and employed the letter form:

> Great people over sea may write to our townsfolks because they have nothing else to do. These Englishmen are strange people; because they can live upon what they call banknotes without working, they think that all the world can do the same. This goodly country never would have been tilled and cleared with these notes...[Mr. F. B.] told us that they have no trees to cut down, no fences to make, no Negroes to buy and to clothe. And now I think on it, when wilt thee send him those trees he bespoke? But if they have no trees to cut down, they have gold in abundance, they say; for they rake it, and scrape it from all parts far and near. I have often heard my grandfather tell how they live there by writing. By writing they send this cargo unto us, that to the West, and the other to the West Indies. But James, thee knowest that it is not by writing that we shall pay the blacksmith, the minister, the weaver, the tailor, and the English shop. (48–9)

The last sentence alludes to the perennial shortage of bills of exchange and paper money in colonial America, which condemned farmers and merchants to fall back on a local barter and exchange economy. James's wife was contrasting the provincial farmer's need to labor to plant and harvest the produce he would later barter for clothes with the tailor or for tea at the English shop, with Englishmen who had "nothing else to do" but write to townsfolk in America because the letters and banknotes they wrote acted in their stead on the material world. Writing letters summoned raw materials to England, like trees from the American farmer's own farm. Writing letters sent out cargoes to all parts far and near, including to the local English shop. Writing letters raked in wealth without work. Merchants sent cargoes of people by underwriting those puffing letters that promoted, to Britons starving under the corn laws, that image of the American farmer that the minister was proposing to James, and which the wife said "travellers. . .as usual observe: 'Here liveth the warm substantial family that never begrudgeth a meal of victuals or a mess of oats to anyone that steps in. Look how fat and well clad their Negroes are'" (49).

The minister indicates that intelligence about America was likewise a commodity that could be bartered for gain, by proposing that James use it to turn writing to Mr. F. B. into a profitable act: "You intend one of your children for the gown; who knows but Mr. F. B. may give you some assistance when the lad comes to have concerns with the bishop. It is good for American farmers to have friends even in England." James could employ a "pleasing" spectacle of America to cultivate a "friendship" with a patron in England that might one day bring his son preferment. Merchants were not the only people who traded in letters to rake in gold. The suggestion here is that even "letters privately written to gratify the curiosity of a friend," as Crevecoeur's letters purported to be, participated in a transatlantic economy based on "epistolary commerce." To correspond over sea was always to barter for gain.

The model for travel letters that Mr. F. B. gives James and the pleasing spectacle of America that the Minister offers for his imitation are both undercut in the course of the letter's written conversation. The wife points out, for instance, that Mr. F. B. could hardly be expected to believe the minister's story of the American farmer's "easy subsistence" because this was belied by his experience during his visit: "one half of his time Mr. F. B. poor man, lived upon nothing but fruit pies or peaches and milk," which was all "our orchard and garden afforded" (45). Nor after traveling the colonies and speaking to the contending political factions, does she think he can be expected to indulge "his imagination" with the spectacle of unqualified "political felicity" that the minister suggests the farmer create. As James points out, therefore, the letters he wrote by imitating models of one kind or another left both their intra- and extradiegetic readers "the trouble of sifting the good from the bad" and required each to "select what he may want and reject what may not answer his purpose" (44). Crevecoeur left plenty of scope for sifting. What, for instance, was the well-informed British reader of 1782 or 1783 – the years when the Treaty of Paris which concluded the American Revolution was being negotiated and signed – to make of the minister's description of America as a place where "we have had no war to desolate our fields?" Or how could an attentive British reader swallow the wife's emphasis on the hard labor of American farmers, when her remarks in the same passage indicated that the letters and notes of English merchants had sent cargoes of slaves to clear the forests, cut the trees and make the fences marking the farmer's property line?

The models for epistolary writing that Mr. F. B. and the minister offered James for his imitation were thus, in their way, as delusive as their teaching that writing letters was only a simple matter of talking on paper. Yet, as minister and wife both indicated, the migration of "pleasing" epistolary models from Europe to America, and their re-presentation in manuscript and printed letters by ordinary American settlers for their own gain, advanced men and moved goods. Re-presentation of European epistolary models in transatlantic correspondences was the *sine qua non*, even among people in the lower ranks, for participation in a transatlantic economy based on intelligence, epistolary commerce, patronage and trade.

Crevecoeur too was trading in letters for gain. When he and his British bookseller represented the printed *Letters from an American Farmer* as "letters privately written to gratify the curiosity of a friend and made public because they contain much authentic information little known on this side of the Atlantic" (35), they made it clear that James had written a series of relatively self-contained letters, each devoted to a different question about America that his correspondent put to him in letters from England. Composing each letter as a more or less self-contained unit of writing gave Crevecoeur maximum flexibility in turning the manuscript letters he carried with him to London into the money he needed to get himself and his son back to France. For it enabled Crevecoeur to negotiate publication for one or more of his manuscript letters by the sheet, in any one of a variety of ephemeral print forms – periodical, pamphlet or book – all of which offered the possibility of further serial publication. Some of the *Letters* also appeared singly in periodicals; and the fact that in 1782 Crevecoeur and his printers were also contemplating further serial publication in book form is made clear in the Advertisement: "Should our farmer's letters be found to afford matter of useful entertainment to an intelligent and candid public, a second volume, equally interesting with those now published, may soon be expected" (36). There were more manuscript letters in the farmer's suitcase.[12]

---

12 Collected in Crevecoeur, *More Letters.*

Here, as in letter manuals, it is more useful to think in terms of variable collections of letters than in terms of an organic "book."[13] In the so-called "ephemeral" forms of print that were heavily dependent on the letter form, one might even argue that the unit of production was not "the book" but the sheet. People who wished to keep newsletters, newspapers or pamphlets – all printed on a quarter, half or whole sheet of paper, or on a sheet that had been folded to form six or eight print pages – subsequently had them bound into a volume in whatever order they chose and with whatever other printed or manuscript material they wished. In America, people often bought "books" as sheets of printed matter; if they wished, they could have them bound for display for an additional fee, according to what they were willing to spend on the binding. In England, a "book" was merely part of a novel, periodical, history or conduct book: it was the number of printed sheets – or printed epistles – that could conveniently be sold separately as a volume at a price that its targeted audience could afford. Like periodicals, books and novels were forms of serial publication. Writers could no more count on readers (especially provincial ones) purchasing or being able to obtain all the books of a novel or history, than they could count on readers reading all the papers of a periodical. Like each letter in a correspondence and like each issue of a periodical therefore, each book in a novel had both to stand on its own, and to establish continuities by pointing beyond itself to other actual or potential books in the series. Composed of variable units, the eighteenth-century "book" was thus a more flexible, adaptable and serial commodity than its more "organic" later offspring.

We should not be surprised, therefore, to find Crevecoeur also capital-izing on this intrinsic instability by exploiting possibilities of imitative rewriting that, as we saw, were inseparable from epistolography. When he got to France, Crevecoeur produced a two-volume version of the *Letters*, called *Les lettres d'un cultivateur Americain* (1784), that was quite different from the English version. As Grantland Rice has pointed out, Crevecoeur "realigned the *Letters* as letters to cater to the Parisian *philosophes*," and as a "sensational defense of American democracy."[14] Crevecoeur rewrote his letters as political circumstances demanded, allowing them to take on what Elizabeth Hackendon Cook has called "serial national identities," as

---

13 In accordance with an essentially modernist conception of books in general, critics have sought organic connections among the letters in order to read them as a novel. See Rice, "Crevecoeur," 94; Asselineau and Allen, *Crevecoeur*, 74; Philbrick, *Crevecoeur*, 75.

14 Rice, *Transformation of Authorship*, 122.

he and they migrated between France, Canada, America, England, France, America and France.[15] Considered from the point of view of the letter manuals and epistolary practices we have examined, however, this was less a "personal" or "psychological" decision, than yet another instance of a widespread conventional method of translating letters and letter-collections from culture to culture, and from one cultural register to another. Serial national identities produced by imitative rewriting and changing combinations of letters were characteristic, not only of the ephemeral forms of print that borrowed, adapted or translated fictional foreign plots but also, as we saw, of the migration of letter-collections and letter-writing manuals between France, England and the American provinces. As James, the simple American farmer, copied imported letter-writing models to participate in profitable transatlantic commerce, Crevecoeur, the more sophisticated and learned letter-writer, demonstrated that imitation was always, at its best, also variation and creative transformation of models or "precedents" of epistolary writing that could be changed repeatedly to "fit" local conditions as they circulated among regions and countries.

THE SPECTATOR LETTERS[16]

Like the letter manuals we considered in Part II, *The Spectator* was a fragmentary text that was much imitated in the provinces into the early nineteenth century. Written and compiled by two of the many provincials who migrated to London to earn their bread by writing, it was also first constructed as a model of metropolitan good breeding by Scottish and American provincials.[17] As such, as we will see, it also served as a letter manual.

Criticism has traditionally followed Dr. Johnson's "Life of Addison" in reading *The Spectator* as "a series of essays," and Macauley in concluding from it that "Addison is *The Spectator*."[18] Johnson's apparent dismissal of the letters has been authoritative too. Drawing attention to Addison's notable "deficiency in conversation" (he was, according to Chesterfield, "the most timorous and awkward man he ever saw"), Johnson praised Addison's "Essays on Wit and the Pleasures of the Imagination and

15 Cook, *Epistolary Bodies*, 147.
16 For a fuller version of the analysis here, Bannet, "Epistolary Commerce."
17 Miller, *Formation of College English*.
18 Johnson, "Life of Addison," 217–18 and Macauley, "Addison," *Edinburgh Review*, July 1843.

Criticism on Milton" as "the product of his former studies." And observing that Addison "made little use" of letters because "his materials were more," he deftly marginalized Steele's more typically epistolary offerings by attributing them to "a negligence which kept him always in a hurry." If Steele called for letters from his readers, Johnson implied, it was only because he lacked the diligence and learning to produce enough essays.

In fact, it was not what Johnson himself described as "the superadded literature and criticism," but the periodical's letters and "commerce of discourse" (no. 1) which represented for its contemporary audiences what *The Spectator* was about. During the years of its publication, Steele, not Addison, was thought to be the author of the papers, more than half of which consisted of letters. And far from constituting random fillers, these were organized as a letter manual, that was recommended as a source of models in other manuals throughout the eighteenth century.[19] For instance, the "General Directions for Writing Letters," which was much reprinted, advised manual users to "read and transcribe frequently letters selected from *The Spectator, Guardian,* and *Tatler*" so that "by degrees, art and study will correct the defects of nature."[20] Benjamin Franklin made the same recommendation in his "Idea for an English School." Johnson tells us this too, in his own fashion, when he attributes the enduring importance both of Steele's *Tatler* and of *The Spectator* to their "perceptible influence on the conversation of that time." Before *The Tatler* and *The Spectator*, Johnson observed, "England had no masters of common life" to "survey the tracks of daily conversation and free it from thorns and pickles" and to "adjust the practice of daily intercourse by propriety and politeness."[21] What Castiglione and della Casa had been to a society of courtiers, *The Tatler* and *The Spectator* were to an age when a gentleman was, in Steele's phrase in *The Tatler*, "a man of conversation" – and thus *ipso facto*, a writer of letters.[22]

---

19 Addison's involvement in the journal only became known after Addison's death, from Tickell's collection of his works. Addison began to be elevated over Steele and sanctified for his virtue, Christianity and purity of style only during the second half of the eighteenth century. This elevation of Addison, together with the practice of publishing careful "Selections" of the "Beauties" of *The Spectator* which began at the same time, were arguably attempts to save the periodical from its politics, which had been virulently attacked by Steele's Tory opponents during the periodical's lifetime. See Bloom and Bloom, *Addison and Steele*; Knight, *Joseph Addison and Richard Steele.* Donald F. Bond has counted the papers that include letters in his Introduction to *The Spectator.*

20 Taken here from *The Court Letter-Writer,* 44.

21 "Life of Addison," 208–10.   22 *Tatler,* no. 21.

Oral conversation, written conversation, and conversation in the word's broader eighteenth-century sense of "having dealings, sociability, commerce, intercourse, intimacy," were Steele's topics of choice, as literature and criticism, religion, stoicism and death, and what we would now call "theory," were Addison's. There was overlap, of course: one sometimes developed or corrected a theme or vein of humor launched by the other, and both men invited their readers to become correspondents and included letters in their texts. But if one accepts modern editorial attributions of particular *Spectator* papers, Addison typically wrote what *The Spectator* called "Speculations" – more or less learned contemplations of a deep, abstruse, visionary or conjectural nature – and more infrequently, "Essays," which he defined as reflections offered without order or method, attempting a subject not treated before (nos. 249, 287). Steele, on the other hand, typically wrote what *The Spectator* called "Discourses" – in the now obsolete senses of talk, narration or conversation communicating thought – about the well-bred proprieties and ill-bred follies of oral and written discourse. It makes sense, therefore, that about half *The Spectator* papers contained letters, and that the majority were in papers by Steele.

While demonstrating through his printed correspondence the enormous variety of topics, genres, functions, styles and tones that the letter form was capable of encompassing, Mr. Spectator taught his readers through brief, introductory observations (which Addison called "hints") to read the letters he printed critically on multiple levels – for the character of their writers, for information and instruction, for entertainment, for grammar and spelling, for clarity and perspicuity, for justness of sentiment, for propriety, sincerity and naturalness, for good breeding, for style and for address.

The *Spectator* offered examples of the same standard classes of letters that we saw modeled by John Hill, Thomas Goodman and their successors. Besides large numbers of letters of love and courtship and almost equally large numbers of letters of complaint or reproach, there were letters of petition (for instance, nos. 36, 78, 258, 304, 310); letters of praise or blame (for instance, nos. 8, 52, 53, 134, 188, 271); letters of recommendation (nos. 230, 308, 493); letters of expostulation (nos. 96, 140, 145, 319); letters of condolence (nos. 163, 192, 417); letters of news or intelligence (nos. 127, 129, 187, 277, 324); letters of command (nos. 347, 526, 534); letters of counsel or persuasion (nos. 38, 164, 240, 246); letters of apology (nos. 181, 401); letters conveying benefits (nos. 248, 292); letters of business (nos. 102, 394, 457, 536, 532); and later, letters of dedication. *The Spectator* offered exemplars of correct and incorrect style in each category, and instances of well- and ill-bred ways of "shewing" oneself in one's correspondence. Among letters of complaint or reproach, for instance, there were serious letters, like those in nos. 155 and 137, from a servant complaining of mistreatment by his master and a shop girl forced to listen to lewd suggestions from her male customers, as well as jocular letters, like those in nos. 145 and 148, complaining of gentlemen who loudly whistled operatic tunes in crowded coffee shops, and of "bawlers" who yelled in one's ear. The same series offered the admirable self-representation in no. 82, of a man writing a rational, restrained and well-bred letter of complaint to a friend who had betrayed him to a life of slavery; and the blustering, cruel and senseless diatribe in no. 189 from a father who falsely thought he had been betrayed by his son. It seems that *The Spectator* papers were designed to be rearranged into such series for reading; for before the decision was taken to bind the papers into volumes where the chronological and numerical order prevailed, Addison advised his readers to collect the loose sheets of the periodical into "separate sets" by subject (no. 124). Like other "ephemeral" forms of print that were heavily based on the letter form, *The Spectator* was composed of sheet-length units that could be combined and recombined in different ways.

Many of Mr. Spectator's injunctions about letter-writing were conveyed quite plainly through the conjunction of series of examples with short prefatory "hints," and papers devoted to more general reflections on the kind of discourse in question that enabled readers to understand its governing principles. In the case of letters of recommendation, for instance, Steele's translation in no. 230 of Pliny's exemplary letter recommending a worthy friend, and the two further examples of appropriately written letters of recommendation in no. 493 (one of which is a translation of a letter from Horace to Claudius Nero) are explained and contextualized in no. 493 by a discourse on the evils of using letters of recommendation either to pass on useless servants or to express unjust resentment against the person one was writing about. The points made by Steele's critical comments on the justice and virtues of each model letter are also buttressed by other papers on defamation and commendation in written and oral discourse. Or to take another example: in no. 192, Steele prefaced his letter of consolation and counsel to an excellent young man who had just lost his father by a discourse on the proper grounds of consolation, which presented memorializing and recommending imitation of the virtues of the departed as the proper substance of such letters. Buttressed in no. 349 by Addison's paper on

Phalaris's "Consolatory Letter" to one who had lost his son, these reflections are taken up again in nos. 468, 517 and 518, through discussion of styles appropriate to eulogy and epitaph. More general matters, like the importance of writing clear, correct and grammatical English, were treated in the same way. Mr. Spectator's observation in no. 92 that the letters he received from Fine Ladies were superior both in sense and in spelling to those he received from Pretty Fellows, and his account in no. 105 of Will Honeycombe's embarrassment over misspellings in his youthful letters, were reinforced by discourses on using thoughts and words adapted to the subject (no. 62), against using empty compliments and words which do not say what they mean (no. 103), and against using imported French phrases that made letters incomprehensible (no. 165).

Like Hill or Goodman in their *Secretaries*, Mr. Spectator imitated the French, both in the sense of borrowing and in the sense of rewriting and creative transformation, to define a distinct national character and style. Articulations and differences become evident when we use as an intertext Antoine de Courtin's courtesy manual, *The Rules of Civility* (1678), which was popular in England when Addison and Steele were growing up. Unlike Mr. Spectator, Courtin's injunctions were primarily directed at high society and at the court. But like Mr. Spectator, Courtin linked his conventional precepts for epistolary writing to general precepts for polite behavior and oral conversation – "the same rules to be observed in our behavior and discourse are to be observed in our writing"[23] – and insisted that true politeness consisted of giving the outward forms and graces a solid foundation in sense and morality. Like Mr. Spectator, too, Courtin's treatment of epistolary writing emphasized questions of address and of style.

What characterized the letter for Courtin was less the proper deployment of the formal superscription or subscription, than the proper adjustment of matter and style in the body of the letter to the person being addressed:

Though Letters be generally historical, yet there is a difference between History and them. For in History, matter is the only thing that regulates our style, as being directed to no particular person. . .In Letters, the quality of the person to whom we write determines absolutely our Style: Only sometimes by accident the matter may regulate, when one equal writes to another. . .especially on the subject of Religion, Consultation or Condolence.[24]

---

23 Courtin, *Rules*, 170.   24 *Ibid.*, 221–2.

For Courtin, the ability to "judge and distinguish styles" was the primary skill a man needed to become a competent reader and writer of letters, because the style of a letter signaled the correspondence that the writer was assuming between his own quality or rank and that of the person to whom he was writing. This was a delicate matter in finely graduated, hierarchical societies like France, or indeed like England in the seventeenth and eighteenth centuries. Because a superior writing to an inferior, an inferior writing to a superior, and equals writing to each other, were expected to use different styles, language that would be polite and well-bred in one case, could appear impudent, arrogant, insulting or ridiculous, and therefore ill-bred, in another. A person could get it wrong by misjudging the position in which he stood relative to another, or the "freedoms" that relation allowed, as easily as by missing the stylistic mark.

The Spectator taught its readers the difficult decorums of different correspondences. Mr. Spectator demonstrated, for instance, through his instructions to his employee, John Sly, that a superior was expected to address inferiors and dependents in a plain, assertive and commanding style. But he also showed, through the absurd letter from the Emperor of the Mohocks in no. 347, that it made a man ridiculous to use an imperious and assertive style when writing to an inferior who was in no way dependent on him. Inferiors writing to their betters were expected to use a plain or serious style, and to address their superior with submission, deference, extreme circumspection, and zeal for their welfare. This is the style of Horace's letter of recommendation to Claudius Nero in no. 493, of Mr. Spectator's letters of dedication to noble patrons, and of the letters of petition to Mr. Spectator in nos. 304 or 310. A trusted confidant like M. Chezluy in no. 480 might be permitted a letter contradicting his prince in respectful and informative terms. But if he misjudged the freedom his master was allowing him, like the secretary in no. 394 who corrected the Latin in his master's letter at the latter's request, he was liable to lose his place or his head. Despite his subscription as "Your humble servant," Jack Lightfoot in no. 332 broke all such bounds, not only by excessive familiarity ("Dear Short-Face"), but also by claiming to know better than "Mr. Spec" in a previous paper, and by correcting him in a direct and assertive style inappropriate to their relative status, which made him impudent and ill-bred.

The style reserved for correspondence between equals was particularly hard to get right – first, because there were in fact *several* styles to choose from; and secondly, because among equals, the different degrees of polite familiarity, the style appropriate to the matter, and the capacity, knowledge, temperament and interests of the person or persons one was addressing, all had to be factored in too. *The Spectator's* discourses and correspondences demonstrated the diverse uses of the five styles that Courtin identified: the plain; the serious; the pleasant, jocular or rallying; the grave and modest; and the elevated and sublime. It may be useful to say something about them before considering how they were deployed. Since the grave and modest style was just a mixture of the plain and the serious, and the elevated and sublime style was largely reserved in *The Spectator* for Addison's speculations on religion and death, I will address myself primarily to the other three.

For Courtin, like for Mr. Spectator who devoted several Discourses to it, the safest basic style for written discourse was the plain and simple style, which eschewed figures and ornaments, and aimed for clarity and perspicuity through short sentences and correct spelling, grammar and word usage. This style was considered appropriate to a wide variety of subjects, including relations of fact and news, and was thought to lie within the capacity of everyone. In *The Spectator*, it tended to characterize those who lacked a gentleman's education, whether by virtue of gender or rank. It also had the advantage (as long as one was careful not to fall into the vulgar "naturalness" of low and mean expressions, rude dialects and dullness) of signifying that the writer was being "natural" and "sincere." These were the qualities that Mr. Spectator invariably highlighted in his prefatory hints to letters written in the plain style. He treated it as proof of a letter's credibility, and prompted readers to allow themselves to be persuaded or moved by what the writer had to say.

The serious style, which was the style most admired by later eighteenth-century Scottish belletrists, was the preferred style for most of Mr. Spectator's serious discourses and for letters involving essays, literary criticism, or argument on moral or political subjects. It was more sophisticated and harder to carry off with clarity and ease, because it required longer, balanced sentences carefully linked into a well-informed and well-reasoned argument, and the judicious use of illustrative figures like antithesis, analogy and metaphor. The argument and illustrations had, moreover, to be organized into some striking or new perspective on the subject at hand. It could easily become pompous, labored, jumbled and flat, as the letter-writer in no. 432 demonstrates, by repeating Mr. Spectator's sentiments while vainly trying to imitate his style.

Most difficult to carry off successfully was the jocular or rallying style, which signaled the *sprezzatura*, or "ease" and "negligence" of the true gentleman, and was the style most admired by the New Critics who tended to equate it with "wit." Characterized by the light and jocular treatment of serious subjects, and by the mock-serious treatment of trivial subjects through disproportionate analogies, counterfeit truths, pretended passions, and absurd or fantastic comparisons, the rallying style offered greater freedom than any other. But for this reason, it was most likely to lapse into excessive freedom or into over-familiarity, and thus to give offense. The art of Raillery was an art of brinkmanship: to take the liberty of mocking to the edge of propriety; to reflect familiarly on the character, conversation, conduct or appearance of others without obtruding too far. Raillery had to remain pleasing even to the person or persons being rallied. Courtin and Mr. Spectator therefore both went to great lengths to distinguish raillery, "a naturally pleasant and witty discourse, expressing something agreeable without offense to any man's person or reputation" (no. 264) from "railing"– derision, malice or ridicule directed at a particular person's infirmity or failings. Both set limits to the freedom and familiarity permissible, by insisting, for instance, that raillery should never reflect on men's politics, religion, misfortunes or serious physical defects; transgress the rules of modesty by lewdness or double entendres; offend against the rules of good taste by puns, slapstick, mean comparisons and other forms of false wit; or be used to express personal malice or contempt.

Roger Chartier has pointed out in his discussion of model letters under the ancien régime, that the debate between convention and sincerity, and between constraint and freedom, which runs through the whole literature of civility, also runs through the letters.[25] And of course this is true. But for *The Spectator* at least, what was at issue was not which side of the binary would prevail. As Mr. Spectator tells us, it was the circumstance that it was permissible, even among equals, for a gentleman to speak with complete sincerity and freedom only in the small circle of his most intimate familiars, which made such friendship among men so precious. In other words, in a finely graduated hierarchical society, the carefully elaborated conventions of proximity and distance, of deference, circumlocution and *agréments*, were what constructed sincerity as such, and made it so fascinating and seductive. Likewise, the conventional degrees of constraint on polite sociability were what constructed whatever "freedoms" a particular conversation or correspondence allowed as "freedoms," and made them appear at once so delicious, and so dangerous.

25 Chartier, "Secretaires," in *Correspondence*, 78.

The styles used among equals – and within them, the distinctions which construed the plain style as the height of sincerity and the jocular style as the height of freedom – derived their significance and their inflections from the hierarchies, formalities and constraints they seemed to deny.

What was remarkable, and indeed shocking, about *The Spectator* in these terms is that the letters were generally dressed in one of the styles that were supposedly appropriate only for equals, *regardless* of whether they issued from servants, pretty gentlemen, small shopkeepers, fine ladies, country squires, scholars, clerics, soldiers, titled merchants, sales girls, bar tenders, the old landed aristocracy, apprentices or whores.[26] Some of the letters were written this way "in-house"; those sent in by correspondents were often rewritten, as Mr. Spectator stresses, "to make them my own by dressing them in my own Stile. . .and by adapting them to the Character and Genius of my Paper."[27] For Addison, this rewriting of letters arguably served a conventionally didactic purpose, since Addison thought that the way for a man to improve his taste for polite letters was to read the best exemplars and to "naturally wear himself into the same manner of speaking and thinking" (no. 409). This was in keeping with the place occupied by example and imitation in the period's pedagogical theory, and supported the role of the periodical as a manual and conduct book for letters. But Tories may well have had grounds for thinking that for Steele – whose occasional papers on social and political issues condemned the servility of those who paid court to great men as "slavery" and criticized all precedency that was not supported by merit – *The Spectator*'s rewriting of correspondents' letters in one of the styles designated for equals served what contemporaries described as a more "republican" purpose. To render the sentiments of letter-writers whatever their quality or rank in one of the accepted styles for equals, was to "take off impertinent Prejudices [and] enlarge the mind of those whose Views are confined to their own Circumstances" (no. 428) by enabling members of all the different ranks to voice their thoughts and complaints with an unusual degree of freedom. It was also to represent the dangerous promise embodied in the empire of letters through the very diffusion and dissemination of letter-writing to all manner and ranks of people. Yet, if *The Spectator* laid out the cards on

---

26 McIntosh, *Common and Courtly Language.*
27 No. 442. Letters supposedly sent to *The Spectator* which were not used were later published in Lillie, *Original and General Letters* (1725). These look to me more like early drafts of Steele letters than anything sent to him.

the table in this respect, it also reordered them to represent society as a dynamic series of upwardly mobile hierarchies, as we will see.

To link the "inside" of the paper to its "outside," *The Spectator* cited and adapted characteristic practices of commercial newsletters, newspapers and epistolary periodicals to frame Mr. Spectator's relationship to an audience of "Lookers-On" like himself as an ongoing conversation. Whether handwritten or printed in a script font which imitated handwriting, commercial newsletters were inscribed on sheets of paper that were folded and addressed like personal letters and sent through the post like personal letters. They also preserved "the effect. . . of direct correspondence between individuals" by purporting to be letters written by a gentleman in town who was in the know, to a country gentleman eager for news about what was going on there.[28] Mr. Spectator highlighted the artifice of this device in his first papers through his rallying portrait of himself as the correspondent in Town supposedly in the know, but who is in reality so little known to anyone there, that he has to insinuate himself everywhere and eavesdrop on the conversations of others to have anything to report. Addison and Steele also transmogrified the country gentleman (who was in reality a multitude of provincial gentlemen, each perusing his own personalized commercial newsletter from Town) into a crowd of "Lookers-On." As spectator and looker-on, writer and reader were turned into mirrors of one another, and placed in an immediately reversible corresponding relationship which Mr. Spectator mimed in the Roger de Coverley papers by sending reports from the country back to town. *The Spectator* also sought to interpolate its readers by imitating, and engaging them in, forms of personal correspondence, using the question-and-answer, or statement-and-response format of epistolary journals. This also permitted Mr. Spectator to "introduce a great Variety of Characters," and to structure his own discourse with his readers, responsively, as ongoing conversation.

Letters from readers were not just "letters to the editor" in the modern sense. Readers who wrote letters to eighteenth-century newspapers often figured as correspondents in the sense in which we speak of foreign correspondents today: they sent in news, foreign or domestic, for the benefit of the paper's wider readership. Sometimes these letters of intelligence were written directly to the paper, like the letter *The Leeds Intelligencer* published in 1740 from a reader traveling overland to Edinburgh,

---

28 Wiles, *Freshest Advices*, 9–10.

who wrote back about the unrest he had observed across the country over corn exports. Sometimes they were personal letters received by readers, which were being made available by their recipients to a wider public through the medium of the paper – like the letter received by a Darlington gentleman which brought news of a financial crisis in London in 1772.[29] Mr. Spectator printed both kinds: for instance, there is a letter in no. 129 from a reader on the Western circuit reporting on the delay with which fashions reached distant parts of the country, and letters in nos. 124 or 304 transacting purely personal business through the periodical. There is also criticism of this practice in no. 310 in a petition against publishing personal business which could be of no interest to anyone but the correspondents immediately concerned. Mr. Spectator underlined the paper's role of silent brokerage among correspondents not only by drawing attention to the fact that he was doing it, but also by printing letters responding to other correspondents' letters, rather than to discourses of his own, and by pointing out that many readers thought "the Letters which are sent to *The Spectator* are as good, if not better, than any of his Works."

The numerous letters that Steele included from the impoverished, the bankrupt, and members of the dependent or oppressed lower orders involved brokerage of a different kind. As many of the discourses pointed out, "this sort of Intelligence" was designed to "give a lively image of the chain of Mutual Dependence in humane Society" (no. 428), to show that "the Strong depend on the Weaker" (no. 485), and to ensure that the former did their duty by the latter. Mr. Spectator instructed both the old aristocracy of birth and the new aristocracy of money that it was their duty to lend their patronage and purses to impoverished persons of ability and merit in the lower orders, in order to help them advance, prosper and rise into their own ranks. Together with discourses by Mr. Spectator to this end, there were letters inviting support for charity schools to give the children of the poor an education qualifying them for employment in trade or in domestic service; letters from well-to-do tradesmen describing how they had overcome obstacles and setbacks to rise from poverty; letters from bankrupt tradesmen who had been helped back on their feet by interest-free loans from wealthy merchants; and letters from young gentlemen of sense and ability seeking to advance in the professions, in public office or in the administrative hierarchy,

29 Black, *English Press*, 95.

who complained about the difficulty in obtaining the requisite patronage from "Men of Eminence."

The correspondence Mr. Spectator established among classes of readers (country gentlemen, merchants, clergy, soldiers, men about town) who were given male representatives in the Spectator Club, offered a positive image of mutual dependence and social harmony among the "strong." Critics have traditionally argued that Addison and Steele sought to reconcile the landed interest, represented by Sir Roger de Coverley, with the mercantile interest, represented by Sir Andrew Freeport, within the boundaries of an England divided between Town and Country. But the Spectator Club was broader than this. It consisted, in fact, of all the groups who drove colonization and enabled international trade: the landowner, the merchant, the soldier, the lawyer, the writer, the courtier and the cleric. Here no reconciliation appears necessary, for they shared a common interest. Sir Andrew Freeport, the London Merchant, owns multiple ships, "calls the Sea the *British Common*" and argues that it would be better to "extend Dominion" and "get true Power" overseas by Arts, Industry and Trade than by force of arms. Captain Sentry, the honest soldier, has "behaved himself with great Gallantry in several Engagements" designed to turn the sea into that "British Common" and keep it safe for "Freeport's" ships. Will Honeycomb, the gallant at court, inhabits the seat of government, power, gossip and fashion, however ineptly. The nameless Lawyer from the Inner Temple whose father "sends up every Post Questions relating to Marriage-Articles, Leases and Tenures" is associated primarily with property law and with the acquisition and exploitation of land. Sir Roger – the benevolent, paternalistic landowner and justice of the peace who knows his servants by name, and whose "Tenants grow rich" from agricultural capitalism by trading their surplus produce – is marked out as the goal to which the others are moving.[30] Captain Sentry is his heir, Sir Andrew Freeport becomes rich enough to acquire an estate, the nameless lawyer already has a small estate, and Will Honeycomb retires from court to his land. The goal of those engaged in transatlantic commerce, in war and in the professions that supported them was to be well-to-do landowners and retire to their estates.

At the same time, the degrees of epistolary competence amongst letter-writers even from the same social rank, created a hierarchy of its own. The

---

30 But see Paulson, *Quixote in England*, which treats Sir Roger as a Quixote. I read the style as rallying rather than railing.

hierarchy it created was a hierarchy of letteracy and education, that supplemented and secretly rivaled those of wealth and birth. Here, as Michael Ketcham put it, "we find a social structure being created out of a literary structure," and a new social hierarchy being formed. The part that Mr. Spectator plays in constructing this hierarchy is not stated but shown. Steele outlined the paradoxical principles underlying the double role that he invisibly plays in selecting and orchestrating all the periodical's epistolary commerce and written conversation, when he described polite conversation in *Tatler* 21 as "a continual Feast" in which "the Man of Conversation":

helps some, and is helped by others, in such a Manner, that the equality of Society is perfectly kept up, and every Man obliges as much as he is oblig'd. It is the greatest and justest Skill in a Man of Superior Understanding to know how to be on a level with his Companions...The most necessary Talent in a Man of Conversation, is a good Judgement. He that has this to Perfection is Master of his Companion without letting him see it, and has the same Advantage over Men of any other Qualification whatsoever, as one that can see would have over a blind Man of ten Times his Strength.

Two versions of polite conversation are juxtaposed here.

In the first version, conversation is an exchange dominated by no one. Each participant seeks to please and be pleased, and to maintain equality in the group by helping others to sustain a mutually entertaining and profitable interchange, in which everyone becomes in turn a listener and an actor. As Steele observed, it was "an impertinent and unreasonable Fault in Conversation for one Man to take up all the Discourse," and thus something for a well-bred man, like Mr. Spectator, strenuously to avoid (no. 428). Steele borrowed this view of conversation from courtesy books and from salon culture where, as Steele said, the Man of Conversation was "what we ordinarily intend by a fine Gentleman." Mr. Spectator taught this model of conversation through his discourses, and used it to structure the "continual Feast" of written conversation offered by his correspondents. He extended it not only across ranks through the "friendly Correspondence" modeled in the Spectator Club and Roger de Coverley papers, but to trade itself. This model of conversation underlies the "good correspondence" that Addison celebrated at the Royal Exchange "between those wealthy Societies of Men that are divided from one another by Seas and Oceans" (no. 69). The Feast produced in England when "the Fruits of Portugal are corrected by the Products of Barbadoes, the Infusion of a China Plant sweetn'd with the Pith of an Indian Cane," is described as the effect of a pleasant and profitable "mutual Intercourse" in which each nation obliged others and became obliged to others, by helping others and being helped by others to useful goods. *The Spectator* thus treated the old courtly model of civil conversation among gentlemen as a model for managing extant diversity, "animosity" and conflict among nations and ranks. This model seemed to allow each to develop "a kind of Dependence on one another" which would enable them to "unite together in one common Interest."

But this first kind of Conversation and the "good correspondence" it created between parties depended on the management of the man of superior understanding, who made himself their master, regardless of their qualifications or rank, while seeming to be "on a level with them." In this second version, conversation is a covert form of competition, in which the Man of Superior Understanding uses the rules of civility to gain an advantage over his companions unbeknownst to them. The most necessary talent of the Man of Conversation in this regard was what Steele called judgment, and Addison, echoing him in *Spectator* 225, "discretion":

The discreet Man finds out the Talents of those he Converses with, and knows how to apply them to proper Uses. Accordingly, if we look into particular Communities and Divisions of Men, we may observe that it is the Discreet Man, not the Witty, nor the Learned, nor the Brave who guides the Conversation, and gives Measures to the Society. A Man with great Talents, but void of Discretion, is like Polyphemus in the Fable, Strong and Blind, endued with an Irresistible Force which for want of Sight is of no use to him.

Picking up Steele's image of blindness and insight, Addison described discretion as the judgment a man showed in "knowing how to pick and cull his Thoughts for Conversation" and what to "shew" or "conceal." This is a quality demonstrated consistently in *The Spectator* only by Mr. Spectator himself. Mr. Spectator not only makes a parade of his invisibility and a display of concealing more than he reveals of himself; he also guides the periodical's conversation and gives measures to society through judicious silences and "hints" which prove their discretion by how easy they have been to overlook. Mr. Spectator's prefatory hints show the uses to which each correspondent's letter should be put, while teaching readers as if he taught them not. Yet his lancing judgments on his correspondents' epistolary style also provide the measure according to which Mr. Spectator emerges as the correspondent whose style never errs. They also create a hierarchy of epistolary competence in which he proves the master of his companions. Mr. Spectator generally presents letters in silence when they evoke his scorn, disbelief, contempt or indifference, to avoid insulting his correspondents. He draws attention to his silences only to modestly disclaim knowledge of the subject at hand or to display his well-bred reluctance to monopolize the discourse by turning entire papers over to correspondents' letters. He thus places himself on a level with his correspondents, while managing the correspondence among different ranks without giving offense. Yet by passing over in discreet silence – with a few speaking exceptions – the role he has played in writing or rewriting his correspondents' letters, he also proves himself so much their master, that it remains undecidable which of his correspondents, *if any*, were capable of conveying the sentiments they "meant to express" without his secret, secretarial help.

In assuming this role, Mr. Spectator was both displaying and modestly concealing his own design. Peter France and Anne Bryson have each shown that "the assimilation of good commerce and good sociability," now generally associated with attempts to integrate trade and gentility, was initially a feature of seventeenth-century courtly culture. The art of conversation, and the art of pleasing, were the currency used to negotiate advancement at court.[31] Like many of their impoverished genteel or would-be genteel contemporaries, Addison and Steele took these arts to a different marketplace to obtain gainful employment and rise in the world. At a time when the need for clerks, secretaries and writers in government and trade was growing rapidly and when the number of letters carried by the post office was doubling each decade, Mr. Spectator sought to demonstrate to his readers that "Letters are of Use in every Station of Life" (no. 353). He also traded on the arts of conversation and of epistolary writing himself, by turning the rules of civility by which men had established their credit at court into a commercial proposition via a "Paper of News." Mr. Spectator was not, therefore, conveying the values of any class but his own.

Mr. Spectator was showcasing the many ways in which secretaries and men of letters (in the *literal* sense) could help and oblige others, while obliging and enriching themselves. He showed potential political patrons the value to the public weal of secretaries and men of discretion like himself, who knew how to please and accommodate themselves to all societies, and who had the "Talent" to create "a good Correspondence" among men. He showed the value – both to "great men" and to wealthy tradesmen like Hezekiah Thrift in no. 509 who knew how to "deliver" his "useful Knowledge" only in "homely Maxims"– of employing men like

31 France, *Politeness*, 101; Bryson, *From Courtesy to Civility*, 123–4; also Burke, *Art of Conversation*.

himself, who were skilled in epistolary correspondence, to convey what they "meant to express" in the polished style of gentlemen, and to write letters for them which showed breeding, sense and ability, whatever the topic or circumstance. To readers like the footman in no. 71, Mr. Spectator showed the relevance to those even in the lowest ranks, who hoped to rise in the world and pass as gentlemen, of learning what he had to teach them about becoming men of conversation, and masters of epistolary style.

BENJAMIN FRANKLIN'S SECRET LETTER TO HIS SON

We turn at last to a pupil of Mr. Spectator's and to a writer famous for his secrecy, who composed a letter in Jonathan Shipley's country house in England in 1771 addressed to his son, William, in America, which eventually became Part I of his *Autobiography*. Franklin's letter to his son offers an object lesson in how, at a critical moment in a contentious environment where his private letters were regularly opened and frequently published, a clever and secretive man went about communicating a politically dangerous decision to his son in disguised form, while alerting him to what he was doing.

As William Spengeman has pointed out, the *Autobiography* as a whole was a transatlantic performance: it was "begun when Franklin was still a loyal British subject, written in England not in America, modeled on the styles of Bunyan and Defoe and on the genre of advice to apprentices; prompted initially by demands from London editors, composed largely in Europe and published first in French translation in Paris."[32] But Franklin stressed that the transatlantic letter to his son which composed the first part was entirely distinct both in addressee and in purpose from the later sections:

Thus far was written with the Intention express'd in the Beginning and therefore contains several little family Anecdotes of no Importance to others. What follows was written many Years after in compliance with the Advice contain'd in these Letters, and accordingly intended for the Publick.[33]

The letters from Abel James and Benjamin Vaughan which Franklin inserted in the *Autobiography* between the letter to his son in Part I and the subsequent narratives further separate the two. James' and Vaughan's letters indicated the didactic purposes that they desired Franklin's account

---

32 Spengeman, *New World of Words*, 178–9.   33 *Autobiography*, 72.

of his life to serve "for the Publick," and thus how the original "Intention" was altered in the later parts. These inserted letters also invite us to read the first letter to his son as a more or less self-contained unit, and to ask what was the "Intention express'd at the Beginning" that was related to these "little family Anecdotes." This intention and the way the letter conveyed it can conveniently be made visible by reference to the devices of contemporary portraiture.

In all but the earliest of the many half- and three-quarter-length English and American portraits for which he sat, Benjamin Franklin invariably chose to be represented by means of a conventional European iconography as a man of letters. His face calm, impassive and a little world weary, Franklin always posed beside or behind a desk in a dark interior surrounded by the emblems of his character. Franklin's scientific achievements composed the backgrounds of these portraits – in those by Mason Chamberlin, Benjamin Wilson, James Ardell, Edward Savage and Charles Wilson Peale, they are represented by the lightening outside the conventional window behind Franklin's head and occasionally by an instrument off to the side; in David Martin's portrait, they are represented by the shadowy bust of Newton rooted on the desk, but observing Franklin from amidst the drapery in a corner of his Craven Street study. By contrast, the instruments of writing – the handwritten sheets, the inkwell, the quill pen, and sometimes the handsomely bound volumes – occupy the very foreground of these portraits, in all but one case literally intervening between the spectator and Franklin's sturdy, prosperously clad body. In Peale's portrait, the huge white quill pen anchored in an elaborate inkwell on the desk bottom right rises diagonally to quite a third of the body seated behind it, while an arm rests firmly on the handwritten letters to Peter Collinson which constitute Franklin's *Experiments and Observations in Electricity.* In the portraits by Martin and Ardell, the table's burden of manuscript letters and books, or of books, letters, inkwell and quill pen, lie between the spectator and the man. In each case, the light falls on the face, on the hands, on the white feathers of the quill pen and on sheaves of handwritten letters that are often, undecidably, just written or just read.

If as Jonathan Richardson explained in 1725, "to sit for one's picture is to have an Abstract of one's Life written and published, and ourselves consigned to Honour or Infamy,"[34] then the implements of correspondence

---

34 Quoted in Fortune and Warner, *Franklin and his Friends*, 14.

in Franklin's portrait might be described as the Abstract of the Abstract of his life. From this point of view, it makes sense that, in consultation with a series of painters, Franklin repeatedly chose to foreground the implements of correspondence in these portraits. The bulk of Franklin's surviving papers consists of letters, many of them transatlantic. The instruments of correspondence also constituted a fulcrum and symbol for all the different facets and phases of his life. In the eighteenth century, to act as a printer and as a postmaster was in each case to control and disseminate correspondence; while to act as a political journalist and as a man of science, as a tradesman and procurer of government supplies, as a colonial agent, diplomat and plenipotentiary, and as a *habitué* of *salons* and of philosophical societies was, in each case, to take on the character of a correspondent oneself.

If, as Wayne Craven has observed, "the primary concern of portraiture was the creation of a visual biography,"[35] Franklin's letter to his son, which was contemporaneous with the later portraits, offered a verbal portrait that gave equal prominence to the instruments of correspondence by representing them as "the Means I made use of to emerge from the Poverty and Obscurity in which I was born and bred, to a State of Affluence and some Degree of [Fame] Reputation in the World" (1). Noting at the outset that "Prose Writing has been of great Use to me in the course of my Life, and was a Principal Means of my Advancement" (12), Franklin structured his letter as an account of how he had "acquir'd" from "imported books" the knowledge and style required for effective prose writing and conversable correspondence, and how these acquisitions had progressively gained him reputation and wealth. Larzer Ziff has argued that Franklin selected episodes to exemplify "the *social* advantages that adhere[d] to the possession and reading of books," and the way books constituted "his passport to society and hence commercial and political advancement."[36] But Franklin also underscored – with remarks like "This was one of the first good Effects of my having learnt a little to scribble" (64), "This was another Advantage gain'd by my being able to Write" (67) – that the episodes were likewise selected to focus attention on his skill as a prose writer, and to indicate how this earned him an early reputation, gained him his first public post as clerk of the Assembly, ensured the sales of the *Pennsylvania Gazette*, and enabled him to realize his projects for the public good. Contrasting his own success with the

35 Craven, "Colonial American Portraiture," 102.   36 Ziff, *Writing the New Nation*, 88.

failure of those like John Collins, James Ralph, Hugh Meredith or old Keimer, who buried their writing abilities in indolence, ignorance or drink, Franklin stressed the industry which led him to make time for study in the midst of trade and to spend his leisure hours practicing writing with like-minded peers. For as much or more than his industry as a "mechanick" or printer, it was his industry as a writer that had proved "the Means of obtaining Wealth and Distinction" (75).[37]

In having himself represented in the portraits with "the Principal Means of my Advancement" before him (often held in his hands) and the symbols of his international reputation behind him, Franklin was careful to underscore this success. The lush velvet coats and rich wigs in the Martin, Wilson, Ardell and Chamberlin portraits, the expensive banyan and elaborate silver inkstand in the portrait by Peale, indicated that Franklin's industry as a reader and writer had brought him wealth and social, as well as scientific and political, distinction. But while making the same point verbally in the letter to his son, Franklin also intimated that he potentially stood on the brink of "a fatal reverso," in which it could all come undone. The direction from which this fatal reverso might come is suggested by his rather curious reading list.

Whether or not it represents what Franklin actually read as a youth (and it is unlikely to represent all he read), the short reading list at the beginning of Franklin's autobiographical letter to his son has the same function as the emblems in the portraits. As the emblems provide carefully selected terms of reference to guide the spectator's reading of Franklin's calm, impassive and world-weary face, so the book list provides terms of reference for his son's reading of the proffered episodes from his father's life. Unlike the emblems in the portraits, however, the book list does not present a register of safe scientific pursuits. The books by Bunyan, Mather, Defoe, Locke, and Collins, and the Port Royale logic, symbolized a nonsectarian filiation with the seventeenth-century radicals, dissenters and philosophers in England and France who opposed absolute monarchy and religious prescription by an established church, and who risked or suffered persecution, exile or punishment as a result. Plutarch's *Lives* (which he "read abundantly and to great Advantage"), Xenophon's *Socrates* and Greenwood's *Grammar* represented a debt to the great civic humanists of ancient Greece and Rome who risked or paid with their lives for pursuing virtue, opposing tyranny and supporting

---

37 For a variant of this argument, Simpson, "Printer as Man of Letters."

freedom of thought. Steele's *Spectator* and Shaftesbury's *Characteristics*, which were key texts for Freemasons throughout the eighteenth century, indicated (among other things) a lifelong filiation with Freemasonry which was closely identified at the time with traits now treated as unique to Franklin: secrecy; the cultivation of a polite and fraternal sociability; the establishment of correspondences across ranks and nations; the cult of reason and of scientific investigation as practiced by the Royal Society, linked to an older, persecuted, neoplatonic and illuminist tradition that sometimes surfaced as deism; reinvigoration of the emblematic tradition; and the pursuit of benevolence, good works and projects for social reform.[38]

As the sitter for a portrait was able to particularize or adapt the conventional objects, dress and poses used in the visual biography – for instance, by selecting the particular view onto which the conventional window would give to represent his or her particular achievements, or the wig that best indicated his actual or desired social status – so Franklin's letter to his son shows him personalizing and adapting his borrowings from the books on his list. While sometimes modeling the method of reading this invited from his son (for instance, by describing how his "rewording" improved on the style he borrowed from the *Spectator*), Franklin assumed that his son would recognize the ongoing allusions in his letter and be able to make further connections on his own. For example, Franklin's explanation of why he gave up argument by the Socratic method he had acquired from Greenwood's *Grammar* in favor of "a Habit of expressing my self in Terms of modest Diffidence" which "has been of great Advantage to me when I have had occasion to inculcate my Opinions and persuade Men into the Measures that I have been from time to time engag'd in promoting" (16), assumed that William would be able to recognize the extensive, unspoken use he had made of Shaftesbury in determining how best to attain "the Chief Ends of Conversation" which were "to inform or be informed, to please or to persuade" (16). Franklin's argument against a "dogmatical Manner in advancing your Sentiments" on the grounds that it "creates Contradiction" and fails either to please or to persuade, paraphrases Shaftesbury and Mr. Spectator, while allying Franklin to the norms of polite conversation promulgated by both.[39] Franklin's citation of Pope's "Men should

38 Stevenson, *Origins of Freemasonry*; Jacob, *Radical Enlightenment* and *Living the Enlightenment*; Lemay, *Deism, Masonry and the Enlightenment*; Weisberger, *Speculative Masonry*.
39 Klein, *Shaftesbury and the Culture of Politeness*.

be taught as if you taught them not" also recalled Shaftesbury's caveat that "the Temper of the Pedagogue suits not the Age," and that a man would be more persuasive by "secretly advising and giving instruction" than by "laying his claim openly."[40]

Franklin's next paragraph, which describes him as "try[ing] my Hand" at personated discourses for the first time in the Silence Dogood Letters, offers an example of such techniques. For Shaftesbury, the key to "secretly advising and giving instruction" in personated letters was recognition: he insisted that readers were unlikely to feel either convinced or refuted if they did not recognize their features in the characters, and their arguments in the personated text. This use of recognition was what Franklin was trying his hand at in the Silence Dogood letters, when he wrote "an anonymous Paper under a feign'd Name" (18) in which he imitatively transformed the persona of the propertied London widow in *Spectator* no. 573 into Silence Dogood, the widow and servant of a provincial Puritan clergyman. The reasons for his choice and the raillery involved, depended on the reader's recognition of the letters' silent allusions to those "Books in polemic and practical Divinity" that proliferated in Boston, and to the way the Mathers, Foxecroft and Colman treated their wives and daughters. As Laurel Thatcher Ulrich has shown, this was distinctive among Puritans in a patriarchal age, for they educated their wives and daughters quite extensively themselves, gave them the run of their libraries and strongly encouraged them to write. In *Undoubted Certainties* and *Bethiah*, published in Boston in 1720 and 1722, shortly before Silence Dogood took up her pen, Cotton Mather insisted publicly that though women were "People who make no noise in the world, People hardly known to be in the World. . .and under all Covers imaginable," they ought to be listened to with particular attention; for "those who may not *speak in Church*, does our Glorious Lord Employ to *Speak*, to *Speak* to Us, and *Speak* by what we see in them, such things as we ought certainly to take much Notice of."[41] Silence Dogood alludes to these distinctive practices in her first letter by describing her education by a Puritan clergyman who was both father and husband to her and who gave her the run of his library. She alludes to such assertions by affirming that she made no noise in the world – "spending my leisure Time either in some innocent Diversion with the neighboring Females, or in some shady Retirement with the best of Company, *Books*" – until,

---

40 Shaftesbury, "Advice to Authors," in *Characteristics*, 33, 70, 87, 90.
41 Ulrich, "Vertuous Women Found," 33, 34.

believing that she was a person who ought to be taken notice of, she took up her pen to "reprove the Faults of others." From the Mathers' point of view, then, Silence Dogood was just about *the* most annoying persona Franklin could have chosen to reprove the Clergy. She was the voice of their wives and daughters speaking of virtue and charity as they had enjoined, but not as they would have wished.

In his discussion of Zoffany, whose opus included one of Franklin's favorite portraits of himself, Ronald Paulson described this method of representation as offering "a plainly public iconography but a private meaning."[42] Like Franklin, or indeed like Mr. Spectator,[43] Zoffany introduced "practical jokes and personal reflections" into his paintings, which would be visible only to those in the know who could (for instance) recognize the faces of Zoffany's personal enemies in his paintings of the Last Supper. Mixtures of what Paulson calls *claritas* and *difficultas* were common in emblematic representations which assumed that meaning lay in a "transaction" between viewer and viewed, and that the work's meanings would be recovered through conversation on "social occasions in which the viewers verbalize[d] and interpret[ed], interacting with each other and with the complex of the visual-verbal image."[44] Like Zoffany's representations, Franklin's letters mixed *claritas* – or what Breitwieser characterizes as an "unremitting stylistic lucidity"[45] – with a *difficultas* that called, like a crossword puzzle, for the recognition and deciphering of citations and allusions. The "private meanings" of these public letters were secreted in full public view and reserved, like Lacan's Purloined Letter, for those who knew enough to look. By impeding or retarding the consumption of the text, the letters' allusive intertextuality drew the reader's eye back, again and again, to the composition of the text. As in the Franklin portraits, the manuscript letters and the instruments of composition were held up for examination and placed between the reader and the meaning of the man.

In 1771, the "private meanings" of Franklin's letter to his son, which foregrounded these issues of reading and writing, were likewise secreted in full public view, and reserved for those who understood that a letter should be read like the writings of old Janus, which "possesses such

---

42 Paulson, *Emblem and Expression*, 138.
43 For instance, while appearing entirely general in its application, Addison's discussion *Spectator*, vol. III, about paying for the lying-in of poor women who had been seduced and left with child, privately rallied Steele for his womanizing and noted proclivity for getting himself into this situation.
44 Paulson, *Emblem and Expression*, 33.   45 Breitwieser, *Mather and Franklin*, 178.

remarkable *Opticks*, as to look two ways at once," both for its public and its hidden transcript, and for its bearing on the future and the past. For the inattentive government clerk copying the letter to put it with the other intercepted Franklin letters in the British Archive, there would be Franklin's impersonation of a tired old man looking back at the incidents of his early life, and contemplating with smug satisfaction how far he had come and how well he had done for himself in the British empire. For William, there would be recognition of the implications of those "family Anecdotes of no Importance to others," and of the emblematic dissenter and republican reading list that frames the account. There would also be some hints in his first paragraphs, such as "I should have no Objection to a Repetition of the same Life from its Beginning, only asking the Advantages Authors have in a second Edition of correcting some Faults in the first" (1). For looked at "two ways at once," it becomes apparent that what William's father had sent him *was* that "second Edition" of his life which "corrected some Faults of the first."

Heretofore, both in his private letters and in the letters he wrote for the British press, Franklin's position had essentially been that of his closest collaborators in London – Thomas Pownall, Richard Jackson and William Strahan – and that of American-born loyalists like Joseph Galloway, Thomas Hutchinson, and his son, William, who was, as Franklin put it, "a thorough Government man."[46] Like them, Franklin had argued that preserving America's union with Britain was necessary for the well-being of both countries. Like them, he had sought to discourage "tumults" in America and to stave off rebellion and war, while urging on parliament and on the Board of Trade a more "coherent, rational and mutually beneficial political reconstruction of the English-speaking world."[47] Heretofore too, as his enemies liked to point out, Franklin had been a beneficiary of the British patronage system: he had acquired the Postmastership of half of America for himself and the Governorship of New Jersey for his son; he had used the patronage system to obtain land in Nova Scotia, and was trying to use it again to obtain vast tracts in the Ohio Valley. Only two years before, in a letter he wrote for the British press, Franklin had also defended American placeholders like himself, his son and Thomas Hutchinson, by arguing that "being loyal subjects to their Sovereign, the Americans think they have as good a right to enjoy offices under him in America, as a Scotchman has in Scotland or an

---

46 Benjamin to William Franklin, London, Oct. 6, 1773.
47 Bailyn, *Ordeal of Thomas Hutchinson*, 79.

Englishman in England" and that American placeholders had "never yet been taught to believe that the interests of their king and his subjects are so contrary and incompatible that an honest man cannot serve one without betraying the other."[48] Franklin had even been considering the possibility of making England his permanent home. The open break with these positions would not come until 1773, when Franklin was publicly humiliated by the Privy Council (purportedly for publishing Hutchinson's letters), deprived of his postmastership, and obliged to leave England to avoid arrest and imprisonment. In the summer of 1771, Franklin was not yet ready for an open break, though he clearly saw one coming; nor could he, as he pointed out, go back and change what he had said and done in the past: a "Repetition of the same Life" in which he could "change some sinister Accidents and Events for others more favorable" was "not to be expected." But "the next Thing most like living one's Life over again" was "a Recollection of that Life. . .and the putting it down in Writing" (1–2). Writing made possible that repetition and correction of the same life that life did not afford. Franklin could go back, in writing, to the beginnings of it all, in the little village of Ecton in Northamptonshire, and to an analogical moment of crisis which had split the Franklin family in 1682. He could "recollect" in "family Anecdotes" that the course that he and his son had been following heretofore was only one of the options that they had inherited from their British forebears; and he could reframe what it meant for him or for his son to say "I am a Briton."

In 1682, under James II, there had been Franklins who agreed to conform to the political and religious correctness of the day. These included Franklin's uncle Thomas, who "qualify'd himself for the business of Scrivener" and rose from a smithy to become "a considerable Man in County affairs," first through the patronage of the local "lord of the manor" and later through that of Lord Halifax. For uncle Thomas, like for Franklin heretofore, writing had been the means to wealth and political advancement within the British patronage system. But there had also been other Franklins who had chosen nonconformity; and when conventicles were outlawed in England, had removed to America at the urging of "some considerable Men of their Acquaintance." "Recollecting" that Benjamin and his son were directly descended from those nonconformist Franklins linked them to another tradition of

---

48 *Franklin's Letters to the Press*, 154–5; for the attacks that this was answering, *ibid.*, 153–4.

Britons – represented by Bunyan, Mather and Locke on his reading list – who had found their interests so "contrary and incompatible" with English kings that they chose imprisonment or exile over advancement through conformity, and agreed to obey English monarchs only as long as these ruled them, as Locke put it, "to their Good." Recollecting that he was heir to a tradition that taught Britons to believe that the interests of their king and his subjects could be incompatible, and that men should face exile, imprisonment or death rather than serve one and betray the other, and using it to correct and reframe the course of his life, indicated the precariousness of the success story that Franklin seemed to be presenting. In its second edition, as Franklin was careful to point out, the story of his life was not the story of his meteoric rise to affluence and fame, but the story of a life suspended between "continuing that happiness" and "a fatal Reverso, which I may experience as others have done" (2).

In the public success story, Franklin's progress had resembled that of his uncle Thomas: like his uncle, he had learned the business of writing and had risen from a humble mechanic to affluence and reputation through the patronage of "men of the first Distinction." But by 1771, Franklin had come to understand that, for him – unlike for his son, perhaps – the road to advancement in England was blocked. He wrote to William in 1768: "there has been talk of getting me appointed undersecretary to Lord Hillsborough; but with little likelihood, as it is a settled point here that I am too much of an American."[49] In the spring of 1771, he gave William an account of an awkward interview with Lord Hillsborough in which the latter had refused to acknowledge him as American agent and had, in effect, cut him out of direct dealings with the Board of Trade. Franklin addresses this issue of his advancement in the second, corrected edition of his life which he said he was writing for his son's "imitation," by "recollecting" that the patrons responsible for his meteoric advancement and success had never been Englishmen. The episodes he selected from his early life showed that he owed both his rise to affluence and his public posts exclusively to the patronage of Americans – American Quakers like Denham; American investors like Meredith; American friends in the Pennsylvania Assembly, like William Allen; American printers like the elder Bradford. Franklin also recounts how he had courted Englishmen, to show that all he had ever received

49 January 9, 1768. In *Writings*, 830.

from them in return were flattering courtesies, trickery or deceit. His representations of his treatment by British officials, from Governor Keith to the British military officer for whom he collected wagons, echo his complaints in other letters of this time about his treatment at the hands of British officials like Hillsborough or Governor John Penn. Franklin represents Englishmen in the autobiographical letter of 1771 as having taken advantage of his abilities and of his willingness to be a "thorough government man" when it suited them, while failing to do their part in return. For him, the letter suggests, British patronage had proved a broken reed.

If the external letter was the narrative of an old man "indulg[ing] the inclination so natural to old men, to be talking of themselves and their own past actions" (2), the internal letter intimated to his son over sea that in 1771, for the reasons he was giving and despite the risks, Franklin had chosen sides in the conflict between Britain and America. Should the threads of correspondence between Britain and America eventually be severed by independence and war, Franklin was signaling to his son that he would choose to advance along the American path that was still open to him, and advising his son to "imitate" him in that regard.

Even interpreted thus, Franklin's letter to his son can be recontextualized as part of the exemplary narrative of American character and nation-building that James' and Vaughan's letters were inviting him to publish. Clearly the choice between British or American identity was a crucial issue faced by all British-Americans during the 1770s, and choosing to be American, the first step towards American nationhood. Franklin's secret internal narrative was therefore as fit for inclusion in a Life that was designed to show, as Vaughan put it, that "all that has happened to you is also connected with the detail of the manners and situation of a rising people," as the external narrative demonstrating what James called "the spirit of industry and early attention to business, frugality and temperance."

But Franklin's insertion of the two letters from James and Vaughan also break the narrative plain. They are real parts of Franklin's life and correspondence which not only figure as the autobiography of this *Autobiography*, but also invite us to read the beginning of the *Autobiography* as composed of a series of three discontinuous letters: the letter to his son and the two juxtaposed letters from his friends. Read in this way, it is perhaps not insignificant that the first thing that the first interpolated letter does is remind us of the dangers of engaging in transatlantic correspondence at this time: "My dear and Honored friend: I have often been desirous of writing to thee, but could not be reconciled to the thought, that the letter might fall into the hands of the British, lest some printer or busy-body should publish some part of the contents, and give our friend pain, and myself censure." This might be described as an invitation to reread the preceding letter by Franklin to see how he met that challenge.

Vaughan's letter controls our reading of the *Autobiography* in a different way. It prevents us from perusing it merely as the reminiscences of the self-indulgent old man in the first letter, and instructs us to consider this *Life* as the work of an "author [of] the immense revolution of the present period" and as the example of a great man whose Life will contribute to "the forming of future great men." But placed where it is, *in medias res* rather than among the *Autobiography*'s prefatory materials, Vaughan's allusions to Franklin in these terms also represents a confirmation of the wisdom of the choice he made in the internal letter to his son. This confirmation appears all the more poignant when we "recollect" that William, who failed to "imitate" his father as instructed, subsequently saw his career as a "government man" among the British come to naught.

AFTERWORD

This chapter has shown that letter manuals can alter, and indeed add to, our understanding of canonical texts. I offer this as a final illustration of the overall argument of this book, which is that letter manuals provide a heretofore largely untapped box of tools, which change the ways in which we can understand and read manuscript, printed and "literary" letters.

Familiarity with the commonplaces proper to the different classes of letters, allows us to read eighteenth-century letters both in terms of how they repeated or varied what was commonly said in each class of letter, and in terms of what they omitted from or added to the expected forms. Appreciation of the variations and creative transformations of the expected commonplaces introduced by skilled or witty writers afforded the letterate eighteenth-century reader what might be called an informed aesthetic pleasure, while even minor departures from the commonplaces were interpreted as significant statements, often far beyond their proportion in the epistolary text. Letter manuals familiarize us not only with the commonplaces proper to each class of letter, but also with the relatively small number of models in terms of which letterate people learned to write, read, evaluate and understand epistolary writing, and with the ways in which style, tone, rank and material presentation figured in the writing and interpretation of letters. They also make us aware of the culture of intertextual fragments which dominated education and the scene of writing, as well as of the many ways in which writers could rewrite, use and manipulate fragments, context and framing, both within letters and within compilations, to convey different messages.

The study of letter manuals adds to what we know from recent work on anthologies, miscellanies and commonplace books, about the fragmentary, discontinuous, heterogeneous and collaborative forms of writing that were so prominent both in the early modern period and in the eighteenth century. It helps us to better understand how to read and interpret such texts. Particularly noteworthy here, it seems to me, is the way both changing versions of the "same" manual by the same publisher, and changing transatlantic manual "series," subvert our modernist notion of print as a fixed and reifying form. Manuals show how printers and compilers used selection, reordering, reframing, abridgement and clustering to change both the composition and the meaning of their London "copy" texts, to alter their proposed target audiences, cultural registers and conduct book teachings, and to adapt letters and manuals to changing times and different local circumstances. This allows us to see how the "same" culture could be reproduced differently in different parts of Britain and of the British Atlantic world. Letter manuals indicate that in the provinces "anglicization" and exceptionalism went hand in hand, while offering a method with a solid material basis that might profitably be used for analyzing local abridgements or provincial compilations of other kinds of texts. Relatively little has been done with eighteenth-century compilations, abridgements or adaptations as yet.[50]

Letter manuals also indicate the importance of social practices in constructing the imaginary attached to epistolary writing as a form of communication that replicated conversation or speech. Letter manuals taught and represented the many ways in which voice, manuscript and print were deployed as complementary modes in epistolary writing. They show that letters were shape changers, that traveled from speech, through the "silent speech" of manuscript or print, back to speech at their point of oral delivery. By representing letters in conventional terms as written conversations that could make the absent present, by arguing that words placed scenes "in idea" before the mind, and by inviting writers to imagine their correspondents were present before them as they wrote,

---

50 Important recent exceptions are Tennenhouse, "Americanization of *Clarissa*," and Price, *Anthology*.

letter manuals extended Enlightenment notions of "society" in imagination to those at a distance.

This opens other potentially fruitful domains of inquiry. For instance, the notion of letters as written conversation enables us to rethink the relations that pertained between model letters in manuals, letters as an increasingly common form of "written conversation" in everyday life, and letters in epistolary novels from a different place. We might, for instance, profitably view the letters in epistolary novels as a particularly salient form of Bakhtin's argument that novels in general offer heterogeneous "images of speech" and read fictive correspondences between characters in novels as images of the written epistolary conversations in society at large – while recognizing that both in manuals and in novels, art was also imitating arts and influencing "real" everyday forms of written conversation and speech. Some epistolary novels can also be read as tackling issues, such as those relating to secrecy and publicity, that were also tackled in letter manuals and that, as we saw in Chapter 6, were inseparable from the culture of letters itself.

The story of efforts to facilitate communication among different parts of the empire by disseminating standard, polite epistolary norms via manuals and schools, offers intriguing *aperçus* into the pressures placed upon different social groups both in England and in the provinces to qualify themselves as epistolary writers. It lifts the curtain on some of the social realities faced by people on either side of the Atlantic. But as we have seen, the story of education and "normalization" was also the story of creative transformations both in the cultural provinces of empire, and across all domains of the literary and epistolary cultures. Both in manuals and in letters, repetition and difference went hand in hand. Imitation and compilation were means of instruction and technes of writing that at once transmitted the same conventional discursive forms and cultural norms to anyone who wished to learn, and produced that kaleidoscopic proliferation of fractals, variants, combinations and mutations which prevented the same from remaining identical with itself. Together, imperious laws, the norms of politeness and the very conventionality of commonplaces and forms of address in epistolary writing, permitted something else to be seen and heard, even while virtually forcing anyone who wished to speak truly or boldly through letters to do so in hiding, and between the lines. As products and agents of social, commercial, domestic, professional and epistolary norms, letter manuals were therefore doubly empowering – as gateways into the opportunities of empire, and as means of escaping its dominion and its constraints.

Bibliography

PRIMARY MATERIALS

Epistolary manuals

Note: I have listed together manual titles and editions of manuals which are versions of each other, correcting the ESTC and Evans where necessary. I have listed only editions that I have examined. The most frequently reprinted British and British-American manuals are in bold.

A Gentleman of Fortune. *The New Art of Letter-Writing, divided into two parts: the first containing Rules and Directions for writing letters on all Sorts of Subjects; with a Variety of Examples, equally elegant and instructive; the Second a Collection of Letters on the most interesting Occasions in Life*, 2ⁿᵈ ed. London: Printed for O. Osborne, 1762.

[Anon.]. *A Select Collection of Original Letters Written by Eminent Persons on Various entertaining Subjects and on many Important Occasions from the Reign of Henry VIII to the Present Time*, 2 vols. London: For J. and J. Rivington, 1755.

[Anon.]. *Classical English Letter-Writer; or Epistolary Selections*. Philadelphia: Published by Caleb Richardson, 1816.

[Anon.]. *The Accomplished Letter-Writer or Universal Correspondent, containing Familiar Letters on all the most common Occasions of Life* . . . London: Printed for T. Caslon and J. Ashburner, 1779.

[Anon.]. *The Accomplish'd Letter-Writer; or the Young Gentleman and Ladies Polite Guide to an Epistolary Correspondence* . . . Newcastle-upon-Tyne: Printed by T. Saint, 1787.

[Anon.]. **The Academy of Complements** London: Printed by Tho. Leach, 1663 5ᵗʰ edition: Printed for Tho. Passinger, 1685.

[Anon.]. **The New Academy of Complements;. . . . . .** *erected for Ladies, Gentlewomen, Courtiers, Gentlemen* . . . London: Printed for John Churchill, 1713. . . . *or the Compleat English Secretary*, London: Printed for R. Ware; C. Hitch and J. Hodges, 1748. Glasgow: Printed by J. and M. Robertson, 1789. . . . *or the Lover's Secretary*, Dublin: Printed by Thomas Browne, 1743.

London: Printed for J. Bew, 1784. *The American Academy of Compliments; or the Complete American Secretary* Philadelphia: Deshong and Folwell, 1796. Hudson, NY: A. Stoddard, 1804. Hudson, NY: A. Stoddard, 1805.

[Anon.]. *The British Letter-Writer: or, Letter-Writer's Complete Instructor, containing A Course of Letters on the most Useful, Important, Instructive and Entertaining Subjects . . .* London: Printed for J. Cooke, n.d.

[Anon.]. *The Columbian Letter-Writer, or young lady and gentleman's guide to epistolary Correspondence.* Alexandria: Printed by S. Snowden, 1811.

[Anon.]. *The Complete Letter-Writer or Polite English Secretary.* [Crowder's] 2nd ed. London: Printed for Stanley Crowder and H. Woodgate, 1756. London: Printed for Stanley Crowder and Henry Woodgate, 1757. London: Printed for Stanley Crowder and Henry Woodgate, 1759. 11th ed. London: Printed for Stanley Crowder and Benjamin Collins in Salisbury, 1767. 12th ed. London: Printed for Stanley Crowder and Benjamin Collins in Salisbury, 1768. 14th ed. London: Printed for Stanley Crowder and Benjamin Collins in Salisbury, 1772. 15th ed. London: Printed for Stanley Crowder and Benjamin Collins in Salisbury, 1775. 16th ed. London: Printed for S. Crowder and Cha. Collins in Salisbury, 1778. 19th ed. London: Printed for James Salisbury, 1800. 19th ed. London: Printed for J. Scatcherd and B. C. Collins, Salisbury 1800. **As** *The Complete Letter-Writer, containing Familiar Letters on the Most Common Occasions of Life. . .* Edinburgh: Printed by John Reid, 1768. Edinburgh: Printed by David Patterson, 1776. Edinburgh: Printed by and for W. Darling, 1778. Edinburgh: Printed for Alex. Donaldson, 1781. Edinburgh: Printed for P. Anderson, 1781. Edinburgh: Printed by W. Darling, 1789. Boston: Printed and sold for John West Folsom, 1790. New York: Printed and sold by William Durrell, 1793. Philadelphia: Printed for Jacob Johnson, 1795. Hartford: Printed for and sold by Oliver D. And I. Cooke, 1796. 4th ed.: Printed by Th. Cushing, 1797. **As** *The American Letter-Writer: Containing A Variety of Letters on the most common Occasions of life.* Philadelphia: Printed and sold by John M'Culloch, 1793.

[Anon.]. *The Complete Letter-Writer; or Polite English Secretary,* Vol. II. London: Printed for S. Crowder and B. C. Collins, Salisbury, 1789.

[Anon.]. *The Correspondent, A Selection of Letters from the best authors, together with some originals, adapted to all the periods and occasions of life, calculated to form the epistolary style of youth of both sexes; to impart a knowlee of the world and letters; and to inspire sentiments of virtue and morality.* 2 vols. London: Printed for T. Cadell, Jun. and W. Davies, 1796.

[Anon.]. *The Court Letter-Writer: or the Complete English Secretary for Town and Country,* London, 1773.

[Anon.]. *The Ladies Complete Letter-Writer; teaching the Art of Inditing Letters on every Subject that can call for their Attention as Daughters, Wives, Mothers, Relations, Friends or Acquaintance.* London: Printed for the Editor and sold by T. Lownds, 1763.

[Anon.]. *The Mirrour of Complements, or a Manuell of Choice, requisite and compendious Curiosities, wherein Gentlemen, Ladies, Gentlewomen and all others, may practice Complemental and amorous expressions in speaking or writing Letters, upon any Subject or Occasion.* 4th ed. London, 1650.

[Anon.]. *The New Art of Letter-Writing.* London, 1762.

[Anon.]. *The New Complete Letter-Writer; or The Art of Correspondence* Worcester, Mass.: Printed by Isaiah Thomas, 1791. New York: Printed by John Tiebout, 1800. Boston: Printed by Samuel Etheridge for Daniel Brewer, 1803. **As** *The New Letter-Writer; or The Art of Correspondence* Whitehaven: Printed for John Dunn, [1775?]. **As** *The Complete Letter-Writer; or the Art of Correspondence* Trenton: Printed and published by James Oram, 1811. New York: Printed and published by George Long, 1815.

[Anon.]. *The New Universal Letter-Writer: or Complete Art of Correspondence-* Philadelphia: Printed and sold by D. Hogan, 1800. 2nd ed. Philadelphia: Published and sold by D. Hogan, 1804. 4th ed. Philadelphia: Published and sold by D. Hogan, 1812. 5th ed. Philadelphia: Published and sold +by D. Hogan, 1816. 6th ed. Philadelphia: Published and sold by D. Hogan, 1818.

[Anon.]. *Polite Epistolary Correspondence. A Collection of Letters On the most Instructive and Entertaining Subjects . . . to which are prefix'd Two Introductory Letters shewing The Necessity and Use of such a Collection; particularly in the instructing of Youth to indite Letters well on all Occasions.* London: Printed for Richard Adams, 1748.

[Anon.]. *An Useful and Entertaining Collection of Letters upon Various Subjects,* London: Printed for W. Bickerton, 1745.

[Anon.]. *Wit's Cabinet: or, a companion for young men and ladies,* 16th ed. Printed for J. Clarke and A. Wilde, 1737.

Blount, Thomas, Gent. *The Academie of Eloquence, Containing a Compleat English Rhetorique Exemplified, With Commonplaces and Formes, digested into an easie and Methodical way to speak and write fluently, according to the mode of the present times. Together with Letters both Amorous and Moral, upon Emergent Occasions.* London, 1654.

Brown, George, Rev. *The New English Letter-Writer; or Whole Art of General Correspondence* London: Printed for Alex. Hogg, [1770?]. London: Printed for Alex. Hogg, [1780?].

The New and Complete English Letter-Writer; or Whole Art of General Correspondence London: Printed for Alex. Hogg, [1770?].

Care, Henry, *The Female Secretary: or Choice new Letters, Wherein each degree of Women may be accommodated with Variety of Presidents for the expressing themselves aptly and handsomly on any Occasion proper to their Sex.* London: Printed by Thomas Ratcliffe and Mary Daniel for Henry Million, 1671.

Cooke, Thomas, Rev. A. B (or A. M.), *The Universal Letter-Writer; or New Art of Polite Correspondence*. London: For J. Cooke, 1771/2. London: For Osborne and Griffin; and Gainsborough: Mozeley, 1788. London: For J. Cooke, [1795?]. **As:** *The New and Complete Universal Letter-Writer* New

York: Printed and sold by G. and R. Waite, 1809. **As:** *The New and Complete Letter-Writer, or New Art of Polite Correspondence.* No place but adapted to the US; printed for the Booksellers, 1803. Poughkeepsie, NY: Printed by Bowman, Parsons & Potter, 1806. Brattleborough, VT: Published by William Fessenden, 1814. New York: Published by Evert Duyckson, 1817. Philadelphia: Published and sold by J. Carson, 1818.

The New and Complete Universal Letter-Writer or Young Secretary's Instructor. London: For C. Cooke, [1790?].

Day, Angel. *The English Secretary, or Methods of writing Epistles and Letters, with a Declaration of such Tropes, Figures and Schemes as either usually or for Ornament sake are therein required.* (1599). Rpt. Gainesville: Scholars Facsimiles and Reprints, 1967.

De la Serre. *The Secretary in Fashion or, An Elegant and Compendious way of Writing all manner letters, Composed in French by the Sire De la Serre.* 5th ed. London: Printed for Peter Parker, 1673.

Dilworth, H. W., M. A. *The Familiar Letter-Writer; or Young Secretary's Complete Instructor*: London: Printed for G. Wright, 1758. **As: *The Complete Letter-Writer or Young Secretary's Instructor*** New York: Printed by Samuel Campbell, 1775. Glasgow: Printed by Peter Tait, bookseller, 1783. New York: Printed for Benjamin Gomez, 1793. New York: Printed for T. Allen, 1794. New York: Printed for Evert Duyckinck, 1795. New York: Printed by Samuel Campbell, 1795. New Haven: From Sidney's Press for Increase Cooke, 1809.

Du Bois, Lady Dorothea. *The Lady's Polite Secretary, or New Female Letter-Writer.* London: Printed for J. Coote and T. Evans, 1771.

Fisher, George, Accomptant. *The Instructor; or, young man's best companion* London: Printed for A. Bettesworth, C. Hitch, R. Ware, J. Clark, S. Birt, J Hodges, *c.* 1735. London: Printed for James Hodges, 4th ed., 1737. London: Printed for S. Birt, 5th ed., 1740. London: Printed for J. Hodges, 5th ed., 1740. London: Printed for C. Hitch, 6th ed. 1742. London: Printed for C. Hitch and L. Hawes, H. Woodfall, J. Fuller, R. Balwin, W. Johnson, S. Crowder and Co, B. Law and Co and C. Ware, 17th ed., 1763. Edinburgh: Printed and sold by Gavin Auston, 1763. Burlington: Printed and sold by Isaac Collins, 1775 (Am.). Walpole, NH: Printed by I. Thomas and David Carlisle, for I. Thomas in Worcester, and Andrews, D. West, E. Larkin Jr. in Boston, 1794. Wilmington: Printed and sold by Peter Brynberg, 1797. **As** *The American Instructor, or Young Man's Best Companion* 9th ed. Philadelphia: Printed by B. Franklin and D. Hall, 1748. 10th ed., Philadelphia: Printed by B. Franklin and D. Hall, 1753. 12th ed. New York: Printed and sold by H. Gaine, 1760. 15th ed. Philadelphia: Printed and sold by John Dunlap. Boston: Printed for J. Boyle and J. D. M'Dougall, 1779. Philadelphia: Printed and sold by J. Crukshank, 1787. **As:** *The Instructor: or American Young Man's Best Companion* 30th ed.: Printed at Worcester by I. Thomas for I. Thomas, J. Boyle, E. Battelle, W. Green, B.

Larkin and J. Condy in Boston, 1785. Philadelphia: Printed and sold by John Bioren, 1801.Philadelphia: Printed and sold by John Bioren, 1810.

Fordyce, David. *The New and Complete British Letter-Writer, or Young Secretary's Instructor in Polite Modern Letter-Writing.* London: Printed for C. Cooke, n.d.

[Fulwood, William]. *The Enimie of Idleness: Teaching the maner and Stile how to indite, compose and write all sorts of Epistles and letters, as well by Answer as otherwise.*

Gildon, Charles. *The Postboy Robb'd of his Mail: or the Packet Broke Open, consisting of Letters of Love and Gallantry and all Miscellaneous Subjects.* Both volumes in one. 2nd ed. London, 1706.

Goodman, T. *The Experienced Secretary or Citizen and Country Man's Companion* London: Printed for N. Boddington, 1699. 4th ed. London: Printed for N. Boddington, 1707. **As:** *The Young Secretary's Guide: or A Speedy Help to Learning,* by Thomas Hill with running title within as above. Boston: Printed by B. Green and J. Allen, 3rd ed. 1703. Boston: Printed by T. Fleet for S. Gerrish, 4th ed. 1713. Boston: Printed by J. Allen for N. Buttolph, 5th ed. 1718. Boston: Reprinted for N. Boone, 6th ed. 1727. Boston: Printed by T. Fleet and sold by the booksellers, 1730.

Hallifax, Charles, *Familiar Letters on Various Subjects of Business and Amusement* 5th ed. London: Printed for L. Davis, C. Reymers, R. Baldwin, W. Johnson, 1758.

Haywood, Eliza. *Epistles for the Ladies.* London: Printed and published by T. Gardner, 1749.

Hill, John, Gent. *The Young Secretary's Guide or Speedy Help to Learning.* 7th ed. London: Printed for H. Rhodes, 1696. 8th ed. London: Printed for H. Rhodes, 1697. 9th ed. London: Printed for H. Rhodes, 1698. 20th ed. London: Printed for H. Rhodes, 1719. London: Printed for and sold by A. Wilde, 1764. Boston: Printed by G. Green for Nicholas Buttolph, 1707 [T. for J. Hill]. 24th ed. Boston: Printed and sold by Thomas Fleet, 1750. **As** *The Secretary's Guide or Young Man's Companion. In Four Parts.* Philadelphia: Printed and sold by Andrew Bradford, 1718. New York and Philadelphia: printed and sold by William Bradford, 1728. New York: Printed and sold by William Bradford, 1729. Philadelphia: Printed and sold by Andrew Bradford, 1737.

Henry Hogg, A. M. *The New and Complete Universal Letter-Writer; or Whole Art of Polite Correspondence.* London: Printed for Alex Hogg, *c.* 1790.

Henry Hogg, A. M. and Rev. George Brown, A. M., *The New and Complete Universal Letter-Writer: or, Whole art of General and Polite Correspondence.* London: Printed for Alex. Hogg, 1800.

Johnson, Charles. *The Complete Art of Writing Letters, Adapted to all Classes and Conditions of Life.* 6th ed. London: Printed for T. Lowndes and T. Evans, 1779.

Johnson, Samuel, *A Compleat Introduction to the Art of Writing Letters; universally adapted to all Classes and Conditions of Life*. London: Printed for Henry Dell and J. Staples, 1758.

Knox, Vicesimus. *Elegant Epistles, being a copious Collection of Familiar and Amusing Letters for the Improvement of Young Persons and for General Entertainment*. Dublin, 1983.

Lipsius, Justus. *Principles of Letter-Writing (Epistolica Institutio)*. Ed. and tr. R. V. Young and M. Thomas Hester. Carbondale: Southern Illinois University Press, 1996.

Marchant. I. B. *The Merchant's Avizo*. London, 1607.

Magee, R. *Magee's London Letter-Writer, being the Complete Art of Fashionable Correspondence*. Philadelphia: R. Magee, [1810?].

Mather, William, *A Very useful manual, or, The Young Man's Companion*, London: Printed by T. Snowden, 1681. **As:** *The Young Man's Companion* London: Printed for S. Clark, 8th ed., 1710. New York: William and Andrew Bradford, 1710 (incomplete). New York: Printed and sold by William and Andrew Bradford, 1719. London: Printed for S. Clark, 18th ed. 1727.

Newbery, John. *Letters on the most common as well as important Occasions of Life*. London: Printed for J. Newbery, 1756.

Porny, Mr. Frenchmaster at Eton College, *Models of Letters in French and English*. Philadelphia: Published by Thomas Bradford, 1795.

Richardson, Samuel. *Letters Written to and For Particular Friends On the most Important Occasions, Directing not only the Style and Forms To be Observed in the Writing Familiar Letters; But How to Think and Act Justly and Prudently in the Common Concerns of Human Life* . . . London: Printed for C. Rivington, 1741.

Serre, Puget de la, *Secretary in Fashion; or a compendious and Refined Way of Expression in all manner of Letters*, tr. John Massinger, 1640; 5th ed. 1773.

Seymour, George. *The Instructive Letter-Writer and Entertaining Companion*. London: Printed for W. Domville, 1769.

Shepard, Sylvanus. *The Natural Letter-Writer*. [US]: Printed for the author, 1812. [US]: Printed for the public, 1813.

S. S., Gent. *Secretaries Studie: Containing new familiar Epistles, Wherein Ladies, Gentlemen, and all that are ambitious to write and speak elegantly, and elaborately, in succinct and faceitious strein, are furnished with fit Phrases, Emphaticall expressions, and various directions for the most polish'd and judicious way of inditing Letters*. London: Printed by T. H. for John Harrison, 1652.

Tavernier, John, *The New and most Complete Polite Familiar Letter-Writer*. Berwick: Printed by R. Taylor, 1768.

Voiture, *Familiar and Courtly Letters to Persons of Honour and Quality, made English by John Dryden, Tho. Cheek, Mr. Dennis, Henry Crowmwell, Mr. Raphson, to which is added A Collection of Letters of Friendship and other Occasional Letters, written by Mr. Dryden, Mr. Wycherly, Mr. Congreve, Mr. Dennis and other hands*. 2 vols. London: Printed for S. Briscoe, 1695.

3rd ed. London: Printed for S. Briscoe, 1701. London: Printed for S. Briscoe, 1718 (changed content).

Voiture, *The Works of Monsieur Voiture . . . Containing his Familiar Letters to Gentlemen and Ladies. Made English by John Dryden, Thomas Cheek, Henry Cromwell, Mr. Dennis, Thomas Seymour, John Savil, Captain Barker, Mr Raphston, Mr. Thomas Brown; with Three Collections of Letters on Friendship and Several other Occasions: Written by John Dryden, William Wycherly, William Congreve, Mr. Dennis, Dr——, Mr. Thomas Brown, Mr. Edward Ward, and Facetious Letters out of Greek, Latin and French.* 2 vols. London: Printed for Sam Briscoe, 1705. London: Printed for Sam Briscoe, 1725. Dublin: Printed for R. Main, 1753.

Wallace, James. *Every man his own Letter-Writer: or The New Complete Art of Letter-Writing made Plain and Familiar to every Capacity.* London, 1782 [?].

Other primary printed sources

Allen, Charles. *The Polite Lady; or a Course of Education, In a Series of Letters,* London, 1760.

[Anon.]. *The Accomplish'd Merchant.* London, n.d.

[Anon.]. *The Art of Complaisance or the Means to Oblige in Conversation.* 2nd ed. London: Printed for John Starkey, 1677.

[Anon.]. *The Gentlemans Companion: or a Character of True Nobility and Gentility.* London: Printed by T. M. for Thomas Sawbridge, 1676.

[Anon.]. *The Royal French Grammar: By Which One may in a Short Time Attain the French Tongue in Perfection.* London, 1709.

An Historical Miscellany of the Curiosities and Rarities in Nature and Art, 5 vols. London, 1794–1800.

Austen, Jane. *Pride and Prejudice.* Harmondsworth: Penguin, 1985.

Behn, Aphra. *Love Letters Between a Nobleman and His Sister.* London, 1708.

Bingham, Caleb, A. B. *The American Preceptor, being a new Selection of Lessons for Reading and Speaking, designed for the use of Schools.* Boston: Printed by Manning and Loring, 1794.

Blair, Hugh. *Lectures on Rhetoric and Belles Lettres.* 2 vols. Rpt. Carbondale: Southern Illinois Press, 1965.

Brightland, John, *A Grammar of the English Tongue, with Notes Giving the Grounds and Reasons of Grammar in General, to which are now added, The Arts of Poetry, Rhetoric, Logic etc, Making a Compleat System of an English Education for the Use of Schools of Great Britain and Ireland.* 2nd ed. London: Printed by R. Brugis for John Brightland, 1712.

Buchanan, John. *The British Grammar.* London, 1762.

Burr, Esther. *The Journal of Esther Edwards Burr, 1754–1757.* Ed. Carol F. Karlsen and Laurie Crumpacker. New Haven: Yale University Press, 1984.

Burt, Edmund. *Burt's Letters from the North of Scotland.* Ed. Andrew Simmons. Edinburgh: Birlinn Press, 1998.

Campbell, Robert. *The London Tradesman, Being a Compendious View of all the Trades, Professions, Arts, both Liberal and Mechanic, now being practised . . .* London, 1747.

Cockin, William. *The Art of delivering Written Language.* London, 1775.

Collier, Mary, *Letters from Felicia to Charlotte,* 2 vols. London, 1755.

Constable, John. *Reflections upon Accuracy of Style.* London: For J. Osborn, 1734.

Crevecoeur, J. Hector St. John. *Letters from an American Farmer and Sketches of Eighteenth-Century America.* Ed. Albert E. Stone. Harmondsworth: Penguin, 1986.

More Letters from an American Farmer. Ed. Dennis Moore. Athens, GA: University of Georgia Press, 1993.

Curwen, Samuel. *Journal and Letters of Samuel Curwen.* Ed. George Atkinson Ward. Boston, 1842.

De Courtin, Antoine. *The Rules of Civility, newly revised.* London, 1678.

Defoe, Daniel, *The Great Law of Subordination consider'd; or the Insolence and Unsufferable Behaviour of Servants in England.* London, 1724.

Delaney, Mrs. *The Autobiography and Correspondence of Mrs. Delaney,* 2 vols. Ed. Sarah Chauncey Woolsey. Boston, 1879.

Digges, Thomas Attwood. *Letters of Thomas Attwood Digges, 1742–1821.* Ed. Robert H. Elias and Eugene D. Finch. Columbia, SC: University of South Carolina, 1982.

Dilworth, Thomas. *A New Guide to the English Tongue.* 1740. Rpt. of 1793 ed. Delmar, NY: Scholars Press Facsimiles and Reprints, 1978.

Dodsley, Robert. *The Preceptor.* 3rd ed. with additions and improvement. London, 1758.

Eddis, William. *Letters from America.* Ed. Aubrey C. Land. Cambridge, Mass.: Harvard University Press, 1969.

Edgeworth, Maria. *Patronage.* London: Pandora, 1986.

[Falconer, John]. *Cryptomenysis Patefacta: Or the Art of Secret Information Disclosed Without a Key.* London, 1685.

Fleetwood, William, *The Relative Duties of Parents and Children, Parents and Wives, Masters and Servants,* London, 1705.

Foster, Hannah. *The Coquette.* Boston, 1797.

Fothergill, John. *Chains of Friendship: Selected Letters of Dr. John Fothergill of London, 1735–1780.* Cambridge, Mass.: Harvard University Press, 1971.

Franklin, Benjamin, *The Papers of Benjamin Franklin,* ed. Leonard W. Labaree. New Haven: Yale University Press, 1969.

"The Examination of Doctor Benjamin Franklin before an August Assembly, relating to the Repeal of the Stamp-Act," in *Pamphlets and the American Revolution* Delmar, NY: Scholars Facsimiles and Reprints, 1976.

The Autobiography of Benjamin Franklin: a Genetic Text. Ed. J. A. Leo Lemay and P. M. Zoll. Knoxville: University of Tennessee Press, 1981.

Benjamin Franklin's Letters to the Press, 1758–1775. Ed. Verner W. Crane. Chapel Hill: University of North Carolina Press, 1950.

Gisbourne, Thomas. *An Enquiry into the duties of the Female Sex.* London, 1797.

Gordon, William, *The Universal Accountant and Complete Merchant*, 2 vols. Edinburgh, 1765.

Griffith, Elizabeth. *The Delicate Distress*. Ed. Cynthia Booth Ricciardi and Susan Staves. Lexington: University of Kentucky Press, 1997.

Guazzo, Stephen, *The Art of Conversation*. London: Printed for J. Brett, 1738.

Hulton, Anne. *Letters of a Loyalist Lady, 1767–1776*. Ed. H. M. and C. M. T. Cambridge Mass.: Harvard University Press, 1927.

Johnson, Samuel. *Lives of the English Poets*, 2 vols. London: Oxford University Press, 1912.

    The Rambler.

Journal of the Commissioners for Trade and Plantations. London: His Majesty's Stationary Office, 1920.

Kames, Henry Home, Lord. *Elements of Criticism*. New York, 1873.

Laurens, Henry. *The Papers of Henry Laurens*. Ed. Philip M. Hamer. Columbia, SC: University of South Carolina Press, 1968.

Lillie, Charles. *Original and General Letters sent to The Tatler and The Spectator during the Time those Works were Publishing, None of which have before been printed*. London, 1725.

Locke, John. *Some Thoughts concerning Education*. Ed. John W. and Jean S. Yolton. Oxford: Clarendon Press, 1989.

Lowth, Robert. *A Short Introduction to English Grammar*. London, 1762.

Luckumbe, Philip. *The History and Art of Printing*. 1771.

Mainwaring, Edward. *Institutes of Learning*. 1737. Rpt. Menston: The Scolar Press, 1968.

Mason, John. *An Essay on the Power and Harmony of Prosaic Numbers* (1749) Rpt. Menston: The Scolar Press, 1967.

    An Essay on Elocution and Pronunciation. 1748. Rpt. Menston: The Scolar Press, 1968.

Mason, William, *La Plume Volante; or the art of short-hand improv'd*, 5th ed. London: [1719?].

Milns, William. *Plan of Instruction for Private Classes*. New York, 1794.

Montagu, Lady Mary Wortley, *An Additional Volume to the Letters of the Right Honourable Lady M—y W—y M—u, Written during her Travels in Europe, Asia and Africa*. London, 1767.

Montesquieu, *The Spirit of the Laws*, tr. Anne M. Cohler, Basia Carolyn Miller and Harold Samuel Stone. Cambridge: Cambridge University Press, 1989.

Mortimer, Thomas. *The Elements of Commerce, Politics and Finances, in Three Treatises, Designed as a Supplement to the Education of British Youth after they quit the public University or private Academies*. London, 1772.

Murray, Lindley. *English Grammar*. York, 1795. Rpt. Menston: The Scolar Press, 1968.

North, Roger. *The Gentleman Accomptant*. 2nd ed. London, 1715.

Pinckney, Eliza Lucas. *The Letterbook of Eliza Lucas Pinckney, 1739–1762*. Ed. Elise Pinckney Chapel Hill: University of North Carolina Press, 1972.

Postlethwayt, Malachy. *The Universal Dictionary of Trade and Commerce*, 2 vols. London, 1755.

Priestley, Joseph. *A Course of Lectures on the Theory of Language and Universal Grammar*. London, 1762. Rpt. Menston: The Scolar Press, 1970.

Rice, John. *An Introduction to the Art of Reading with Energy and Propriety*. 1965. Rpt. Menston: The Scolar Press, 1969.

Rollin, Charles. *The Method of Teaching and Studying the Belles Lettres*, 4 vols. London, 1734.

Rolt, Richard. *A New Dictionary of Trade and Commerce*, 2nd ed. London, 1761.

Sancho, Ignatius. *Letters of the Late Ignatius Sancho*. Ed. Vincent Carretta. Harmondsworth: Penguin, 1998.

A Scottish Firm in Virginia, 1767–1777. Ed. T. M. Devine. Edinburgh: Clark Constable Ltd, 1984.

Scotus Americanus, "Informations Concerning the Province of North Carolina, addressed to Emigrants from the Highlands and Western Isles of Scotland" (1773) in *Some Tracts Concerning North Carolina*, ed. William Boyd, Raleigh, NC, 1927.

Shaftesbury, *Characteristics of Men, Manners, Opinions and Times*. Cambridge: Cambridge University Press, 1999.

Sheridan, Thomas. *A Course of Lectures on Elocution, together with two Dissertations on Language*. 1762. Rpt. New York: Benjamin Blom Inc., 1968.

The Adams Family Correspondence. Ed. Richard Alan Ryerson. Cambridge, Mass.: Harvard University Press, 1993.

The Spectator. Ed. Donald F. Bond. Oxford: Clarendon Press, 1965.

The Tatler. Ed. Donald F. Bond. Oxford: Clarendon Press, 1987.

[Thicknesse, Philip], *A Treatise on the Art of Decyphering and of Writing in Cypher with an Harmonic Alphabet*. London, 1772.

Thomas, Isaiah. *The History of Printing in America*. Albany, NY, 1874.

Timperley, Charles, *Encyclopedia of Literary and Typographical Anecdote*. London, 1842.

Walker, John. *Elements of Elocution*. 2 vols. 1781. Rpt. Menston: The Scolar Press, 1969.

Walpole, Horace. *Selected Correspondence*. London: G. Bell 1914.

Walsh, William. *Letters and Poems, Amorous and Gallant*. London, 1692.

Ward, Ned. *The London Spy*. London: Folio Society, 1955.

Watts, Thomas. *An Essay on the Proper Method for forming a Man of Business*. London, 1716.

Webster, Noah. *Dissertations on the English Language*. 1789.

Webster, William. *An Attempt towards rendering the Education of Youth more Easy and Effectual*. London, 1726.

[Wilkins, John], *Mercury, or the Secret and Swift Messenger*. London, 1641.

Young, E., Schoolmaster in London. *The Compleat English Scholar in Spelling, Reading and Writing*. London: For T. Longman, 1752.

SECONDARY SOURCES

Adams, Percy G. *Travel Literature and the Evolution of the Novel.* Lexington: University of Kentucky Press, 1983.

Altman, Janet Gurkin. *Epistolarity: Approaches to a Form.* Columbus: Ohio University Press, 1982.

"Political Ideology in the Letter Manual," *Studies in Eighteenth-Century Culture*, 18 (1989): 105–21.

Amory, Hugh and David D. Hall (eds.). *A History of the Book in America. Vol. I: The Colonial Book in the Atlantic World.* Cambridge: Cambridge University Press, 2000.

Amussen, Susan Dwyer. *An Ordered Society: Gender and Class in Early Modern England.* Oxford: Blackwell, 1988.

Anderson, Benedict. *Imagined Communities: Reflections on the Origins and Spread of Nationalism.* London: Verso, 1983.

Anderson, Howard *et al.* (eds.). *The Familiar Letter in the Eighteenth Century.* Laurence: University of Kansas Press, 1966.

Armitage, David. *Greater Britain 1516–1776: Essays in Transatlantic History.* Aldershot: Ashgate, 2004.

Armstrong, Nancy. *Desire and Domestic Fiction.* Oxford: Oxford University Press, 1987.

Austin, Frances. "Letter-Writing in a Cornish Community in the 1790s," in Barton and Hall (eds.), *Letter-Writing as a Social Practice.*

Backscheider, Paula. *Spectacular Politics: Theatrical Power and Mass Culture in Early Modern England.* Baltimore: The Johns Hopkins University Press, 1993.

Backscheider, Paula and Timothy Dyksal (eds.). *The Intersections of the Public and Private Spheres in Early Modern England.* London: Frank Cass, 1996.

Bailey, Richard W. *Images of English: A Cultural History of the Language.* Ann Arbor: University of Michigan Press, 1991.

Bailyn, Bernard. *The Peopling of British North America.* New York: Knopf, 1986.
Education in the Forming of American Society. New York: Norton, 1960.
The Ordeal of Thomas Hutchinson. Cambridge, Mass.: Harvard University Press, 1964.

Bailyn, Bernard and John B. Hench (eds.). *The Press and the American Revolution.* Worcester: American Antiquarian Society, 1980.

Bakeless, John. *Turncoats, Traitors and Heroes.* New York: de Capo, 1998.

Bannet, Eve Tavor. *The Domestic Revolution: Enlightenment Feminisms and the Novel.* Baltimore: The Johns Hopkins University Press, 2000.

"The Marriage Act of 1753," *Eighteenth-Century Studies*, 30: 3 (Spring 1997): 233–54.

"Empire and Occasional Conformity: David Fordyce's *Complete British Letter-Writer*," *Huntington Library Quarterly*, 66: 1&2 (2003): 55–79.

"Secret History: Talebearing Inside and Outside the Secretorie," *The Languages of History*, ed. Paulina Kewes. Sp. Ed., *Huntington Library Quarterly*, vol. 68 (2005): nos. 1 & 2.

"Epistolary Commerce in Steele's Spectator," in Don Newman (ed.). *Emerging Discourses in The Spectator*. Delaware: University of Delaware Press, (2005): 220–47.

"Haywood's *Spectator* and the Female World," in D. Newman and M. Wright (eds.). *Fair Philosopher*. Bucknell (forthcoming).

Barber, Giles, "Books from the Old World to the New: The British International Trade in Books in the Eighteenth Century," *Studies in Voltaire and the Eighteenth Century*, 151 (1976): 185–224.

Barton, David and Nigel Hall (eds.). *Letter-Writing as a Social Practice*. Philadelphia: John Benjamins Publishing Co., 2000.

Basye, Arthur Herbert. *The Lords Commissioners of Trade and Plantations*. New Haven: Yale University Press, 1925.

Batten, Charles I. *Pleasurable Instruction: Form and Convention in Eighteenth-Century Travel Literature*. Berkeley: University of California Press, 1978.

Bauman, Zygmunt. *Legislators and Interpreters*. Cambridge: Polity Press, 1987.

Baxter, W. T. *The House of Hancock: Business in Boston, 1724–1775*. Cambridge, Mass.: Harvard University Press, 1945.

Bazerman, Charles. "Letters and the Social Grounding of Differentiated Genres," in Barton and Hall (eds.), *Letter-Writing as a Social Practice*.

Beale, Peter. "Nations in Garrison," in W. Speed Hill (ed.), *New Ways of Looking at Old Texts*. Binghamton, NY: Renaissance English Text Society, 1993.

Beales, Ross and E. Jennifer Monaghan. "Literacy and School-Books." in Amory and Hall (eds.), *The Colonial Book in the Atlantic World*.

Beckett, John. "Estate Management in Eighteenth-Century England," in John Chartres and David Kay (eds.). *English Rural Society, 1500–1800*. Cambridge: Cambridge University Press, 1990.

Benedict, Barbara. *Making the Modern Reader: Cultural Mediation in Early Modern Literary Anthologies*. Princeton: Princeton University Press, 1996.

Black, Jeremy. *The English Press in the Eighteenth Century*. Philadelphia: University of Pennsylvania Press, 1987.

Bloom, Edward A. and Lilian D. Bloom. *Addison and Steele: The Critical Heritage*. London: Routledge, 1980.

Borsay, Peter. "The English Urban Renaissance: The Development of Provincial Urban Culture," in Borsay (ed.). *The Eighteenth-Century Town: A Reader in English Urban History, 1688–1820*. London: Longman, 1990.

Botein, Stephen. "The Anglo-American Book Trade before 1776," in William Royce *et al* (eds.). *Printing and Society in Early America*.

Breitweiser, Michael Robert. *Cotton Mather and Benjamin Franklin*. Cambridge: Cambridge University Press, 1984.

Brewer, John. *The Sinews of Power: War, Money and the English State, 1688–1783*. New York: Knopf, 1989.

Brooks, Christopher. "Apprenticeship, Social Mobility and the Middling Sort, 1550–1800," in *The Middling Sort of People: Culture, Society and Politics in England, 1550–1800*. New York: St. Martin's Press, 1994.

Brown, Richard D. *Revolutionary Politics in Massachusetts: The Boston Committee of Correspondence and the Towns, 1772–1774*. Cambridge, Mass: Harvard University Press, 1970.

  The Idea of an Informed Citizenry in America, 1650–1870. Chapel Hill: University of North Carolina Press, 1996.

Bryson, Anna. *From Courtesy to Civility: Changing Codes of Conduct in Early Modern England*. Oxford: Clarendon Press, 1998.

Burchell, R. A. (ed). *The End of Anglo-America: Historical Essays in the Study of Cultural Divergence*. Manchester: Manchester University Press, 1991.

Burke, Peter. *The Art of Conversation*. Ithaca: Cornell University Press, 1993.

Bushman, Richard. *The Refinement of America*. New York: Knopf, 1992.

  "American High Style and Vernacular Cultures," In Jack P. Greene and J. R. Pole, (eds.). *Colonial British America*. Baltimore: The Johns Hopkins University Press, 1984.

Calder, Angus. *Revolutionary Empire: The Rise of the English-speaking Empires from the Fifteenth Century to the 1780s*. London: Pimlico, 1998 (revised ed.).

Calhoun, Craig (ed.). *Habermas and the Public Sphere*. Cambridge Mass.: the MIT Press, 1992.

Cannon, John. *Aristocratic Century*. Cambridge: Cambridge University Press, 1984.

Canny, Nicholas and Anthony Pagden, *Colonial Identity in the Atlantic World, 1500–1800*. Princeton: Princeton University Press, 1987.

Cavallo, Guglielmo and Roger Chartier (eds.). *A History of Reading in the West*. Amherst: University of Massachusetts Press, 1999.

Chartier, Roger (ed.). *Correspondence: Models of Letter-Writing from the Middle Ages to the Nineteenth Century*. Princeton, NJ: Princeton University Press, 1997.

Clark, Charles E. *The Public Prints: The Newspaper in Anglo-American Culture, 1665–1740*. Oxford: Oxford University Press, 1994.

  "Early American Journalism," *History of the Book in America*, vol. I. Cambridge: Cambridge University Press, 2000.

Clark, J. C. D. *English Society, 1688–1832: Ideology, Social Structure and Political Practice during the Ancient Regime*. Cambridge: Cambridge University Press, 1985.

Clive, John and Bernard Bailyn, "England's Cultural Provinces: Scotland and America," *William and Mary Quarterly*, 3rd ser., 11 (April 1954): 200–13.

Cohen, Michele. *Fashioning Masculinity: National Identity and Language in the Eighteenth Century*. London: Routledge, 1996.

Cohen, Murray, *Sensible Words: Linguistic Practice in England, 1640–1785*. Baltimore: The Johns Hopkins University Press, 1977.

Cohen, Patricia Cline. *A Calculating People: The Spread of Numeracy in Early America*. Chicago: Chicago University Press, 1982.

"Reckoning with Commerce: Numeracy in Eighteenth-Century America," in John Brewer and Roy Porter (eds.), *Consumption and the World of Goods*. London: Routledge, 1993.

Cohen, Sheldon. *A History of Colonial Education, 1607–1776*. New York: John Wiley, 1974.

Coleman, Joyce. *Public Reading and the Reading Public in Late Medieval England and France*. Cambridge: Cambridge University Press, 1996.

Colley, Linda. *Britons: Forging the Nation 1707–1837*. New Haven: Yale University Press, 1992.

Cook, Elizabeth Hackendorn. *Epistolary Bodies: Gender and Genre in the Republic of Letters*. Stanford: Stanford University Press, 1996.

Corfield, P. J. *The Impact of English Towns, 1700–1800*. Oxford: Oxford University Press, 1982.

Power and the Professions in Britain, 1700–1850. London: Routledge, 1995.

"Class by Name and Number in Eighteenth-Century Britain," *History*, 72 (1987): 38–61.

Crain, Patricia. "Print and Everyday Life in the Eighteenth Century," in Scott E. Cooper, Joanne D. Chaison and Jeffrey D. Groves (eds.). *Perspectives on American Book History*. Amherst: University of Massachusetts Press, 2000.

Crane, Mary Thomas. *Framing Authority: Sayings, Self and Society in Sixteenth-Century England*. Princeton: Princeton University Press, 1993.

Craven, Wayne, "Colonial American Portraiture: Iconography and Methodology," in Ellen G. Miles (ed.). *The Portrait in Eighteenth-Century America*. Newark: University of Delaware Press, 1993.

Cremin, Lawrence A. *American Education: The Colonial Experience, 1607–1783*. New York: Harper & Row, 1970.

Cressy, David. 'Literacy in Context: Meaning and Measurement in Early Modern England," in John Brewer and Roy Porter (eds.). *Consumption and the World of Goods*. London: Routledge, 1993.

Crowley, Tony. *Standard English and the Politics of Language*. Urbana: University of Illinois Press, 1989.

Language in History: Theories and Texts. London: Routledge, 1996.

Davidoff, Leonore and Catherine Hall, *Family Fortunes: Men and Women of the English Middle Class, 1780–1850*. Chicago: Chicago University Press, 1987.

Davidson, Cathy (ed.). *Reading in America: Literature and Social History*. Baltimore: The Johns Hopkins University Press, 1989.

Davis, Richard Beale. *A Colonial Southern Bookshelf: Reading in the Eighteenth Century* Athens, GA: University of Georgia Press, 1979.

Daybell, James (ed.). *Early Modern Women Letter-Writers, 1450–1700*. Basingstoke: Palgrave, 2001.

Derrida, Jacques. *La Carte postale de Socrates à Freud*. Paris: Flammarion, 1980.

De Wolfe, Barbara (ed.). *Discoveries of America: Personal Accounts of British Emigrants to North America during the Revolutionary Era.* Cambridge: Cambridge University Press, 1997.

Dickerson, Oliver Morton. *American Colonial Government, 1696–1765: A Study of the Board of Trade in its Relation to the American Colonies.* Cleveland, OH: The Arthur Clark Col., 1912.

Dickson, P. G. M. *The Financial Revolution in England, 1688–1756.* New York: St. Martin's Press, 1967.

Dierks, Konstantin. "Letter-Writing, Gender and Class in America." Dissertation, Brown 1999.

Ditz, Toby. "Formative Ventures: Eighteenth-Century Commercial Letters and the Articulation of Experience," in Rebecca Earle (ed.), *Epistolary Selves.*

"Secret Selves and Credible Personas: The Problematics of Trust and Public Display in the Writings of Eighteenth-Century Philadelphia Merchants," in Robert Blair St. George (ed.). *Possible Pasts.*

Dobson, David. *Scottish Emigration to Colonial America, 1607–1785.* Athens, GA: University of Georgia Press, 1994.

Earle, Peter. *The Making of the English Middle Class: Business, Society and Family Life in London, 1660–1730.* Berkeley: University of California Press, 1989.

Earle, Rebecca (ed.). *Epistolary Selves: Letters and Letter-Writers, 1600–1945.* Aldershot: Ashgate, 1999.

Ellis, Joyce M. *The Georgian Town, 1680–1840.* Basingstoke: Palgrave, 2001.

Ellis, Kenneth. *The Post Office in the Eighteenth Century.* Oxford: Oxford University Press, 1958.

Enders, Jody. "Music, Delivery and the Rhetoric of Memory in Guillaume de Machaut's Remède de Fortune." *PMLA*, 103: 3 (May 1992): 450–64.

Ezell, Margaret. *Social Authorship and the Advent of Print.* Baltimore: The Johns Hopkins University Press, 1999.

Favret, Mary A. *Romantic Correspondence: Women, Politics and the Fiction of Letters.* Cambridge: Cambridge University Press, 1993.

Feather, John. *The Provincial Book Trade in England.* Cambridge: Cambridge University Press, 1985.

Fender, Stephen. *Sea Changes: British Emigration and American Literature.* Cambridge: Cambridge University Press, 1992.

Fergus, Jan. "Provincial Servants' Reading in the late Eighteenth-Century," in James Raven, Helen Small and Naomi Tadmor (eds.). *The Practice and Representation of Reading in England.* Cambridge: Cambridge University Press, 1996.

Fischer, David Hackett. *Albion's Seed: Four British Folkways in America.* Oxford: Oxford University Press, 1989.

Fliegelman, Jay. *Declaring Independence: Jefferson, Natural Language and the Culture of Performance.* Stanford: Stanford University Press, 1993.

Fortune, Brandon Brame and Deborah Warner. *Franklin and his Friends.* Philadelphia: University of Pennsylvania Press, 1999.

Fowler, Dorothy Ganfield. *Unmailable: Congress and the Post Office*. Athens, GA: University of Georgia Press, 1977.

France, Peter. *Politeness and its Discontents*. Cambridge: Cambridge University Press, 1992.

Frazer, Peter. *The Intelligence of the Secretaries of State and their Monopoly of Licensed News, 1660–88*. Cambridge: Cambridge University Press, 1956.

Fry, Michael. *The Scottish Empire*. Edinburgh: Birlinn, 2001.

Fuller, Wayne E. *The American Mail*. Chicago: University of Chicago Press, 1972.

Gauci, Perry. *The Politics of Trade: The Overseas Merchant in State and Society, 1660–1720*. Oxford: Oxford University Press, 2001.

Gillis, Christina Marsden. *The Paradox of Privacy: Epistolary Form in Clarissa*. Gainsville: University of Florida Press, 1984.

Gilmore, William J. *Reading Becomes a Necessity of Life: Material and Cultural Life in Rural New England, 1780–1835*. Knoxville: University of Tennessee Press, 1989.

Gilroy, Amanda and W. M. Verhoeven (eds.). *Epistolary Histories: Letters, Fiction, Culture*. Charlottesville: University Press of Virginia, 2000.

Goldberg, Jonathan. *Writing Matter: From the Hands of the English Renaissance*. Stanford: Stanford University Press, 1990.

Goldgar, Anne. *Impolite Learning: Conduct and Community in the Republic of Letters, 1680–1750*. New Haven: Yale University Press, 1995.

Goldsmith, Elizabeth C. *Exclusive Conversations: The Art of Interaction in Seventeenth-Century France*. Philadelphia: University of Pennsylvania Press, 1988.

Gonda, Caroline. *Reading Daughters' Fictions 1709–1834*. Cambridge: Cambridge University Press, 1996.

Goodman, Dena. *The Republic of Letters: A Cultural History of the French Enlightenment*. Ithaca: Cornell University Press, 1994.

Gorlach, Manfred. "Regional and Social Variation," in Roger Lass (ed.). *The Cambridge History of the English Language*. Cambridge: Cambridge University Press, 1999.

Grandqvist, Raoul, *Imitation as Resistance: Appropriations of English Literature in Nineteenth-Century America*. Madison: Fairleigh Dickinson University Press, 1995.

Grasso, Christopher. *A Speaking Aristocracy: Transforming Public Discourse in Eighteenth-Century Connecticut*. Cambridge, Mass.: Harvard University Press, 1992.

Green, Jack P. *Imperatives, Behaviors and Identities: Essays in Early American Cultural History*. Charlottesville: University Press of Virginia, 1992.

Periphery and Center, 1607–1788. Athens, GA: University of Georgia Press, 1986.

The Intellectual Construction of America: Exceptionalism and Identity from 1492 to 1800. Chapel Hill: University of North Carolina Press, 1993.

Green, Katherine Sobba. *The Courtship Novel, 1740–1834*. Lexington: University Press of Kentucky, 1991.

Griffin, Dustin. *Literary Patronage in England, 1650–1800*. Cambridge: Cambridge University Press, 1996.

Griffin, Robert J. (ed.). *The Faces of Anonymity: Anonymous and Pseudonymous Publication from the Sixteenth to the Twentieth-Century*. New York: Palgrave Macmillan, 2003.

Grillo, R. D. *Dominant Language and Hierarchy in Britain and France*. Cambridge: Cambridge University Press, 1991.

Gustafson, Sandra M. *Eloquence is Power, Oratory and Performance in Early America*. Chapel Hill: University of North Carolina Press, 2000.

Haber, Samuel. *The Quest for Authority and Honor in the American Professions, 1750–1900*. Chicago: University of Chicago, 1991.

Habermas, Jürgen, *The Structural Transformation of the Public Sphere*, trans. Thomas Burger and Frederick Lawrence. Cambridge, Mass.: The MIT Press, 1989.

Hall, David. "The Uses of Literacy in New England, 1600–1850," in William L. Joyce *et al* (eds.). *Printing and Society in America*. Worcester: American Antiquarian Society, 1983.

Hancock, David. *Citizen of the World: London Merchants and the Integration of the British Atlantic Community, 1735–1785*. Cambridge: Cambridge University Press, 1995.

Hanson, Laurence. *Government and the Press, 1695–1763*. Oxford: Oxford University Press, 1936.

Harrison, Jane E. *Until Next Year: Letter-Writing and the Mails in the Canadas, 1640–1830*. Quebec: Canadian Museum of Civilization, 1997.

Hay, Douglas *et al* (eds.). *Albion's Fatal Tree: Crime and Society in Eighteenth-Century England*. New York: Pantheon, 1975.

Hay, Douglas and Nicholas Rogers. *Eighteenth-Century English Society: Shuttles and Swords*. Oxford: Oxford University Press, 1997.

Hecht, Jean. *The Domestic Servant Class in Eighteenth-Century England*. London: Routledge, 1956.

Hill, Bridget. *Servants: English Domestics in the Eighteenth Century*. Oxford: Clarendon Press, 1996.

Hoffman, Ross J. S. (ed.). *Edmund Burke: New York Agent*. Philadelphia: The American Philosophical Society, 1956.

Holderness, B. A. *Preindustrial England: Economy and Society 1500–1750*. Totowa, NJ: Rowman and Littlefield, 1976.

Holmes, Geoffrey. *Augustan London: Professions, State and Society, 1680–1730*. London: George Allen and Unwin, 1982.

Hornbeak, Katherine Gee. The Complete Letter-Writer in English, 1568–1800, *Smith College Studies in Modern Languages*, 15 (April–July, 1934).

Houston, *Scottish Literacy and the Scottish Identity: Illiteracy and Society in Scotland and Northern England, 1600–1800*. Cambridge: Cambridge University Press, 1985.

How, James. *Epistolary Spaces: English Letter-Writing from the Foundation of the Postoffice to Richardson's Clarissa.* Aldershot: Ashgate, 2003.

Howell, Wilbur Samuel. *Eighteenth-Century British Logic and Rhetoric.* Princeton: Princeton University Press, 1971.

Howland, John. *The Letter-Form and the French Enlightenment: The Epistolary Paradox.* New York: Peter Lang, 1991.

Hume, Robert D. "Editing a Nebulous Author: The Case of the Duke of Buckingham," *The Library,* 4:3 (Sept. 2003): 249–77.

Hunt, Margaret R. *The Middling Sort.* Berkeley: University of California Press, 1996.

Irving, William Henry. *The Providence of Wit in the English Letter-Writers.* Durham, NC: Duke University Press, 1955.

Jacob, Margaret C. *The Radical Enlightenment: Pantheists, Freemasons and Republicans.* London: George, Allen and Unwin, 1981.

Living the Enlightenment: Freemasonry and Politics in Eighteenth-Century Europe. Oxford: Oxford University Press, 1987.

Jagodzinski, Cecile M. *Privacy and Print: Reading and Writing in Seventeenth-Century England.* Charlottesville: University of Virginia Press, 1999.

Jardine, Lisa. "Reading and the Technology of Textual Effect: Erasmus' Familiar Letters and Shakespeare's *King Lear,*" in James Raven, Helen Small and Naomi Tadmore (eds.). *The Practice and Representation of Reading in England,* Cambridge: Cambridge University Press, 1996.

John, Richard R. *Spreading the News: The American Postal System from Franklin to Morse.* Cambridge, Mass.: Harvard University Press, 1995.

Joyce, William L. *et al.* (eds.). *Printing and Society in Early America.* Worcester: American Antiquarian Society, 1983.

Kammen, Michael G. *A Rope of Sand: The Colonial Agents, British Politics and the American Revolution.* Ithaca: Cornell University Press, 1968.

Kaufmann, Victor, *Post Scripts: The Writer's Workshop.* Cambridge, Mass.: Harvard University Press, 1994.

Keeble, N. H. *The Literary Culture of Nonconformity in the Later Seventeenth Century.* Athens, GA: University of Georgia Press, 1987.

Kennedy, George A. *Classical Rhetoric and its Christian and Secular Tradition from Ancient to Modern Times.* Chapel Hill: University of North Carolina Press, 1980.

Kerber, Linda. *Women of the Republic: Intellect and Ideology in Revolutionary America.* Chapel Hill: University of North Carolina Press, 1980.

Ketcham, Michael. *Transparent Designs: Reading, Performance and Form in the Spectator Papers.* Athens, GA: University of Georgia Press, 1985.

Kewes, Paulina. *Authorship and Appropriation: Writing for the Stage in England, 1660–1710.* Oxford: Clarendon Press, 1998.

Kiebowicz, Richard B. *News in the Mail: The Press, Post Office and Public Information, 1700–1860.* New York: Greenwood, 1989.

Klancher, Jon. *The Making of English Reading Audiences.* Madison: University of Wisconsin Press, 1987.

Klein, Lawrence E. *Shaftesbury and the Culture of Politeness*. Cambridge: Cambridge University Press, 1994.

"Gender, Conversation and the Public Sphere in Early Eighteenth-Century England," in Judith Still and Michael Worton (eds.). *Textuality and Sexuality: Reading Theories and Practices*. Manchester: Manchester University Press, 1993.

Konwiser, Henry M. *Colonial and Revolutionary Posts*. Richmond, VA: Dietz, 1931.

Knight, Charles A. *Joseph Addison and Richard Steele: A Reference Guide, 1730–1991*. New York: G. K. Hall, 1994.

Knowles, Gerry. *A Cultural History of the English Language*. London: Arnold, 1997.

Kussmaul, Ann. *A General View of the Rural Economy of England, 1538–1840*. Cambridge: Cambridge University Press, 1990.

Landsman, Ned. "The Provinces and the Empire: Scotland, the American Colonies and the Development of a British Colonial Identity," in Lawrence Stone (ed.). *An Imperial State at War: Britain from 1789–1815*. London: Routledge, 1994.

From Colonials to Provincials: American Thought and Culture, 1680–1760. New York: Twayne, 1997.

Landsman, Ned (ed.). *Nation and Province in the First British Empire*. Lewisburg: Bucknell University Press, 2001.

Langford, Paul. *A Polite and Commercial People: England 1727–1783*. Oxford: Clarendon Press, 1989.

Leith, Dick and George Myerson. *The Power of Address: Explorations in Rhetoric*. London: Routledge, 1989.

Lemay, J. A. Leo (ed.). *Deism, Masonry and the Enlightenment*. Newark: University of Delaware Press, 1987.

Lerer, Seth. *Courtly Letters in the Age of Henry VIII: Literary Culture and the Arts of Deceit*. Cambridge: Cambridge University Press, 1997.

Looby, Christopher. *Voicing America: Language, Literary Form and the Origins of the United States*. Chicago: University of Chicago Press, 1996.

Love, Harold. *Scribal Publication in Seventeenth-Century England*. Oxford: Clarendon Press, 1993.

Lowenthal, Cynthia. *Lady Mary Wortley Montagu and the Eighteenth-Century Letter*. Athens, GA: University of Georgia Press, 1994.

Madsen, David L. *Early National Education, 1776–1830*. New York: John Wiley, 1974.

Magnusson, Lynne. *Shakespeare and Social Dialogue*. Cambridge: Cambridge University Press, 1999.

Manning, Susan. "Introduction." *Letters from an American Farmer*. Oxford: Oxford University Press, 1997.

Marshall, Alan. *Intelligence and Espionage in the Reign of Charles II, 1660–85*. Cambridge: Cambridge University Press, 1994.

Marshall, Peter, "Empire and Authority in the Later Eighteenth-Century," *Journal of Imperial and Commonwealth History*, 15 (1987): 105–22.

Marshall, Peter and Glyn Williams (eds.). *The British Atlantic Empire Before the American Revolution*. London: Frank Cass, 1980.

Marotti, Arthur F. and Michael D. Bristol (eds.), *Print, Manuscript and Performance*. Columbus: Ohio State University Press, 2000.

McIntosh, Carey. *The Evolution of English Prose, 1700–1800: Style, Politeness and Print Culture*. Cambridge: Cambridge University Press, 1998.

Common and Courtly Language: The Stylistics of Social Class in Eighteenth-Century Literature. Philadelphia: University of Pennsylvania Press, 1986.

McKenzie, Alan T. (ed.). *Sent as a Gift: Eight Correspondences from the Eighteenth-Century*. Athens, GA: University of Georgia Press, 1993.

McKenzie, D. F. "Speech–Manuscript–Print," in Dave Oliphant and Robin Bradford (eds.). *New Directions in Textual Studies*. Austin: Harry Ransom Humanities Research Center, 1990.

Mee, John. "Examples of Safe Printing: Censorship and Popular Radical Literature in the 1790s," in Nigel Smith (ed.). *Literature and Censorship*. New York: Boydell and Brewer, 1993.

Michael, Ian. *The Teaching of English from the Sixteenth-Century to 1870*. Cambridge: Cambridge University Press, 1987.

Miller, Peter N. *Defining the Common Good: Empire, Religion and Philosophy in Eighteenth-Century Britain*. Cambridge: Cambridge University Press, 1994.

Miller, Thomas. *The Formation of College English*. Pittsburgh: University of Pittsburgh Press, 1997.

Mitchell, Linda. *Grammar Wars*. Aldershot: Ashgate, 2001.

Mohr, James. "Calculated Disillusionment: Crevecoeur's Letters Reconsidered." *South Atlantic Quarterly*, 69 (1970): 354–63.

Money, John. "Teaching in the Market Place," in Brewer and Porter (eds.). *Consumption and the World of Goods*.

Moss, Ann. *Printed Commonplace Books and the Structure of Renaissance Thought*. Oxford: Clarendon Press, 1996.

Myers, Robin and Michael Harris (eds.). *Fakes and Frauds: Varieties of Deception in Print and Manuscript*. Detroit: Omigraphics Inc., 1989.

North, Douglass C. "Institutions, Transaction Costs and the Rise of Merchant Empires," in James D. Tracy (ed.). *The Political Economy of Merchant Empires*. Cambridge: Cambridge University Press, 1991.

Norton, Mary Beth. *Liberty's Daughters*. Ithaca: Cornell University Press, 1980.

O'Brien, Patrick. "Inseparable Connections: Trade, Economy, Fiscal State and the Expansion of Empire, 1688–1815," in P. J. Marshall (ed.). *The Oxford History of the British Empire*, Vol. II: *The Eighteenth Century*. Oxford: Oxford University Press, 1998.

O'Day, Rosemary. *The Family and Family Relationships 1500–1900: England, France and the United States of America*. New York: St. Martin's Press, 1994.

Education and Society, 1500–1800: Social Foundations of Education in Modern Britain. London: Longman, 1982.

The Professions in Early Modern England, 1450–1800. London: Longman, 2000.

Olson, Alison Gilbert. *Making Empire Work: London and American Interest Groups, 1690–1790*. Cambridge, Mass.: Harvard University Press, 1992.
"The Board of Trade and London-American Interest Groups in the Eighteenth-Century," in Peter Marshall and Glyn Williams (eds.). *The British Atlantic Empire before the American Revolution*. London: Frank Cass, 1980.

Pagden, Anthony. *Lords of all the World: Ideologies of Empire in Britain, Spain and France, c. 1500–1800*. New Haven: Yale University Press, 1995.

Parkes, M. B. *Pause and Effect: An Introduction to the History of Punctuation in the West*. Berkeley: University of California Press, 1993.
Scribes, Scripts and Readers: Studies in the Communication, Presentation and Dissemination of Medieval Texts. London: Hambledon Press, 1991.
"The Influence of the Concepts of Ordinatio and Compilatio on the Development of the Book," in Parkes (ed.), *Medieval Learning and Literature: Essays Presented to Richard William Hunt*. Oxford: Clarendon Press, 1976.

Patterson, Annabel. *Censorship and Interpretation: The Condition of Writing and Reading in Early Modern England*. Madison: University of Wisconsin Press, 1984.

Paulson, Ronald. *Emblem and Expression: Meaning in English Art of the Eighteenth Century*. Cambridge, Mass.: Harvard University Press, 1975.
Don Quixote in England. Baltimore: The Johns Hopkins University Press, 1998.

Perry, Ruth. *Women, Letters and the Novel*. New York: AMS Press, 1980.

Peters, Julie Stone. *Theater of the Book, 1480–1880: Print, Text and Performance in Europe*. Oxford: Oxford University Press, 2000.

Phillbrick, Thomas. *St John De Crevecoeur*. New York: Twayne, 1970.

Phillipson, "Culture and Society in the Eighteenth-Century Province: The Case of Edinburgh and the Scottish Enlightenment," in Lawrence Stone (ed.). *The University in Society*, 2 vols. Princeton: Princeton University Press, 1974: II, 407–48.

Plomer, H. R., *A Dictionary of the Printers and Booksellers who were at Work in England, Scotland and Ireland from 1668 to 1725*. Oxford: Oxford University Press, 1989.

Pollard, M. *Dublin's Trade in Books, 1550–1800*. Oxford: Clarendon Press, 1989.

Pollock, Linda A. "Living on the Stage of the World: The Concept of Privacy among the Elite in Early Modern England," in *Rethinking Social History: English Society 1570–1920 and its Reinterpretation*. Manchester: Manchester University Press, 1993.

Portelli, Alessandro. *The Text and the Voice: Writing, Speaking and Democracy in American Literature*. New York: Columbia University Press, 1994.

Potkay, Adam. *The Fate of Eloquence in the Age of Hume*. Ithaca: Cornell University Press, 1994.

Potter, Lois. *Secret Rites and Secret Writing: Royalist Literature, 1641–1660*. Cambridge: Cambridge University Press, 1989.

Pred, Allan R. *Urban Growth and the Circulation of Information: The US System of Cities, 1790–1840.* Cambridge, Mass.: Harvard University Press, 1973.

Price, Leah. *The Anthology and the Rise of the Novel: From Richardson to George Eliot.* Cambridge: Cambridge University Press, 2000.

Raven, James. *Judging New Wealth: Popular Publishing and Responses to Commerce in England, 1750–1800.* Oxford: Clarendon Press, 1992.

London Booksellers and American Customers: Transatlantic Literary Community and the Charleston Library Society, 1748–1811. Columbia, SC: University of South Carolina Press, 2002.

"Commodification and Value: Interactions in Book Traffic in North America, c. 1750–1820," in *Across Boundaries: The Book in Culture and Commerce.* Delaware: Oak Knoll Press, 2000.

Raven, James, Helen Small and Naomi Tadmor (eds.). *The Practice and Representation of Reading in England.* Cambridge: Cambridge University Press, 1996.

Redford, Bruce. *The Converse of the Pen: Acts of Intimacy in the Eighteenth-Century Familiar Letter.* Chicago: University of Chicago Press, 1986.

Remer, Rosalind. *Printers and Men of Capital: Philadelphia Book Publishers in the New Republic.* Philadelphia: University of Pennsylvania Press, 1996.

Rice, Grantland S. *The Transformation of Authorship in America.* Chicago: University of Chicago Press, 1997.

"Crevecoeur and the Politics of Authorship in Republican America," *Early American Literature*, 28: 2 (1993): 91–119.

Richards, Cynthia. "Fair Trade: The Language of Love and Commerce in Mary Wollstonecraft's *Letters Written during a short Residence in Sweden, Norway and Denmark,*" in *Studies in Eighteenth-Century Culture*, 30. Ed. Timothy Erwin and Ourida Mosefai. Baltimore: The Johns Hopkins University Press, 2001.

Robertson, Jean. *The Art of Letter-Writing: An Essay on the Handbooks published in England during the Sixteenth and Seventeenth Centuries.* London: Hodder & Stoughton, 1943.

Robinson, Howard. *The British Post-Office: A History.* Princeton: Princeton University Press, 1948.

Carrying British Mails Overseas. New York: New York University Press, 1964.

Royce, William L., David Hall, Richard D. Brown and John B. Hench (eds.). *Printing and Society in Early America.* Worcester: American Antiquarian Society, 1983.

Sacks, David Harris. *The Widening Gate: Bristol and the Atlantic Economy, 1450–1700.* Berkeley: University of California Press, 1991.

Saintsbury, George. *A Letter Book.* London: G. Bell & Sons, 1922.

Salmon, Vivian, "Orthography and Punctuation," in Roger Lass (ed.). *The Cambridge History of the English Language.* Cambridge: Cambridge University Press, 1999.

Scott, James C. *Domination and the Arts of Resistance: Hidden Transcripts.* New Haven: Yale University Press, 1990.

Sheldahl, K. (ed.). *Education for the Mercantile Counting House*. New York: Garland, 1989.

Shields, David S. *Civil Tongues and Polite Letters in British America*. Chapel Hill: University of North Carolina Press, 1997.

"The Manuscript in the British-American World of Print," *American Antiquarian Society*, 102: 2 (1993): 403–16.

Siebert, Frederick Seaton. *Freedom of the Press in England, 1476–1776: The Rise and Decline of Government Controls*. Urbana: University of Illinois Press, 1952.

Simonton, Deborah. "Apprenticeship: Training and Gender in the Eighteenth-Century," in Maxine Berg (ed.). *Markets and Manufacture in Early Industrial Europe*. London: Routledge, 1991.

Simpson, Lewis P. "The Printer as a Man of Letters," in Brian M. Barbour (ed.). *Benjamin Franklin: A Collection of Critical Essays*. Englewood Clifts: Prentice Hall, 1979.

Siskin, Clifford. *The Power of Writing: Literature and Social Change in Britain 1700–1830*. Baltimore: The Johns Hopkins University Press, 1998.

Smith, Olivia. *The Politics of Language, 1791–1819*. Oxford: Clarendon Press, 1984.

Smith, Wilson (ed.). *Theories of Education in Early America, 1655–1819*. Indianapolis: Bobbs-Merrill, 1973.

Solomon, Harry M. *The Rise of Robert Dodsley: Creating the New Age of Print*. Carbondale: Southern Illinois University Press, 1996.

Sommerville, C. John. *The News Revolution in England: Cultural Dynamics and Daily Information*. Oxford: Oxford University Press, 1996.

Sosin, Jack M. *Agents and Merchants*. Lincoln, NB: University of Nebraska Press, 1965.

Spacks, Patricia Meyer. *Privacy: Concealing the Eighteenth-Century Self*. Chicago: University of Chicago Press, 2003.

Spengeman, William. *A New World of Words: Redefining Early American Literature*. New Haven: Yale University Press, 1994.

St. George, Robert Blair (ed.). *Possible Pasts: Becoming Colonial in Early America*. Ithaca: Cornell University Press, 2000.

Steele, Ian. *The English Atlantic, 1675–1740: An Exploration of Communication and Community*. Oxford: Oxford University Press, 1986.

Politics of Colonial Policy: The Board of Trade in Colonial Administration 1696–1720. Oxford: Clarendon Press, 1968.

Stevenson, David. *The Origins of Freemasonry: Scotland's Century, 1590–1710*. Cambridge: Cambridge University Press, 1988.

Stewart, Keith. "Towards Defining an Aesthetic for the Familiar Letter in Eighteenth-Century England," *Prose Studies*, 5 (1982): 179–92.

Stiverson, Cynthia Z. and Gregory A. Stiverson, "The Colonial Retail Book Trade: Availability and Affordability of Reading Material in Mid-Eighteenth-Century Virginia," in William L. Joyce, David D. Hall, Richard D. Brown and John B. Hench (eds.). *Printing and Society in America*. Worcester: American Antiquarian Society, 1983.

Stone, Lawrence (ed.). *An Imperial State at War: Britain from 1689 to 1815.* London: Routledge, 1994.

Tadmor, Naomi. *Family and Friends in Eighteenth-Century England.* Cambridge: Cambridge University Press, 2001.

—— "Even my wife read to me: Women, Reading and Household Life in the Eighteenth Century," in James Raven *et al.* (eds.). *The Practice and Representation of Reading in England.* Cambridge: Cambridge University Press, 1996.

Tennenhouse, Leonard. "The Americanization of Clarissa," *Yale Journal of Criticism*, 11: 1 (1998): 177–96.

—— "A Language for the Nation: A Transatlantic Problematic," in W. M. Verhoeven (ed.). *Revolutionary Histories: Transatlantic Cultural Nationalism, 1775–1815.* Houndmills: Palgrave, 2002.

Todd, Janet. "The hot brute drudges on: Ambiguity and Desire in Aphra Behn's *Love Letters*," *Women's Writing*, 1:3 (1994): 277–90.

Traister, Bruce. "Criminal Correspondence." *Early American Literature*, 37:3 (Dec. 2002): 469–97.

Ullman, H. Lewis. *Things, Thoughts, Words and Actions.* Carbondale: Southern Illinois University Press, 1994.

Ulrich, Laurel Thatcher. "Virtuous Women Found: New England Ministerial Literature, 1698–1735," *American Quarterly*, 28 (1976): 20–40.

Vickery, Amanda. *The Gentleman's Daughter: Women's Lives in Georgian England.* New Haven: Yale University Press, 1998.

Wahrman, Dror. *Imagining the Middle Class: The Political Representation of Class in Britain, c. 1710–1840.* Cambridge: Cambridge University Press, 1995.

Warner, Michael. *The Letters of the Republic: Publication and the Public Sphere in Eighteenth-Century America.* Cambridge, Mass.: Harvard University Press, 1990.

—— "The Mass Public and the Mass Subject," in Craig Calhoun (ed.). *Habermas and the Public Sphere.* Cambridge, Mass.: MIT Press, 1993.

Watson, Nicola. *Revolution and the Form of the British Novel, 1790–1825.* Oxford: Clarendon Press, 1994.

Weinbrot, Howard D. *Britannia's Issue.* Cambridge: Cambridge University Press, 1993.

Weisberger, R. William. *Speculative Masonry and the Enlightenment.* New York: Columbia University Press, 1993.

Weiss, Harry. *American Letter-Writers 1698–1943.* New York: New York Public Library, 1945.

White, Harold Ogden, *Plagiarism and Imitation during the English Renaissance: A Study of Critical Distinctions.* Cambridge, Mass.: Harvard University Press, 1993.

Wiles, R. M. *Freshest Advices: Early Provincial Newspapers in England.* Columbus: Ohio State University Press, 1965.

Williams, Julie Hedgepath. *The Significance of the Printed Word in Early America.* Westport: Greenwood Press, 1999.

Wilson Allen, Gay and Roger Asselineau. *St John de Crevecoeur*. New York: Viking, 1987.

Wilson, Kathleen. *The Sense of the People: Politics, Culture and Imperialism in England, 1715–1785*. Cambridge: Cambridge University Press, 1995.

Wilson, R. G. *Gentlemen Merchants: The Merchant Community in Leeds, 1700–1830*. Manchester: Manchester University Press, 1971.

Winans, Robert B. *A Descriptive Catalogue of Book Catalogues Separately Printed in America, 1693–1800*. Worcester: American Antiquarian Society, 1981.

Winn, James Anderson. *A Window in the Bosom: The Letters of Alexander Pope*. Hamden: Archon Books, 1977.

Wood, Gordon, *The Radicalism of the American Revolution*. New York: Knopf, 1992.

Woolf, Edwin. *The Book Culture of a Colonial American City: Philadelphia Books, Bookmen and Booksellers*. Oxford: Clarendon Press, 1988.

Wrightson, Keith. "Class," in David Armitage and Michael J. Braddick (eds.). *The British Atlantic World 1500–1800*. Houndmills: Palgrave, 2002.

Yeazell, Ruth. *Fictions of Modesty: Women and Courtship in the English Novel*. Chicago: University of Chicago Press, 1991.

Zaczek, Barbara Maria. *Censored Sentiments: Letters and Censorship in Epistolary Novels and Conduct Material*. Newark: University of Delaware Press, 1997.

Ziff, Larzer. *Writing the New Nation: Prose, Print and Politics in the Early United States*. New Haven: Yale University Press, 1992.

Index

Lightning Source UK Ltd.
Milton Keynes UK
11 June 2010

155447UK00001B/45/P